P9-CRP-950

INTERNATIONAL ENCYCLOPEDIA OF

Marriage and Family

Editor in Chief

James J. Ponzetti, Jr.
University of British Columbia

Associate Editors

Raeann R. Hamon
Messiah College

Yvonne Kellar-Guenther
University of Colorado

Patricia K. Kerig
University of North Carolina at Chapel Hill

T. Laine Scales
Baylor University

James M. White
University of British Columbia

INTERNATIONAL ENCYCLOPEDIA OF

Marriage and Family

SECOND EDITION

Volume 4: Sh–Za, Index

James J. Ponzetti, Jr
Editor in Chief

MACMILLAN
REFERENCE
USA™

New York • Detroit • San Diego • San Francisco • Cleveland • New Haven, Conn. • Waterville, Maine • London • Munich

International Encyclopedia of Marriage and Family

James J. Ponzetti, Jr.

For more information, contact
Macmillan Reference USA
300 Park Avenue South, 9th Floor
New York, NY 10010
Or you can visit our Internet site at
http://www.gale.com

Macmillan Reference USA
300 Park Avenue South, 9th Floor
New York, NY 10010

Macmillan Reference USA
27500 Drake Road
Farmington Hills, MI 48331-3535

LIBRARY OF CONGRESS CATALOGING-IN-PUBLICATION DATA

International encyclopedia of marriage and family / James J. Ponzetti, Jr., editor in chief. — 2nd ed.
p. cm.
Rev. ed. of: Encyclopedia of marriage and the family. c1995.
Includes bibliographical references and index.
ISBN 0-02-865672-5 (set : alk. paper) — ISBN 0-02-865673-3 (v. 1 : alk. paper) — ISBN 0-02-865674-1 (v. 2 : alk. paper) — ISBN 0-02-865675-X (v. 3 : alk. paper) — ISBN 0-02-865676-8 (v. 4 : alk. paper)
1. Marriage—Encyclopedias. 2. Family—Encyclopedias. I. Ponzetti, James J. II. Encyclopedia of marriage and family.

HQ9 .E52 2003
306.8'03—dc21

2002014107

Printed in the United States of America
10 9 8 7 6 5 4 3 2 1

SHYNESS

Shyness refers to passivity, emotional arousal, and excessive self-focus in the presence of other people (Jones, Cheek, and Briggs 1986). It also frequently involves negative self-evaluations, social avoidance, and withdrawal. From a practical point of view, the importance of shyness derives from its consequences. Shy persons, for example, are often excessively uncomfortable and anxious in social situations. Moreover, because of such discomfort, chronic shyness often leads to failures to capitalize on the occupational and interpersonal opportunities available to the shy person. Scientifically, shyness affords the opportunity to observe the complex interplay of personal and situational context factors in the evolution of social interactions.

State versus Trait Shyness

Typically, a distinction between two characterizations of shyness is drawn. The immediate emotional/cognitive experience of shyness—arousal and heightened self-consciousness in response to social threat—defines what is known as *state or situational shyness*. This type of shyness may be experienced by virtually anyone from time to time, especially in certain social situations. For example, people are generally more shy in situations involving strangers than when interacting with friends or family members. By contrast, *trait shyness* refers to the chronic tendency to experience state shyness more frequently or at lower levels of social threat (Buss 1980). For some people state shyness dissipates when the circumstances giving rise to it change, whereas trait shyness is a personality dimension leading to frequent and intense experiential shyness over time and across situations (Russell, Cutrona, and Jones 1986). The specific level of state shyness experienced by persons high in trait shyness also varies from one situation to the next, but remains higher for them than for persons low in trait shyness.

The Experience of State Shyness

State shyness consists of converging processes in the *cognitive* (e.g., self-focus, thoughts of escape, dread, preoccupation with the self, concern with one's performance), *affective* (e.g., anxiety, shame, embarrassment), *behavioral* (e.g., nervous gestures, inhibited speech, dysfluency, nervous and excessive verbalization), and *physiological* (e.g., sweating, heart palpitations, elevated blood pressure, dry mouth) domains of experience. These experiences are often sufficiently unpleasant to lead to withdrawal from or avoidance of many social situations, but they also compound the distress of shyness by distracting from skilled and self-confident social interactions.

The origins of state shyness are twofold. First, certain situations in which one's identity is at issue under conditions of uncertainty, and situations that elicit awareness of the self as the object of others' attention, give rise to the experience of shyness (Buss 1980). Relevant situations include those involving evaluations, public performances, novelty, high status/attractive people, formality (e.g., weddings, funerals), self-presentations, and being the center of attention. The necessity of meeting and interacting with strangers at social gatherings is a prototypical example of an experience involving several of these factors. The second contributing factor is trait shyness. Specifically, some people are predisposed to experience state shyness by virtue of their personality and characteristic ways of coping with social demands. Thus, state shyness is a joint function of the level of trait shyness and situational characteristics.

State shyness is related to other social emotions such as shame, audience anxiety, and embarrassment. All involve some degree of social withdrawal, but shyness also differs from these other emotions by virtue of its situational elicitors and the specific components of the experience. For example, shame arises from the public detection of an immoral or undesirable behavior whereas shyness involves vacillation between interest and fear in social situations (Izard 1972). One unpleasant consequence of shyness is that it often results in negative interpersonal and emotional judgments in which the shy person is perceived not only as reticent, but also as unfriendly, arrogant, or even hostile.

Trait Shyness

Origins of trait shyness. As a relatively stable personality characteristic, one important issue is how trait shyness develops. Research and theory suggests two major sources of trait shyness (Buss 1984). First, trait shyness often reflects a genetic predisposition toward inhibition and excessive anxiety. Several studies have found evidence of a high degree of inheritablity for shyness (e.g., Plomin and Rowe 1979). Alternatively, shyness may emerge because of disruptions or problems in development, most especially those involved in the establishment of a personal identity during adolescence (e.g., Asendorpf 1989; Buss 1984).

Social inhibition is a developmental precursor of shyness and is relatively stable over time (Kagan, Reznick, and Snidman 1988). Inhibition in an infant is often manifested as stranger anxiety, which is common at about nine months of age. Not all infants are excessively afraid of strangers, and even those who are often become much less so during the second year. For a minority, however, inhibition continues and resembles the avoidant and reticent behavior of shy adults. Children with a chronically inhibited social interaction style beyond age three are usually labeled as shy. Thus, the idea that some children are born with the biological foundation for shyness is further supported by research showing that inhibition is consistent across situations and is related to specific physiological responses: Shy-inhibited children tend to have higher and less variable heart rates and larger pupil dilation during cognitive tasks than uninhibited children (Garcia-Coll, Kagan, and Reznick 1984).

Alternatively, shy children may be conditioned for inhibition by parents or others (Asendorpf 1989). For example, being intimidated, harassed, or rejected may encourage a wariness of others as a means of avoiding being hurt. This is especially so if shy expressions are also modeled or reinforced by parents. More commonly, uncertainty and anxiety associated with establishing a personal identity in adolescence may initiate shyness (Buss 1984). The transition from elementary to secondary school, the relative increase in peer influence as compared to parental/family influences, and accommodation to social and role expectations are illustrative of the identity transformations that may be implicated in the initiation of acquired shyness. Consequently, although some children may be born with a readiness for inhibition and physiological arousal in social situations, this inclination may at least partially actualize through environmental/developmental factors involving both learning and stress.

On the other hand, in one study shyness at age two predicted parenting practices at age four such as a lack of encouragement of independence, but parenting practices at age two did not predict shyness at age four (Rubin et al. 1999). This suggests that the experiential contribution to the development of shyness may be a parental response to existing shyness rather than shyness resulting from differences in parenting behaviors.

Developmental manifestations of trait shyness. Another important issue regarding trait shyness is how it is expressed at various stages in the life cycle. Being shy during childhood does not automatically mean that an individual will remain shy throughout life. On the other hand, shyness appears to stabilize by approximately eighth or ninth grade, and adolescent shyness has been found to predict significantly adult shyness as much as twenty-five years later (Morris, Soroker, and Burruss 1954). During adolescence, shyness is likely to be intensified by the physical impact of puberty as well as changes in social context in the adolescent's life that may contribute to disturbances in self-image. In this regard, junior high school students more frequently describe themselves as shy than do elementary school students (Simmons and Rosenberg 1975).

Shyness among adults involves inhibited social behavior that impedes the development of friendships and romantic and work relationships (Jones and Carpenter 1986). For example, shy adults tend to have selective memory for unpleasant social interactions, underestimate their own social skill, and assume responsibility for failure, but not for success (Halford and Foddy 1982; Jones and Briggs 1984; Jones and Carpenter 1986). Also, shy adults are less effective in asking for help, expressing opinions, and coping with stress, and more likely to engage in negative self-evaluations (DePaulo et al. 1989; Eisenberg, Fabes, and Murphy 1995; Jones, Briggs, and Smith 1986).

Longitudinal data indicates that individuals identified as shy and reserved in late childhood differed in marital and family experiences thirty years later (Caspi, Elder, and Bem 1988). For example, shy males were more likely than their male age cohorts to delay marriage and parenthood to a later point in life, whereas shy girls were more likely to pursue conventional marital, childbearing, and homemaking endeavors than their less shy counterparts.

In work-related situations, chronically shy persons tend to achieve lower occupational status and stability (Caspi, Elder, and Bem 1988). Also, shy adults fail to take advantage of the employment opportunities available to them and are less confident and active in occupational endeavors (Phillips and Bruch 1988). For elderly adults, shyness is associated with greater life disruption as a result of retirement, widowhood, and other changes toward the end of the life cycle (Hansson 1986). However, because the social roles of the elderly have fewer effects on other people and the evaluations of others are not as important to the elderly, shyness may have fewer or less dramatic consequences as people grow older.

Variations in Shyness

Shyness appears to vary in conjunction with gender. Gender role stereotypes may play a role in the development of adolescent shyness. Shyness is considered to be a feminine trait; therefore, it is not surprising that girls report more self-conscious shyness after age eleven than boys (Simmons and Rosenberg 1975). Stereotypes make it more acceptable for girls to be shy and shyness may be a more serious problem for boys because they are expected to take the initiative in social encounters (Porteus 1979). Research also suggests cultural variation in shyness. For example, one research group (Pilkonis and Zimbardo 1979) found self-labeled shyness to be highest among samples of Japanese, Taiwanese, and Indian national groups and lowest among samples of Jewish Americans, Israelis, and Mexicans. The origin of such variation has not been determined, however.

Shyness and Adjustment

Another important issue that has not been fully resolved is the point at which shyness ceases to be an everyday problem common to many people and becomes a form of psychopathology. There is evidence that shyness is related to introversion and neuroticism more or less equally (Briggs 1988). However, although studies indicate a convergence between shyness and various diagnoses such as anxiety disorder, social phobia and avoidant personality, most research suggests that shyness results in such debilitating conditions in only a small number of cases (e.g., Prior et al. 2000). Moreover, shyness tends to be most seriously problematic during life transitions (e.g., going away to college or changing jobs) that require social skill and assertiveness to acquire new social networks and relationship partners as compared to more stable periods of life (Jones and Carpenter 1986). Finally, there is also evidence that both "everyday" shyness and its variants of greater clinical significance can be successfully treated with psychological and other forms of intervention (Cappe and Alden 1986).

See also: ANXIETY DISORDERS; DEVELOPMENTAL PSYCHOPATHOLOGY; PEER INFLUENCE; SEPARATION ANXIETY; TEMPERAMENT

Bibliography

Asendorpf, J. B. (1989). "Shyness as a Final Common Pathway for Two Different Kinds of Inhibition." *Journal of Personality and Social Psychology* 57:481–492.

Briggs, S. R. (1988). "Shyness: Introversion or Neuroticism?" *Journal of Research in Personality* 22:290–307.

Buss, A. H. (1980). *Self-Consciousness and Social Anxiety.* San Francisco: Feemon.

Buss, A. H. (1984). "Two Kinds of Shyness." In *Self-Related Cognitions in Anxiety and Motivation,* ed. R. Schwarzer. Hillsdale, NJ: Erlbaum.

Cappe, R. F., and Alden, L. E. (1986). "A Comparison of Treatment Strategies for Clients Functionally Impaired by Extreme Shyness and Social Avoidance." *Journal of Consulting and Clinical Psychology* 54:796–811.

Caspi, A.; Elder, G. H., Jr.; and Bem, D. J. (1988). "Moving away from the World: Life-Course Patterns of Shy Children." *Developmental Psychology* 24:824–831.

DePaulo, B. M.; Dull, W. R.; Greenberg, J. M.; and Swaim, G. W. (1989). "Are Shy People Reluctant to Ask for Help?" *Journal of Personality and Social Psychology* 56:834–844.

Eisenberg, N.; Fabes, R. A.; and Murphy, B. C. (1995). "Relations of Shyness and Low Sociability to Regulation and Emotionality." *Journal of Personality and Social Psychology* 68:505–517.

Garcia-Coll, C.; Kagan, J.; and Reznick, J. S. (1984). "Behavioral Inhibition in Young Children." *Child Development* 55:1005–1019.

Hansson, R. O. (1986). "Shyness and the Elderly." In *Shyness: Perspectives in Research and Treatment,* ed. W. H. Jones, J. M. Cheek, and S. R. Briggs. New York: Plenum.

Halford, K., and Foddy, M. (1982). "Cognitive and Social Skill Correlates of Social Anxiety." *British Journal of Clinical Psychology* 21:17–28.

Izard, C. E., ed. (1972). *Patterns of Emotions: A New Analysis of Anxiety and Depression*. New York: Academic Press.

Jones, W. H., and Briggs, S. R. (1984). "The Self-Other Discrepancy in Social Shyness." In *The Self in Anxiety, Stress, and Depression,* ed. R. Schwarzer. Amsterdam, The Netherlands: North Holland.

Jones, W. H.; Briggs, S. R.; and Smith, T. G. (1986). "Shyness: Conceptualization and Measurement." *Journal of Personality and Social Psychology* 51:629–639.

Jones, W. H., and Carpenter, B. N. (1986). "Shyness and Social Behavior." In *Shyness: Perspectives on Research and Treatment,* ed. W. H. Jones, J. M. Cheek, and S. R. Briggs. New York: Plenum.

Jones, W. H.; Cheek, J. M.; and Briggs, S. R., eds. (1986). *Shyness: Perspectives on Research and Treatment*. New York: Plenum.

Kagan, J.; Reznick. J. S.; and Snidman, N. (1988). "Biological Bases of Childhood Shyness." *Science* 240:167–171.

Morris, D.; Soroker, M.; and Burruss, A. (1954). "Follow-Up Studies of Shy Withdrawn Children: A. Evaluation of Later Adjustment." *American Journal of Orthopsychology* 24:743–754.

Phillips, S. D., and Bruch, M. A. (1988). "Shyness and Dysfunction in Career Development." *Journal of Counseling Psychology* 35:159–165.

Pilkonis, P. A., and Zimbardo, P. G. (1979). "The Personal and Social Dynamics of Shyness." In *Emotions in Personality and Psychopathology,* ed. C. E. Izard. New York: Plenum.

Plomin, R., and Rowe, D. C. (1979). "Genetic and Environmental Etiology and Social Behavior in Infancy." *Developmental Psychology* 15:62–72.

Porteus, M. A. (1979). "Survey of the Problems of Normal 15-Year-Olds." *Journal of Adolescence* 2:307–323.

Prior, M.; Smart, D.; Sanson, A.; and Oberklaid, F. (2000). "Does Shy-Inhibited Temperament in Childhood Lead to Anxiety Problems in Adolescence?" *Adolescence* 39:461–468.

Rubin, K. H.; Nelson, L. J.; Hastings, P.; and Asendorpf, J. (1999). "The Transaction between Parents' Perceptions of Their Children's Shyness and Their Parenting Styles." *International Journal of Behavioral Development* 23:937–958.

Russell, D.; Cutrona, C. E.; and Jones, W. H. (1986). "A Trait-Situational Analysis of Shyness." In *Shyness: Perspectives on Research and Treatment,* ed. W. H. Jones, J. M. Cheek, and S. R. Briggs. New York: Plenum.

Simmons, R., and Rosenberg, R. (1975). "Sex, Sex Roles, and Self-Image." *Journal of Youth and Adolescence* 4:229–258.

WARREN H. JONES

SIBLING RELATIONSHIPS

Relationships with extended kin, spouses, parent and child, and siblings are all affected by a changing social world. Family size (one indicator of sibling structure) is shrinking in many societies. The International Database of the U.S. Bureau of the Census (2001) reports an all-time low of 2.76 children per woman, down from 4.17 in 1960. Growing up with fewer siblings (or none, as is mandated in much of China) has profound implications in terms of intrafamily relationships, inheritance possibilities, and obligations and responsibilities for family members.

Dimensions of the sibling relationship. Sibling relationships can be analyzed according to a number of factors, including position within the sibling system, roles assumed by different siblings, family norms for children's expected behavior, the extent of coalition formation within the sibling system, and the functions siblings perform for each other. Expected behavior for siblings may depend on where the child is in the sibling hierarchy (oldest, middle, or youngest child) and whether the child is male or female. At all ages, sisters are reported to be, and report themselves to be, closer to one another than are brothers or cross-sex sibling pairs. Position and sex may dictate role behavior (e.g., who assumes outside versus inside chores or acts as caretaker for younger siblings). Coalitions foster sibling solidarity, counter the power of parents or other sibling subgroups, and develop to strengthen siblings' positions in times of conflict. Siblings serve many functions for one another. Some of these include serving as a "testing ground" for one another when experimenting with new behaviors or ideas before exposing them to parents or peers; serving as teachers; practicing negotiation skills; and learning the consequences of cooperation and conflict and the benefits of commitment and loyalty. Older siblings may serve a protective function, "translate" parental and peer meanings for younger brothers and sisters, and act as pathbreakers when new ideas or behaviors are introduced into the family. For example, parents may object less when a younger son decides to get his ear pierced, or a younger sister decides to have the small of her back tattooed, because an older sibling already weakened parental resistance. Lastly, it is within the sibling group that children first experience feelings of fairness and justice. Siblings compete for resources within the family, and if resources (such as affection, time, attention from parents, space, or material goods) are scarce, children watch closely to ensure that they are getting their fair share (Ihinger 1975). What appears to distinguish middle childhood sibling behavior of children in the United States from its non-Western counterpart is that it reflects a family system based upon independent relationships. It mirrors the prototypical Western family as a culture of individualism (as compared to a culture of collectivism). The consequence of such behavior is intergenerational and interpersonal independence (Kagitcibasi 1996).

Sibling Similarities and Differences

Despite commonalties of shared factors such as social class; physical and mental health of family members; the parental relationship; the emotional climate of the family; and the child-rearing skills, values, and attitudes of parents, siblings are a good deal different from one another. Only about 50 percent of siblings' genetic background is shared. In terms of weight and height, they are about 50 percent similar, and the correlation between siblings and their IQ scores is only .47 as children and .31 as adults (Dunn and Plomin 1990). By comparing the shared and nonshared family experiences of siblings, it can be seen that differential treatment and expressions of affection and interest by parents and other kin, perceptions of this differential treatment by siblings, and the effects of peer groups and school experiences coalesce to create a separate "life" for each child growing up in the same family.

Siblings in Non-Western Cultures

Siblings have important and unique roles and functions to perform within the family. These vary, however, according to the cultural context. In Western societies, the sibling relationship tends to be identified by biological or genealogical criteria and it is typically less important than the spousal or parent-child relationship. In contrast, in some non-Western societies, a sibling may be more important than a spouse; in others, cousins may be considered siblings (Adams 1999). Victor Cicirelli (1994) cautions that it is important to be aware of how sibling is defined in the particular culture that is being discussed. For example, in the Malo culture of New Hebrides in Oceania, all cousins of the same sex, the parent's siblings of the same sex, and grandparents of the same sex are considered to be siblings. In the Marquesas culture of Oceania, however, only full biological siblings are identified as siblings.

Many important family functions, such as taking care of younger children and teaching them basic household and occupational skills, are carried out by siblings in non-Western societies. Childcare is usually a shared activity that takes place in the context of other activities such as doing chores, participating in games or play, or just lounging. Sibling caretaking serves several major functions for a family and community. It supports parents who must spend their time in vital subsistence tasks, serves as a training ground for parenting, provides exposure to important superordinant and subordinate role behavior that will have to be carried out later in adulthood (e.g., male and female roles), and stresses interdependence—an important characteristic of the group in which the children will live (Weisner 1982). Thus, interdependence and mutual support between siblings is highly valued and is learned at very early ages (Nuckolls 1993). A family system that is characterized by a *culture of collectivism* develops from such interdependence. So strong is this interdependence that in much of the world siblings are a major influence in the life course of their brothers and sisters. As adults, they may help arrange marriages and provide marriage payments for each other. "They share life crisis and rite of passage ceremonies essential to their cultural and social identity; they take on ritual and ceremonial responsibilities for each other essential to community spiritual ideas" (Weisner 1982, p. 305). This culture of collectivism persists even in the face of social change. A study of adolescents found that youth in Asia and Latin America (collectivistic cultures) held stronger family values and higher expectations regarding their obligations to assist, respect, and support their families than did their European counterparts (Fulgini, Tseng, and Lam 2000).

Interdependence does not, however, eliminate conflict and disharmony. In non-Western societies, whether descent is traced through the mother or father's lineage, two distinct dimensions of adult sibling relationships have been identified. One of these is *competition* for inheritance and property-holding; the other is joint *obligation* to parents. Within a patrilineal society there are a variety of ways property can be transmitted. Family property may be inherited by the first-born son or the last-born son, or given to all sons partially. Yet another way of property distribution involves giving sons undivided shares so that siblings have to stay and work together for their collective interests and property. In matrilineal societies, family property passes through the female line but males still have rights of inheritance. Tension over the division of family property often occurs between a man and his wife's brothers (Adams 1999).

In Taiwan there is a unique family structure called *take-turn stem families* where siblings make an arrangement, according to a timeline, in which parents will live with them. Siblings take turns and cooperate to support and take care of their parents. Caring for parents often brings siblings into close and frequent contact with each other.

Age and sex are major determinants of sibling status in most parts of the world. An ancient Confucian code for family socialization in Chinese society was as follows: "Fathers should be kind to their children, and sons should be obedient to their parents, and older brothers should love their younger siblings, and younger brothers should respect their older ones." Following this code, children (especially the first son or daughter) were socialized to provide material and emotional support for one another at an early age. Older brothers replaced parental roles and inherited parental authority in the absence of a father whereas older sisters served as a backup system of caregiving for younger siblings. However, sisters had no control or power over them, especially younger brothers. Younger brothers and sisters were expected to obey and respect their older siblings, particularly the big brother, as if he were in the parental position (Tsai 1998). Modernization and economic development have modified these norms. When the one-child policy was first introduced in China in 1979, its aim was to prevent rapid population growth. In urban areas, particularly, this policy succeeded, with a dramatic decline in the Chinese birth rate. The fertility rate was 5.8 per woman in 1960; 5.3 in 1970; 2.5 in 1980; and 1.82 in 2000 (Census Bureau 2001; World Bank 1984, 1993). However, changing a society's norms about how many children to have when male children are more highly valued than female children is problematic when the odds are high that the one and only child conceived will turn out to be a girl. Increasing rates of infanticide, the crippling of first-born girls in order to get permission to have a second child, among other considerations, brought about a slight relaxation of this policy for parents with special needs: if, for example a child was disabled or the first-born was a girl (Shen 1996). There are profound consequences for a society's families when a large majority of couples have only one child. Over time family structure and relationships are transformed when there are no kin to call brother, sister, uncle, aunt, or cousin.

In the following section the focus is on one Western society, the United States. However, although the details vary, similar interpersonal processes of conflict, competition, cooperation, learning, and teaching take place within the sibling group, just as in non-Western societies.

Sibling Relationships across the Life Span

In the United States, sibling relationships are dynamic and vary depending on the stage in the life cycle; they are no less important during old age than when children are toddlers or adolescents. However, what one expects from and what one gives to a sibling in old age is different from expectations and exchanges at earlier ages.

Research on infant and preschool siblings. There is growing recognition that siblings play potentially important roles in socializing each other's social, emotional, and cognitive development. One example of the effects of this socialization role is the finding that older siblings are not as accommodating to young children as adults are and thus encourage the development of pragmatic skills in their younger siblings. In other words, older siblings will make younger children perform such tasks as tying their own shoes and getting their own bowl of ice cream.

Psychologists studying the interaction patterns of preschool children and their infant siblings report that the arrival of a newborn in the family has immediate consequences for older siblings' adjustment and behavior. Bed-wetting, withdrawal, aggressiveness, dependency, and anxiety are among the most problematic behaviors reported in these studies (Dunn 1995). Positive roles for older siblings include the opportunity to learn caretaking skills and serving as models for appropriate social and cultural behaviors. Numerous studies find that young siblings benefit from observing and imitating their older brothers and sisters. This happens because older siblings "engage in activities during interaction that are within the scope of actions that the younger child is capable of reproducing immediately or slightly after observation" (Zukow 1989, p. 85).

Sometime between their third and fourth year, older siblings begin to take a more active interest in younger siblings, and brothers and sisters become both more effective companions and antagonists at this age. Older siblings demonstrate a clear understanding of how to provoke and annoy a younger child as early as age two. Countering this negative tendency is an increasing interest in alleviating the distress of others during the second year. There is some evidence that the way mothers talk to an older sibling about a newborn child is associated with the quality of the behavior between the children over time (Dunn 1995). Children become increasingly more involved with their older siblings during the preschool years.

Relationships between sisters are reported to be closer than those between brothers and those between a brother and a sister. The two girls pictured are sisters, living in Cambodia. DAN LAMONT/CORBIS

Sibling relationships in middle childhood. American children become more egalitarian during the middle childhood years. When fifth- and sixth-grade children were asked about the relationship with their siblings, the quality noted most was companionship. This was followed by antagonism, admiration of sibling, and quarreling (Furman et al. 1989). These positive and negative qualities of the relationship were independent of one another, illustrating the ambivalence and complexity of sibling interaction. Younger siblings report feeling more affection, closeness, and respect for older siblings than the reverse.

Brothers and sisters tend to influence each other's gender role development. Boys with sisters score higher on expressiveness than boys with brothers, and girls with brothers score higher on competitiveness and assertiveness (Sulloway 1996). Boys with only brothers are reported as being more violent than boys with sisters (Straus, Gelles, and Steinmetz 1980).

A study of the relation between parental behaviors and sibling behaviors found that negative parental care (hostile/detached behavior) was associated with sibling quarreling/antagonism among children in middle childhood. Differential treatment by mothers is associated with more conflicted and hostile sibling relationships (Boer, Goedhart, and Treffers 1992).

Adult sibling relationships. A large majority (about 80%) of adult Americans have at least one living brother or sister (Connidis and Campbell 1995). Because of their shared past, and because they are typically close in age, siblings are potential sources of financial, physical, emotional, and psychological support and assistance in old age. Some of the topics related to adult siblings that have been investigated include the frequency of contact, feelings of solidarity and closeness, use of siblings as confidants, and types of support and assistance exchanged.

Those who study adult sibling relationships report four consistent findings. First, sibling contact and closeness is greater between sisters than in brother-brother or brother-sister combinations. Overall, women are more likely to be the ones to initiate and maintain kin ties, including those with siblings. Second, geographic proximity is a key factor in predicting the extent of adult sibling interaction. When siblings live close to one another they maintain contact, exchange goods and services, and support one another to a greater degree than when they live apart. Third, there is a curvilinear relationship between age and feelings of closeness, contact, and meaningfulness of the sibling tie. Relations are close during early and middle childhood, they decrease slightly during adolescence and middle age, and increase as individuals near the end of the life cycle. Almost two-thirds of adults report that they are close to their grown-up siblings and 78 percent feel they get along well with them (Cicirelli 1991). Fourth, sibling ties appear to be more salient for the unmarried and childless than for those who are currently married and those with children (Campbell, Connidis, and Davies 1999; White 2001).

In the process of studying sibling relationships, when methodological analyses are complex and include or control for the large variety of factors that influence adult sibling interaction (marital status, presence and number of children, number of siblings, income and educational status, age, presence of living parents, and race/ethnicity), the complexity of sibling interaction becomes evident. For example, one longitudinal study reported that giving and receiving help and assistance increasingly declined between the ages of twenty and seventy, then took an upturn—for siblings living close to one another. No upturn was evident for those who lived twenty-six miles away or further. When siblings lived close by, help was given more often by those with higher education; when there were more siblings in the family, help was more often given by sisters; and help was less likely to be given when parents were still alive (White 2001).

One similarity between the adult siblings in the United States and Taiwanese siblings discussed earlier is a reported closeness between siblings who provide care for elderly parents. When there is an emotionally close sibling network, the likelihood is much higher that *all* siblings will share in the support and care (Matthews 1987).

Some life experiences affect sibling closeness, improve relations, or increase the frequency of contact among adult siblings. Ingrid Connidis (1992) found that sibling ties were heightened when divorce, widowhood, or health problems occurred. However, when siblings married or had children, the relationship did not change. Lynn White (2001), on the other hand, found that getting married and having children decreased sibling contact and exchange among siblings.

Gary Lee and Marilyn Ihinger-Tallman (1980) examined whether sibling relations increased the morale of elderly persons. They found that siblings acted as companions, provided emotional support, shared reminiscences, and validated each other's sense of self, but they did not influence each others' degree of life satisfaction, disappointment, or pleasure in life. This finding underlies the more common "benign" exchanges that occur among elderly siblings. Although they may hold high regard for one another, sociability usually consists of telephone calls and visits to one anothers' homes: just sitting around talking and discussing matters of mutual interest—ordinary as opposed to exciting conversations (Scott and Roberto 1981; Allan 1977). Reminiscences are particularly valued because siblings were witnesses to the changes that took place during an individual's life (Connidis 1992). In a now-classic study, Bert Adams (1968) suggested that such mundane contacts are sufficient to meet the general obligation adult siblings have to maintain the relationship.

Stepsiblings and Half-Siblings

Half-siblings. The number of households that include either a half- or stepsibling increased 21.4 percent between 1980 and 1990 (Statistical Abstract of the United States 1994). Demographers predict that 33 percent of all children will live with a stepparent before the age of eighteen, and the predominant type of family form will be a stepfamily by the year 2010 (Visher, Visher, and Pasley 1997).

Stepsiblings. When children from different family backgrounds are brought together to live in the same household, the new situation contains more ambiguities and fewer guidelines than exist for full brothers and sisters who live in first-marriage families. For example, they generally have had few opportunities to get to know and adjust to one another before living together; remarried family boundaries are more fluid and children may come and go, visiting a parent, perhaps moving in for a period of time; stepsiblings have no shared family "history" that helps to develop common habits, values, customs, and expectations; and changes in family size, place in the family, status, and role expectations may precipitate strong emotional reactions in children. However, children tend to be adaptable and, in general, stepsibling relationships are characterized by positive affect even though they are not as close as those of full siblings (Ganong and Coleman 1995). Marilyn Ihinger-Tallman (1987) proposed seven conditions under which stepsiblings develop positive feelings for one another: frequent contact; shared experiences; family conditions fostering intimacy and interdependency; similarities in age, sex, values, and family culture; mutual benefit from association; perceived equality or equity of the children's changed circumstances and new living arrangements; and a minimum of competition over scarce resources (e.g., parental time).

According to Lawrence Ganong and Marilyn Coleman (1994) half-siblings who live together commonly call themselves brother and sister, rarely using the term *half.* Only when children have little to do with each other (i.e., they do not share vacations or other time together) do they tend to use the term *half-sibling.* Anne Bernstein (1997) proposed several factors that help develop strong relationships between half-siblings. These include a parental remarriage that is well established; a larger age gap between half-siblings; a shared residence; fewer children belonging to each spouses; sharing a mother as opposed to sharing a father; same sex; and similar temperaments.

Conclusion

The focus on cross-cultural sibling relationships centered primarily on the Far East, where scholars have concentrated attention on structural and cultural factors (i.e., birth-order, gender effects, inheritance, and socialized interdependencies). From an observation of the shifts in family size and structure, one might conclude that the values of individualism and utilitarianism that characterize family relationships in Western societies will erode the traditional values that are at the basis of non-Western societies (e.g., a preference for many children and for sons, an emphasis on interdependence and community). Testing this supposition, Cigdem Kagitcibasi (1996) examined several cross-cultural studies and concluded that in spite of global changes in social structure and economic changes, the collectivistic cultures that emphasize interdependence among family members continues, at least in the Far East (i.e., Japan, China, Taiwan, and Hong Kong). He did observe in both Western and non-Western societies that a change in family relationships is occurring in the patterns of interdependence: material or instrumental support is decreasing whereas emotional interdependence in increasing. Other scholars find that the traditional values of the importance of children and family obligations remain intact in the Far East in various degrees (Cho and Shin 1996; Shen 1996). Whether the patterns of interdependence and obligation among siblings will change or remain stable remains to be seen.

Focus on one Western nation, the United States, found that social science investigators have tended to examine sibling relationships at the interactional level, focusing on different stages of the life cycle. Growing up with their siblings, stepsiblings, and half-siblings, children act (either positively or negatively) as socializing agents, caretakers, playmates, teachers and role models. Across the life span, the majority of individuals report feeling close to their siblings, yet only a minority depend on these kin for intimate companionship or for financial, emotional, or physical assistance when they are adults. However, certain life experiences (e.g., never marrying, having no children, becoming widowed, or experiencing divorce) can produce closer contact and greater feelings of closeness among siblings. For the majority of people, interactions with siblings are positive and lead to the development of an affectionate life-long bond.

One could characterize sibling relationships in the United States as reflecting a culture of individualism that creates both intragenerational and interpersonal independence. This individualism and independence has, in most cases, resulted in affection, concern, and interest in brothers and sisters but with no accompanying obligation or responsibility for frequent contact or mutual aid (Rossi and Rossi 1990).

See also: ACADEMIC ACHIEVEMENT; AUNT; BIRTH ORDER; CHILDCARE; COMMUNICATION: FAMILY RELATIONSHIPS; CONFLICT: FAMILY RELATIONSHIPS; COUSINS; DEVELOPMENT: COGNITIVE;

DEVELOPMENT: EMOTIONAL; DEVELOPMENT: SELF; FAMILY BUSINESS; FAMILY ROLES; FAVORITISM/DIFFERENTIAL TREATMENT; GIFTED AND TALENTED CHILDREN; KINSHIP; ONLY CHILDREN; PRIMOGENITURE; SELF-ESTEEM; STEPFAMILIES; UNCLE

Bibliography

Adams, B. N. (1968). *Kinship in an Urban Setting*. Chicago: Markham.

Adams, B. N. (1999). "Cross-Cultural and U.S. Kinship." In *Handbook of Marriage and the Family,* 2nd edition, ed. M. B. Sussman, S. K. Steinmetz, and G. W. Peterson. New York: Plenum Press.

Allan, G. (1977). "Sibling Solidarity." *Journal of Marriage and the Family* 39:177–183.

Bernstein, A. (1997). "Stepfamilies from Siblings' Perspectives." In *Stepfamilies: History, Research, and Policy,* ed. I. Levin and M. Sussman. New York: Haworth Press.

Boer, F.; Goedhart, A. W.; and Treffers, P. D. A. (1992). "Siblings and Their Parents." In *Children's Sibling Relationships: Developmental and Clinical Issues,* ed. F. Boer and J. Dunn. Hillsdale, NJ: Erlbaum.

Campbell, L. D.; Connidis, I. A.; and Davies, L. (1999). "Sibling Ties in Later Life."*Journal of Family Issues* 20:114–148.

Cho, B. E., and Shin, H. Y. (1996). "State of Family Research and Theory in Korea." In *Marriage and Family Review,* ed. M. B. Sussman and R. S. Hanks. New York: Haworth Press.

Cho, W. S. (1996). "The Chinese Society and Family Policy for Hong Kong." In *Marriage and Family Review,* ed. M. B. Sussman and R. S. Hanks. New York: Haworth Press.

Cicirelli, V. (1991). "Sibling Relationships in Adulthood: A Lifespan Perspective." *Marriage and Family Review* 16:291–310.

Cicirelli, V. (1994). "Sibling Relationships in Cross-Cultural Perspective." *Journal of Marriage and the Family* 56:7–20.

Connidis, I. A. (1992). "Life Transitions and the Adult Tie: A Qualitative Study." *Journal of Marriage and the Family* 54:972–982.

Connidis, I. A., and Campbell, L. D. (1995). "Closeness, Confiding, and Contact among Siblings in Middle and Late Adulthood." *Journal of Family Issues* 16:722–745.

Dunn, J. (1995). *From One Child to Two.* New York: Ballantine Books.

Dunn, J., and Plomin, R. (1990). *Separate Lives: Why Siblings are So Different.* New York: Basic Books.

Fulgini, A. J.; Tseng, V.; and Lam, M. (2000). "Attitudes toward Family Obligations among American Adolescents with Asian, Latin American, and European Background." *Child Development* 70:1030–1044.

Furman, W.; Jones, L.; Buhrmester, D.; and Adler, T. (1989). "Children's, Parents' and Observers' Perspectives on Sibling Relationships." In *Sibling Interaction Across Cultures: Theoretical and Methodological Issues,* ed. P. G. Zukow. New York: Springer-Verlag.

Ganong, L., and Coleman, M. (1994). *Remarried Family Relationships.* Thousand Oaks, CA: Sage.

Ganong, L., and Coleman, M. (1995). "Adolescent Stepchild-Stepparent Relationships: Changes over Time." In *Stepparenting: Issues in Theory, Research, and Practice,* ed. K. Pasley and M. Ihinger-Tallman. Westport, CT: Praeger.

Ihinger, M. (1975). "The Referee Role and Norms of Equity: A Contribution toward a Theory of Sibling Conflict." *Journal of Marriage and the Family* 37:515–524.

Ihinger-Tallman, M. (1987). "Sibling and Stepsibling Bonding in Stepfamilies." In *Remarriage and Stepparenting: Current Research and Theory,* ed. K. Pasley and M. Ihinger-Tallman. New York: Guilford.

Kagitcibasi, C. (1996). *Family and Human Development across Cultures: A View from the Other Side.* Hillsdale, NJ: Erlbaum.

Lee, G., and Ihinger-Tallman, M. (1980). "Sibling Interaction and Morale: The Effects of Family Relations on Older People." *Research on Aging* 2:367–391.

Matthews, S. H. (1987). "Provision of Care to Old Parents: Division of Responsibility among Adult Children." *Research on Aging* 9:45–60.

Nuckolls, C. W. (1993). *Siblings in South Asia: Brothers and Sisters in Cultural Context.* New York: Guilford.

Rossi, A. S., and Rossi, P. H. (1990). *Of Human Bonding: Parent-Child Relations across the Life Course.* New York: Aldine de Gruyter.

Scott, J. P., and Roberto, K. A. (1981). "Sibling Relationships in Later Life." Paper presented at the annual meeting of the National Council on Family Relations, Milwaukee, WI, October 13–17.

Shen, T. (1996). "The Process and Achievements of the Study on Marriage and Family in China." In *Marriage and Family Review,* ed. M. B. Sussman and R. S. Hanks. New York: Haworth Press.

Straus, M.; Gelles, R. J.; and Steinmetz, S. (1980). *Behind Closed Doors: Violence in the American Family.* New York: Doubleday.

Sulloway, F. J. (1996). *Born to Rebel: Birth Order, Family Dynamics, and Creative Lives*. New York: Pantheon Books.

Tsai, W. H. (1998). *Marriage and the Family: The Sociology of Family*. Taipei, Taiwan: Wu-Nan Publishing.

Visher, E. B.; Visher, J. S.; and Pasley, K. (1997). "Stepfamily Therapy from the Client's Perspective." In *Stepfamilies: History, Research, and Policy*, ed. I. Levin and M. B. Sussman. New York: Haworth Press.

Weisner, T. S. (1982). "Sibling Interdependence and Child Caretaking: A Cross-Cultural View." In *Sibling Relationships: Their Nature and Significance across the Lifespan*, ed. M. E. Lamb and B. Sutton-Smith. Hillsdale, NJ: Erlbaum.

White, L. (2001). "Sibling Relationships Over the Life Course: A Panel Analysis." *Journal of Marriage and the Family* 63:555–568.

World Bank. (1984). World Tables. New York: Oxford University Press.

World Bank. (1993). World Tables. New York: Oxford University Press.

Zukow, P. G. (1989). "Siblings as Effective Socializing Agents: Evidence from Central Mexico." In *Sibling Interaction Across Cultures: Theoretical and Methodological Issues*, ed. P. G. Zukow. New York: Springer-Verlag.

Other Resource

U.S. Bureau of the Census. (2001). *The International Database*. Available from http://www.census.gov/ipc/www/.

MARILYN IHINGER-TALLMAN
YING-LING (AMY) HSIAO

SIKHISM

Sikhism originated in the Punjab region, in northwest India, five centuries ago. It is the youngest of all independent religions in India, where the Sikhs are less than 2 percent (1.8%) of India's one billion people. What makes Sikhs significant is not their numbers but their contribution in the political and economic spheres. The global population of the Sikhs is approximately 20 million, which is slightly more than the worldwide total of Jewish people. About 18 million Sikhs live in the state of Punjab, while the rest have settled in other parts of India, including the substantial communities of Sikhs now established in Southeast Asia, East Africa, the United Kingdom, and North America through successive waves of emigration. During the last century, a quarter million Sikhs have settled in the United States of America. The observant male Sikhs are easily recognized by their beards and turbans—which are the very symbols of their faith.

The Origins and Development of Sikhism

Sikhism is rooted in a particular religious experience, piety, and culture and informed by a unique inner revelation of its founder, Guru Nanak (1469–1539). It evolved in response to three main elements. The first of these was the ideology based on religious and cultural innovations of Guru Nanak and his nine successors. The second was the rural base of the Punjabi society. The third significant element was the period of Punjab history. All three elements combined to produce the mutual interaction between ideology and environment in the historical development of Sikhism.

During the period of the ten Gurus (*Preceptors*), three key events took place in the evolution of Sikhism. The first was the establishment of the first Sikh community at Kartarpur in west Punjab during the last two decades of Guru Nanak's life. To ensure its survival, Guru Nanak formally appointed a successor before he passed away in 1539. Thus, a lineage was established, and a legitimate succession was maintained intact from the appointment of the second Guru, Angad (1504–1552), to the death of Guru Gobind Singh (1666–1708), the tenth and the last Guru of the Sikhs. The second event was the compilation of the canonical scripture, the *Adi Granth* (AG) in 1604 by the fifth Guru, Arjan (1563–1606). It provided a framework for the shaping of the Sikh community. The third was the founding of the institution of the *Khalsa* (pure) by Guru Gobind Singh in 1699, an order of loyal Sikhs bound by common identity and discipline.

The inauguration of the *Khalsa* was the culmination of the canonical period of the development of Sikhism. The most visible symbols of Sikhism known as *the Five Ks*—namely uncut hair, a wrist ring, a short sword, a comb for the topknot, and breeches—are mandatory to the Khalsa. Guru Gobind Singh terminated the line of personal Gurus before he passed away in 1708, and installed the Adi Granth as *Guru Eternal for the*

This Sikh girl lives in a large settlement of American Sikhs in New Mexico. The Sikh Gurus were ahead of their time on issues of gender equality. As early as the sixteenth century, women were granted equal rights to conduct prayers and other religious ceremonies. BUDDY MAYS/CORBIS

Sikhs. Thereafter, the authority of the Guru was to vest in the scripture, the Guru Granth Sahib, and the corporate community itself.

Family in Sikh Thought and Practice

Guru Nanak stressed the way of the householder as the ideal pattern of life for the seeker of liberation, rejecting the ascetic alternative. His successors upheld the same ideal of normal family life, expressing it in their own lives as well as in their teachings. The third Guru, Amar Das (1479–1574) proclaimed: "Family life is superior to ascetic life in sectarian garb because it is from householders that ascetics meet their needs by begging" (AG, p. 586). To understand the family relationships, caste and gender issues need to be addressed from the Sikh perspective.

In Punjabi society, family life is based upon broad kinship relationships. Every individual is a member of a joint family, a *biradari* (brotherhood), a *got* (exogamous group), and a *zat* (endogamous group). Like most other Indians, Sikhs are endogamous by caste (*zat*) and exogamous by subcaste (*got*). Descent is always patrilineal, and marriages link two groups of kin rather than two individuals. The cultural norms of honor (*izzat*) and modesty play a significant role in family relationships within the framework of patriarchal structures of Punjabi society. The Gurus employ the term *pati* that essentially refers to the core of a person, encompassing honor, self-respect, and social standing.

Guru Nanak and the succeeding Gurus emphatically proclaimed that divine Name is the only sure means of liberation for all four castes: the *Khatri* (originally *Kshatriya,* warrior), the *Brahmin* (priest), the *Shudra* ("servant") and the *Vaishya* (tradesman). In the Gurus' works, the Khatris are always placed above the Brahmins in caste hierarchy, while the Shudras are raised above the Vaishyas. This was an interesting way of breaking the rigidity of the centuries-old caste system. All the Gurus were Khatris, and this made them a top-ranking caste in Punjab's urban hierarchy, followed by *Aroras* (merchants) and *Ahluvalias* (brewers). In rural caste hierarchy, an absolute majority (64%) among the Sikhs are *Jats* (peasants), who are followed by *Ramgarhias* (artisans), *Ramdasias* (cobblers) and *Mazhabis* (sweepers). Although Brahmins are at the apex in Hindu caste hierarchy, Sikhs place them distinctly lower on the caste scale. This is partly due to the strictures that the Sikh Gurus laid upon Brahmin pride and partly to the reorganization of Punjabi rural society that confers dominance on the Jat caste.

Doctrinally, caste has never been one of the defining criteria of Sikh identity. In the Sikh congregation, there is no place for any kind of injustice or hurtful discrimination based upon caste identity. Sikhs eat together in the community kitchen, worship together, and share the same sacramental food in the *gurdwara* (Sikh place of worship). However, caste still prevails within the Sikh community as a marriage convention. Most of the Sikh marriages are arranged between members of the same endogamous caste group. Nevertheless, intercaste marriages are now taking place frequently among the professional Sikhs in India and abroad.

The Sikh Gurus offered their vision of gender equality within the Sikh community and took practical steps to foster respect for womanhood. They were certainly ahead of their times when they championed the cause of women with equal access in spiritual and temporal matters. Guru Nanak raised a strong voice against the position of inferiority assigned to women in contemporary society: "From women born, shaped in the womb, to woman betrothed and wed; we are bound to women by ties of affection, on women man's future depends. If one woman dies he seeks another; with a woman he orders his life. Why then should one speak evil of women, they who give birth to kings?" (AG, p. 473). Guru Nanak brought home to the harsh critics of women the realization that the survival of the human race depends upon women whom they unjustifiably ostracized within the society. Guru Amar Das abolished the prevalent customs of "veil" and *sati* (self-immolation) by widows, and permitted widows to remarry. He further appointed women as Sikh missionaries. Indeed, Sikh women have equal rights with men to conduct prayers and other ceremonies in the gurdwaras.

The Gurus were addressing the issues of gender within the parameters set by traditional patriarchal structures. In their view, an ideal woman plays the role of a good daughter or sister, a good wife and good mother within the context of family life. They condemned both women and men alike who did not observe the cultural norms of modesty and honor in their lives. In this context, the images of *immoral woman* and *unregenerate man* are frequently encountered in the scriptural texts. There is thus no tolerance for any kind of premarital or extramarital sexual relationships. In particular, Guru Nanak was deeply anguished over the rape of women when Babur's army invaded India in 1526. He employs the Punjabi phrase "stripping of one's honor" to describe the rape of women by the Mughal army. In fact, rape is regarded as a violation of women's honor in the Punjabi culture. It amounts to the loss of family honor, which in turn, becomes the loss of one's social standing in the community. The notion of family honor is intimately linked with the status of women in Punjabi society.

Two Sikh men in India wear beards and turbans, visible signs of their commitment to their faith. ARVIND GARG/ CORBIS

The *Anand* Marriage Ceremony

The third Guru, Amar Das, proclaimed: "They are not said to be husband and wife, who merely sit together. Rather, they alone are called husband and wife who have one soul in two bodies" (AG, p. 788). This proclamation has become the basis of the Sikh engagement and marriage process, which traditionally emphasizes a spiritual commitment between two partners over any material or physical advantages of the union. At every step, tradition surrounding Sikh marriages seeks to insure the spiritual compatibility of the couple to be married.

To this end, Sikh marriages are arranged by the family of the prospective couples. Although the involvement of the couple themselves has increased over time, the involvement and input of the family has remained vital. This emphasis on family, reflected in every aspect of Sikh life, from the communal eating halls of the gurdwaras to the common practice of identifying oneself through one's parentage, is among the most important precepts of Sikhism. At every stage in the Sikh process of engagement and marriage, the opinion of each partner's family is respected, considered, and valued.

A Sikh wedding, according to the *Anand* (Bliss) rite, takes place in the presence of the Guru Granth Sahib, and the performance of the actual marriage requires the couple to circumambulate the sacred scripture four times to take four vows. Before the bridegroom and the bride make each round, they listen to a verse of the wedding hymn (AG, pp. 773–74) by the fourth Guru, Ram Das (1534–1581), being read by a scriptural reader.

Then they bow before the Guru Granth Sahib and get up to make the round while professional musicians sing the same verse in the congregation. During the process of their clockwise movement around the scripture four times, they take the following four vows: (1) To lead an action-oriented life based on righteousness and to never shun obligations of family and society; (2) to maintain a bond of reverence and dignity between them; (3) to keep enthusiasm for life alive in the face of adverse circumstances and remain detached from worldly attachments; and (4) to cultivate a "balanced approach" in life, avoiding all extremes. The pattern of circumambulation in the Anand marriage ceremony is in fact the re-actualization of the primordial movement of life in which there is no beginning and no end. The continuous remembrance of the four marital vows makes the life of the couple blissful.

The standard manual of *Sikh Code of Conduct, Sikh Rahit Maryada,* explicitly states: "No account should be taken of caste; a Sikh woman should be married only to a Sikh man; and Sikhs should not be married as children." This is an ideal arrangement. In actual practice, however, a large majority of Sikh marriages take careful account of the prospective partner's caste. In initial inquiries, the choosing of a partner requires that the marriage should be arranged with a member of the same zat, but that it must exclude got of the father, the mother, the father's mother, and the mother's mother. In addition, rural Sikhs maintain the custom of village exogamy, such that marriages should not be arranged between two families of the same village. It further ensures that a married daughter does not live in her father's village, strengthening the rule that inheritance in Punjabi village families is always through the male lineage. The custom of village exogamy still operates even when the families move to towns or overseas locations. Most rural Sikhs living in the diaspora know the identity of their "ancestral village," and hence they normally observe this custom (McLeod 1997).

The situation with urban Sikhs is entirely different. By tradition, the Khatris are large-scale traders, and they live in the big cities to conduct their business. The small-scale traders among the Sikhs are mostly Aroras. Both of these groups are not too rigid about caste requirements in choosing a marriage partner. The Khatri and Arora families frequently intermarry, and there is no custom of city exogamy among them. Marriages between cousins (i.e., marrying mother's sister's son or daughter, or marrying father's sister's son or daughter) are also possible. This is due to the influence of Muslim culture on these groups, who moved to India from Pakistan at the time of partition in 1947. Further, marriages between Hindus and Sikhs are common in the case of Khatri and Arora families.

Changing Trends in Sikh Marriages

Sikh marriage patterns are showing signs of significant changes in the following areas. First, a difference between the education of the groom and the bride is narrowing. This preference for comparable educational qualifications in the selection of prospective partners, leading ultimately to the earning capacity of both spouses, shows the growth of individualism and decline in joint families and kinship ties. Such marriages have become possible due to the impact of economic and educational factors, including the processes of urbanization and modernization. Second, a favorable attitude towards intercaste marriages shows the decline of caste ties. Caste as a principle of endogamy is, however, losing its importance more in urban cities than in rural villages. The Singh *Sabha* reforms within Sikhism in the last century have enhanced this process. Third, young men and women now marry later than they did in earlier times. Finally, obtaining the consent of the young man and the woman in matrimonial alliances, favoring widow remarriage, agreeing to divorce as a last resort, and getting married again after divorce, are the practices that indicate the impact of Western urban influences (Rajagopalan and Singh 1967).

Another tradition has been an important part of the Sikh marriage process. The fundamental respect for the judgement of family is reflected in the ancient practice of not meeting one's partner between the time of engagement and the time of marriage. It is understood that, at the time of engagement, a spiritual commitment to one's fiancé(e) has been made. Respect for the family makes impossible any second-guessing of that commitment. Over many centuries, this practice expanded and became tradition, so that even when the family is unavailable or uninvolved, the custom of not meeting one's fiancé(e) before the marriage ceremony continues. In recent decades, however, many young Sikhs have chosen not to follow this established tradition, and the rigid procedure surrounding Sikh arranged marriages is on the decline. Nevertheless, for many devout Sikhs, the above practice continues to be an important reflection of their faith and tradition. To be forced to ignore or violate long-standing tradition by meeting one's fiancé(e) between the engagement and the ceremony could cloud the sanctity of the marriage process in the minds of those devout Sikhs involved.

In the diaspora, Sikh marriages are undergoing significant changes. The second-generation Sikhs are raising questions concerning the traditional form of marriage. Like their peer groups from other religious faiths, they tend to follow the idea of romantic love in choosing their partners. They frequently date prospective mates to test their compatibility in standard situations. Living in a complex multiethnic environment, they are exposed to people of different faiths and cultures. Not surprisingly, this results in occasional marriages between Sikh and non-Sikh partners. These marriages provide new challenges to both partners to make necessary adjustments in their lives.

Conclusion

In Sikh households, the selection of a marriage partner is arranged formally with parental approval. The idea of romantic love is gaining some popularity among contemporary youth, but economic, educational, and family considerations are still among the important factors in most decisions to marry. Caste endogamy is on the decline among Sikh professionals. Doctrinally, women enjoy complete equality, but in actual practice they have yet to achieve equal representation within various Sikh organizations. In the pluralistic societies of the postmodern world, where emphasis is being placed upon liberty, diversity, tolerance, and equality of race and gender, Sikh ideals are thoroughly in place and congenial to the developing values of the society.

See also: INDIA; RELIGION

Bibliography

Jyoti, S. K. (1983). *Marriage Practices of the Sikhs: A Study of Intergenerational Differences*. New Delhi: Deep & Deep.

McLeod, W. H. (1995). *Historical Dictionary of Sikhism*. Lanham, MD: Scarecrow Press.

McLeod, W. H. (1997). *Sikhism*. London: Penguin Books.

Rajagopalan, C., and Singh, J. (1967). "Changing Trends in Sikh Marriage." *The Journal of Family Welfare* 14(2):24–32.

Singh, H., ed. (1992–1998). *The Encyclopaedia of Sikhism*, Vols. 1–4. Patiala: Punjabi University.

Singh, J. (1968). "Sikh Marriage in Transition." *Social Action: A Review of Social Trends* 18(3):224–230.

Singh, K. (1996). "The Condition of Women as Depicted in the Adi Guru Granth." *Journal of Sikh Studies* 20(2):9–15.

Singh, K., trans. (1994). *Sikh Rahit Maryada: The Code of Sikh Conduct and Conventions*. Amritsar: Dharam Parchar Committee, SGPC.

Singh, P. (2000). *The Guru Granth Sahib: Canon, Meaning and Authority*. New Delhi: Oxford University Press.

Talib, G. S., trans. (1984–1990). *Sri Guru Granth Sahib*, Vols. 1–4. Patiala: Punjabi University.

PASHAURA SINGH

SINGLE-PARENT FAMILIES

Single-parent families can be defined as families where a parent lives with dependent children, either alone or in a larger household, without a spouse or partner. There was a rapid and drastic increase in the number of single-parent families in the latter half of the twentieth century. This change has been used by some to argue that we are witnessing the breakdown of the family (defined as a married couple residing with their dependent offspring) with negative effects for children, families, and society (Popenoe 1996). Others suggest that single-parent families have been present in all societies over time and should not be viewed as deviant or problematic, but rather as an alternative family form (Coontz 1997). Regardless of how family diversity is viewed, the increase in and prevalence of families headed by one parent has a major influence on the social, economic, and political context of family life.

Demographic Trends

Globally, one-quarter to one-third of all families are headed by single mothers, calling into question the normativeness of couple headed families. Developed countries, in particular, are experiencing an increase in single-parent families as divorce becomes more common. The United States has the highest percentage of single-parent families (34% in 1998) among developed countries, followed by Canada (22%), Australia (20%), and Denmark (19%). In developing countries, divorce is not as common, but desertion, death, and imprisonment produce single-parent families, primarily headed by women (Kinnear 1999). Rates vary country to country from a low of less than 5 percent in Kuwait to a high of over 40 percent in Botswana and Barbados. In countries such as Ghana, Kenya, Rwanda, Cuba, Puerto Rico, Trinidad, and Tobago more than 25 percent of households are headed by women.

There was a dramatic increase in single-parent families in the United States in the last three decades of the twentieth century; only 13 percent of families were headed by a single parent in 1970. Over one-fourth of children in the United States lived with a single parent in 1996, double the proportion in 1970. Approximately 84 percent of these families are headed by women. Of all single-parent families, the most common are those headed by divorced or separated mothers (58%) followed by never-married mothers (24%). Other family heads include widows (7%), divorced and separated fathers (8.4%), never-married fathers (1.5%), and widowers (0.9%). There is racial variation in the proportion of families headed by a single parent: 22 percent for white, 57 percent for black, and 33 percent for Hispanic families.

Historically, single-parent families were the result of parental death; about one-fourth of children born around the turn of the nineteenth century experienced the death of a parent before they reached age fifteen (Amato 2000). The factors most commonly related to the contemporary U.S. single-parent family are changing social and cultural trends, increased rates of divorce and nonmarital childbearing, increased employment opportunities for women, decreased employment opportunities for men (especially African-American men), and the availability of welfare benefits that enable women to set up their own households (Rodgers 1996). It has been estimated that 50 percent of children born in recent cohorts will spend some part of their childhood with a single parent as a result of separation, divorce, or out-of-marriage births.

The U.S. divorce rate steadily and dramatically increased in the thirty year period 1965 to 1995. In 1965 the divorce rate was 2.5 per 1,000 people, increasing to an all time high of 5.0 in 1985 and declining to 4.4 in 1995. The United States has one of the highest divorce rates in the world, twice that of Denmark, Canada, or the United Kingdom. The divorce rate is highest among lower income couples. Divorce is somewhat higher for African-American couples, with 10.5 percent divorced in 1993, compared to 8.8 of white couples and 7.3 of Hispanic couples. Developing regions of the world are also experiencing an increase in the divorce rate, although the proportions remain low in most regions of Asia and Africa.

Most children live with one parent as the result of divorce, but by 1996 the single-parent home was as likely to involve a never married as a divorced parent. Unmarried women in the United States accounted for nearly one in three births in 1995, compared with one in five in 1980 and one in ten in 1970. The percentage of births to single women varies across race. In 1995, 20 percent of all births to Asian and Pacific Islanders were to single women, compared to 25 percent for white women; 41 percent for women of Hispanic origin; 57 percent for Native American, Eskimo, and Aleut women; and 70 percent for African-American families.

For the most part the increase in births to unwed mothers is the consequence of unplanned, accidental pregnancy coupled with the decision not to marry. This includes teenage mothers who are less likely to marry than pregnant teens in the past, as well as adult women who delay marriage while pursuing educational and career opportunities, increasing the probability of pregnancy outside of marriage. Teens account for almost 13 percent of all births in the United States (23% for African Americans, 23% for Native Americans, and 17% for Hispanic Americans, 11% of white births). Approximately one million adolescent girls become pregnant each year, with half ending in birth. The majority of these pregnancies (67%) involve an adult male over the age of twenty.

Since 1990, births have declined among African-American teens and risen among white teens, who comprise two-thirds of teen mothers. The factors contributing to teen pregnancy and childbirth include lack of close contact with adult role models; peer pressure; family poverty; the perception among many teens that few opportunities for success are available; and inadequate sex education, especially about contraception and family planning (Sidel 1998). Girls who have a positive self-image, high expectations and aspirations for the future, and good relationships with their parents are much less likely to get pregnant than others. The United States has one of the highest rates of teen pregnancy in the world, with 53 births per 1,000 women aged nineteen and younger compared to countries at the lower end of the spectrum such as Denmark (nine births per 1,000), Netherlands (six births per 1,000), and Japan (four births per 1,000). Worldwide adolescents give birth to over 14 million children annually.

Another form of parenthood outside of marriage involves single women choosing to bear or adopt and raise children alone. Technological developments allowing insemination without intercourse contribute to women's choices in this regard. Women choosing to conceive children in this manner include lesbians, who may raise their children as a single parent or with a same-sex partner; and heterosexual women who are in their thirties, single, and want children before they are past childbearing age (Burns and Scott 1994). Although an increase in nonmarital childbirth has occurred among well-educated and professional women, it is more commonly found among women with lower levels of education and income.

The rate of births to women outside of marriage in the United States is similar to rates found in Canada, France, the United Kingdom, and other industrialized countries. In Sweden, nonmarital childbirth is twice as high as in the United States, while in Japan only one percent of all births occur outside of marriage. Several Central American countries have high rates of nonmarital births ranging from 67 percent in Guatemala and El Salvador to 53 percent in Honduras. Four factors explain the rate of births outside marriage in these countries: male migration, male mortality, machismo, and pro-natalist attitudes and policies (Kinnear 1999).

Mother-Only and Father-Only Families

Single-parent families are generally categorized by the sex of the custodial parent (mother-only or father-only families). Mother-only families include widows, divorced and separated women, and never-married mothers. In the case of divorce, mothers are usually given custody in the United States and other developed countries. In Italy, in 1997, for example, 90 percent of children whose parents divorced went into the custody of their mothers. Since the vast majority of single parents are mothers, most of the research focuses on female-headed families. However, regardless of sex, single parents share similar problems and challenges (Grief 1985).

In the past, father-only families formed as a result of widowhood, desertion by the mother, or wives refusing custody. There has been a 25 percent increase in the number of single fathers in the United States—from 1.7 to 2.1 million—from 1995 to 1998. In 1997, Canadian fathers received sole custody in 11 percent of the cases and joint custody in 28 percent. The increase in father-only families is due, in part, to the efforts of fathers to obtain custody of their children. Although most fathers in the United States do not request custody during divorce proceedings, about one-half to two-thirds of those who do are awarded custody. In 1995 2.5 million U.S. children resided with a single father, an increase from 1 percent of children in 1970 to 4 percent. Single fathers in the United States are twice as common in white families (16%) as compared with black families (8%). Although single fathers are slightly better educated than single mothers, on average, both groups are less likely to be college graduates and more likely to have dropped out of high school than married parents.

There are an estimated one million noncustodial mothers in the United States, with 75 percent voluntarily giving up custody. The primary reasons women give up custody include: inadequate financial resources, child's preference for living with the father, difficulty in controlling the children, threats of legal custody battles, and physical or emotional problems experienced by the mother. Almost all (97%) noncustodial mothers actively maintain a relationship with their children (Herrerias 1995).

Fathers increase their chances of getting custody when they pay child support, when the children are older, and when the oldest child is male. Single fathers report that they feel competent as primary parents and, in taking responsibility for the activities of caregiving usually assigned to mothers, are able to develop intimate and affectionate relationships with their children (Risman 1986). Other factors supporting their transition into

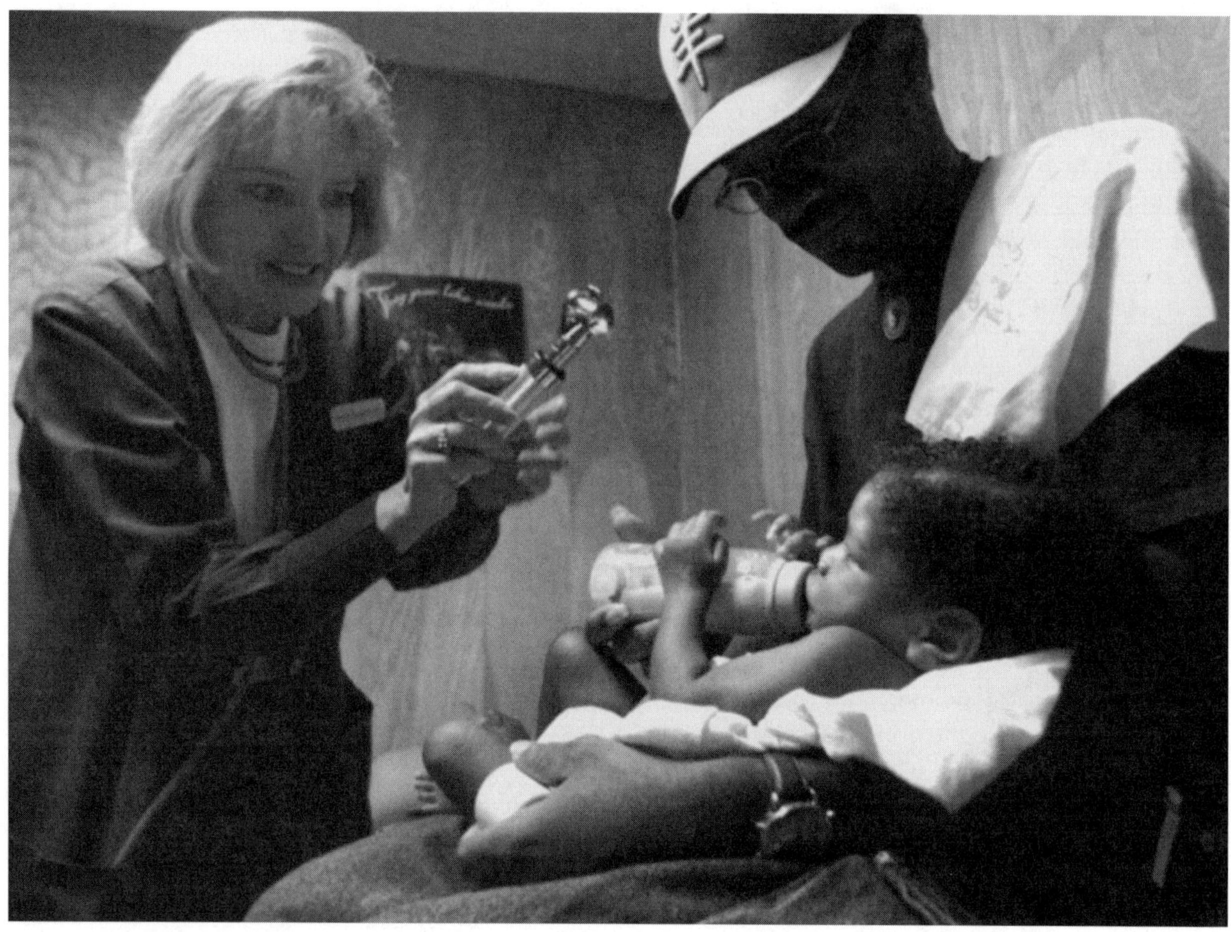

A single father in Texas takes his son for a check-up. Single fathers report that they feel competent as primary caregivers and are able to develop affectionate relationships with their children. A/P WIDE WORLD PHOTOS

primary parenthood include financial security, prior involvement in housework and child care during the marriage, satisfaction with child-care arrangements, and a shared sense of responsibility for the marital breakup (Greif 1985).

Challenges of Single-Parenting

Parenthood is challenging under the best of conditions. With one parent, the challenges are multiplied. Coping with childrearing for single parents becomes more difficult because of responsibility overload, when one parent makes all the decisions and provides for all of the family needs; task overload, when the demands for work, housework, and parenting can be overwhelming for one person; and emotional overload, when the single parent must always be available to meet both their own and their children's emotional needs. Alone or in combination these result in problems for the single parent, including loneliness, anxiety, and depression.

Support from friends and relatives can offset the effects of overload, with friends offering a buffer against loneliness and relatives giving more practical help (Gladow and Ray 1986). One difficulty is asking for help in a society that defines the family as an autonomous unit responsible for its own circumstances and well-being. However, few single parents can successfully raise children alone, despite the social expectation that noncustodial parents (usually the father) should only be responsible for supplemental financial support, while the custodial parent (usually the mother) takes on both parenting and economic roles (Goldscheider and Waite 1991). Some suggest that the ideal of an independent family head represents a Eurocentric view which is challenged by an African-American model of motherhood (Hill Collins 1994). In this model the importance of caring for and supporting children in the context of community development and social activism is emphasized. Children are cared for and raised by their own mothers (bloodmothers), other women in the community (othermothers), and relatives. African-American children are more likely to live with a grandmother than are white and Hispanic children.

The Effects on Children

In the United States, the effects of single-parent family life on children fall into two categories: (1) those attributed to the lower socioeconomic status of single parents and (2) the short-term consequences of divorce that moderate over time. Four factors are predictive of U.S. children's adjustment to the divorce of their parents: the passage of time, the quality of the children's relationship with their residential parent, the level of conflict between parents, and the economic standing of the children's residential family. In the first few years after a divorce, the children have higher rates of antisocial behavior, aggression, anxiety, and school problems than children in two parent families. However, some of these problems may be attributed to a decrease in available resources and adult supervision; many of the negative effects disappear when there is adequate supervision, income, and continuity in social networks (McLanahan and Sandefur 1994).

In mother-only families, children tend to experience short- and long-term economic and psychological disadvantages; higher absentee rates at school, lower levels of education, and higher dropout rates (with boys more negatively affected than girls); and more delinquent activity, including alcohol and drug addiction. Adolescents, on the other hand, are more negatively affected by parental discord prior to divorce than by living in single-parent families and actually gain in responsibility as a result of altered family routines (Demo and Acock 1991). Children in single-mother homes are also more likely to experience health-related problems as a result of the decline in their living standard, including the lack of health insurance (Mauldin 1990). Later, as children from single-parent families become adults, they are more likely to marry early, have children early, and divorce. Girls are at greater risk of becoming single mothers as a result of nonmarital childbearing or divorce (McLanahan and Booth 1989). Although the research findings are mixed on long-term effects, the majority of children adjust and recover and do not experience severe problems over time (Coontz 1997).

A common explanation for the problems found among the children of single parents has been the absence of a male adult in the family (Gongla 1982). The relationship between children and noncustodial fathers can be difficult and strained. Fathers often become disinterested and detached from their children; in one study more than 60 percent of fathers either did not visit their children or had no contact with them for over a year. The loss of a father in the family can have implications beyond childhood (Wallerstein and Blakeslee 1989). However, the lack of a male presence may not be as critical as the lack of a male income to the family. The economic deprivation of single-parent family life, in combination with other sources of strain and stress, is a major source of the problems experienced by both parents and children.

Economics of Single-Parent Family Life

The most profound effect of divorce is economic deprivation for mother-only families. For example, in the United States, the custodial mother's and children's standard of living is reduced by 30 percent on average while the noncustodial father's standard of living increases by 15 percent (Hoffman and Duncan 1988). The typical pattern for both middle-class and working-class newly divorced mothers in Western societies is to move into inadequate apartments in undesirable neighborhoods due to the scarcity of affordable housing that will accommodate children (Wekerle 1985). The result is that they often leave their social networks and sources of support at the same time that they are forced to enter the labor force or increase their working hours. For single parents the housing/employment issue is one of affordability and geographic proximity and access to jobs that pay a living wage (Mulroy 1995). In addition, teenage mothers face economic adversity with the interruption of their education. As teen mothers move into adulthood they often remain unskilled, unemployed, and unemployable (Sidel 1998).

Child support, money paid by the noncustodial parent to the custodial parent toward the support of the children, does not offset the economic deprivation experienced by single-parent families. Since mothers retain custody in the majority of cases, fathers are typically ordered to pay child support. However, award levels have consistently accounted for less than half of the expense of supporting a child, representing about 10 percent of the noncustodial father's income. According to one study, a father's child support payments average less than his car payments (Pearce 1990). Despite recent U.S. legislation (Family Support Acts of 1988 and 1994), many fathers do not pay court-ordered child support payments. In 1997, 68 percent of custodial mothers with children under the age of eighteen received full (42%) or partial (27%) child support payments, leaving a third without any payment. The average amount received by U.S. mothers in 1997 was $3,700, an increase of $400 from 1994. Women below the poverty level are the least likely to be awarded or to receive child support. Black and Hispanic mothers are even less likely to be awarded support or to benefit from payments (Rodgers 1996).

When the situation is reversed and custody is granted to the father, mothers are ordered to pay lower child support awards since fathers tend to have higher incomes. Mothers still pay an average of $3,300 to custodial U.S. fathers, although only one-third pay in full. Compared to noncustodial mothers who do not pay support, mothers who pay support earn a higher income, have more regular visitation with their children, are consulted more by the fathers, and have more positive feelings about their arrangement (Greif 1986).

The economics of single-parent family life mean that single mothers are disproportionately represented among the poor. Among U.S. households headed by single mothers in 1998, one-third lived below the poverty line, compared to 12 percent of male-headed families. In 1999, 42 percent of children living in female-headed families were poor, compared to 18 percent in male-headed families, and 8 percent in couple-headed families. Overall, women with dependent children comprise two-thirds of the poor population, a phenomenon referred to as the "feminization of poverty." This is especially pronounced for African-American and Hispanic women who head families, with 43 and 51 percent, respectively, living below the poverty line, compared to 31 percent of white mothers who head families. African-American (14.7%) and Hispanic (16.8%) single fathers are also more likely to be living below the poverty line than their white male counterparts (10.8%).

Around the world women make up the majority (70%) of the 1.3 billion people who live in poverty. The United Nations Commission on the Status of Women (1996) estimates that women constitute almost 60 percent of the world's population, perform two-thirds of all working hours, receive only one-tenth of the world's income, and own less than 1 percent of the world's wealth. The poverty of families headed by women can be attributed to the fact that women's roles are primarily domestic (mother, homemaker), undervalued, and unpaid. In addition, when women work for wages they make significantly less than their male counterparts. Even full-time employment does not guarantee financial security, given the structure of the labor force, the lower wages paid in female-dominated occupations, and the lower human capital investment of single mothers (education, training, and work experience). However, even when controlling for education and work place experience, women earn less than men, a global pattern that holds true across all racial and ethnic groups throughout the occupations. In the developed world, the United States and Canada have the highest wage gap (75%) and the Scandinavian countries have the lowest (80% to 94%).

Gender differences in earnings are exacerbated by race; in 1995, the median income for full-time year-round work in the United States was $22,900 for white women, $20,700 for African-American women, and $17,200 for Hispanic women. Whereas the majority of single mothers worked for wages in 1997 (79%), one-third were employed part-time or part-year only. Single fathers, on the other hand, were more likely to be working full-time (77%), with only 17 percent working part-time or part-year. In addition, single mothers are more likely than other employees to experience layoffs, they receive fewer fringe benefits, and they pay higher expenses for childcare (Kinnear 1999). In developing countries, families are often disrupted as parents leave home to find work. For example, Filipina women regularly migrate to Hong Kong to work as domestics on multiple-year contracts managed by the government. They leave their children in the Philippines and send money for their support since the wages earned in Hong Kong ($325 month) exceed what they could earn at home ($125 month).

The income of mothers heading families, supplemented by child support and transfer payments, is used to support the family. In the United States child support and alimony together account for about 10 percent of the total income of white mothers and for about 3.5 percent of the income of African-American mothers. However, alimony or spousal support is awarded in less than 15 percent of all divorce cases, is received in less than 7 percent, and has been virtually eliminated in marriages ending in fewer than five years (Weitzman 1985).

Another source of support essential to the ability of single parents to manage the demands of work and home is child care. A disruption in childcare arrangements can be stressful for any family in which both parents work; for the single-parent family, it can create an immediate crisis. Single mothers report that childcare is one of the most difficult obstacles in their efforts to provide for their families through paid employment (Kamerman and Kahn 1988). European and Scandinavian countries are ahead of the United States in developing government subsidized comprehensive childcare programs. France and Sweden, in particular, provide a model of supporting working mothers, with resulting low rates of poverty among mother-only families, along with modest levels of public dependency (Garfinkle and McLanahan 1994). Japan also provides high-quality, affordable day care for working mothers; poor families receive the service free (Rodgers 1996).

Public Assistance for Single-Parent Families

An alternative or supplement to paid employment for U.S. single parents is public assistance in the form of Temporary Aid to Needy Families (TANF), formerly Aid to Families with Dependent Children (AFDC). This means-tested program, established in 1935 as part of the Social Security Act, was originally designed to support mothers and children who had lost a male earner in the family, allowing the mother to stay at home. Historically, welfare policy was based on a distinction between worthy women who were dependent through no fault of their own (widows) and undeserving mothers who were divorced or never married. Program regulations were developed in ways that reflected this distinction, along with racist assumptions about the role of immigrant and African-American women within both the family and the paid labor force.

Welfare reform and the resulting TANF program represent a change in societal views about women's roles in the family and at work. The assumption is that mothers can and should work to support their families and that public support should be temporary and supplemental. TANF placed a lifetime limit of five years on welfare eligibility, required that within five years one-half of a state's caseload was to be enrolled in jobs or job-related activities, and excluded college education from the list of qualified work and training activities. As a result, the welfare rolls dropped dramatically from 14.2 million in 1994 to 7.6 million in 1998, a decline of more than 40 percent. At the same time the number of children living at the lowest levels of poverty (less than $6,401 in 1997) grew by 400,000 between 1995 and 1997.

Only about half of all mother-only families receive welfare benefits at any given time. In recent years the rate of participation in at least one public assistance program plummeted from 45 percent in 1993 to 38 percent in 1997. Regardless, public assistance, including non-cash transfers, maintains families well below the U.S. poverty line.

Other developed countries, particularly those in Western Europe, have maintained the goal of supporting mothers to stay at home if they wish. In Great Britain, for example, mothers are not pressured to find work outside the home, and child allowances, national health services, and access to public housing are provided. In Norway single parents receive a child allowance, a child care cash benefit, an education benefit, a housing allowance, and transitional and advanced cash benefits. While most single parents (90%) have incomes less than half the median family income, only 9 percent of all children in single-parent families fall below the poverty line. Developing countries are less likely to have formalized assistance programs in place, although there are grassroots efforts such as the AIDS Support Organization in Uganda to aid widows and their children and Dwip Unnayam Sangstha in Bangladesh to help divorced and widowed women and their children.

Views of Single-Parent Families

Societal views about single-parent families are expressed in social policies and agendas. U.S. policies, especially those relating to welfare, child care, and family/work support, reflect disapproval of families needing public support, single-parent families in particular. Divorced or "broken" families as they are sometimes called are seen as deviant and a threat to the social order (Faust and McKibben 1999). Other Western countries support the well-being of children regardless of the number of parents with programs such as guaranteed child-support payments, health insurance, child care, maternity and parenting benefits, and housing subsidies. Although all families are well-supported, couple-headed families are valued over other family forms.

In many areas of the Third World single mothers are socially ostracized and seen as having inferior status (Kinnear 1999). In the case of widowhood, women are not allowed to inherit property or possessions in many countries where other sources of support are not provided. In the past, unmarried women (with or without children) would have been cared for by the family system, which has been weakened as a result of urbanization. In these patriarchal societies men and women do not share equally the limited resources available to families. Development, especially strategies based on capitalism, worsens the situation for women.

Societal views are also expressed in public discourse about women living outside of marriage and family who fail to live up to the ideals of motherhood imposed through legal and public policies. Feminists argue that efforts to control women's sexuality and enforce mothers' economic dependence upon men are part of a backlash designed to limit women's mobility and freedom (Silva 1996). Rather than attempt to force women into a traditional mold, more institutional support for the new type of dual-earner and single-parent family prevalent today is needed.

See also: ACADEMIC ACHIEVEMENT; ADOLESCENT PARENTHOOD; ADOPTION; CHILDCARE; DIVORCE: EFFECTS ON CHILDREN; FAMILY POLICY; FATHERHOOD; HEALTH AND FAMILIES; HOUSING; JUVENILE DELINQUENCY; LONELINESS; MOTHERHOOD; NONMARITAL CHILDBEARING; POVERTY; SOCIOECONOMIC STATUS; STRESS; WIDOWHOOD; WORK AND FAMILY

Bibliography

Amato, P. R. (2000). "Diversity within Single-Parent Families." In *Handbook of Family Diversity,* ed. D. Demo, K. R. Allen, and M. A. Fine. New York: Oxford University Press.

Burns, A., and Scott, C. (1994). *Mother-Headed Families and Why They Have Increased.* Hillsdale, NJ: Erlbaum.

Collins, P. H. (1994). "The Meaning of Motherhood in Black Culture." In *The Black Family: Essays and Studies,* ed. R. Staples. Belmont, CA: Wadsworth.

Coontz, S. (1997). *The Way We Really Are: Coming to Terms with America's Changing Families.* New York: Basic Books.

Demo, D. H., and Acock, A. C. (1991). "The Impact of Divorce on Children." In *Contemporary Families: Looking Forward, Looking Back,* ed. A. Booth. Minneapolis, MN: National Council on Family Relations.

Faust, K. A., and McKibben, J. N. (1999). "Marital Dissolution: Divorce, Separation, Annulment, and Widowhood." In *Handbook of Marriage and the Family,* ed. M. B. Sussman, S. K. Stenimetz, and G. W. Peterson. New York: Plenum.

Garfinkel, I., and McLanahan, S. S. (1994). "Single-Mother Families, Economic Insecurity, and Government Policy." In *Confronting Poverty : Prescriptions for Change,* ed. S. H. Danziger, G. Sandefur, and D. H. Weinberg. Cambridge, MA: Harvard University Press.

Gladow, N. W., and Ray, M. P. (1986). "The Impact of Informal Support Systems on the Well-Being of Low-Income Single Parents." *Family Relations* 35:113–123.

Goldscheider, F. K., and Waite, L. J. (1991). *New Families, No Families?* Berkeley: University of California Press.

Gongla, P. A. (1982). "Single-Parent Families: A Look at Families of Mothers and Children." *Marriage and Family Review* 5:5–27.

Greif, G. L. (1985). *Single Fathers.* Lexington, MA: D. C. Heath.

Greif, G. L. (1986). "Mothers Without Custody and Child Support." *Family Relations* 35:87–93.

Herrerias, C. (1995). "Noncustodial Mothers Following Divorce." *Marriage and Family Review* 20:233–55.

Hoffman, S. D., and Duncan, G. J. (1988). "What are the Economic Consequences of Divorce?" *Demography* 25:641–645.

Kamerman, S. B., and Kahn, A. J. (1988). *Mothers Alone: Strategies for a Time of Change.* Dover, MA: Auburn House.

Kinnear, K. L. (1999). *Single Parents: A Reference Handbook.* Santa Barbara, CA: ABC-Clio.

Mauldin, T. A. (1990). "Women Who Remain above the Poverty Level in Divorce: Implications for Family Policy." *Family Relations* 39:141–46.

McLanahan, S., and Booth, K. (1989). "Mother-Only Families: Problems, Prospects, and Politics." *Journal of Marriage and the Family* 5:557–580.

McLanahan, S., and Sandefur, G. (1994). *Growing Up with a Single Parent: What Hurts, What Helps*. Cambridge, MA: Harvard University Press.

Mulroy, E. A. (1995). *The New Uprooted: Single Mothers in Urban Life*. Westport, CT: Auburn House.

Pearce, D. M. (1990). "Welfare Is Not for Women: Why the War on Poverty Cannot Conquer the Feminization of Poverty." In *Women, the State, and Welfare,* ed. L. Gordon. Madison: University of Wisconsin Press.

Popenoe, D. (1996). *Life Without Father*. New York: Free Press.

Risman, B. J. (1986). "Can Men 'Mother'? Life as a Single Father." *Family Relations* 35:95–102.

Rodgers, H. R., Jr. (1996). *Poor Women, Poor Children: American Poverty in the 1990s*. Armonk, NY: M. E. Sharpe.

Sidel, R. (1998). *Keeping Women and Children Last: America's War on the Poor*. New York: Penguin.

Silva, E. B. (1996). *Good Enough Mothering?: Feminist Perspectives on Lone Mothering*. New York: Routledge.

Wallerstein, J., and Blakeslee, S. (1989). *Second Chances: Men, Women, and Children a Decade After Divorce*. New York: Ticknor and Fields.

Weitzman, L. J. (1985). *The Divorce Revolution: The Unexpected Social and Economic Consequences for Women and Children in America*. New York: Free Press.

Wekerle, G. (1985). "From Refuge to Service Center: Neighborhoods That Support Women." *Sociological Focus* 18:79–96

KATHRYN M. FELTEY

SINGLES/NEVER MARRIED PERSONS

Just as the age at first marriage has increased over the past few decades, so too has the proportion of adults living together outside of traditional marriage, as well as the number of men and women who are delaying or forgoing marriage. This has resulted in a great number of men and women spending a significant amount of their adult years single. The U.S. Census Bureau (1999) reports that between 1975 and 1999, the percentage of people who had never married rose from 22 percent to 28 percent. For adults between the ages of thirty and thirty-four, the increase during this period has been from 6 percent to 29 percent for men, and from 9 percent to 21 percent for women.

With age, the percentage of the population that has never married decreases. In Canada and the United States, between 5 and 10 percent of older adults have never been married. As in most societies where approximately 90 to 95 percent of adults do marry, marriage remains the normative and expected life choice, and the connection between marriage and adulthood continues to be reaffirmed.

Social and Historical Context of Singlehood

Most cultures, past and present, have viewed adulthood as synonymous with being married and having children, and being single as a transitional stage that preceded these significant and expected adult roles. Different historical and cultural contexts have significantly affected the propensity, desire, and ability to marry, as well as opportunities and circumstances inside and outside of marriage. Yet historically, as now, a significant minority of the population remained single.

How the never married have been viewed has also varied with time and place. For example, in the early New England states, social and economic sanctions were placed upon women and men who did not marry. At the same time, between 1780 and 1920 in parts of the United States and Europe, singlehood was often seen as a respectable alternative to marriage for women, if these women were willing to devote their lives to the service of others (Chambers-Schiller 1984). Between 1880 and 1930, a bachelor subculture emerged in the United States. Although never married men during this period had more freedom than never married women, they were generally viewed as social outcasts or societal threats (Chudacoff 1999).

During the 1970s, several social factors converged to create a new and more positive recognition of singlehood: more women in higher education, expanding career and job opportunities for women, and increased availability and acceptable of birth control. These societal changes provided women with greater freedom and independence and contributed to a shift in attitudes about the desirability and necessity of marriage. Subsequent scholarship is greatly indebted to the pioneering work of people like Margaret Adams (1978), Marie Edwards and Eleanor Hoover (1974), and, perhaps best known, Peter Stein (1975, 1976, 1981), for examining singlehood as a meaningful and multidimensional lifestyle in its own right and the social factors that brought about this new recognition.

Although singlehood is less stigmatized today than in the past, being part of a married heterosexual couple remains the typical and expected lifestyle choice and, therefore, the status of being never married remains somewhat ambiguous or marginalized. Never married individuals are seen as violating societal expectations for "appropriate" gender role behavior. Even the term *never married* is structured as a negative. For those who remain single, it is difficult to locate positive role models to support and validate their singlehood choice or circumstance. Further, the perception of singlehood tends to differ by age or stage of life. Being single is a normative and expected social role in youth and early adulthood. However, with increased age, the likelihood of marrying diminishes, and the meaning of singlehood often changes as it is seen as a less expected but more permanent state.

The never married in later life are subject to stereotypes that portray older adults in general, as well as those associated with individuals who have failed to marry (Rubinstein 1987). In Anglo-American culture, the terms *spinster* and *old maid* for women, and *confirmed bachelor* for men, may have become outdated, yet their stereotypical meanings persist. Single women particularly may be seen in a negative light, perhaps because expectations remain strong that women will fulfil the nurturing and caring roles most often associated with being married—that of wife, mother, grandmother, and care provider for other family members.

Peter Stein (1981) identifies four categories of never married based upon attitudes toward this single status—voluntary/temporary singles, voluntary/stable singles, involuntary/temporary singles, and involuntary/stable singles. Although individuals can move between and among these categories over their lifetime, whether singlehood is perceived as a choice or circumstance, or is seen as temporary or permanent, can influence one's satisfaction with being single, and one's overall well-being.

The voluntary and stable singles tend to be single by choice and generally satisfied with their decision. This category includes those who have a lifestyle that precludes traditional heterosexual marriage, such as members of religious orders, as well as gay and lesbian single adults. It is difficult to obtain accurate statistics, but the evidence suggests that gays and lesbians comprise between 4 and 6 percent of adults in the United States, Canada, and other Western countries. Research finds that long-term relationships are common among this population, particularly among lesbians. However, regardless of their commitment to a significant partner, these relationships are outside the boundaries of traditional heterosexual marriage, and these individuals are, by societal definition, never married.

The involuntary and stable singles tend to be dissatisfied with their singlehood, but feel it is permanent. This group includes many well-educated, professionally successful women for whom finding a suitable mate is often a problem of demographics—a lack of older, single, well-educated men. This category tends to be the most difficult for successful adjustment to permanent singlehood.

Stein's foundational work highlights the diversity that exists within the never married population, as well as the importance of choice in remaining single for life satisfaction. Research supports this diversity. Many never married individuals make a positive and conscious choice to remain single (O'Brien 1991), while others look upon their singlehood as less desirable, resulting from circumstances beyond their control (Austrom 1984). The former group tends to be more satisfied with being single than the latter.

Stein (1976) identifies push and pull factors—pushes away from marriage and pulls toward singlehood. For individuals who feel that marriage restricts self-realization and limits involvement with other relationships and that singlehood affords greater freedom of choice and autonomy, permanent singlehood is often seen as the marital status of choice. Barbara Simon's (1987) study of older single women finds that most of these women had declined marriage proposals, typically because of their fear of becoming subordinate to a husband.

The salience of these pushes and pulls varies by factors such as age, financial well-being, sexual orientation, as well as the strength and availability of supportive ties to family and friends.

Psychosocial Characteristics of the Never Married

The never married are a diverse and complex group. They differ by sexual orientation, age, health status, ethnicity, and living arrangements, and are as varied as married persons by social class background, education, occupation, and income level. The life satisfaction of the never married, in general, is similar to the married and better than for other unmarried groups, particularly the divorced. The health status of single men tends to be poorer than for married men, while never married women tend to enjoy better health than other women. In later life, the never married are more likely to face economic insecurity (particularly older women) and weaker social support networks (particularly older men) than are their married counterparts. Marcia Bedard (1992) and others contend that the happiness of single people is related to meeting their social and economic needs, not to the issue of being single.

The literature finds other gender differences in how singlehood is experienced, and these differences tend to be complicated by age. Although current older single women tend to be significantly disadvantaged in economic terms, younger and middle-aged single women tend to have high general ability scores, are highly educated, and have high-status occupations. The situation for single men tends to be different. Many men who remain unmarried are often "those at the very bottom of the social scale, with no women available who are sufficiently low in status" (Unger and Crawford 1992, p. 386).

Never married women tend to manage their lives better than do single men. Studies suggest that single men are more depressed, report lower levels of well-being and life satisfaction and poorer health, and are more likely to commit suicide than single women. It may be that single women's greater ability to maintain close and supportive ties over their lifetime with family members, particularly siblings, and with friends, contributes to their greater overall well-being.

In general, however, never married people report satisfaction in terms of friendships, general health, standard of living, and finances. They are more likely to live with others, such as siblings or other relatives, than are the widowed or divorced, and less likely to be lonely when compared to the other unmarried groups. Although the social networks of the never married tend to be smaller than for the married, the majority of never married individuals are socially active, with friends, neighbors, and relatives, as well as dating partners. Family ties are often central in the lives of the never married, particularly never married women, whose roles include caring for parents, being a lifelong companion to siblings, and serving as a surrogate mother to siblings' children (Allen and Pickett 1987). Friendship ties also take on great significance in the lives of many never married adults, particularly women, across their life course (Campbell, Connidis, and Davies 1999).

Nevertheless, people who remain single throughout their lives still face difficulties. The availability of a willing sexual partner, particularly in later life, is more likely to be a problem for the unmarried than for married couples. Further, for those who live alone, the financial costs tend to be greater than for those who share a household. Also, because most informal support is provided by a spouse and/or adult children, the never married in later life are more likely than the married to have to rely on formal support. When caregiving needs increase, never married older women in particular have a greater likelihood of requiring placement in a long-term care facility than older married women or those with children.

Culture, Ethnicity, and the Never Married

Research is scarce that recognizes culture or ethnicity in the study of the never married. However, the existing literature suggests that the rates of nonmarriage have been increasing across different racial and ethnic groups—groups that have traditionally seen most men and women marry. The U.S. Bureau of the Census (1999) reports that the major increase in the never married population in the United States has occurred among blacks, rising from 32 percent in 1975 to 44 percent in 1999. The nonmarriage rates for other cultural groups have also been increasing. For example, although historically the marriage rates of Asian women were very high, native-born Chinese-American and Japanese-American women had, by the end of the twentieth century, lower rates of marriage than did native-born European-American women.

Susan Ferguson (2000) asked never married native- and foreign-born Chinese-American and Japanese-American women their reasons for remaining unmarried. The women in her study discussed how their feelings about their parents' traditional marriage and their role as the eldest daughter deterred them from marrying and having children. They also talked about the lack of available partners because of family pressure to marry a good Chinese-American or Japanese-American man. Pressure also existed to pursuit an advanced education. The opportunities presented to them with advanced degrees and career gave them an independence that they did not feel would be possible if married to more traditional Asian men. Ferguson (2000, p. 155) concludes that "these never married women are not only challenging the traditional marriage of their parents and the cultural expectations to marry within the Chinese-American and Japanese-American communities but also are challenging the pro-marriage norms and gender role expectations of the dominant culture."

Other research on the marital behavior of Japanese women also finds a link between greater economic independence for women and an increased likelihood of remaining single. James Raymo (1998) contends that economic independence may reduce the appeal of marriage and may be used to "buy out of marriage." He suggests that a significant increase in the number of Japanese women who remain single could have important demographic, social, and economic consequences. More research is needed to better understand the lives of never married women and men within and across different cultures, and whether social and demographic changes that are occurring in other countries will also challenge traditional cultural expectations of marriage as the normative lifestyle choice.

Conclusion

The increase in those remaining single may, in part, reflect changes in social attitudes and structures related to marriage and singlehood. The lives of the never married are varied and complex. Similarities and differences that exist between the never married and other marital groups are more likely to be influenced by individual characteristics such as gender, age, social class, ethnicity, sexual orientation, and level of education, than by marital status group membership. Further research that examines how these and other factors intersect to shape the lives of the never married within and across different cultures and social contexts will help us to learn more not only about those who remain single, but also about the structure and experiences within marriage, families, and social roles and relationships more broadly.

See also: CHILDLESSNESS; COHABITATION; DATING; LONELINESS; SEXUALITY; SOCIAL NETWORKS

Bibliography

Adams, M. (1978). *Single Blessedness.* New York: Penguin.

Allen, K. R., and Pickett, R. S. (1987). "Forgotten Streams in Family Life Course: Utilization of Qualitative Retrospective Interviews in the Analysis of Lifelong Single Women's Family Careers." *Journal of Marriage and the Family* 49:517–526.

Austrom, D. R. (1984). *The Consequences of Being Single.* New York: Peter Lang.

Bedard, M. (1992). *Breaking with Tradition: Diversity, Conflict and Change in Contemporary American Families.* Dix Hills, NY: General Hall.

Campbell, L. D.; Connidis, I. A.; and Davies, L. (1999). "Sibling Ties in Later Life: A Social Network Analysis." *Journal of Family Issues* 20(1):114–148.

Chambers-Schiller, L. (1984). *Liberty, a Better Husband: Single Women in America: The Generations of 1780–1840.* New Haven, CT: Yale University Press.

Chudacoff, H. P. (1999). *The Age of the Bachelor: Creating an American Subculture.* Princeton, NJ: Princeton University Press.

Edwards, M., and Hoover, E. (1974). *The Challenge of Being Single.* New York: Signet Books.

Ferguson, S. (2000). "Challenging Traditional Marriage: Never Married Chinese American and Japanese American Women." *Gender and Society* 14(1):136–159.

O'Brien, M. (1991). "Never Married Older Women: The Life Experience." *Social Indicators Research* 24:301–315.

Raymo, J. (1998). "Later Marriages or Fewer? Changes in the Marital Behaviour of Japanese Women." *Journal of Marriage and the Family* 60:1023–1034.

Rubinstein, R. L. (1987). "Never Married Elderly as a Social Type: Re-evaluating Some Images." *The Gerontologist* 27(1):108–113.

Simon, B. L. (1987). *Never Married Women*. Philadelphia: Temple University Press.

Stein, P. J. (1975). "Singlehood: An Alternative To Marriage." *Family Coordinator* 24:489–503.

Stein, P. J. (1976). *Single*. Englewood Cliffs, NJ: Prentice Hall.

Stein, P. J. (1981). "Understanding Single Adulthood." In *Single Life: Unmarried Adults in Social Context,* ed. P. J. Stein. New York: St. Martin's Press.

Unger, R., and Crawford, M. (1992). *Women and Gender: A Feminist Psychology*. New York: McGraw-Hill.

Other Resources

U. S. Bureau of the Census. (1999). *Current Population Reports*. From Statistical Abstract of the United States, 1999. Available from http://www.ameristat.org.

LORI D. CAMPBELL

SLOVAKIA

Marriage and family have always been considered fundamental social values among the Slovak population. Nearly 90 percent of all inhabitants consider the family to be the most important value in their lives (European Values Study 1999/2000). This feeling was formed under the strong influence of Christianity (according to the last census in 2001, 69% of all inhabitants are Roman Catholic). Approximately 90 percent of the adult population marry at least once in their life. The family based on matrimony is a culturally, religiously, and legislatively accepted form of cohabitation. Basic family legal relationships are regulated by the Act No. 94/1963 (Coll.) on Family.

Marriage

The main purpose of marriage is to create a harmonious, solid, and permanent association for man and woman. Slovak law stipulates that the minimum age for marriage is eighteen years. Younger persons are allowed to marry only by permission of the court. The lowest age permitted for marriage is sixteen years, and a serious reason for requesting permission to marry must be declared (e.g., pregnancy).

Marriage requires the consent of both the man and the woman. This consent must be stated before a church or civil authorities and two witnesses. Marriages performed either by the church or state authorities are equally valid. Before 1992, only marriages in front of the state authorities were considered valid.

Cohabitation of a couple based on matrimony is preferred to any other form of cohabitation in Slovakia. Only 11.5 percent of Slovak inhabitants consider marriage an outdated institution (European Values Studies 1999/2000). Slovak family law does not recognize common-law partnerships as legal conjugal relations. Although some couples cohabitate without marrying, the partners do not have the same legal rights and responsibilities as those who officially marry. Only some rights based on the civil code (e.g., heritage rights, rights to a common dwelling) apply in cohabiting cases, but not the mutual responsibility to provide for subsistence as in the case of married couples.

Selection of Partners

Slovakia was predominantly rural until the middle of the twentieth century. Custom and social status determined how people would find their future wife or husband, usually in the same or nearby village and from a family of similar social level. The parents were the ones who decided who would be their future son- or daughter-in-law. In the urban areas these rules were not so precise nor were they strictly followed. Urban marriages were also more heterogeneous (Štefanek 1944).

Social progress, supported by urbanization and industrialization, promoted new values that were considered important in the process of the selection of a partner. The significance of wealth and the parents' aims receded and the personal interests of the young couple became a priority.

During the period of socialism (1948–1989) economic self-sufficiency, as the basic prerequisite for getting married and establishing a family, became less important. Social policy became supportive, especially towards young families. These policies enhanced access to housing and allowed for state loans on favorable terms to newlyweds.

FIGURE 1

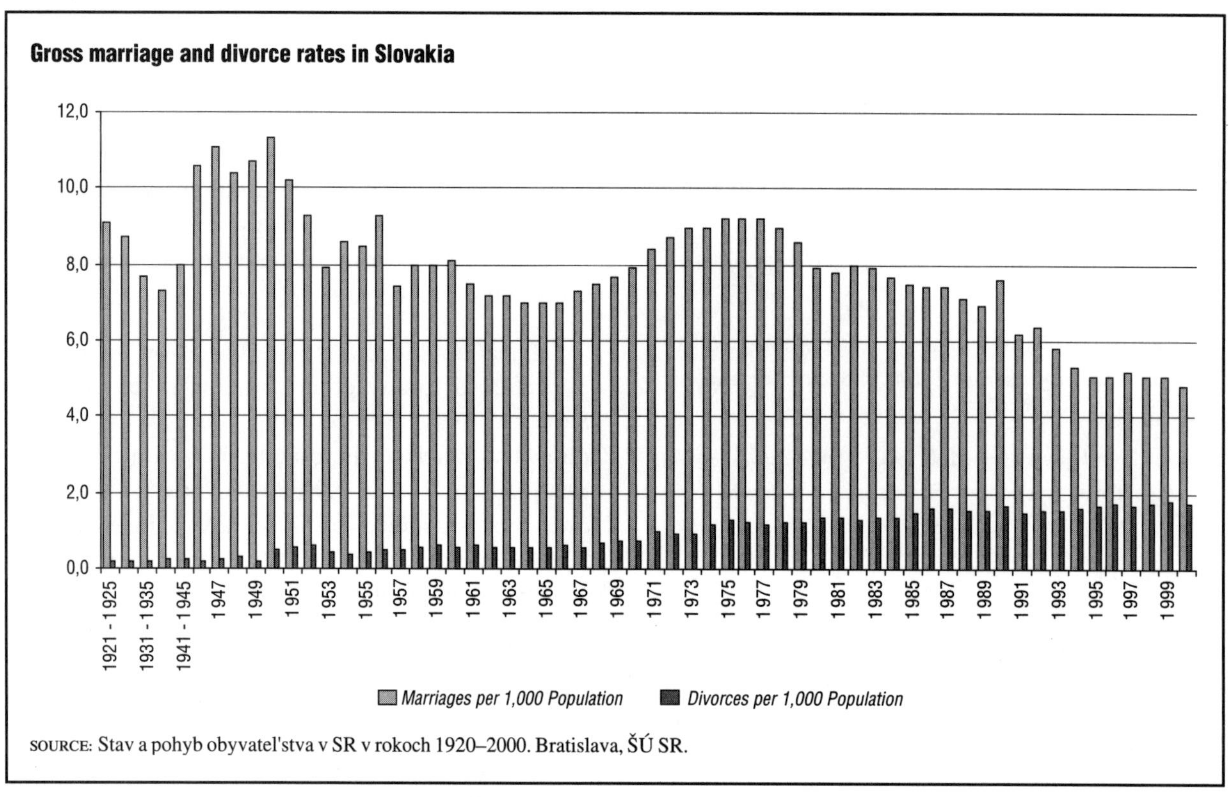

SOURCE: Stav a pohyb obyvatel'stva v SR v rokoch 1920–2000. Bratislava, ŠÚ SR.

These measures and the lack of sexual education, as well as the fact that contraception was neglected, resulted in marriages at early ages. Approximately 50 percent of brides became pregnant before their wedding (Vagac 2000). Many of these were students without their own independent income. It became an expectation that the parents of a young couple would provide assistance, usually financial. Approximately 90 percent of young families depended on such assistance (Bútorová 1996).

Before 1990, the average age for brides was about twenty-one years at marriage (first marriages) and about twenty-three years for bridegrooms. During the 1990s, the average age of women and men at their first marriage rose, and by 1999 the average age of brides was 23.1 years, whereas the average age of bridegrooms rose to 25.6 years. About 85 percent of women and 83 percent of men were living in their parents' home before marriage (Bútorová 1996). These changes were caused both by the increased opportunity to study, to travel, and gain employment abroad after the disappearance of the *Iron Curtain* and by the deterioration of living conditions among young people. Despite the fact that unmarried cohabitation of young couples is not the preferred form, it has become increasingly common.

Termination of Marriage

A marriage may be terminated for one of two reasons: the death of the other spouse or divorce in a court of justice. In the latter case, the process of divorce can only begin after a request for divorce is submitted to the court by one of the spouses. The court must take into account the needs of dependent children. In its decision, the court must define parents' rights and responsibilities with respect to children, as well as decide custody of the children and the way in which each of the parents will contribute to their children's upbringing.

The divorce rate is showing a slow but continuous increase over time. The marriage rate, on the other hand, is approximately half of what it was in the 1980s, which reflects demographic processes, and has continued to decline since the early 1990s. The reason for this is the deterioration in economic and social conditions in the country. The high rate

FIGURE 2

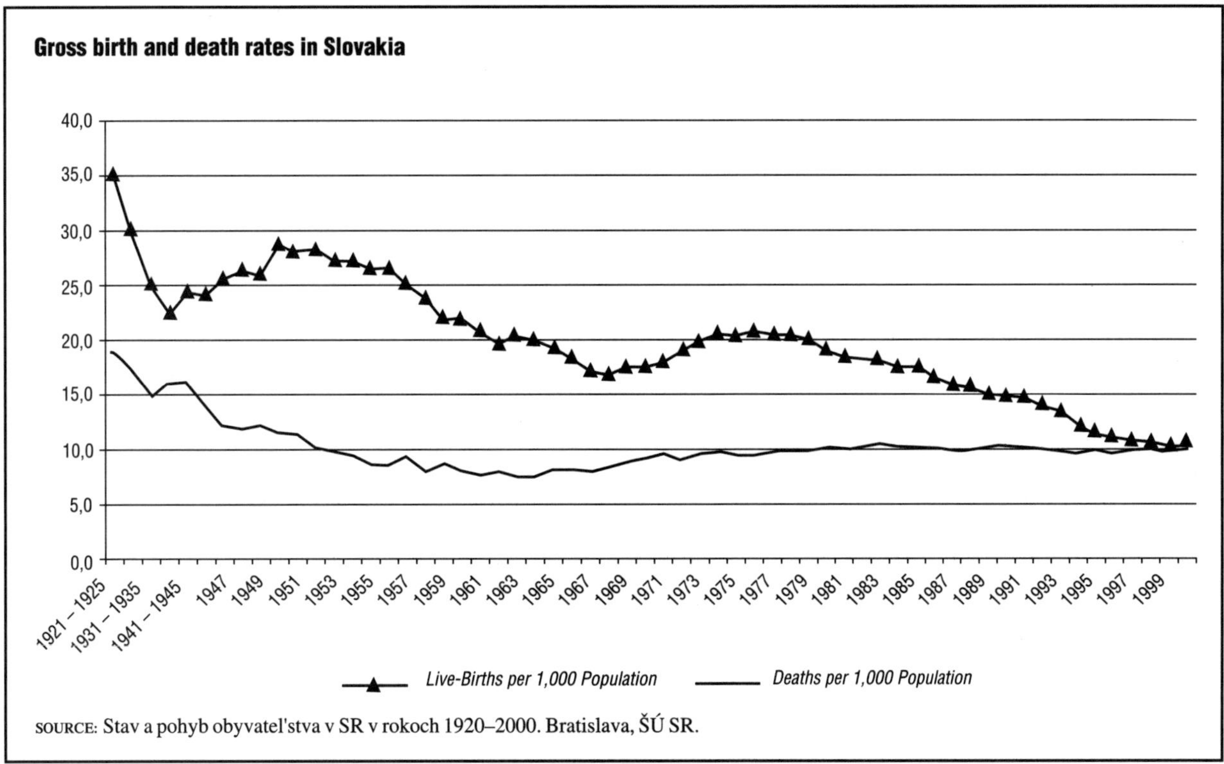

SOURCE: Stav a pohyb obyvatel'stva v SR v rokoch 1920–2000. Bratislava, ŠÚ SR.

of unemployment, the collapse of former social policy measures (such as housing and services for families), and new professional opportunities for young people have contributed to this phenomenon.

Changes in the Family

Following World War II, changes in the family included changes in the size of the family, relations between individual family members, division of labor, and the economic activity of family members and their family roles, as well as to intergenerational coexistence.

Changes in the reproductive behavior in Slovakian families started long before the World War II. A large percentage of the population adopted the ideal of the still-dominant two-children family model. Families with two children made up 18.6 percent of all families in 1961, and increased to 26.7 percent by 1991. Families with more than three children have been in decline (15.4% in 1961, 11.5% in 1991) whereas families with only one child have been increasing in number. Between 1980 and 1991 the share of childless households increased from 36.7 per cent to 39.6 percent. Concomitantly, belief in the importance of children in a family for a marriage to be considered a fulfilled and happy one declined. In 1992, 88.2 percent of respondents indicated that children were an important condition for a happy marriage, whereas in 1999 only 68.8 percent expressed the same opinion (European Values Study 1999/2000).

Agriculture was the main source of subsistence for the largest portion of the Slovak population until halfway through the twentieth century. The division of duties between spouses and their responsibilities to the children were determined by their primary economic activity. "The father is the real head of the family and enjoys the authority of master and ruler of the house. . . . The wife of the household was not only the mother, cook, and guardian of cleanliness, but also coworker on the field, in the shed and in the yard. . . . Children from an early age were involved in household chores and farm work according to their age" (Štefanek 1944, p. 76).

Extensive industrialization started in Slovakia after World War II. Collectivization and the mechanization of agriculture resulted in an exodus of the work force from agriculture. Young men were the first to leave agriculture, later followed by the women. Men found new jobs in industry and

TABLE 1

Children born out of wedlock in Slovakia

Year	Children born out wedlock Total	per 1000 population	% of total births	By order (in %) 1st	2nd	3rd +
1950	5,538	1.60	5.4	57.6	18.3	24.1
1955	4,738	1.26	4.7	59.8	18.4	21.8
1960	4,189	1.00	4.7	49.6	17.9	32.5
1965	4,506	1.03	5.3	49.8	17.0	33.2
1970	5,048	1.11	6.2	55.5	17.8	26.7
1975	5,177	1.09	5.3	61.1	16.7	22.2
1980	5,490	1.10	5.7	64.6	16.6	18.8
1985	5,967	1.16	6.6	62.1	19.0	18.9
1990	6,134	1.15	7.6	26.8	31.0	42.2
1995	7,788	1.45	12.6	55.4	21.6	23.0
1996	8,486	1.57	14.0	52.1	22.0	25.9
1997	8,982	1.67	15.1	51.4	22.0	26.6
1998	8,881	1.65	15.3	53.5	22.5	24.0
1999	9,568	1.77	16.9	54.0	22.0	24.0
2000	10,132	1.88	18.3	.	.	.

SOURCE: Stav a pohyb obyvatel'stva v SR v rokoch 1950-2000. Bratislava, ŠÚ SR.

women found work in the service sector in nearby towns. Beginning in the 1960s, a high proportion of commuters was typical in Slovak rural areas. By the end of the 1980s, there were villages in which 90 percent of economically active people commuted to work. After returning home from their work, people would work on their household plots: they grew crops and vegetables and reared animals, to produce both food and additional income for the family.

Single persons and childless couples would commute daily or weekly. After the birth of a child or children they often moved to the city because it offered better infrastructure and greater opportunities. (As a rule, people moved within short distances from their village to the nearby district capital.) In the urban centers they had access to various services. Highly educated parents wanted their children to have better access to various after-school activities (educational and recreational). The number of families who owned a second home also increased. On weekends, urban dwellers went back to their villages where they did gardening in order to improve their economic situation.

Since the 1970s it became a characteristic feature of rural and urban families in Slovakia for both parents to be employed. The economic activity of women was primarily motivated by the need to obtain additional income for the family. At the end of the 1990s, the majority of wives preferred being employed to the role of a housewife, even if their husbands' earnings were sufficient to support the family.

Family Contacts and Relations

Family law and policy are based on the nuclear family. Nevertheless, relations with kin play an important role in the everyday life of families in Slovakia. Members of larger families provide assistance in difficult situations. Social contact is frequent among relatives and is not limited by the boundaries of the settlement where the family lives.

Standard of Living

There were no significant differences in the standard of living between rural and urban families, or small and large families, or families with more highly educated parents and less well educated parents, until the end of the 1980s. Remuneration from paid work was essentially the same, but income was supplemented by benefits of various kinds. Family allowances were paid for all children until they attended school, prices of food were heavily subsidized, and education was free at all levels. Travel costs were also subsidized, rent for housing was reduced for families with children (the more children in a family, the greater the reduction), and there was income-tax relief for parents and state loans for young families on favorable terms. (The principal was written off by a certain amount at the birth of each additional child.) All of these measures helped families increase their income indirectly and, in this way, allowed for an appropriate standard level of living for all families regardless of their size.

After 1990 most of these benefits were phased out. The economic situation of the majority of Slovak families, especially the young ones, began to deteriorate. At the beginning of the twenty-first century, there is a high rate of unemployment (about 20%) and many families are living on social benefits. The reduction of income from paid work has led to higher involvement of family members in other activities around the home, particularly those focused on the production of food. This is more common in rural areas, where the unemployment rate is higher than in urban centers. Many fathers, particularly from less-developed regions, work in places distant from the family dwelling, and often abroad. Mothers usually stay at home and care for children as well as the household and garden. The father's absence and the mother's heavy workload result in the fact that children are often left on their own. The absence of fathers is also frequent in well-to-do families where fathers are so deeply involved in their business activity that there is no time for the children.

The gap between rich and poor families has increased. The financial situation of families is difficult, especially in the economically marginal regions of Slovakia. There are some families in which no family member has had a paid job in over two or three years—sometimes longer.

Conclusion

Political, economic, social, and demographic processes in the twentieth century affected family relationships and their function. Changes in family roles accompanied such developments as an increase in the educational level of women, the massive entry of women into the labor market, birth control, shrinking of families, and changes in intergenerational relationships and multigenerational coexistence. In spite of these changes, the family remains the basic social network for individual relationships and family solidarity. At the beginning of the twenty-first century the family is still an important social value in the life of the majority of Slovak people.

See also: CZECH REPUBLIC

Bibliography

Bodnárová, B. (2001). "Nezamestnanost a jej dôsledky na rodinu." (Unemployment and its impact on the family). In *Rodina v spolocenskch premenách Slovenska* (Family within the changing society in Slovakia). Preöov, Slovakia: Filozofická fakulta Preöovskej Univerzity (Faculty of Art of University of Preöov).

Bodnárová, B.; Filadelfiová, J.; and Gurán, P. (2001). "Slovakia—National Report." In *Demographic Conditions on Family and Social Policies in CEE Countries,* ed. B. Bodnárová and J. Filadelfiová. Bratislava: Bratislava International Centre for Family Studies.

Bútorová, Z., ed. (1996). *On a ona na Slovensku. ensk údel ocami verejnej mienky* (She and he in Slovakia. Women's deal reflected by public opinion). Bratislava: Focus, Centrum pre sociálnu a marketingovú analzu.

European Values Study. (1999/2000). Bratislava: Tilburg University-Sociologick ústav SAV.

Európsky dotazník hodnôt 1991 (European Questionnaire on Values 1991). *Vsledky komparatívneho vskumu podla Európskeho dotazníka hodnôt—Slovensko 1991* (Results of the Comparative Research by the European Questionnaire of Values-Slovakia 1991). (1991). Bratislava: stav Sociálnych Analz (Institute of Social Analyses).

Filadelfiová, J.; Gurán, P.; Skorová, D.; Leoncikas, T.; äkobla, D.; and Dûambazovic, R. (1999). *The Possibilities and Limits of Family in Today's Europe.* Bratislava: Bratislava International Centre for Family Studies.

Filová, B., and Mjartan, J., eds, (1975). *Slovensko. Lud—II. cast* (Slovakia. People, Vol. 2). Bratislava: Obzor.

Gurán, P., and Filadelfiová, J. (1997). *Rodina a obec v strednej Európe* (Family and community in Central Europe). *Záverecná správa* (research report). Bratislava: S.P.A.C.E.

Scítanie ludu, domov a bytov SR (Population Census in Slovakia). (1961, 1970, 1980, and 1991 editions). Bratislava: šú SR (Statistical Office of the Slovak Republic).

Štefánek, A. (1944). *Základy sociografie Slovenska (Sociographic Background of Slovakia).* Bratislava: Editio Academiae Scientiarium et Artium Slovacae.

Stav a pohyb obyvatelstva v SR v rokoch (Size and mobility of population in the Slovak Republic). (1920–2000 editions). Bratislava: šú SR (Statistical Office of the Slovak Republic).

Vagac, L., ed. (2000). *National Human Development Report. Slovak Republic 2000.* Bratislava: United Development Programme and Center for Economic Development Bratislava.

Zákon o rodine (Act on Family). c. 94/1963 Z.z. (Act No. 94/1963 [Coll.] on Family).

BERNARDÍNA BODNÁROVÁ
JARMILA FILADELFIOVÁ

SOCIAL EXCHANGE THEORY

The Social Exchange Framework was formally advanced in the late 1950s and early 1960s in the work of the sociologists George Homans (1961) and Peter Blau (1964) and the work of social psychologists John Thibaut and Harold Kelley (1959). Over the years, several exchange perspectives, rather than one distinct exchange theory, have evolved. The exchange framework is built upon the combination of the central tenets of behaviorism and elementary economics where human behavior is envisaged as a function of its payoff. The framework is primarily concerned with the factors that mediate the formation, maintenance, and breakdown of *exchange relationships* and the dynamics within them.

Core Assumptions Made Within the Exchange Framework

Embedded within the exchange framework are core assumptions about the nature of individuals and about the nature of relationships (Sabatelli and Shehan 1993). These are summarized as follows:

(1) Individuals seek rewards and avoid punishments.

(2) When interacting with others, individuals seek to maximize profits for themselves while minimizing costs. Because it is not possible to know the actual rewards and costs involved in interacting with another before interactions occur, individuals guide their behavior through their expectations for rewards and costs.

(3) Individuals are rational beings and, within the limitations of the information that they possess, they calculate rewards and costs and consider alternatives before acting.

(4) The standards that individuals use to evaluate rewards and costs differ from person to person and can vary over time.

The assumptions about the nature of exchange relationships are as follows:

(1) Social exchanges are characterized by interdependence, that is, the ability to obtain profits in a relationship is contingent on the ability to provide others with rewards.

(2) Social exchanges are regulated by norms like reciprocity, justice, and fairness.

(3) Trust and commitment result from the emergent experiences of individuals within relationships and help to stabilize relationships over the longer term.

(4) The dynamics of interaction with relationships and the stability of relationships over time result from the contrasting levels of attraction and dependence experienced by the participants in the relationship.

Major Contemporary Concepts

The major exchange concepts can be classified as falling into the following broad categories:

Rewards, costs, and resources. Exchange theories make use of the concepts of rewards and costs (which were borrowed from behavioral psychology) and resources (which were borrowed from economics) when discussing the foundation of the interpersonal exchange. Rewards and resources refer to the benefits exchange in social relationships. Rewards are defined as the pleasures, satisfactions, and gratifications a person enjoys from participating in a relationship (Thibaut and Kelley 1959). Resources, on the other hand, are any commodities, material or symbolic, that can be transmitted through interpersonal behavior (Foa and Foa 1980) and give one person the capacity to reward another (Emerson 1976). The costs of social exchange relationships can involve punishments experienced, the energy invested in a relationship, or rewards foregone as a result of engaging in one behavior or course of action rather than another (Blau 1964).

Satisfaction with exchange relationships: outcomes and comparison levels. Satisfaction with an exchange relationship is derived, in part, from the evaluation of the outcomes available in a relationship. Outcomes are equal to the rewards obtained from a relationship minus the costs incurred. Although it is generally the case that the higher the level of outcomes available, the greater the satisfaction, these concepts are not equivalent. To account for satisfaction, both the experiences of the outcomes derived from the relationship and the expectations that individuals bring to their relationships are taken into account (Nye 1979; Sabatelli 1984; Thibaut and Kelley 1959).

The concept of Comparison Level (CL) was developed by Thibaut and Kelley to explain the contributions that previous experiences and expectations make to the determination of how satisfied an individual is with a relationship. Individuals come to their relationships with an awareness of societal norms for relationships and a backlog of experiences. The CL is influenced by this information and, thus, reflects (a) what individuals feel is deserved and realistically obtainable within relationships, and (b) what individuals feel is important for them to experience within a relationship. When the outcomes derived from a relationship exceed the CL (particularly highly valued outcomes or ones that are important to individuals), global assessments of a relationship are likely to be high (Nye 1979; Sabatelli 1984; Thibaut and Kelley 1959).

Relationship stability: comparison level for alternatives, dependence, and barriers. According to exchange theorists, satisfaction with a relationship alone does not determine the likelihood that a relationship will continue. Thibaut and Kelley (1959) developed the concept of comparison level of alternatives (CLalt), defined as the lowest level of outcome a person will accept from a relationship in light of available alternatives, to explain individuals' decisions to remain in or leave a relationship. The CLalt is an individual's assessment of the outcomes available in an alternative to the present relationship. When the outcomes available in an alternative relationship exceed those available in a relationship, the likelihood increases that person will leave the relationship.

Hence, staying in or leaving a relationship is not simply a matter of how rewarding that relationship is. Relationships that are rewarding are more likely to be stable because a high level of outcomes reduces, in terms of expectations, the likelihood of a better alternative existing. Unsatisfactory relationships, in turn, may remain stable for the lack of a better alternative. These relationships have been conceived of as *nonvoluntary relationships* by Thibaut and Kelley (1959). Married individuals who stay in violent relationships can be thought of as participating in a nonvoluntary relationship—that is, the relationship stays stable in spite of the violence because of the absence of better alternatives (Gelles 1976).

The CLalt is also related to the experience of dependence. Dependence is defined as the degree to which a person believes that he or she is subject to or reliant on the other for relationship outcome. The degree of dependence evidenced is determined by the degree to which the outcomes derived from a relationship exceed the outcomes perceived to be available from existing alternatives. Dependence may be experienced as one of the costs of participating in a relationship, but this is probably determined in part by the level of satisfaction experienced with the relationship. Dependence, in other words, is tolerated in highly rewarding relationships.

Dependence is further influenced by the barriers that increase the costs of dissolving an existing relationship (Levinger 1982). Levinger proposes the existence of two types of barriers—internal and external—that discourage an individual from leaving a relationship by fostering dependence even if attraction is low. Internal barriers are the feelings of obligation and indebtedness to the partner that contribute to dependence by increasing the psychological costs of terminating the relationship. Internal constraints might involve the moral belief that a marriage, for example, is forever or that children should be raised in a home with both parents present. External barriers are things like community pressures, legal pressures, and material or economic considerations that foster dependence by increasing the social and economic costs of terminating a relationship.

Norms regulating exchange relationships: exchange orientations and rules. Exchange relationships are governed by both *normative* and *cognitive* exchange orientations that delineate acceptable and appropriate behavior. Normative orientations refer to the societal views on acceptable and appropriate behavior in relationships. These norms refer to the broader consensus that exists within a culture about how exchange relationships should be structured.

Cognitive orientations represent the beliefs, values, and relationship orientations that an individual associates with various types of exchange relationships (McDonald 1984). These orientations serve as the standards for interpersonal behavior that an individual brings to his or her personal relationships. Among the more prominent of the cognitive orientations discussed in the exchange literature are the norms of distributed justice, or fairness, norms of reciprocity, and norms of equity (Blau 1964; Homans 1961; Walster, Walster, and Berscheid 1978). Each of these has to do with the expectation that within a close and intimate relationship, the rewards experienced by partners should be more or less proportionately distributed. When these norms are violated, as when housework is unfairly distributed within a marriage, people are apt to complain more about the relationship and pressure their partners to restore a more just and fair pattern of exchange (Berardo, Shehan, and Leslie 1987).

Trust and commitment. Trust refers to the belief on the part of individuals that their partners will not exploit or take unfair advantage of them. When relationships conform to the norms of reciprocity and when the pattern of exchange is perceived as being fair, individuals are more likely to come to believe that they will not be exploited (Blau 1964; McDonald 1981). Trust is proposed to be important in relationship development because it allows individuals to be less calculative and to see longer-term outcomes (Scanzoni 1979). Put another way, through trust an individual is able to expect fairness and justice in the long-term and therefore does not have to demand it immediately.

Commitment is characterized as central in distinguishing social and intimate exchanges from economic exchanges (Cook and Emerson 1978). Commitment involves the willingness of individuals to work for the continuation of their relationships (Leik and Leik 1977; Scanzoni 1979). Exchange theorists would expect commitment to develop within a relationship when partners experience high and reciprocal levels of rewards that facilitate the experience of trust (Sabatelli 1999). Commitment builds stability into relationships by increasing partners' dependence on their relationships—in part because the emergence of commitment is thought to be accompanied by a reduction of attention to alternative relationships (Cook and Emerson 1978; Leik and Leik 1977; Scanzoni 1979).

Exchange dynamics. The exchange framework also provides insight into the dynamics found within intimate relationships. In particular, the exchange framework has been used to explain the patterns of power and decision-making found within relationships. Fundamental to the exchange views of power are the assumptions that dependence and power are inversely related, and resources and power are positively and linearly related (Huston 1983; McDonald 1981; Thibaut and Kelley 1959). This is to suggest that exchange theorists address the bases of power by focusing on the constructs of resources and dependence. The partners least interested in their relationships tend to have the greater power in large part because they are less dependent on the relationships. The partners with the greater resources, also, tend to be the ones with the greater power—here largely because they have relatively greater control over the outcomes available to the partners. In other words, the essential point of the discussion of the patterns of interaction observed within exchange relationships is that the relative levels of involvement, dependence, and resources contribute importantly to the different patterns of interaction observed within relationships.

See also: EQUITY; FAMILY THEORY; FILIAL RESPONSIBILITY; INTERGENERATIONAL RELATIONS; RELATIONSHIP INITIATION; RELATIONSHIP THEORIES—SELF-OTHER RELATIONSHIP; SPOUSE ABUSE: THEORETICAL EXPLANATIONS; THERAPY: COUPLE RELATIONSHIPS; TRUST

Bibliography

Berardo, F. M.; Shehan, C. L.; and Leslie, G. R. (1987). "A Residue of Tradition: Jobs, Careers, and Spouses' Time in Housework." *Journal of Marriage and the Family* 49:381–390.

Blau, P. M. (1964). *Exchange and Power in Social Life.* New York: John Wiley & Sons.

Cook, D., and Emerson, R. (1978). "Power and Equity and Commitment in Exchange Networks." *American Sociological Review* 43:721–739.

Emerson, R. (1976). "Social Exchange Theory." In *Annual Review of Sociology,* ed. A. Inkeles, J. Colemen, and N. Smelser. Palo Alto, CA: Annual Reviews.

Foa, E. B., and Foa, U. G. (1980). "Resource Theory: Interpersonal Behavior as Social Exchange." In *Social Exchange: Advances in Theory and Research,* ed. K. J. Gergen, M. S. Greenberg, and R. H. Willis. New York: Plenum Press.

Gelles, R. J. (1976). "Abused Wives: Why Do They Stay?" *Journal of Marriage and the Family* 38:659–668.

Homans, G. (1961). *Social Behavior: Its Elementary Forms.* New York: Harcourt, Brace & World.

Huston, T. L. (1983). "Power." In *Close Relations,* ed. H. H. Kelley, E. Berscheid, A. Christensen, J. H. Harvey, T. Huston, G. Levinger, E. McClintock, I. A. Peplau, and D. R. Peterson. New York: Freeman.

Leik, R., and Leik, S. (1977). "Transition to Interpersonal Commitment." In *Behavioral Theory in Sociology,* ed. R. Hamblin and J. Kunkel. New Brunswick, NJ: Transaction.

Levinger, G. (1982). "A Social Exchange View on the Dissolution of Pair Relationships." In *Family Relations: Rewards and Costs,* ed. F. I. Nye. Beverly Hills, CA: Sage.

McDonald, G. G. (1981). "Structural Exchange and Marital Interaction." *Journal of Marriage and the Family* 43:825–839.

Nye, F. I. (1979). "Choice, Exchange, and the Family." In *Contemporary Theories About the Family,* ed. W. Burr, R. Hill, F. I. Nye, and I. Reiss. New York: The Free Press.

Sabatelli, R. M. (1984). "The Marital Comparison Level Index: A Measure for Assessing Outcomes Relative to Expectations." *Journal of Marriage and the Family* 46:651–662.

Sabatelli, R. M. (1999). "Marital Commitment and Family Life Transitions: A Social Exchange Perspective on the Construction and Deconstruction of Intimate Relationships." In *Handbook of Interpersonal Commitment and Relationship Stability,* ed. W. H. Jones and J. M. Adams. New York: Plenum Press.

Sabatelli, R. M., and Shehan, C. (1993). "Exchange and Resource Theories." In *Sourcebook of Family Theories and Methods,* ed. P. Boss, W. Doherty, R. LaRossa, W. Schuum, and S. Steinmetz. New York: Plenum Press.

Scanzoni, J. (1979). "Social Exchange and Behavioral Interdependence." In *Social Exchange in Developing Relationships,* ed. R. Burgess and T. Huston. New York: Academic Press.

Thibaut, J. W., and Kelley, H. H. (1959). *The Social Psychology of Groups.* New York: John Wiley & Sons.

Walster, E.; Walster, G. W.; and Berscheid, E. (1978). *Equity: Theory and Research.* Boston, MA: Allyn & Bacon.

RONALD M. SABATELLI

SOCIALIZATION

Socialization is not a process unique to childhood. According to the sociological theory known as *symbolic interactionism,* socialization is required for each new role an individual acquires over the life-course. Nevertheless, most of us generally understand socialization to mean the process of creating socially responsible beings out of primarily *asocial* beings—that is, infants and children (asocial in the sense that they are ignorant of the rules and roles of society and must acquire these over time). Socialization is considered to be more general than either *enculturation* or *acculturation.* Enculturation refers to the specific process of transmitting a particular culture from one generation to another (e.g., minority members of a society teaching their children about minority issues such as discrimination). Acculturation refers to the process of acquiring a new or different culture (e.g., as an immigrant to another country).

Several articles outline Western models of socialization. These include chapters by Gary Peterson and his colleagues (Peterson and Haan 1999; Peterson and Rollins 1987). First, what exactly do we mean by *socialization*? One component—probably the one most of us think of initially—is the process that "transforms a biological organism into a human being" (471). The other component is the process that "confronts adults with a new set of experiences and responsibilities" (471). Daphne Bugental and Jacqueline Goodnow (1998) defined socialization as "the continuous collaboration of 'elders' and 'novices'—of 'old hands' and 'newcomers' in the acquisition and honing of skills important for meeting the demands of group life" (389).

Ross Parke and John Buriel (1998) described socialization as "the process whereby an individual's standards, skills, motives, attitudes, and behaviors change to conform to those regarded as desirable and appropriate for his or her present and future role in any particular society" (463). Each of these definitions leaves open the possibility that adults, in addition to children, can be socialized into new roles and responsibilities. Thus, late twentieth century conceptions of socialization suggest that parents, as well as children, are socialized by others referred to as *socialization agents.*

There are many theories that address both the transition to parenthood and parental involvement, as well as the socialization of children (e.g., social learning, symbolic interactionism). There are, however, relatively few theoretical models that focus on the socialization of parents (e.g., Wapner 1993), despite the fact that parenthood has a powerful influence on the development of the adult, to say nothing of the child. Existing developmental models of parent socialization typically use conception or the birth of the child as the starting point in parental development. Furthermore, most approaches focus on parental-child relations in infancy, childhood, or adolescence, ignoring ongoing parent-child relations across the life-course (for an exception see Pillemer and McCartney 1991). The focus of this entry is primarily on socialization—both formal and informal—of children in different contexts, and in different countries around the world.

Unidirectional Models of Socialization

Who are these agents—or forces—of socialization? Early twentieth century models of socialization ignored the fact that parents can be socialized, too, and only looked at the effects of parents on children. This approach is known as a *parent-effects model* (i.e., a unidirectional or one-way effects model from parent to child). This model of socialization stems from a *mechanistic* paradigm (e.g., Reese and Overton 1970), in which the individual is the unit of analysis. In particular, models of this kind focus on the parent as actor, or agent, and the child as reactor. Research conducted from this perspective follows the *social mold* tradition, in which parents are seen as the agents that mold children's behavior. The best example of research in this tradition is Diana Baumrind's (1971) typology of parenting styles—in which parent effects (i.e., parenting styles) determine child outcomes.

Parent effects. For much of the twentieth century, Western parenting theorists and researchers have focused primarily on two essential dimensions of parenting style: *support* (also known as warmth or acceptance) and *control* (Baumrind 1971; Peterson and Haan 1999). It is hypothesized that parenting style falls anywhere along the *continuum of support,* from low support of children to high support of children. At the same time, parenting style can also fall anywhere along the independent or *orthogonal dimension* of control, from low control to high control. Thus, parenting style can be categorized as low in support and control (i.e., *permissive-neglecting*); low in support but high in control (i.e., *authoritarian*); high in support but low in control (i.e., *permissive-indulgent*); or high in support and high in control (i.e., *authoritative*).

Research in the United States, cross-sectional and longitudinal, has consistently found that a parenting style high in both support and control (i.e., authoritative parenting) is associated with children's and adolescent's higher academic achievement and social competence (e.g., Peterson and Haan 1999). A permissive parenting style (i.e., permissive-neglecting or permissive-indulgent) is associated with children who are lower in both academic achievement and social competence, and higher in aggression or impulsiveness. These children may be either neglected by parents who are unwilling or unable to meet the developmental needs of their children, or spoiled by overly indulgent parents who cater to their children's wants instead of their needs. Finally, a parenting style low in support but high in control (i.e., authoritarian) is associated with lower academic achievement and social competence in children. As an extreme example of control, the use of corporal punishment, either at home or at school, is a hotly debated topic. Although many parents and teachers around the world follow religious and traditional dictums such as "spare the rod," and "an eye for an eye," corporal punishment of children is contrary to the International Convention on the Rights of the Child (1989), ratified by every country in the world except Somalia and the United States. Sweden, followed to date by eight other European countries and Israel, was the first country in the world to make spanking or other corporal punishment of children illegal in 1979. According to Swedish law, "Children are to be treated with respect for their person and individuality and may not be subjected to corporal punishment or any other humiliating treatment." Nevertheless, corporal punishment remains widespread in many homes and schools (e.g., Kenya; Human Rights Watch 1999) around the world.

Child effects. Richard Bell (1968), reacting against parent-effects models, suggested that children also influence parents. Thus, a unidirectional *child-effects model* (i.e., from child to parent) was developed. In this model of socialization, the child is the actor and the parent is the reactor. Children's individual differences in age, gender, and personalities can evoke different behaviors and treatment from parents in addition to other socialization agents. An example of research based in this tradition is Alexander Thomas and Stella Chess's (1977) classic work in child temperament. Children can be classified as *easy, slow-to-warm-up,* and *difficult* based on nine dimensions of temperament (e.g., activity level, emotional intensity), with easy children being the most compliant to parental requests and difficult children the least. Subsequently, many researchers have focused on qualities of infants and children that evoke different responses in parents, or different parental outcomes.

Of all the factors that influence how children are treated (e.g., temperament, health status, aptitude), gender is arguably the most salient. For example, in several South Asian countries, there is a clear preference for male children due to economic and religious factors (Khan and Khanum 2000). Strong preferences exist for sons in Bangladesh, China, India, Korea, and Pakistan, although no such preferences are found in Sri Lanka or Thailand (Abeykoon 1995). Parents view sons as economic assets (e.g., old-age security) and daughters as economic liabilities (e.g., dowries). Both Confucianism and Hinduism have been cited as religions that foster preferences for male offspring (Abeykoon 1995). In the Hindu tradition, only sons can pray for the souls of dead parents. Indicators of gender preference in South Asia include abnormal sex ratios at birth (i.e., more female fetuses aborted), and higher mortality rates for female offspring (e.g., infanticide, higher rates of malnutrition, less access to health care).

Gender inequality also exists in education, with the greatest gender disparity occurring in developing countries with overall low rates of enrollment. UNESCO tracks gender parity in education, with a goal of worldwide gender parity for the year 2005. Since 1980, gender disparity in education has widened not only in Afghanistan (i.e., under the Taliban regime, although this pattern would be expected to reverse now that the Taliban are no longer in power) but also in Pakistan. The countries with the worst record for gender parity in education are found primarily in sub-Saharan Africa (e.g., Chad, Guinea, and Senegal) and in the Arab states (e.g., Yemen and Sudan). In these countries, only six to eight girls are enrolled in primary school for every ten boys enrolled in primary school. Countries with a more moderate gap in gender disparity include Angola and Mozambique in sub-Saharan Africa, Iraq and Saudi Arabia in the Middle East, China and Indonesia in South Asia, and Brazil and Guatemala in South and Central America, respectively.

Age is another factor that influences how children are socialized. Psychologists and anthropologists have concluded that the transition from informal parental socialization to more formal socialization (e.g., education) typically occurs during the period known as the *5-to-7 shift,* which marks the end of young childhood and the beginning of middle childhood (Konner 1991). Among other things, changes in brain development (e.g., *myelinization,* or the coating of neurons with myelin sheaths, resulting in better motor coordination and memory) occur between the ages of two and six, paving the way for formal learning. Not surprisingly, UNICEF reports that, around the world, compulsory education begins between the ages of five (e.g., Barbados and United Kingdom) and seven (e.g., Ethiopia and Sweden).

Around fifteen years of age, adolescents are deemed ready to leave school to enter the work force as adults (i.e., compulsory education ends at age fourteen in Turkey, fifteen in Japan, sixteen in Canada). Addressing child labor, the International Labour Organization (ILO) has set the General Minimum Age for full-time labor participation at age fifteen, or not less than compulsory school age. In highly industrialized societies, which require longer periods of education and training, adolescents often attend post-secondary institutions for anywhere from two years (i.e., a two-year diploma) to four years (i.e., a four-year degree), and in some cases for several additional years (for graduate degrees, e.g., M.S., Ph.D.). Educational demands of technological societies are so high, that at least one researcher proposed an additional stage of the life cycle: *Emerging adulthood* (age eighteen to twenty-five)—a period distinct from both adolescence and young adulthood—which entails on-going formal socialization (Arnett 2000).

Other Models of Socialization

According to Western researchers and theorists, unidirectional models of socialization are not comprehensive enough, in that such models are too simplistic and do not explain enough of the variance in outcome variables. Instead, parent-child socialization is sometimes explained using a *bidirectional-effects model.* Effects go both ways in a reciprocal manner—from parent to child *and* from child to parent. This bidirectional, or two-way, model of socialization stems from an *organismic* paradigm (e.g., Reese and Overton 1970). From this perspective, child and parent interact in a dance of socialization with neither one nor the other the actor/reactor. Instead, child and parent act on each other and react to each other in a mutual, synchronous interaction. Rather than the individual as the unit of analysis, the parent-child *dyad* is the unit of analysis.

Interactional models. Examples of research based in this tradition include Mary Ainsworth's (1989) work on maternal sensitivity and *child attachment* (i.e., close emotional tie or bond between a child and caregiver). Ainsworth first observed mothers interacting with their babies in England, then in Uganda, and finally in the United States. It was while she was working in Uganda in the 1950s that she noticed that some children seemed to be more securely attached to their mothers than other children were. She also noticed that whereas some mothers were sensitive and responsive to the needs of their children, others were not. On her return to the United States, Ainsworth began to systematically study the relationship between mother's behavior and children's style of attachment. Ainsworth and her colleagues (1978) developed the *strange situation test,* a series of short episodes in which babies are alternatively left and rejoined by their mothers.

Babies' style of attachment could be determined based on their reactions to the *separation* and *reunion* episodes. Babies who were upset when their mother left, but settled down when she returned, were classified as having a *secure* attachment. Babies who were upset on separation from their mother, and who could not seem to settle down again on her return, were classified as having an *insecure-resistant* attachment. Finally, babies who were not particularly upset by separation from their mother, and did not seek contact with her on her return, were classified as having an *insecure-avoidant* attachment. A fourth category on attachment has also been documented: *insecure-disorganized* attachment, in which children seem fearful of their mother and show contradictory behavior toward her (Main and Solomon 1990). Ainsworth concluded that caregivers who were sensitive and responsive had children who were securely attached, whereas insensitive and unresponsive caregivers had children who were insecurely attached.

Although most children worldwide appear to have secure attachments to their caregivers (65%), cross-cultural research indicates some interesting differences (van IJzendoorn and Kroonenberg 1988). British babies are the most likely to be securely attached (75%), with Chinese babies the least likely to be securely attached (50%). With regard to insecure-avoidant attachment, German babies are the most likely (35%) and Japanese babies the least likely (5%) to show this pattern of attachment. Insecure-resistant attachment tends to be more likely among Israeli babies (29%) and less likely among Swedish babies (4%). Cultural differences, such as an emphasis on independence in Germany, for example, may account for some of these reported differences. Nevertheless, the strange situation test may not be an appropriate or ecologically valid measure of attachment across cultures.

Multidirectional models. Theorists have argued that even bidirectional models of socialization are not complex enough. *Multidirectional-effects models* were developed to explain child and parent outcomes within an ecological context. These multidirectional-effects models stem from a *contextual* paradigm (e.g., Reese 1991), in which child and parent interact over time and within familial, societal, and historical contexts. From this perspective, factors beyond the parent-child dyad affect both individual and dyadic outcomes. In these models, the system (e.g., the family) is the usual unit of analysis. Examples of theories based in this perspective include Urie Bronfenbrenner's (1979) *ecological model* and *family systems theory.* Research conducted using this approach includes studies on the effect of the marital relationship on the parent-child dyad, the workplace on the parent's relationship with the child, or the society on both child and parent (e.g., Parke and Buriel 1998).

One of the essential ways in which children are socialized into adult roles is by means of compulsory education, followed in many cases by job training or higher education. Although education and labor participation are clearly related in a developmental sense (education first, then work), they can interfere with each other. For the most part, involvement in one (e.g., education) precludes involvement in the other (e.g., labor). Thus, children and adolescents are primarily involved in education, and young and middle-aged adults are typically involved in labor, either in or outside the home. (Although many older adults cannot afford to retire, some financially secure older adults use retirement as an opportunity to return to educational pursuits such as *Elderhostel,* an educational program for older adults interested in life-long learning.)

Exceptions to compulsory school attendance are found in disadvantaged families and countries. Homeless families or those living in poverty may not be able to afford to send children to school (e.g., books, uniforms, transportation) and may rely on the income of their school-aged children for the household. Thus, extreme poverty interferes with the progression of education/labor participation typically found in industrialized countries. According to the ILO, between 1 and 200 million children worldwide are estimated to be child laborers (children under the age of fifteen who work full-time), with the worst forms of child labor including child slavery (i.e., forced labor) and child prostitution. Children around the world also work as child soldiers, child domestics, and child farm workers. In addition to the danger, pain, and stress associated with child labor, working keeps these children from attending school and reaching their potential.

As previously mentioned, most cultures around the world assign some degree of responsibility to children during the 5-to-7 shift. Anthropologists have examined children's responsibilities as a function of the type of society the child inhabits (e.g., Konner 1991). Responsibility given to children takes primarily two forms: instruction and chores. Children in *hunter-gatherer societies* such as the !Kung are assigned neither formal instruction nor chores. Instead, they spend most of middle childhood not only tagging along and observing adults at their work, but also playing and socializing (Konner 1991). In *agricultural societies,* where families often rely on the labor of their children, formal task assignment is the typical pattern, sometimes in the form of an apprenticeship (e.g., Ghana, Mexico). Industrial societies, because of the demands of the labor market, typically assign formal instruction to children (i.e., compulsory education) for anywhere from five (e.g., Cuba, Vietnam) to twelve years (e.g., Belgium, Germany).

Conclusion

Thus, in the area of socialization, there has been a steady progression from unidirectional-effects models—first, from parent to child, and then from child to parent—to bidirectional-effects models, and finally to multidirectional-effects models. The latter are more complex, more ecologically valid (e.g., Bronfenbrenner 1979), but more difficult to test empirically (e.g., Peterson and Haan 1999). Nevertheless, it seems reasonable that models of socialization should reflect more sophisticated contextual theoretical approaches. To return to the earlier question: Who are the agents or forces of socialization? According to the best thinkers in the area of socialization, the agents or forces of socialization are legion. They include parents, children, teachers, peers, institutions, the media, and society.

Parents socialize children—but children also socialize parents. Peers, according to Judith Harris's (1995) model of peer group socialization, may socialize children even more so than parents. Likewise, parents' families and friends socialize parents. Furthermore, the media, historical events (e.g., war, famine, industrialization), socioeconomic status, family structure, culture—all of these influence both parents and their children. By leaving these important factors out of our models of socialization, we limit the complexity of our theoretical models and thus our ability to explain important outcomes. Finally, socialization occurs in many different contexts (i.e., at home, in the workplace) as well as over the life-course.

See also: ACCULTURATION; CHILDHOOD; GLOBAL CITIZENSHIP; MIGRATION; RITES OF PASSAGE; SYMBOLIC INTERACTIONISM

Bibliography

Abeykoon, A. T. P. L. (1995). "Sex Preference in South Asia: Sri Lanka an Outlier." *Asia-Pacific Population Journal* 10:5–16.

Ainsworth, M. D. S. (1989). "Attachments beyond Infancy." *American Psychologist* 44:709–716.

Ainsworth, M. D. S.; Blehar, M. C.; Waters, E.; and Wall, S. (1978). *Patterns of Attachment: A Psychological Study of the Strange Situation.* Hillsdale, NJ: Erlbaum.

Arnett, J. J. (2000). "Emerging Adulthood." *American Psychologist* 55:469–480.

Baumrind, D. (1971). "Current Patterns of Parental Authority." *Developmental Psychology Monograph* 4 (1, Pt. 2):1–103.

Bell, R. Q. (1968). "A Reinterpretation of the Direction of Effects in Studies of Socialization." *Psychological Review* 75:81–95.

Bronfenbrenner, U. (1979). *The Ecology of Human Development.* Cambridge, MA: Harvard University Press.

Bugental, D. B., and Goodnow, J. J. (1998). "Socialization Processes." In *Social, Emotional, and Personality Development,* ed. N. Eisenberg. Vol. 3: *Handbook of Child Psychology,* 5th edition. New York: Wiley.

Harris, J. R. (1995). "Where Is the Child's Environment? A Group Socialization Theory of Development." *Psychological Review* 102:458–489.

Human Rights Watch. (1999). *Spare the Child: Corporal Punishment in Kenyan Schools.* New York: Author.

Khan, M. A., and Khanum, P. A. (2000). "Influence of Son Preference on Contraceptive Use in Bangladesh." *Asia-Pacific Population Journal* 15:43–56.

Konner, M. (1991). *Childhood.* Boston: Little, Brown.

Main, M., and Solomon, J. (1990). "Procedure for Identifying Infants as Disorganized/Disoriented during the Ainsworth Strange Situation." In *Attachment in the Preschool Years: Theory, Research, and Intervention,* ed. M. T. Greenberg, D. Cicchetti, and E. M. Cummings. Chicago: University of Chicago Press.

Parke, R. D., and Buriel, R. (1998). "Socialization in the Family: Ethnic and Ecological Perspectives." In *Social, Emotional, and Personality Development,* ed. N. Eisenberg. Vol. 3: *Handbook of Child Psychology,* 5th edition. New York: Wiley.

Pillemer, K., and McCartney, K., eds. (1991). *Parent-Child Relations throughout Life.* Hillsdale, NJ: Erlbaum.

Peterson, G. W., and Haan, D. (1999). "Socializing Children and Parents in Families." In *Handbook of Marriage and Family,* 2nd edition, ed. M. B. Sussman, S. K. Steinmetz, and G. W. Peterson. New York: Plenum.

Peterson, G. W., and Rollins, B. C. (1987). "Parent-Child Socialization." In *Handbook of Marriage and the Family,* ed. M. B. Sussman and S. K. Steinmetz. New York: Plenum.

Reese, H. W. (1991). "Contextualism and Developmental Psychology." *Advances in Child Development and Behavior* 23:187–230.

Reese, H. W., and Overton, W. F. (1970). "Models of Development and Theories of Development." In *Life-Span Developmental Psychology,* ed. L. R. Goulet and P. B. Baltes. New York: Academic Press.

Thomas, A., and Chess, S. (1977). *Temperament and Development.* New York: Brunner/Mazel.

van IJzendoorn, M. H., and Kroonenberg, P. M. (1988). "Cross-Cultural Patterns of Attachment: A Meta-Analysis of the Strange Situation." *Child Development* 59:147–156.

Wapner, S. (1993). "Parental Development: A Holistic, Developmental Systems-Oriented Perspective." In *Parental Development,* ed. J. Demick, K. Bursik, and R. DiBiase. Hillsdale, NJ: Erlbaum.

HILARY A. ROSE

SOCIAL NETWORKS

Married couples and families do not exist in isolation, but are embedded in a network of social relationships and culture. Even prior to marriage, relations with family members, friends, and acquaintances can influence dating activities and romantic relationships. When individuals become a couple, they must deal with the demands of both their own social ties and those of their spouses. Couples informally negotiate the degree to which they will maintain separate friendships, balance their own and their partner's family relationships, and engage in social activities as a couple. Relationships with marital partners, friends, and families change as individuals and couples age. It is increasingly clear that social relationships help to shape the basic nature of married life. In examining social relationships, some researchers use the terms *social network* and *social support* interchangeably (Schonauer et al. 1999).

Defining Social Networks

Personal social networks are typically defined as "a collection of individuals who know and interact with a particular target individual or couple" (Milardo 1988, p. 20). Researchers can assess the structural characteristics of an individual's network such as *network size, role composition* (the number of individuals, including family, friends, or work associates, in the network), or *network density* (interconnectedness among members). *Content characteristics* of networks describe the nature of linkages between the individual and network members such as relationship satisfaction, feelings of closeness, or reciprocity. *Functional characteristics* of networks describe linkages in which a given person serves some function for the focal individual, such as providing social support or informal help (Laireiter and Baumann 1992).

The social networks of couples have been investigated in three major ways. Using an *individual* perspective, researchers have defined a couple's social ties in terms of the separate personal networks maintained by each partner. At the *dyadic* level, a couple's network has been viewed as those network members jointly shared by the couple. A *configural* approach conceptualizes a couple's network as a composite of the shared and separate ties contributed by both partners. Individual, dyadic, and configural perspectives differ in their assumptions about the role of network structure for couples, and each perspective has certain advantages and limitations (Stein et al. 1992).

There is no one correct definition of a social network, but rather different network delineation strategies yield different data about social relationships. In studying the social context of marital and family life, researchers distinguish between the structure, content, and function of social network relationships. Researchers who study married couples must also decide if they are interested in the separate networks of marital partners, the degree of overlap between the partners' social ties, or some composite picture of the couple's network relations.

Social Network Structure: Relationship Opportunities and Constraints

The structure of social networks is critical for understanding opportunities and constraints in the development and maintenance of social relationships. Friends and family can introduce an individual to others who may have the potential for friendship or romantic involvement. Existing network ties can also limit opportunities to form new relationships, given that a person has only a finite amount of time and energy to engage in social relationships. Researchers typically acknowledge the reciprocal influence of married couples and their social networks—namely, that network ties influence the development and maintenance of a couple's relationships and that being "a married couple" affects the nature of their social network ties.

Some individuals withdraw from network relationships as they become romantically involved, but network withdrawal is probably not a universal phenomenon. Instead, different types of networks (e.g., interactive versus close associates) and different network sectors (e.g., family, close friends, peripheral friends) undergo various changes as partners become more involved in a dating relationship (Johnson and Leslie 1982). For example, to assess the interactive networks of college-age dating couples, Robert Milardo, Michael Johnson, and Ted Huston (1983) had respondents keep daily logs for two ten-day periods separated by a ninety-five–day span. Respondents in later stages of couple involvement reported that they interacted with fewer total network members than respondents in earlier stages of involvement. However, longitudinal data results found no significant differences in total network size between respondents whose dating relationships had become more involved and respondents whose dating relationships had deteriorated. In fact, there was an increase in the number of family members and of intermediate friends in the network of dating couples who increased in romantic involvement.

As couples become increasingly interdependent in their personal lives, they develop increasingly interdependent social networks (Milardo 1982). Studies investigating couples' networks have assessed the degree of overlap between network members listed by both husbands and wives. Shared networks of family were found to be a particularly valuable source of support (Veiel et al. 1991). However, husbands and wives in the study rarely shared the same network member as their closest confidant. These findings suggest the importance of both individual and shared network ties as supportive resources for married couples.

Catherine Stein and her colleagues (1992) found that couples with different types of networks reported significantly different levels of marital satisfaction and individual well-being. For example, couples whose conjoint networks featured a relatively large number of friends for both husbands and wives also reported significantly higher levels of marital satisfaction than couples in some of the other network types. However, husbands reported significantly higher levels of depression than wives in this type of network. Postulating a direct relationship between separate friendships and individual well-being would suggest that friends might help wives with feelings of depression in a way that men's separate friendships do not. Such findings suggest that conjoint network structure may have different implications for the marital relationship and the psychological well-being of individual partners.

Gender Differences in Social Networks

Developing and maintaining network ties requires a set of interpersonal skills and the desire and opportunity to use those skills. Men and women often differ in the nature of their interpersonal exchanges and in their opportunities for social interaction (Dykstra 1990). Research indicates that men and women structure their personal networks differently and that networks may serve different functions for husbands and wives. For example, wives generally report larger networks of kin and greater network interconnectedness than husbands (Antonucci and Akiyama 1987).

Claude Fischer and Stacey Oliker (1983) suggest that age and lifestyle stage account for network differences, with young married men having larger networks than their wives, and the reverse being true for older married couples. Studies of middle-aged and older adults indicate that married men are more likely to report their wives as their primary confidants and sources of support, whereas women are more likely to report confidants other than their husbands and to rely on friends and children as sources of support (Antonucci and Akiyama 1987). Women are more likely than men to request assistance from network members in general (Butler, Giodano, and Neren 1985).

Network composition may affect women's opportunities for social contact outside of the home, such as participation in the labor force. Although a number of factors influence work force participation, social network connections can play a critical role in finding and securing paid employment. As women's networks tend to have larger proportions of kin compared to their male counterparts, the networks of women may lack the heterogeneity of members needed to provide unique information and help in finding a job (Wellman and Wortley 1990). Research has shown that women who have large, diverse social networks are more likely to be working for pay as compared with women whose networks are less diverse (Stoloff, Glanville, and Bienenstock 1999).

Cultural Differences in Social Networks

Ethnicity, race, and culture have also been shown to shape social network ties. Network characteristics such as network size, composition, frequency of contact, and interconnectedness among members have been found to differ for people from different ethnic, racial, and cultural backgrounds. However, overall research findings in this area tend to be inconsistent. Recent studies compare the social networks of minority populations with those of Caucasians with little attention given to comparisons across a variety of ethnic or cultural groups.

In his overview of the features of social networks of people in the United States, Peter Mardsen (1987) found that whites had the largest networks, Hispanics had intermediate-sized networks, and African Americans had the smallest networks. This study also found that African Americans had a smaller proportion of kin and less gender diversity in their networks than white respondents.

Other studies support the findings that African-American social networks tend to be smaller than those of whites or other non-European groups (Pugliesi and Shook 1998). However, some research has shown that African Americans have more kin members in their networks and that their networks often include members from church and religious communities (Ajrouch, Antonucci, and Janevic 2001; Kim and McKenry 1998; Roschelle 1997). It may be that differences in assessing social network ties account for some of the inconsistent findings.

There is evidence to suggest that Hispanics have highly interconnected networks that include kin and friends and have strong church and school ties (Wilkinson 1993). For example, Thomas Schweizer and his colleagues (1998) found that both Euro-American and Hispanic participants had networks that were homogenous with regard to ethnicity. In addition, when compared to Euro-American networks, the networks of Hispanic participants were dominated by family ties, with most kin members living in the same neighborhood.

Relationship Processes in Social Networks

Family theories such as the *Double ABCX Model* (McCubbin and Patterson 1983) underscore the importance of social networks in helping individuals cope with family crises. Network relationships are not only important sources of support in times of stress, but the nature of family crises may themselves necessitate changes in the structure and quality of network ties. For example, social network members provide emotional and instrumental support during times of bereavement following the death of a family member (Suitor and Pillemer 2000). Structural characteristics, such as network composition and the interconnectedness among network members, are thought to play a role in mourning and adjustment to the death of a spouse (Blackburn, Greenburg, and Boss 1987).

How do networks of family and friends shape the nature of relationships between couples and families? Couples and families typically have regular and frequent contact with relatives and friends. Friends and relatives provide couples and individual partners with both emotional support and a variety of different kinds of tangible assistance (Stein and Rappaport 1986). However, there may be some negative outcomes when couples use their networks to help them deal with marital distress.

Danielle Julien and Howard Markman (1991) examined associations among spouses' problems, the support partners sought within and outside of marriage, and levels of individual and marital adjustment. Husbands' support was a particularly relevant component of wives' marital satisfaction, and marital distress was associated with less mobilization of spouses' support. Mobilization of support from network members was associated with greater marital distress. Discussing marital problems with outsiders was associated with low marital adjustment. The authors speculated that network members may provide alternative resources, reducing spouses' motivation to address each other to solve personal problems.

Contact with close network ties can also lead to social comparisons about the nature of relationships and marriage. People can use information and observations of other couples or individual partners to evaluate their own feelings, behaviors, and expectations for couples and marital relations. Social comparisons can provide information about the equity of one's relationship relative to others, validate the correctness of one's attributions or expectations, or reduce uncertainty.

In an exploratory study, Sandra Titus (1980) found that more than half of the thirty married couples in her sample reported explicitly comparing their own marriage with friends' marriages during interactions with friends or their spouses. Social comparisons were more common in younger couples with children less than five years of age and more common among wives than husbands. Social comparisons seemed to establish a frame of reference for marital expectations, helped couples identify issues to discuss in their own marriages, and helped couples to evaluate or affirm the quality of their marriages.

Renate Klein and Robert Milardo (2000) examined the role that network members play in couples' perceptions of how they manage relationship conflict. After identifying one controversial issue in their relationship, partners were independently asked to delineate their social networks in terms of members who they thought would approve of their point of view (*supporters*) and those who would disapprove of their position (*critics*). The number of perceived supporters identified by respondents was positively related to their belief that their position in the conflict was legitimate, justified, and reasonable (*self-legitimacy*). The number of perceived critics was related to a decreased sense of self-legitimacy for men, but not for women. These preliminary findings suggest that the social comparison process may be different for men and women as they manage relationship conflict. It may be that men's sense of legitimacy in relationship conflict is related to a lack of network critics, whereas women's feelings of conflict legitimacy are related to having supporters to validate their point of view.

Social Networks and Aging

Changes in social networks as a function of the aging process have been the focus of research. There is evidence to suggest that as people age, their social networks tend to grow smaller and are composed largely of kin (Lang 2000; Sluzki 2000).

As individuals age and view their future as time-limited, they are likely to seek relationships that provide the most emotional impact and short-term benefits and discontinue those relationships that are less satisfying (Carstensen, Isaacowitz, and Charles 1999). Thus, the motivation to seek and maintain social contacts is thought to be linked to an individual's perceptions of their future.

The gerontological literature documents the importance of families, particularly adult daughters, in caring for elders (see Dwyer and Coward 1992). However, as more couples in the United States choose not to have children, the family members available for support and care become more limited. In a study by Melanie Gironda, James Lubben, and Kathryn Atchison (1999), elders without children generally reported less contact with other relatives and family members than those elders with children. It appears that elders without children may renew old friendships or relations with distant kin in later life if geographic location permits (Sluzki 2000). Thus, the social networks of some elders may largely consist of *recycled* or *renewed* relationships with people who share a long personal history, if not an extended period of sustained interaction.

Conclusion

Social network analysis has helped researchers to more systematically describe different kinds of social relationships that exist and develop within the context of marriage and family life. Yet, researchers are only beginning to examine the complex, reciprocal influence of network forces on family relationships and marital ties. More methodological and conceptual work is needed to understand the network conditions that best help to nurture and support the many aspects of marriage and the family.

See also: COMMUNICATION: COUPLE RELATIONSHIPS; DATING; ELDERS; FAMILY ROLES; FICTIVE KINSHIP; FRIENDSHIP; INFIDELITY; MARITAL QUALITY; NEIGHBORHOOD; RELATIONSHIP DISSOLUTION; RELATIONSHIP INITIATION; RELATIONSHIP MAINTENANCE; RENEWAL OF WEDDING VOWS; SINGLES/NEVER MARRIED PERSONS; STRESS

Bibliography

Ajrouch, K. J.; Antonucci, T. C.; and Janevic, M. R. (2001). "Social Networks among Blacks and Whites: The Interaction between Race and Age." *Journal of Gerontology* 56B:S112–S118.

Antonucci, T. C., and Akiyama, H. (1987). "An Examination of Sex Differences in Social Support among Older Men and Women." *Sex Roles* 17:737–749.

Blackburn, J. A.; Greenburg, J. S.; and Boss, P. G. (1987). "Coping with Normative Stress from Loss and Change: A Longitudinal Study of Rural Widows." *Journal of Gerontological Social Work* 11:59–70.

Butler, T.; Giodano, S.; and Neren, S. (1985). "Gender and Sex-Role Attributions as Predictors of Utilization of Natural Support Systems during Personal Stress Events." *Sex Roles* 13:515–524.

Carstensen, L. L.; Isaacowitz, D. M.; and Charles, S. T. (1999). "Taking Time Seriously: A Theory of Socioemotional Selectivity." *American Psychologist* 54:165–181.

Dwyer, J. W., and Coward, R. T., eds. (1992). *Gender, Families, and Elder Care.* Thousand Oaks, CA: Sage.

Dykstra, P. A. (1990). "Disentangling Direct and Indirect Gender Effects on the Supportive Network." In *Social Network Research,* ed. C. P. Kees, M. Knipscheer, and T. C. Antonucci. Amsterdam: Swets and Zeitlinger.

Fischer, C. S., and Oliker, S. J. (1983). "A Research Note of Friendship, Gender, and the Life Cycle." *Social Forces* 62:124–133.

Gironda, M.; Lubben, J. E.; and Atchison, K. A. (1999). "Social Networks of Elders without Children." *Journal of Gerontological Social Work* 31:63–84.

Johnson, M. P., and Leslie, L. (1982). "Couple Involvement and Network Structure: A Test of the Dyadic Withdrawal Hypothesis." *Social Psychology Quarterly* 45:34–43.

Julien, D., and Markman, H. J. (1991). "Social Support and Social Networks as Determinants of Individual and Marital Outcomes." *Journal of Social and Personal Relationships* 8:549–568.

Kim, H. K., and McKenry, P. C. (1998). "Social Networks and Support: A Comparison of African Americans, Asian Americans, Caucasians, and Hispanics." *Journal of Comparative Family Studies* 29:313–334.

Klein, R., and Milardo, R. M. (2000). "The Social Context of Couple Conflict: Support and Criticism from Informal Third Parties." *Journal of Social and Personal Relationships* 17:618–637.

Laireiter, A., and Baumann, U. (1992). "Network Structures and Support Functions: Theoretical and Empirical Analyses." In *The Meaning and Measurement of Social Support,* ed. H. Veiel and U. Baumann. New York: Hemisphere.

Lang, F. R. (2000). "Endings and Continuity of Social Relationships: Maximizing Intrinsic Benefits within Personal Networks When Feeling Near to Death." *Journal of Social and Personal Relationships* 17:155–182.

Mardsen, P. V. (1987). "Core Discussion Networks of Americans." *American Sociological Review* 52:122–131.

McCubbin, H. I., and Patterson, J. M. (1983). "The Family Stress Process: The Double ABCX Model of Adjustment and Adaptation." *Marriage and Family Review* 6:7–37.

Milardo, R. M. (1982). "Friendship Networks in Developing Relationships: Converging and Diverging Social Environments." *Social Psychology Quarterly* 45:162–172.

Milardo, R. M. (1988). "Families and Social Networks: An Overview of Theory and Methodology." In *Families and Social Networks,* ed. R. M. Milardo. Newbury Park, CA: Sage.

Milardo, R. M.; Johnson, M. P.; and Huston, T. L. (1983). "Developing Close Relationships: Changing Patterns of Interaction between Pair Members and Social Networks." *Journal of Personality and Social Psychology* 44:964–976.

Pugliesi, K., and Shook, S. L. (1998). "Gender, Ethnicity, and Network Characteristics: Variation in Social Support Resources." *Sex Roles* 38:215–238.

Roschelle, A. R. (1997). *No More Kin: Exploring Race, Class, and Gender in Family Networks,* Thousand Oaks, CA: Sage.

Schonauer, K.; Achtergarde, D.; Suslow, T.; and Michael, N. (1999). "Comorbidity of Schizophrenia and Prelingual Deafness: Its Impact on Social Network Structures." *Social Psychiatry and Psychiatric Epidemiology* 34:526–532.

Schweizer, T.; Schnegg, M.; and Berzborn, S. (1998). "Personal Networks and Social Support in a Multiethnic Community of Southern California." *Social Networks* 20:1–21.

Sluzki, C. E. (2000). "Social Networks and the Elderly: Conceptual and Clinical Issues, and a Family Consultation." *Family Process* 39:271–284.

Stein, C. H.; Bush, E. G.; Ross, R. R.; and Ward, M. (1992). "Mine, Yours, and Ours: A Configural Analysis of the Networks of Married Couples in Relation to Marital Satisfaction and Individual Well-Being." *Journal of Social and Personal Relationships* 9:365–383.

Stein, C. H., and Rappaport, J. (1986). "Social Network Interviews as Sources of Etic and Emic Data: A Study of Young Married Women." In *Stress, Social Support, and Women,* ed. S. E. Hobfoll. New York: Hemisphere.

Stoloff, J. A.; Glanville, J. L.; and Bienenstock, E. J. (1999). "Women's Participation in the Labor Force: The Role of Social Networks." *Social Networks* 21:91–108.

Suitor, J. J., and Pillemer, K. (2000). "When Experience Counts Most: Effects of Experiential Similarity on Men's and Women's Receipt of Support during Bereavement." *Social Networks* 22:299–312.

Titus, S. L. (1980). "A Function of Friendship: Social Comparisons as a Frame of Reference for Marriage." *Human Relations* 33:409–431.

Veiel, H. O. F.; Crisland, M.; Strosreck-Somschor, H.; and Herrie, J. (1991). "Social Support Networks of Chronically Strained Couples: Similarity and Overlap." *Journal of Social and Personal Relationships* 8:279–292.

Wellman, B., and Wortley, S. (1990). "Different Strokes from Different Folks: Community Ties and Social Support." *American Journal of Sociology* 96:558–588.

Wilkinson, D. (1993). "Family Ethnicity in America" In *Family Ethnicity: Strength in Diversity,* ed. H. P. McAdoo. Newbury Park, CA: Sage.

CATHERINE H. STEIN
MARCIA G. HUNT

SOCIOECONOMIC STATUS

Social inequality is a fundamental characteristic of the fabric of society. Rich or poor; advantaged or disadvantaged; privileged or underprivileged: each contrast speaks to differences among people that are consequential for the lives they lead.

Whether in describing patterns of inequality or examining the consequences of inequality, the results depend upon how inequality is conceptualized and measured. Socioeconomic status is among the most prominent concepts in inequality research. The term *socioeconomic status* refers to the relative hierarchical placement of a unit (e.g., an individual, a community) along a gradient stratified by social and economic resources.

Theoretical Background

The sociologist Max Weber (1958) conceptualized inequality along three related tracks—class, status, and party. Each was understood as a basis for power and influence. Whereas class focused on economic resources and partly referred to political clout, status was understood as honor and prestige. For Weber, status groups were hierarchically arrayed on the basis of distinctive lifestyles, consumption patterns, and modes of conduct or action.

In North America, the sociologist Talcott Parsons (1970) has been most influential in delineating the theoretical underpinnings of socioeconomic status. First, Parsons understood the idea of status as a position in the social structure, as part of the social differentiation in society (different occupations, different family positions). Although Parsons associated status with position (a status is occupied, such as accountant, and a role is performed, as in financial auditing), the concept carries with it a hierarchical referent as in Weber's notion of honor and prestige.

A status is evaluated, and this social evaluation is central to Parsons's contribution to the idea of socioeconomic status. Social status was, for him, the core notion of social stratification, or rank. This differential evaluation in terms of honor and prestige lay at the heart of inequality. In social relations with others, status distinctions affect how people interrelate. For Parsons, income and wealth were important, but secondary to social status or honor.

Second, Parsons understood family units as the key component of stratification. Families were assumed to be units of solidarity sharing similar interests. He also assumed that families had a single breadwinner. That is, the concept of the head of a family was central to his understanding of the family unit.

Although there is a tendency to interpret this idea of a single breadwinner as sexist, various reasons at the time gave some plausibility to the assumption. First, the inequities of domestic labor meant that most families had one principal wage earner, and this was typically the male head of the household. Second, many families had made investments in a single earner, either via decisions about geographic mobility or support for education (in both cases, women's careers typically were de-emphasized). Third, Parsons and others assumed that family members had a shared interest not only in their own well-being, but also in the well-being of their children. These ideas were the basis of the thinking that the family was the key unit of stratification and that the male head of the household was the principal determinant of the family's social status.

Finally, Parsons and his followers (Kingsley Davis and Wilbert Moore, in particular) developed the functional theory of stratification. The core premise of this theory was that society had to differentially evaluate positions so that members of society would be motivated both to pursue the training necessary for the most important positions and, once in those positions, to perform them as well as possible. Encouraging the most qualified and competent people in a society to perform the most important jobs required that jobs be differentially ranked. Differences in socioeconomic status were one way to understand this necessary hierarchy.

Measurement

Socioeconomic implies at least two dimensions to inequality—social and economic. Although these two dimensions are understood as closely associated, they nevertheless incorporate two different aspects of stratification. The economic dimension is best represented by money or wealth as reflected in employment income, home ownership, and other financial assets (e.g., pension plans, property ownership). The social dimension incorporates education, occupational prestige, authority, and community standing.

The very earliest measures of socioeconomic status in North America relied on community reputation. A family's social standing as judged by others was used to differentiate between upper, middle, and lower classes. Although the term *class* was used, this was a very North American usage that understood classes as loose aggregates of families who shared similar social and economic traits. However, this early measurement tradition rested mainly in community studies. As social scientists started to focus more on entire societies, a different measurement technique was essential.

In 1947, Cecil North and Paul Hatt conducted a study in the United States in which they asked people to judge the prestige of different occupations. This study marked a watershed in the measurement of socioeconomic status. Prestige studies typically ask respondents to judge the social standing of about one hundred occupations. However, working independently, Bernard Blishen in Canada and Otis Dudley Duncan in the United States devised a way to combine the prestige scores of occupations with the typical incomes and educations of occupational incumbents. For example, Duncan's Socio-economic Index (SEI) was constructed by weighting an occupation's median education and income on the metric of occupational prestige (via a regression equation that can be simplified as follows: Prestige = a + B1[Income] + B2[Education] where each variable represents an occupational average). SEI scores were developed for all of the major occupations and allowed researchers to assign a person an SEI score based on one variable, occupation.

In the United States, prestige studies done in 1947, 1963, 1971, and 1989 have been used to generate SEI scores. Although the hierarchical placement of a few specific occupations has changed over time, the relative placement of most occupations is stable. This stability in the prestige hierarchy has meant that specific scales of socioeconomic status can be used with confidence long after they are first constructed.

More recently, scholars of inequality in North America, in particular, have moved away from single scales of socioeconomic status to amalgam measures. Rather than relying on a summary SEI score, contemporary researchers are often asking a set of questions related to socioeconomic status (SES). Thus, for example, many researchers now measure SES by combining (often through factor analysis or some analogous statistical method) measures of at least three of the following: an individual's education, earnings, home ownership, occupation, and net worth. In measuring the SES of a family, a frequent approach is to combine the education, earnings, and occupation of wives and husbands or communal partners (sometimes along with home ownership or net value of a family home).

However, researchers at times want to examine the relative effects of the separate components of SES. Therefore, measures of education and income (for example) are sometimes used separately and are not combined in a scale or index. Important information may be lost in combining education, income, occupation, and residential status. Summative family scales are also not appropriate when scholars seek to compare the relative influence of the SES of spouses or partners on, for example, the educational attainment of their children or the health status of family members.

The old assumption of the male breadwinner, whatever its historical validity, is highly problematic. Family forms have changed (e.g., single parents, gay and lesbian couples). Women's labor force participation and career commitment increased dramatically in the last decades of the twentieth century. The contributions of partners who are not in the paid labor force have been increasingly recognized. For all of these reasons, the use of a family SES measure based on information about a single family member is sometimes inadequate. However, it is also important not to exaggerate the force of this claim because the SES of spouses and partners are often similar. In the British sociological literature, there is a long-running debate on this very issue, although the referent is more often to social class than to SES (see Goldthrorpe 1983).

Individuals or families have their own SES, but they also live and work in contexts that may be defined by different levels of SES. In this sense, the SES context in which a person finds him or herself may be more or less powerful than his or her own individual SES when it comes to predicting outcomes (e.g., job satisfaction, psychological stress). This is often understood as the *ecological* setting or context of people or groups. For example, do children in school classrooms where the SES of their classmates is greater than their own do better academically than would be predicted simply from their own families' SES?

Today, there is no consensus upon exactly how SES should be measured. In modern research, the following considerations are important in devising one or more indicators to measure SES. First, is SES the relevant conceptual approach to inequality? Second, if SES is a core variable, how many indicators should be used, and should these be combined in a scale? Third, what is the validity and reliability of SES measures in comparison to alternatives? Fourth, will measures of SES provide the necessary comparability with other research studies in the area? Fifth, is SES applicable to all members of the population being studied? Especially in this last case, the SES of students, the unemployed, recent migrants, and the retired may be problematic.

When analyzing data, different scholars may or may not treat SES as an ordinal (i.e., ranked [beauty]) or interval (i.e., equal distance between categories [age]) measure. Often, when an ordinal measurement preference is chosen, SES is collapsed into groups, frequently with labels like upper class, middle class, and lower class. The boundaries between these groups are typically relatively arbitrary, there being no natural or theoretical cutting point in deciding at exactly what SES score the boundary should be drawn. Often, for this reason, others choose to assume SES has interval measurement properties, and they use more sophisticated statistical techniques.

In contrast to Europe where the idea of social class was more influential, in North America, seen as the land of opportunity and upward mobility, social status with its hierarchical stress was more prevalent. Among the more important studies in demonstrating the utility of socioeconomic status was the work of Otis Dudley Duncan and Peter Blau on social mobility. Using SEI scores as their basic measure, they were concerned with, among other things, the relative chances of upward mobility across generations for whites and blacks in the United States. More recently this tradition has prospered in North America and elsewhere in the guise of status attainment models, addressing a variety of research questions involving who achieves status and how they do it.

Socioeconomic status has been shown to be significantly, consistently, and universally correlated with a variety of measures of life chances (e.g., occupational attainment), lifestyles (e.g., health status), sociopolitical orientations (e.g., ideological leanings), and modes of action and association (e.g., association memberships). Why these correlations exist remains one of the central questions continuing to be pursued. Simply put, what is it about SES that creates a causal effect and why does this effect occur? It is now well understood that although economic resources are important, it is not so clear exactly why (e.g., is the effect due to access to better nutrition, better information, or more powerful networks?). Similarly, education is an important SES measure, again correlated with many diverse outcomes, but its precise role is often unclear (i.e., is it the cognitive dimension, is it the credential, is it the network of contacts?).

Finally, it is worth noting that although socioeconomic status is most frequently found in the academic literature, it is a term increasingly employed in research outside the academy. For example, the marketing firm A. C. Nielsen (which measures television audience share around the world) uses socioeconomic status as a core measure for differentiating types of viewers. Other marketing firms do likewise in reporting on voter preferences or consumer product choices.

Conclusion

Although its roots in the functional theory of stratification are now obscured, much of North American social science research continues to focus upon stratification (and socioeconomic status) as opposed to inequality. To a significant extent this is because stratification imagery focuses upon gradients, upon higher and lower status, whereas the conceptual perspectives that employ the imagery of inequality (e.g., class, gender differences) stress group conflict. Especially where this gradient approach makes theoretical sense, as in studies of status attainment, the idea of socioeconomic status has been used worldwide.

Debate continues as to whether class or SES is the stronger measure of inequality. Depending upon the theoretical framework and the research question being addressed, SES remains a viable concept. A significant amount of empirical research has demonstrated the power of SES in predicting life chances, lifestyles, sociopolitical orientations, and modes of action and association.

See also: ACADEMIC ACHIEVEMENT; ACCULTURATION; COHABITATION; HOUSING; INTERGENERATIONAL TRANSMISSION; MIGRATION; NAMES FOR CHILDREN; SINGLE-PARENT FAMILIES

Bibliography

Adler, N. E., and Coriell, M. (1997). "Socioeconomic Status and Women's Health." In *Health Care for Women: Psychological, Social, and Behavioral Influences,* ed. S. J. Gallant, G. P. Keita, and R. Royak-Schaler. Washington, DC: American Psychological Association.

Blau, P. M., Duncan, O. D. (1967). *The American Occupational Structure.* New York: John Wiley and Sons.

Davis, K., and Moore, W. (1945). "Some Principles of Stratification." *American Sociological Review* 10:242–249.

Ensminger, M. E.; Forrest, C. B.; Riley, A. W.; Kang, M.; Green, B. F.; Starfield, B.; and Ryan, S. A. (2000). "The Validity of Measures of Socioeconomic Status of

Adolescents." *Journal of Adolescent Research* 15:392–420.

Gerth, H., and Mills, C. Wright, eds. and trans. (1958). *From Max Weber: Essays in Sociology*. New York: Oxford University Press.

Goldthorpe, J. (1983). "Women and Class Analysis: In Defense of the Conventional View." *Sociology* 17:465–88.

Hertzman, C. (2000). "The Case for an Early Childhood Development Strategy." *Isuma, Canadian Journal of Policy Research* 1(2):11–18.

Kawachi, I., and Kennedy, B. P. (1997). "Socioeconomic Determinants of Health: Health and Social Cohesion: Why Care About Income Inequality?" *British Medical Journal* 314 (April 5):1037.

Parsons, T. (1970). "Equality and Inequality in Modern Society, or Social Stratification Revisited." In *Social Stratification*. ed. E. O. Laumann. New York: Bobbs-Merrill.

NEIL GUPPY

SOUTH AFRICA

South Africa, with its 40 million residents, is a multicultural society with eleven official languages. Although most residents (76.7%) speak an indigenous African language (Xhosa 23.4%; Zulu 29.9%; and Sepedi 12%), English is the language that most people understand (Statistics South Africa 1996). Family life must thus also be seen against the background of cultural diversity and extreme socioeconomic differences. Most families—primarily nonwhites—are poor and struggle to satisfy their daily needs. Contributing in complex ways to different types of family structures are traditional practices, historical events—especially the racially discriminatory and disruptive effect of apartheid laws, which placed restrictions on movement, provided inferior education and limited employment opportunities, and enforced compulsory shifting of families—and the demands of modern society (Ross 1995).

When the first whites arrived from Europe in the seventeenth century, there were various dominant black groups with established cultural patterns in the country. After some internal conflicts between whites and black races (for example, the nine border wars on the Cape's eastern boundary between 1778 and 1878 and the Anglo-Zulu war of 1878), two wars were also fought against domination by the United Kingdom, originally from December 1880 to February 1881 and then again from 1899 to 1902 (Davenport 1978). The Union of South Africa, with a white minority government in power, was established in 1910. Afrikaner nationalism (supported by a white group with Afrikaans as its mother tongue) reached a climax with the formation of the Republic of South Africa in 1961. The National Party had come into power in 1948, and this is viewed as the beginning of legal apartheid (*separate development*), which lasted until 1994. With the first true democratic election in 1994, a predominantly black political party came into power and immediately began to transform society at all levels—economical, social, and educational. The main focus of this transformation process had as its objective the empowerment of nonwhite South Africans in particular.

Although the white population flourished economically and progressed in various ways during the greater part of the twentieth century, various factors had a negative effect on nonwhite families. Urbanization increased rapidly, especially after the abolishment of the influx control regulations—legislation prohibiting people from moving and settling freely to any part of the country—in 1986. However, with the precarious circumstances in which many families had to live (in cities and rural areas), as well as physical separation between husband and wife in many cases (primarily as a result of the migrant labor system), large-scale family disruption occurred in traditional black, colored, and Indian families.

The arrival of political freedom and power in 1994 did not automatically bring about economic power for the nonwhite majority. Most nonwhite families still cannot satisfy their basic needs. The consequences of the previous political era are, therefore, still visible in the low educational and living standard of many nonwhite South Africans (uneducated 21.6%; Statistics South Africa 1996). As a result, the high crime statistics are ascribed to, among other things, poor socioeconomic circumstances, high unemployment (24%), circumstantial frustration, and the failure of politicians to meet campaign promises. Signs of tension are evident in many families in high divorce rates (whites 357 per 100,000 of the population; Indians 142 per 100,000;

coloreds 116 per 100,000; and blacks 23 per 100,000; Statistics South Africa 1996), family violence that takes place in many households, and the high rate of teenage pregnancies and out-of-wedlock births. At the same time, the adverse effects of the AIDS epidemic (11% of the population) are already affecting many families and will continue to do so. Given this context, a general description will be given of family structures as they occur in the various population groups.

Family Life in Black Communities

Anthropologically, the black people (77.5% of the population) are viewed as belonging to four ethnic groups, the Nguni, the Sotho, the Tsonga Shangaan, and the Venda. The groups differ in size and origin and have their own cultures, speak their own languages, and have different dialects within the groups.

Black families are traditionally extended, with a dominant father at the head. Large changes in urban families have taken place primarily as a result of urbanization, housing problems, political factors (the migratory labor system), and economic underdevelopment coupled with poverty. However, nuclear families have formed within the high socioeconomic group. The high incidence of out-of-wedlock births has resulted in the replacement of the nuclear family with other structures. In many cases the daughter and child live with the mother, which means that many multigenerational families exist (Steyn 1993).

Economic development in the areas of mining, harbors, and industrial growth resulted in the migrant labor system. This meant that the workers (men) moved to other areas alone to work there to earn an income. A portion of the money was then sent to the family in the rural area. In the course of time, family members were allowed to live together near the workplace under certain conditions. However, traditional family structures could not continue in this industrial environment. Differences between families in urban and rural areas can be ascribed to the effect of industrialization, urbanization, and the migrant labor system (Nzimande 1996).

Although ethnically different, all black families share some characteristics: the importance of children, a happy family life, strong family ties, and the nature and implication of being married (Viljoen 1994). Certain practices, such as polygamy and *lobola* (the giving of something valuable or the payment of money by the groom to the family of the bride), are viewed as strengths because they prevent divorce and marital disintegration. The decrease in the incidence of payment of lobola can be ascribed to the diminishing of parents' authority over their daughters and is an indication of how traditional practices are making way for Western values (Manona 1981). Traditionally, the family unit is viewed as consisting of the husband, wife, and unmarried children, who form part of a larger family structure, the extended family. This is the ideal structure, and when a married son leaves the extended family to begin his own household, the process is known as fission. Viewed over time, black family life can be seen as moving from the extended to the nuclear type. However, the one has not replaced the other.

General extended family patterns are vertical (multigenerational) or horizontal (when brothers with their families live with the oldest brother). A further dimension, also known as *composite families,* occurs when the husband has more than one wife, and they all live together (with their children). These various extended family forms exist in all African cultures (Nzimande 1996). Generally in extended families, there is a wider group of people who are related by blood or marriage and who identify with and care for one another. The extended family is usually more stable than a nuclear family and extends over longer periods. The development and shrinkage of the extended family is affected by fertility, marriages, divorces, and deaths; in many communities it serves as a social service system that cares for and provides support to various categories of dependents. Notwithstanding the longer lifetime of the extended family, its existence is influenced especially by the greater economic independence of individual members, who tend to move out in order to live more independently in their own nuclear family.

Although the nuclear family functions more independently, its members usually do not totally break ties with the family of origin or other important family members. During problems and in times of crises, members of the extended family are still expected to help and support one another. In many nuclear families a niece, nephew, aunt, or uncle is also present because he or she needs support.

The support system in black communities is based upon regulations, values, and socialization patterns through which a feeling of social responsibility and reciprocal support is created and practiced (Nzimande 1996). The main purpose is to maintain the group's character throughout the extended family. There are indications of a continual decrease of family involvement within the extended family system, which results in a decrease of support resources, especially for those who need them. Because the individual worker becomes economically independent, the extended family increasingly becomes a smaller supportive factor for his or her survival.

Some of the strongest influences changing traditional family life in black communities are poverty, poor housing, urbanization, rising divorce rates, and a decline in traditional institutions, customs, and values (Viljoen 1994). Obedience and respect for parents (or parentlike authority) are among the key values and socialization processes of traditional black families that are being affected in particular. This is why a reformulation of the role of the father in the family (in terms of authority and involvement) is one of the most crucial issues in black family life. Along with these factors is the changing external environment, which, in itself, sets new challenges and presents other values for the younger generation of black families.

Family Life in Asian Communities

Between 1860 and 1911, a total of 152,184 Indians (Hindus and Muslims) came to South Africa from various parts of India to work as laborers on sugar plantations in the Durban area. They formed a diverse group in terms of language and culture, and their ranks included twice as many men as women. Although in their native lands some of these people would not have interacted because they belonged to different castes, common work and problems (e.g., poor working conditions and health care) resulted in the demise of the caste system and other traditional practices. Once their working contracts had expired, some continued their involvement in farming, while others moved to towns and cities and began their own businesses, some of which are still thriving as family businesses. Indian families live all over South Africa (2.6% of the population), with the greatest concentration in Natal (Jithoo 1996).

The *joint family* was originally the norm for Indian families. However, nuclear families are increasing as a result of modernization. Poverty and unemployment affected and still affect many families, making it hard for parents to pass down traditional values in the nuclear family within the context of greater freedom of thought and new opportunities (Steyn 1993).

Although many joint families exist today (with the father or senior brother as undisputed head), with different generations living together (with different interests and power structures), there has been a transition to families that are more nuclear, especially in the cities. Unlike typical Western nuclear families, traditional values and obligations bind an Indian nuclear family, and its members maintain good contact with the extended family. Nevertheless, there has been a loss of the traditional understanding that promotes cohesion, solidarity, and loyalty in the joint family. The decrease in the incidence of joint families can be ascribed to an increase in kinds of housing, the building of roads, more professional work opportunities as a result of better educational opportunities, and the influence of Western values, with their emphasis on individuality. One of the greatest challenges for Indian families is to adapt to a changing sociocultural environment. The great distances between children, parents, and grandparents as a result of nuclear family life patterns has resulted in a decline in the traditional values and associated support networks. This places greater demands on family members to adapt as a result of less continuity and more uncertainty. Exposure to the media, a more integrated educational system, and the dominant influence of Western culture have all contributed to a culture of family transition for Indians in South Africa. Nevertheless, although structural changes have occurred in Indian families, many remain conservative, and many traditional values and morals have been maintained (Jithoo 1996).

Family Life in Colored Families

The colored people in South Africa (8.9% of the population) stem from slaves, Asians, Europeans, Khoi, and Africans. Consequently, conspicuous differences exist within the colored group with regard to religion, language, and socioeconomic status (SES). Two distinct groups can be differentiated in terms of SES: the high class with stable family relationships as well as social and economic security,

Obedience and respect for parents play key roles in maintaining stable family life and values in South-African families.
DAVID TURNLEY/CORBIS

and the low socioeconomic class that, as a result of forced moves, inadequate education, and the like, lived in poverty for generations. The low SES group usually lives in precarious conditions that are characterized by social problems, such as street violence, unemployment, overcrowding, many out-of-wedlock pregnancies, and a poverty-stricken lifestyle. These factors usually contribute to feelings of despair and limited expectations for the future (Rabie 1996).

How the colored family originated differs substantially from that of the Indian family. Colored families and African-American families, however, have in common many factors that shaped them. These promoted a high out-of-wedlock birth rate as well as an unstable family life. Today there are large differences in social class within the colored population. The nuclear family is common in the high-income groups, whereas single-parent families, as part of an extended family with a dominant woman, are common in low-income groups. Living together and desertion are also common in low-income groups (Steyn 1993).

The following are some of the most predominant characteristics and contributing factors to the socioeconomic circumstances of many colored households (Rabie 1996). First, poverty entails that housing with associated services is lacking or inadequate. Units are small, and children are often left alone at home unsupervised. In high-density areas, two or more nuclear families live together, which strains normal family relationships and places excessively high demands on families with inadequate resources. These circumstances are thus largely responsible for the prevalence of well-organized gang syndicates in many neighborhoods. Gang activities are common (especially in the Western Cape, where large concentrations of colored people live) and even schoolchildren are recruited to join these complex competing power structures that have a large influence on many households. Gang membership can last until late adolescence and even early adulthood. A second factor is that approximately 43 percent of births take place outside marriage. This has implications for stable supportive relationships.

Supportive networks in poorer communities are mostly built around gender roles (Rabie 1996). Adolescents spend a lot of time with peers of the same gender. In marriages where the relationship between the husband and wife is not one of attachment, the husband spends almost all of his time with his friends, while the wife directs her affection to their children and family. In addition to the economical contributions that these women make to the households and wider network in many cases, these women also hold the families and networks together. They do so on a daily basis, for example, by lending to others or borrowing from others what is needed (e.g., cash, household ingredients) and providing emotional support when necessary.

A substantial proportion of nuclear families have adopted Western lifestyles. In many of these families both parents work, but in other cases, there is a single breadwinner while the wife (in most cases) looks after the family and household.

Family Life in White Communities

Historically, the family life of whites (11% of the population) is similar to that of the Christian, western European style. Although extended families did exist originally, white families were mostly characterized by large nuclear families, with strong family ties, who were involved in their community and church. The husband was traditionally also the undisputed head of the family. Industrialization and urbanization (especially after World War II) brought about large changes in the family life of white people. The nuclear family became more autonomous from the extended family and began to function independently from it (Steyn 1993).

The Incidence of Distinguishable Family Structures

In a comprehensive study involving 1,746 white, 2,024 colored, 2,411 Asian, and 1,199 black families, it became evident that the pure nuclear family is still the most prevalent, although masked differential proportions exist between the groups (Steyn 1993), with the smallest proportion of nuclear families occurring among black people. Although the nuclear structure is the most common among both black and colored people, they make up less than half of the total. Multigenerational families, with either a man (coloreds 11.6% and blacks 16. 2%) or a woman (coloreds 8.2% and blacks 12.6%) as head of the family occur most commonly in these two population groups. For Asians and whites, the incidence of multigenerational families with either a man or a woman as head is 12 percent and 1.2 percent, respectively. The incidence of single-parent families, primarily with the woman as parent, is as follows: coloreds 15 percent, blacks 14.8 percent, Asians 7.7 percent, and whites 6.2 percent. Steyn (1993) concludes that the nuclear family is the predominant family form for whites, while single-parent and multigenerational families are also legitimate family units for both the colored and black communities. For Asians, only the multigenerational family structure (after the nuclear family) has a relatively high incidence.

Another family type that exists is where other relatives live with a family. This occurs mostly among black families (21.3%), followed by Asians (20%), coloreds (18.3%), and whites (6%). The incidence of reconstituted families (man or woman marries for the second time) is as follows: whites 13 percent, blacks 6.1 percent, coloreds 6 percent, and Asians 2.3 percent.

Sean Jones (1991) provides a good description of how the movement of family members between urban and rural areas occurs in families of migrant black workers. This gives families a movable characteristic, with support resources dependent on locality and the nature of the crisis. Research done by Fiona Ross (1995) confirms Jones's description of mobility between areas (rural to cities and vice versa). However, Ross also provides a description of the mobility of family members from colored families within settlements (rural). Support for family members comes from friends, neighbors, and even a fictitious family—the people in the immediate environment who help from time to time in order for the family members to survive. This fluidity questions the existence of the conventional family for these people.

Women in the Labor Market

Most white women enter the labor market after the completion of their education, although a small percentage between the ages of twenty and thirty years stay at home during their childbearing years. An increasing number of women also re-enter the labor market at a later stage. Black women tend to enter the labor market later in life than do others. Many of them are single mothers upon whom high demands are made by the extended family. Colored and Asian women tend to work until the birth of their first child and then remain at home (Gerdes 1997).

Conclusion

The heterogeneity of the South African society is reflected in the many different family structures and ways of family life. Traditions (cultural), changing values, political events, economic developments, modernization, and globalization contribute in a complex way to ever-changing family forms and family relationships. Greater economic independence has resulted in more nuclear families, while poorer conditions force families to unite for the sake of survival and to support one another emotionally and economically.

See also: EXTENDED FAMILIES

Bibliography

Davenport, T. R. H. (1978). *South Africa, A Modern History,* 3rd edition. Johannesburg: Macmillan.

Gerdes, L. C. (1997). "General Perspectives." In *Family Relations,* ed. L. C. Gerdes, T. le Roux, and J. D. van Wyk. Pretoria: Human Sciences Research Council Publishers.

Jithoo, S. (1996). "Family Structure and Support Systems in Indian Communities." In *Marriage and Family Life in South Africa: Research Priorities,* ed. S. Jones. Pretoria: Human Sciences Research Council Publishers.

Jones, S. (1991). "Assaulting Childhood: An Ethnographic Study of Children in a Western Cape Migrant Hostel Complex." Masters thesis. Cape Town: University of Cape Town South.

Manona, C. W. (1981). "Labour Migration, Marriage and Family Life in a Ciskei Village." Masters thesis. Grahamstown, South Africa: Rhodes University.

Nzimande, S. V. (1996). "Family Structure and Support Systems in Black Communities." In *Marriage and Family Life in South Africa: Research Priorities,* ed. L. C. Gerdes. Pretoria: Human Sciences Research Council Publishers.

Rabie, P. J. (1996). "Family Structure and Support Systems in Coloured Communities." In *Marriage and Family Life in South Africa: Research Priorities,* ed. L. C. Gerdes. Pretoria: Human Sciences Research Council Publishers.

Ross, F. C. (1995). *The Support Network of Black Families in Southern Africa.* Pretoria: Human Sciences Research Council Publishers.

Statistics South Africa. (1996). *South African Census.* Pretoria: Central Statistics.

Steyn, A. F. (1993). *Family Structures in the RSA.* Pretoria: Human Sciences Research Council Publishers.

Viljoen, S. (1994). *Strengths and Weaknesses in the Family Life of Black South Africans.* Pretoria: Human Sciences Research Council Publishers.

ABRAHAM P. GREEFF

SPAIN

The Spanish family has been undergoing dramatic changes that started in the 1980s. These changes have influenced not only patterns of interaction, but also society's broader values regarding marital and family life. To understand these changes, it is important to study these families in their immediate social and larger historical context.

Demographic Trends

Spain has a population of approximately 39,508,900 (Eurostat 2001), with fifty provinces in seventeen autonomous regions. The people of Spain are as diverse as the geographical areas they represent. Throughout the centuries, several ethnic groups have maintained their unique cultural and linguistic identities. Among these groups, the *Catalans* reside primarily in the northeast and on the eastern islands and represent 16 percent of the population. Second, the *Galicians* live in the northwestern section of Spain and represent 7 percent of the population. Third, the *Basques* (or Euskal-dun), who represent 2 percent of the population, reside primarily around the Bay of Biscay. Finally, the nomadic Spanish Roma or *Gypsies,* who traditionally have been more numerous in the southern region of Spain (i.e., Almeria, Granada, Murcia), can also be found today in larger cities like Madrid and Barcelona.

The population's natural growth has been moderate (7 per 1,000, or 27,200 people). Most population growth has been due to migration to the country, which accounted for 1.0 per 1,000 population

(40,000 people) in 2000 (European Communities 2001). One of the leading causes of the slow growth is a decrease in fertility rates that began in the 1980s. In 1980 the crude birth rate was 15.3 per 1,000 population; in 1998 and 1999 that rate decreased to 9.2 and 9.5 per 1,000 population, respectively (European Communities 2001 Collection for 1999). In 2000 that number increased slightly to 9.8 per 1,000 population (European Communities 2001).

The decrease in fertility rates is more dramatic when examining the average number of live births during a woman's life. In 1980 the number was 2.2, but it dropped in 1998 and 1999, by which time the numbers stood at 1.15 and 1.18, respectively (European Communities 2001). By 2025 the annual rate of growth is estimated to be –0.4 percent with an approximate population of only 37,648,000 (U.S. Census Bureau 2001).

In trying to understand these numbers, attention must be given to factors affecting the marital relationship as well as the changing role of individuals within the family unit. Over the years Spaniards have been delaying the age at which they marry. In 1975, the average age at first marriage was 26.5 for men and 23.9 for women. In 1995, however, the average age increased to 28.9 for men and 26.8 for women (Pérez-Díaz, Chuliá, and Valiente 2000). During the same period, the average number of marriages per 1,000 individuals also decreased. In 1975 the average rate was of 7.6 per 1,000 population, while the rate in 1980 was 5.9 and in 1999 was 5.2 (European Communities 2001). The divorce rate, however, has remained low when compared to other countries, particularly the United States. In 1998 the average divorce rate per 1,000 individuals was 0.9 compared to 4.3 in the United States (European Communities).

Views regarding cohabitation and the age of emancipation for youth have also changed over the years. In a survey conducted by the Center for Sociological Studies (Centro de Investigaciones Sociólogicas, or CIS) in 1994, 59.2 percent of those interviewed indicated that being married by the church represented the best living arrangement a couple could have. The respondents also indicated at a more personal level that if their neighbors were living together and they were not married, it would not bother them (80.2%). More than half (68.1%) of those interviewed believed the decision to live with someone was a very personal one, and the couple's decision should be accepted (Centro de Investigaciones Sociological 1994).

Meanwhile, researchers have found that young people are also delaying the age at which they leave the family home. In 1987, 84 percent of Spanish youth ages twenty to twenty-four and almost one-half (49%) of individuals ages twenty-five to twenty-nine were still living with their parents. In 1996 the number had increased slightly. Nine out of every ten youth ages twenty to twenty-four were still living with their parents, compared with 62 percent of individuals ages twenty-five to twenty-nine who were also living at home with their nuclear families (as cited by Pérez-Díaz, Chuliá, and Valiente 2000).

The role of women and their active participation the workforce has also played a critical role in Spain's demographic changes. Women are working more outside the home and staying longer in the workforce than any previous generation. According to Víctor Pérez-Díaz and his colleagues (2000), the number of women who completed their formal education and entered the workforce by the end of the 1990s represents two out of every three women ages twenty-five to forty-four (75%), compared to only 30 percent twenty years earlier. However, the critical issue here, according to Julio Iglesias de Ussel (1998), is not that women are working outside the home, but rather that they are staying in the workforce longer. For instance, among women age forty-five to fifty-four, 43 percent of the women interviewed reported still being active in the workforce (as cited by Pérez-Díaz, Chuliá, and Valiente 2000). Access to the public sphere of interaction and its economic implications have empowered women to begin to take control of their own futures and challenged the traditional patriarchal delineation of power within the family.

Nevertheless, is critical to consider the meaning behind these statistics. Why are people delaying the age of marriage? Why have fertility rates decreased so sharply? What seems to fuel the changing role of women in Spanish society?

The Changing Attitudes in Spain

The debate is on whether patterns of interaction are the result of changes in the larger political and/or economic sectors (Alberdi 1999) or, conversely, whether changes in individual/familial perspectives have served as catalysts to larger social change

Spanish families celebrate together by having a picnic on Easter weekend. The town of Fermoselle can be seen in the background . STEPHANIE MAZE/CORBIS

(Pérez-Díaz, Chuliá, and Valiente 2000). This debate remains unresolved. What seems clear, however, is that there has been a gradual and significant shift in attitudes regarding the way Spaniards define their roles and future goals within their interpersonal relationships. A review of the historical context yields a better sense of the magnitude of these changes. During Francisco Franco's government (1939–1975) both the laws of the state and the regulations of the Catholic Church enforced a set of structures aimed to preserve a conservative and patriarchal structure of the family, as well as significant control of the mass media and various institutions (Clark 1990).

Before the creation of the constitution in 1978 and the reforms of the civil code of 1981, Spanish law discriminated heavily against married women. Stringent standards restricted opportunities for women to pursue professional careers, while celebrating their roles as mothers and wives. During Franco's government, Spanish law prohibited wives from taking part in almost all forms of economic opportunity, including employment, ownership of property, or even travel, unless they had the consent of their husbands. These laws were known as *permiso marital* (marital permission) (Clark 1990). The government advocated a policy of *perfecta casada* (the perfect housewife) and *angel del hogar* (angel of the home), reaffirming women's subordinate roles within the family and in society at large. Women, for example, had to enroll in a six-month training program in preparation for motherhood (as cited in Sanchez and Hall 1999). Adultery during this time was a crime, as was abortion. Marriages also had to be canonical in nature. This meant that basically all marriages in Spain had to be sanctioned by the Catholic Church. Since the church did not allow divorce, the difficult process of annulment was the only means of dissolution (Clark 1990).

By the 1960s, social values were changing faster than the existing legal statutes allowed, creating tension between the legal codes and the growing social reality. Many scholars believe that these changes developed as a result of the economic exodus of hundreds of thousands of people from rural settings to new urban centers during that time. In addition, the increasing flow of European tourists to Spain as well as the migration of Spanish workers to other European countries dramatically changed Spain's isolation from the rest of the world (Clark 1990). Soon after Franco's death in 1975, the *permiso marital* was abolished, laws against adultery were cancelled in 1978, and divorce was legalized in 1981 (Clark 1990).

This growing shift in attitudes regarding family roles could be viewed as part of a larger ideological divide experienced by many countries during the industrialization process. The change is a shift from a traditional style of family, which is often hierarchical and patriarchal, to a secular definition, which is often more individualistic and egalitarian in style. A secular style questions the role of women as the primary familial caretaker and homekeeper and challenges hierarchical conceptions of men's and women's relationships (Sanchez and Hall 1999).

In Spain, as in many other countries, these two ideologies co-exist. At one level, Spaniards affirm the right of women to work outside the home, but they still expect women to carry most of the burden of childcare and housework. The same discrepancy is true when comparing the difference in pay between men and women. The average salary for women is only 75 to 80 percent of that of men, depending on the sector of the economy in which they participate. Nevertheless, the dramatic increase of women's participation in the labor markets has significantly challenged traditionalist notions of couple and family relationships.

Ines Alberdi, in her 1999 study of the Spanish family, attributes the growing secular trend to a changing ethic that encompasses the following factors. The first is a growing egalitarian ethic that encourages women to pursue professional jobs and increase participation in the decision-making process in the home. Traditionally, women normally followed values such as personal sacrifice of other goals in the interest of raising children. However, with the improvement in economic conditions and opportunities for professional advancement, the emphasis shifted from the struggle for economic survival to the pursuit of more meaningful and satisfying interpersonal relationships. Alberdi (1999) believes that there is the desire for individual liberty and the pursuit of personal happiness at the heart of this movement toward egalitarian relationships. Although from a general perspective, men and women agree on the benefits of more autonomy in their relationships, many couples have difficulties working out these roles because many men have not been socialized to function in this way. The result is a constant effort to negotiate and renegotiate their individual responsibilities within the relationship. This experience has left many couples questioning the need to increase additional responsibilities either by formalizing their relationship through marriage or by having children. Therefore, couples are delaying the age at which they marry and have children to have the opportunity to pursue their own individual relational and professional interests.

An increasing tolerance toward diverse family forms and patterns of interactions has also supported the development of secular trends in the society. The majority of Spaniards do not see any problems with cohabitation or having children outside the marital relationship. This shift in social expectations and norms has given couples more flexibility and less pressure to conform to traditional standards. As a result, couples are able to explore different types of living arrangements in response to different economic needs and educational opportunities (Alberdi 1999).

Spaniards, amidst all these changes, maintain a strong sense of family loyalty and solidarity. The traditional values of family obligation, similarity of interest, and sympathy for members of the group remain. The challenge, however, is in the application of these values in a society where individual families are increasingly separated from their extended families. Nevertheless, this value remains central to the way many families operate. For instance, a mother may take care of her daughter's children so her daughter can go to work or a grandparent may use part of a pension to help financially support unemployed younger members of the family. It is within this context of the search for individual liberty and desire to be part of the larger group that many Spanish families find themselves today (Alberdi 1999).

More Spaniards are less willing to postpone any opportunity for current happiness for a distant and uncertain future. As opposed to past decades, during which individuals would put aside short-term personal desires to reap the benefits of a better future, contemporary Spaniards are paying more attention to what is available to them in the present. Therefore, it is possible to understand how some of these demographic changes have taken place when considering the reinterpretation of the value of time as well as an increased desire for meaningful and satisfying emotional connections in their interpersonal relationships. These changes represent for many Spaniards new challenges and opportunities, as they attempt to define for themselves what family life will be like in the future.

See also: BASQUE FAMILIES; HISPANIC-AMERICAN FAMILIES; LATIN AMERICA; MEXICO

Bibliography

Alberdi, I., ed. (1995). *Informe sobre la situación de la familia en España* (Report regarding the situation of the family in Spain). Madrid: Ministerios de Asuntos Sociales.

Alberdi, I. (1999). *La nueva familia Española* (The new Spanish family). Madrid: Taurus.

Centro de Investigaciones Sociológicas (Center for Sociological Investigations). (April 1994). *Barómetro de Abril* (April Barometer) Issue Brief No. 2.087. Madrid: Author.

Clark, R. P. (1990). "The Society and Its Environment: Social Values and Attitudes." In *Spain: A Country Study,* ed. E. Solsten and S. W. Meditz. Washington, DC: Library of Congress, Federal Research Division.

Flaquer, L. (1998). *El destino de la familia* (The destiny of the family). Barcelona: Ariel.

Iglesias de Ussel, J. (1998). *La familia y el cambio político en España* (The family and political change in Spain). Madrid: Tecnos.

Miel Landwerlin, G. (1999). *La Postmodernizacion de la familia Española* (The Postmodernization of the Spanish family). Madrid: Acento.

Pérez-Díaz, V.; Chuliá, E.; and Valiente, C. (2000). *La familia Española en el año 2000* (The Spanish family in the year 2000). Madrid: Fundación Argentaria—Visor Dis.

Sanchez, L., and Hall, C. S. (1999). "Traditional Values and Democratic Impulses: The Gender Division of Labor in Contemporary Spain." *Journal of Comparative Family Studies* 30(4):659–685.

Other Resources

European Communities. (2001). "First demographic estimates for 2000." Available from http://europa.eu.int/comm/eurostat.

European Communities. (2001). "First results of the demographic data collection for 1999 in Europe." Available from http://europa.eu.int/comm/eurostat.

European Communities. (2001). "First results of the demographic data collection for 2000 in Europe." Available from http://europa.eu.int/comm/eurostat.

U.S. Census Bureau. IDB Summary Demographic Data for Spain. Available from http://www.census.gov/cgi-bin/ipc/idbsum?cty=SP.

J. ROBERTO REYES

SPANKING

Although *spanking* is a term familiar to most parents, it may be defined differently depending on our personal circumstances. For some, spanking may refer to one or two flat-handed swats on a child's wrist or buttocks, but would not include a beating with a whip or a belt. For others, spanking also includes slaps and pinches to the leg, arm, back, or even the head, as long as no marks are left after a relatively short period of time.

On a broader level, the term *corporal punishment* is sometimes used instead of spanking. One oft-cited definition of corporal punishment is "the use of physical force with the intention of causing a child to experience pain, but not injury, for the purpose of correction or control of the child's behavior" (Straus 1994, p. 4). Shoving, shaking, grabbing, and even keeping a child in an uncomfortable position for a prolonged period of time probably ought also to be included to form a more complete definition. In this entry, *spanking, corporal punishment,* and *physical discipline* will be used interchangeably but will exclude any type of hitting or physical contact that results in injury or marks that last longer than a few hours.

Prevalence of Physical Discipline

Since the late 1940s, when the first national surveys in the United States were published about spanking, it has been consistently found that almost all parents in the United States have occasionally spanked their children. The data have also shown that over 90 percent of children and adults remember being spanked as children. Because so many parents spank their children and the percentage has remained high over the years, most consider spanking to be a cultural norm in the United States. In fact, according to studies in Britain, Canada, China, Israel, Italy, Kenya, Korea, South Africa, and the West Indies, most parents in most countries around the world spank their children at least occasionally.

Many surveys have also gathered data regarding attitudes about spanking and have found that most parents believe that corporal punishment in a nonabusive manner is an acceptable form of discipline. However, toward the end of the twentieth century the number of parents who believe physical discipline is acceptable consistently dropped in many countries. According to Murray A. Straus (2000), in the United States, for example, between the years 1968 and 1998, "the percent agreeing that a 'good hard spanking is sometimes necessary' dropped from near unanimity to 55 percent" (p. 206).

How does one explain the discrepancy between the decrease in the approval of spanking and the continued use of spanking as a form of punishment? One suggestion is that the 30 to 40 percent difference in behavior and attitudes occurs because many parents use corporal punishment as a last resort, when nothing else seems to work. Some parents may reluctantly spank their children because they cannot think of what else to do to show the child the seriousness of his or her misbehavior.

Although spanking is commonplace in many countries, in 1979 Sweden became the first country to outlaw spanking. Since then, at least seven other countries have enacted similar laws to ban corporal punishment (Finland, Denmark, Norway, Austria, Cyprus, Latvia, and Croatia). Several studies have been done in Sweden to attempt to determine the impact of the ban on behavior and attitudes in that country. Some critics of the ban in Sweden point out that Sweden actually showed an increase in the child abuse rate after the law was enacted (e.g., Larzelere and Johnson 1999; Rosellini 1998). Some also suggest that most of the countries that have outlawed spanking are considered permissive in social areas, unlike the United States. As a result, they do not believe the United States should consider a law against corporal punishment.

Those who favor a law like Sweden's point out that surveys in Sweden since 1979 have found dramatic decreases in the use of physical punishment

Russell Baker stands next to his mother, Virginia, holding a paddle used for spankings, 1975. Spanking, once considered a cultural norm in the United States with over 90 percent of parents spanking their children, has dropped in approval in recent years. A survey conducted in 2000 found that only half of all parents approve of spanking as a form of punishment. A/P WIDE WORLD PHOTOS

and parental commitment to the use of physical punishment even though breaking this law does not carry any punishment. The surveys indicate that parents no longer believe they need to use physical punishment to achieve compliance in their children. One study (Durrant 2000) in particular, upon examining youth well-being in Sweden since 1979, found that youth have not become more "unruly, undersocialized, or self-destructive following the passage of the 1979 corporal punishment ban" (p. 451).

Although there is nearly universal use of physical discipline by parents, it should be noted that the effects of spanking may vary from one culture to another. Even if one does interpret the data from Sweden as suggesting a positive result from banning spanking in that country, other studies (e.g., Deater-Deckard et al. 1996) have found that the effects of spanking are likely influenced by the parental, familial, and ethnic context in which the family lives. Some studies actually suggest that in certain cultures, especially collectivist cultures that exist in places like China and Africa, parents' failure to spank their children might indicate to the children that their parents do not care enough about them to discipline them. Thus, findings from one group of subjects must not be generalized to everyone.

In addition to information about attitudes towards spanking and frequency of spanking, studies have also consistently found that:

- Boys are spanked more than girls;
- Mothers spank more than fathers;
- Toddlers and preschoolers are spanked most often,
- Parents from lower income groups spank more often;
- Parents who have more education are less likely to spank;
- Religious conservatives are more favorable towards spanking; and
- Some groups, based on cultural and/or ethnic background are more likely to spank their children.

Although it is helpful to know about these tendencies, one must recognize that they have not been true in every study and are not necessarily indicative of every person who fits in one or more of these groups. In addition, many of the studies have asked questions about harsh physical discipline and not the occasional slap on the buttocks. Most studies have also been retrospective in nature, asking subjects to remember their own childhood or to recall how many times they spanked their children in the past. Due to these limitations on the data, one must be careful not to overgeneralize the findings.

Controversy about the Use of Physical Discipline

Although almost everyone seems to have been spanked while growing up, there continues to be a heated controversy about the efficacy and wisdom of spanking children. Most people, including some child development experts, seem to believe that limited, nonabusive, physical punishment is not harmful to children and is often necessary to teach children respect and obedience. On the other hand, many child development experts and some people are convinced that even moderate amounts of corporal punishment can be harmful to a child and consequently should be avoided at all costs. After decades of discussion in a variety of settings, about the only thing that is certain is that almost everyone seems to hold a strong opinion on whether or not children should be spanked.

In the first half of the twentieth century, most parents in the United States demanded complete obedience on the part of their children and usually followed the adage "spare the rod and spoil the child." As a result, there was little discussion about whether or not it was in the best interest of their children to spank them or use the hickory switch if they misbehaved. Further, corporal punishment was practiced in many public schools in the United States well into the second half of the twentieth century, usually with the blessing of the parents.

However, from mid-century on, experts like Benjamin Spock (1946), Thomas Gordon (1970), T. Berry Brazelton (1969), and others began to speak against the harsh discipline of earlier times and suggested that children were individuals who needed to be treated with rights equal to all other members of the family. Instead of seeing the parent-child relationship as a benevolent dictatorship, they suggested the relationship should be viewed as a democracy. They taught that parents ought to consider their children as friends and treat them as they would their spouse.

These influential opinions, together with several significant social changes in the United States such as increases in violence, child abuse, and divorce, led to a reexamination of the use of physical punishment in schools and in homes during the last quarter of the twentieth century. Some experts have repeatedly claimed that the research on spanking clearly shows that even mild corporal punishment leads to a number of negative outcomes in those who have been spanked. As a result of their efforts, corporal punishment has been banned in virtually all schools, and some states have even considered legislation banning parents from hitting their children in the home. Many other countries around the world seem to be following trends similar to those in the United States. In addition, many other countries have been experiencing some change in views about physical punishment of children.

Since the 1970s, the academic community generally has interpreted the research as saying that corporal punishment in schools or homes is detrimental and should be abolished. Murray A. Straus, author of *Beating the Devil Out of Them* (2000), and Irwin A. Hyman, author of *The Case Against*

Spanking (1997), are two of the key proponents in the movement to abolish spanking in schools and homes in the United States. They believe that corporal punishment is a significant psychological and social problem. Straus claims that there are over eighty different studies dating to the 1950s which link corporal punishment in children to later behavioral problems such as increased violence, aggression, noncompliance, delinquency, antisocial behavior, sexual hang-ups, and depression. He also claims that the research shows that alternative discipline strategies work just as well as corporal punishment and therefore corporal punishment serves no real purpose. Hyman spends much of his time speaking with state legislators and policymakers as he attempts to persuade people that other types of discipline are as effective as spanking and therefore hitting children is never right.

In examining the causal link between corporal punishment and negative outcomes, Straus recognizes that earlier studies did have a serious limitation—they were correlational in nature and therefore did not show which is the cause and which is the effect. Accordingly, one could argue that children are spanked because of behavior problems or that they have behavior problems because they were spanked. However, Straus believes that five studies done between 1997 and 1999 have overcome the flaws of the previous studies and confirmed the findings of the previous eighty studies: that corporal punishment has long-term negative effects on children. Because these studies were based on large and nationally representative samples of U.S. children and were longitudinal in nature, he believes they allow for causal conclusions regarding the link between physical punishment and the negative behavior of children. All of this evidence leads Straus to conclude that all corporal punishment ought to be considered abuse and ought to be against the law.

In contrast to Straus and Hyman, Diana Baumrind (1994, 1996a) believes that the evidence seems to indicate that mild, nonabusive, physical punishment is not harmful when used occasionally, in a loving relationship, and in conjunction with other methods of discipline, most notably with reasoning. She claims that the critical issue is the relationship between the parent and the child. If the child feels as if he or she is in a loving, trusting relationship with his or her parents, then the child usually understands that discipline, and even spanking, is for the good of the child. When this occurs, Baumrind and others claim, there are no long-term negative effects.

Robert Larzelere, along with some of his colleagues (1998), also suggests that spanking is not all bad. In fact, they found that spanking used in conjunction with reasoning was the most effective type of discipline in some situations. Larzelere, like most experts who believe spanking is not always detrimental, believes certain guidelines must be kept in mind if parents choose to use corporal punishment. First, physical discipline should be limited to a couple of slaps applied by the open hand to the buttocks or legs. Second, it should only be used on children between the ages of two and six when other disciplinary methods may not be as effective. Third, it should only be used to back up less aversive disciplinary techniques and as a supplement to positive parenting. Finally, spanking should not be done while the parent is angry because it could escalate to abuse.

Alternatives to Physical Discipline

Although it is beyond the scope of this entry to discuss disciplinary alternatives in depth, several brief comments are warranted. First, parenting experts recommend that parents create a disciplinary plan in advance so that they have discussed how they will respond in a variety of situations. This might eliminate some of the spanking that occurs impulsively and out of anger. Secondly, parents should consider a variety of alternatives such as

- Redirecting children to a more suitable activity;
- Rewarding children who follow the rules;
- Utilizing time-outs for short periods of time;
- Helping children to avoid situations and activities that naturally lead to misbehavior;
- Removing privileges;
- Allowing for natural consequences to result from negative behavior;
- Giving additional chores;
- Grounding older children from certain activities or friends; and
- Above all, communicating and reasoning with children about problem behavior.

Conclusion

What conclusions, then, can be drawn about corporal punishment? First, most parents in most cultures use corporal punishment at least occasionally. Second, experts do not agree about the efficacy or wisdom of physical punishment. Third, if spanking is used, it should be used sparingly and as one part of a total disciplinary program. Fourth, parents must consider the views of the culture when deciding about disciplinary strategies. Finally, no matter what disciplinary approach is taken, parents and caregivers must realize they do influence children by their own attitudes and behaviors.

See also: CHILD ABUSE: PHYSICAL ABUSE AND NEGLECT; CHILD ABUSE: PSYCHOLOGICAL MALTREATMENT; CHILDCARE; CHILDREN'S RIGHTS; CONDUCT DISORDER; CONFLICT: FAMILY RELATIONSHIPS; CONFLICT: PARENT-CHILD RELATIONSHIPS; COPARENTING; DISCIPLINE; JUVENILE DELINQUENCY; PARENTING EDUCATION; PARENTING STYLES

Bibliography

Baumrind, D. (1994). "The Social Context of Child Maltreatment." *Family Relations* 43:360–368.

Baumrind, D. (1996a). "A Blanket Injunction against Disciplinary Use of Spanking is Not Warranted by the Data." *Pediatrics* 98:828–831.

Baumrind, D. (1996b). "The Discipline Controversy Revisited." *Family Relations* 45:405–414.

Brazelton, T. B. (1969). *Infants and Mothers: Differences in Development.* New York: Delacorte Press.

Canter, L., and Canter, M. (1985). *Assertive Discipline for Parents,* rev. edition. New York: Harper and Row.

Deater-Deckard, K., and Dodge, K. A. (1997). "Externalizing Behavior Problems and Discipline Revisited: Nonlinear Effects and Variation by Culture, Context, and Gender." *Psychological Inquiry* 8:161–175.

Deater-Deckard, K.; Dodge, K. A.; Bates, J. E.; and Pettit, G. S. (1996). "Physical Discipline among African American and European American Mothers: Links to Children's Externalizing Behaviors." *Developmental Psychology* 32:1065–1072.

Durrant, J. (2000). "Trends in Youth Crime and Well-Being since the Abolition of Corporal Punishment in Sweden." *Youth and Society* 31:437–455.

Forehand, R., and Kotchick, B. A. (1996). "Cultural Diversity: A Wake Up Call for Parent Training." *Behavior Therapy* 27:187–206.

Gershoff, E. T. (2002). "Corporal Punishment by Parents and Associated Child Behaviors and Experiences: A Meta-Analytic and Theoretical Review." *Psychological Bulletin* 128:539–579.

Gordon, T. (1970). *Parent Effectiveness Training.* New York: Wyden.

Gunnoe, M. L., and Mariner, C. L. (1997). "Toward a Developmental-Contextual Model of the Effects of Parental Spanking on Children's Aggression." *Archives of Pediatric Adolescent Medicine* 151:768–775.

Hyman, I. A. (1997). *The Case against Spanking: How to Discipline Your Child without Hitting.* San Francisco: Jossey-Bass.

Larzelere, R. E. (1996). "A Review of the Outcomes of Parental Use of Nonabusive or Customary Physical Punishment." *Pediatrics* 98:824–828.

Larzelere, R. E., and Johnson, B. (1999). "Evaluations of the Effects of Sweden's Ban on Physical Child Abuse Rates: A Literature Review." *Psychological Reports* 85:381–392.

Larzelere, R. E.; Sather, P. R.; Schneider, W. N.; Larson, D. B.; and Pike, P. L. (1998). "Punishment Enhances Reasoning's Effectiveness as a Disciplinary Response to Toddlers." *Journal of Marriage and the Family* 60:388–403.

McCord, J., ed. (1995). *Coercion and Punishment in Long-Term Perspectives.* New York: Cambridge University Press.

Rosellini, L. (1998). "When to Spank." *U.S. News and World Report,* April 13, 52–58.

Rosemond, J. K. (1994). *To Spank or Not to Spank: A Parents' Handbook.* Kansas City, MO: Andrews McMeel.

Spock, B. (1946). *The Common Sense Book of Baby and Child Care.* New York: Duell, Sloan, and Pearce.

Straus, M. A. (2000). *Beating the Devil Out of Them: Corporal Punishment by American Families,* 2nd edition. Piscataway, NJ: Transaction.

Straus, M. A.; Sugarman, D. B.; and Giles-Sims, J. (1997). "Spanking by Parents and Subsequent Antisocial Behavior of Children." *Archives of Pediatric Adolescent Medicine* 151:761–767.

Whaley, A. L. (2000). "Sociocultural Differences in the Developmental Consequences of the Use of Physical Discipline during Childhood for African Americans." *Cultural Diversity and Ethnic Minority Psychology* 6(1):5–12.

JOHN A. ADDLEMAN

SPOUSE ABUSE

PREVALENCE *Orsolya Magyar*

THEORETICAL EXPLANATIONS *Richard J. Gelles*

PREVALENCE

Over the past two decades, violence by an intimate partner has become identified throughout the world as a serious physical and mental health concern. *Spouse abuse,* in particular, was recognized, at the Fourth World Conference on Women held in Beijing in 1995 as a human rights concern worldwide.

Terms and Definitions

Various terms are used to characterize the violence between intimate partners. For example terms such as *spouse abuse, domestic violence, family violence, partner violence, intimate partner abuse,* and *battering* are popular but they do not differentiate between men and women (Gelles 1995). These terms imply that men are as likely as women to be victims of spouse abuse and suggest that women and men initiate assaults on their partners at approximately the same rate (Straus and Gelles 1986). And roughly equivalent victimization rates have been found for married (e.g., Straus, Gelles, and Steinmetz 1986) and dating (e.g., White and Koss 1991) couples.

However, numerous other sources indicate that women are far more likely than men to be victimized. For example, a National Crime Victimization Survey in the United States (Bachman 1994) found that women were ten times more likely to be injured by their male partners than vice versa. The National Violence Against Women Survey (Tjaden and Thoennes 2001) found that 20.4 percent of women, as opposed to only 7 percent of men, were physically assaulted by their intimate partner at some point in their relationship; thus, women were almost three times more likely to report being victimized by their husband or boyfriend. This type of information supports the shift from gender-neutral terms to terms such as *violence toward women, woman abuse, wife abuse,* or *violence against wives* (Gelles 1995).

In studying wife abuse, violence toward women is typically defined in one of three ways: (1) *overall prevalence,* referring to the percentage of women who have ever been physically assaulted by a partner in an intimate relationship; (2) *overall twelve-month prevalence,* referring to the percentage of women who have been physically assaulted by a partner in an intimate relationship during the previous twelve months; and (3) *current prevalence,* referring to the percentage of women who are currently being physically assaulted by a partner in an intimate relationship.

Early definitions of spouse abuse referred only to the physical injury a husband perpetrated against his wife (Gelles 1974; Martin 1976). More recent research broadened this definition to include sexual abuse, marital rape, emotional or psychological abuse, and coercion. The United Nations Commission on the Status of Women presently defines domestic violence as "any act of gender based violence that results in physical, sexual or psychological harm or suffering to women, including threats of such acts, coercion, or arbitrary deprivation of liberty whether occurring in public or private life" (Fikree and Bhatti 1999).

Prevalence

Given the fact that the most common victims of spouse abuse are wives, in the late twentieth century researchers began to study the prevalence of wife abuse around the world (Campbell 1992). The World Health Organization, though the Department for Injuries and Violence Prevention, created a Violence Against Women database. This database is one of the few current sources for international spouse abuse statistics. It notes that comparisons between studies need to be undertaken cautiously because of differences in definitions, samples and data collection techniques. In addition, variability in reporting violence by the subjects in the studies needs to be considered, due to fear, embarrassment, self-blame, or cultural norms regarding the acceptability of violence. Nevertheless, available studies indicate that between 20 and 50 percent of women in various populations around the world have experienced spouse abuse at some point in their lives (Heise et al. 1994; World Health Organization 2002). These figures support that the physical abuse of women by their intimate partners is indeed a serious international problem.

North America. The 1985 National Family Violence Survey in the United States and a 1987 study of Alberta, Canada, residents produced similar rates of wife abuse; 11.3 percent of U.S. women

(Straus and Gelles 1986) and 11.2 percent of Canadian women (Kennedy and Dutton 1989) were reported to be the victims of spouse abuse in a twelve-month period. More recent findings, however, from the National Violence Against Women Survey (World Health Organization 2002) show twelve-month rates of 1.3 percent (and an overall prevalence rate of 22.1%), whereas a recent report by Statistics Canada (Trainor and Mihorean 2001) reported that both the 1993 Violence Against Women Survey and the 1999 General Social Survey found twelve-month wife abuse rates of 3 percent. The declines in rates of domestic violence in North America may be the result of many factors, including an expansion of the number of resources and services offered to abused women (e.g., shelters), more reporting of the abuse, mandatory arrest laws for men who beat their wives, and better training for police officers and attorneys appointed by the crown; in addition, new treatment programs for men who assault women, and the slowly increasing status of women, both socially and financially, may be contributing to a reduction of this problem (Canadian Centre for Justice Statistics 2001). These interventions are, unfortunately, not available or implemented in many parts of the world, and the high estimates for prevalence rates of spouse abuse around the world reflect lack in services. However, many countries around the world have domestic violence rates similar to North America's, pointing out, perhaps, that there may be other factors involved in this problem.

Central/South America. In Central and South America, research suggests that wife abuse is a significant problem. In Mexico, spouse abuse rates varied from 27 to 40 percent (World Health Organization 2002). A national study of wife abuse in Puerto Rico between 1993 and 1996 noted lifetime prevalence rates of 19.3 percent (World Health Organization 2002). Thirty percent of a Peruvian sample of middle- and low-income women in 1997 reported physical abuse within the past year (World Health Organization 2002), and 22.5 percent of the participants in a study of domestic violence in Santiago, Chile, reported being assaulted in the year preceding the study (World Health Organization 2002). In Leon, the second largest city in Nicaragua, 52 percent of women reported physical abuse from their partner at some point in their lives, with 27 percent being the victim of it during the year before the study (Ellsberg 1999).

Europe. Spouse abuse statistics for European countries are difficult to find. This is unfortunate because the few studies investigating this problem in Europe indicate that the rates of domestic violence are comparable or higher than those found in North America. The largest English survey of men's reports of assaulting their intimate partners found the overall prevalence rate to be over 7 percent (Farrington 1994). A cross-sectional survey of women in Ireland found that 39 percent of women who had ever been in a relationship had in fact experienced spouse abuse (Bradley et al. 2002).

A study of Norwegian women residing in Trondheim, Norway, found that 18 percent had experienced domestic violence at some point in a relationship (Schei and Bakketeig 1989). Similarly, within a Dutch sample, 20.8 percent of the women had, at some point in their lives, experienced physical (and/or sexual) violence by their partner (Romkens 1997). In Switzerland, according to a two-year study from 1994 to 1996, overall prevalence rates for wife abuse are 12.6 percent, whereas twelve-month prevalence rates are 6.3 percent (World Health Organization 2002).

Slightly more than 4 percent of Spanish women over the age of eighteen are reported by the Women's Institute—a women's rights organization—to suffer from daily physical assaults from their husbands (Bosch 2001). Eastern Turkey has perhaps the highest reported prevalence rates in all of Europe; in East and Southeast Anatolia, Turkey, the lifetime prevalence rate of spouse abuse is estimated to be an astonishing 57.9 percent (World Health Organization 2002).

Africa. Prevalence rates of wife abuse are high in Africa, even though the many government organizations have promised to promote the full and equal role of women in society. Domestic violence in Egypt remains a significant social problem (Refaat et al. 2001). In the Meskanena Woreda region of Ethiopia, 45 percent of women were estimated to have been victimized by an intimate partner, and 10 percent had been victimized in the twelve months preceding the study (World Health Organization 2002). Odujinrin (1993) reports that wife beating has a prevalence rate of 31.4 percent in Nigeria. In the Kisii District of Kenya, the prevalence of physical abuse within current relationships appears to be 42 percent (World Health Organization 2002). A twelve-month prevalence rate of wife abuse for Kigali, Rwanda, in 1990 was 21 percent (World Health Organization 2002). 40.4 percent of Uganda's women residing in the Lira and Masaka Districts report being abused by a current husband or boyfriend (World Health Organization 2002). In addition, research has documented that domestic violence is pervasive in South Africa despite government efforts to reduce its prevalence (Kim and Mmatshilo 2002).

Asia. The investigations of domestic violence in Asian countries can be compared only indirectly to those of African nations. Both countries have serious problems with spouse abuse that may covertly be maintaining, as well as definitely emphasizing, the lesser status of women in these developing countries. An estimate of the prevalence of domestic violence in Chinese families living in Hong Kong, through the unique data collection technique of children's recall of their parents' behavior, is 14 percent (Tang 1994). This rate is similar to North American estimates of the prevalence of wife abuse; however, a nationwide survey in Japan found that 58.7 percent of the women respondents experienced physical abuse (Yoshihama and Sorenson 1994). In the year preceding a National Study in the Republic of Korea in 1989, 37.5 percent of the respondents had been physically assaulted by their husband or boyfriend (World Health Organization 2002). Twenty percent of a sample of husbands in Bangkok, Thailand, revealed that they had slapped, hit, or kicked their wife one or more times during their marriage (Hoffman, Demo, and Edwards 1994). An examination of domestic violence in the Jullender district of Punjab found that 75 percent of lower-caste men reported physically abusing their wives, and 22 percent of the higher-caste men also reported physically assaulting their wives (Mahajan 1990, 1–10). A later survey found that the prevalence of wife abuse reported by men across five districts of Northern India between 1995 and 1996 was between 18 percent and 45 percent (Martin et al. 1999). Researchers assessing spouse abuse among women attending health centers in Karachi, Pakistan, found that 34 percent reported being physically assaulted at least once by their partner (Fikree and Bhatti 1999). An overall lifetime prevalence rate of 47 percent, and a twelve-month prevalence rate of 19 percent were obtained from ethnographic and survey data in rural Bangladesh (Schuler et al. 1996). In Israel, the 1992 estimate of the number of women affected by domestic violence was at least 150,000 per year (Eldeson, Peled, and Eiskovotz 1991). A national study in the West Bank and Gaza Strip in 1994 revealed that 52 percent of women had been physically assaulted in an intimate relationship in the twelve months before the study (World Health Organization 2002). Two studies of the prevalence of domestic violence in Papua New Guinea found lifetime prevalence rates of 67 percent, and 56.1 percent, in rural villages and in Port Moresby, respectively (World Health Organization 2002).

Australia. A study to determine the prevalence of wife abuse in women attending general practitioners in Melbourne, Australia, found that among subjects who were currently involved in a relationship, 6 percent had been kicked, bitten, or punched, 4 percent had either been hit, or their spouse had tried to hit them with an object, 4 percent had been severely beaten, 4 percent had been choked, and 1 percent had been injured by their partner's use of a gun or knife (Mazza, Dennerstein, and Ryan 1996). Another investigation found that, in a small city (population: 80,000) in tropical Australia, spouse abuse was the norm, rather than the exception in relationships (Kahn et al. 1980).

The prevalence rates cited above were based on physical abuse only. In actuality, sexual and psychological abuse are important types of abuse that are found either on their own or in varying degrees with physical abuse. Therefore, it is likely that using a definition of wife abuse that included all three types of these victimizations would have provided higher prevalence rates. Another important concept to acknowledge when examining these prevalence rates is that, as reported by Marvin Kahn and colleagues (1980), domestic violence is seen by many cultures as normal. Thus, the reported rates may underestimate the actual problem because this type of behavior may be accepted, or even embraced, in some cultures. Despite these evident limitations, the available statistics reported by victims or their perpetrators still indicate a severe problem in all the countries examined. North American and European prevalence rates are comparable, as are estimates from South America, Africa, and Asia. Although these prevalence rates are beneficial in helping understand the extent of domestic violence, research urgently needs to address the complex array of social, cultural, and psychological factors that influence these rates in countries around the world.

See also: CONFLICT: COUPLE RELATIONSHIPS; CONFLICT: FAMILY RELATIONSHIPS; ELDER ABUSE; INTERPARENTAL VIOLENCE—EFFECTS ON CHILDREN; MARITAL QUALITY; POSTTRAUMATIC STRESS DISORDER (PTSD); POWER: FAMILY RELATIONSHIPS; POWER: MARITAL RELATIONSHIPS; RAPE; THERAPY: COUPLE RELATIONSHIPS

Bibliography

Bachman, R. (1994). *National Crime Victimization Report: Violence Against Women*. Washington, DC: Government Printing Office.

Bosch, X. (2001). "Spain's Government Puts Domestic Violence Plan as Top Priority." *Lancet* 357:1682.

Bradley, F.; Smith, M.; Long, J.; and O'Doud, T. (2002). "Reported Frequency of Domestic Violence: Cross Sectional Survey of Women Attending General Practice." *British Medical Journal* 324:271–274.

Campbell, J. C. (1992). "Prevention of Wife Battering: Insights from Cultural Analysis." *Response to the Victimization of Women and Children* 14:18–24.

Eldeson, J. C.; Peled, F.; and Eiskovotz, Z. (1991). "Israel's Response to Battered Women." *Violence Update* 1(4–5):11.

Ellsberg, M. (1999). "Domestic Violence and Emotional Distress among Nicaraguan Women." *American Psychologist* 54:30–36.

Farrington, D. P. (1994). "Childhood, Adolescent, and Adult Features of Violent Males." In *Aggressive Behaviour: Current Perspectives,* ed. L. R. Huesman. New York: Plenum Press.

Fikree, F. F., and Bhatti, L. I. (1999). "Domestic Violence and Health of Pakistani Women." *International Journal of Gynecology and Obstetrics* 65:195–201.

Gelles, R. J. (1974). *The Violent Home*. Newbury Park, CA: Sage.

Gelles, R. J. (1995). "Spouse Abuse and Neglect." In *Encyclopedia of Marriage and the Family,* ed. D. Levinson. New York: Macmillan.

Heise, L.; Raike, A.; Watts, C.; and Zwi, A. (1994). "Violence Against Women: A Neglected Public Health Issue in Less Developed Countries." *Social Science and Medicine* 39:1165–1179.

Kahn, M. W., and the Behavioral Health Technician Staff. (1980). "Wife Beating and Cultural Context: Prevalence in an Aboriginal and Islander Community in Northern Australia." *American Journal of Community Psychology* 8:727–731.

Kennedy, L. W., and Dutton, D. G. (1989). "The Incidence of Wife Assault in Alberta." *Canadian Journal of Behavioral Science* 21:40–54.

Kim, J., and Mmatshilo, M. (2002). "'Women enjoy punishment': Attitudes and Experiences of Gender-Based Violence among the PHC Nurses in Rural South Africa." *Social Science and Medicine*: 54:1243–1254.

Hoffman, K. L.; Demo, D. H.; and Edwards, J. N. (1994). "Physical Wife Abuse in a Non-Western Society: An Integrated Theoretical Approach." *Journal of Marriage and the Family* 56:131–146.

Mahajan, A. (1990). "Instigators of Wife Battering." In *Violence Against Women,* ed. S. Sood. Jaipur, India: Arihanti.

Martin, D. (1976). *Battered Wives*. San Francisco: Glide.

Martin, L. S.; Ong-Tsui, A.; Maitra, K.; and Marinshaw, R. (1999). "Domestic Violence in Northern India." *American Journal of Epidemiology* 150:417–426.

Mazza, D.; Dennerstein, L.; and Ryan, V. (1996). "Physical, Sexual, and Emotional Violence Against Women: A General Practice-Based Prevalence Study." *Medical Journal of Australia* 164:14–17.

Odujinrin, O. (1993). "Wife Battering in Nigeria." *International Journal of Gynecology and Obstetrics* 41: 159–164.

Refaat, A.; Dandash, K.; Defrawi, M.; and Eyada, M. (2001). "Female Genital Mutilation and Domestic Violence among Egyptian Women." *Journal of Sex and Marital Therapy* 27:593–598.

Romkens, R. (1997). "Prevalence of Wife Abuse in the Netherlands." *Journal of Interpersonal Violence* 12: 99–125.

Schei, B., and Bakketeig, L. S. (1989). "Gynaecological Impact of Sexual and Physical Abuse by Spouse: A Study of a Random Sample of Norwegian Women." *British Journal of Obstetrics and Gynecology* 96: 1379–1383.

Schuler, S. R.; Hashemi, S. M.; Riley, A. P.; and Akhter, S. (1996). "Credit Programs, Patriarchy, and Men's Violence against Women in Rural Bangladesh." *Social Science and Medicine* 43:1729–1742.

Straus, M. A., and Gelles, R. J. (1986). "Societal Change and Change in Family Violence from 1975 to 1985 as Revealed by Two National Surveys." *Journal of Marriage and the Family* 48:465–479.

Straus, M. A.; Gelles, R. J.; and Steinmetz, S. K. (1980). *Behind Closed Doors: Physical Violence in the American Family*. New York: Doubleday/Anchor.

Tang, C. S. (1994). "Prevalence of Spouse Abuse in Hong Kong." *Journal of Family Violence* 9:347–356.

Tjaden, P., and Thoennes, N. (2001). Prevalence and Consequences of Male-to-Female and Female-to-Male Intimate Partner Violence as Measured by the National Violence Against Women Survey. *Violence Against Women* 6:142–161.

Trainor, C., and Mihorean, K., eds. (2001). "Family Violence in Canada: A Statistical Profile 2001." *Statistics Canada,* no. 85–224-XIE. Ottawa, Canada: Minister of Industry.

White, J. W., and Koss, M. P. (1991). "Courtship Violence: Incidence in a National Sample of Higher Education Students." *Violence and Victims* 6:247–256.

Yoshihama, M., and Sorenson, S. B. (1994). "Physical, Sexual, and Emotional Abuse by Male Intimates: Experiences of Women in Japan." *Violence and Victims* 9:63–77.

Other Resource

World Health Organization. (2002). *Prevalence of Physical Violence Against Women.* Available at www5.who.int/violence_injury_prevention/.

ORSOLYA MAGYAR

THEORETICAL EXPLANATIONS

Six theoretical models have been developed to explain spouse abuse and neglect: social learning theory, social situational/stress and coping theory, general systems theory, resource theory, exchange/social control theory, and patriarchy.

Social learning theory proposes that individuals who experienced violence are more likely to use violence in the home than those who have experienced little or no violence. Children who either experience violence themselves or who witness violence between their parents are more likely to use violence when they grow up. This finding has been interpreted to support the idea that family violence is learned. The family is the institution and social group where people learn the roles of husband and wife, parent and child. The home is the primary place in which people learn how to deal with various stresses, crises, and frustrations. In many instances, the home is also where a person first experiences violence. Not only do people learn violent behavior, but they learn how to justify being violent. For example, hearing a father say, "This will hurt me more than it will hurt you," or a mother say, "You have been bad, so you deserve to be spanked," contributes to how children learn to justify violent behavior.

Social situation/stress and coping theory explains why violence is used in some situations and not others. The theory proposes that abuse and violence occur because of two main factors. The first is structural stress and the lack of coping resources in a family. For instance, the association between low income and family violence indicates that an important factor in violence is inadequate financial resources. The second factor is the cultural norm concerning the use of force and violence. In contemporary American society, as well as many other societies, violence is normative (Straus, Gelles, and Steinmetz 1980). Thus, individuals learn to use violence both expressively and instrumentally as a way to cope with a pileup of stressor events.

General systems theory, a social system approach, was developed and applied by Murray Straus (1973) and Jean Giles-Sims (1983) to explain family violence. Here, violence is viewed as a system product rather than the result of individual pathology. The family system operations can maintain, escalate, or reduce levels of violence in families. General systems theory describes the processes that characterize the use of violence in family interactions and explains the way in which violence is managed and stabilized. Straus (1973) argues that a general systems theory of family violence must include at least three basic elements: (1) alternative courses of action or causal flow, (2) the feedback mechanisms that enable the system to make adjustments, and (3) system goals.

The resource theory of family violence assumes that all social systems (including the family) rest to some degree on force or the threat of force. The more resources—social, personal, and economic—a person can command, the more force that individual can muster. However, according to William Goode (1971), the more resources a person actually has, the less that person will actually use force in an open manner. Thus, a husband who wants to be the dominant person in the family, but has little education, has a job low in prestige and income, and lacks interpersonal skills may choose to use violence to maintain the dominant position.

Exchange/social control theory was developed by Richard J. Gelles (1983) on the basic propositions of an exchange theory of aggression. The exchange/social control model of family violence proposes that wife abuse is governed by the principle of costs and rewards. Drawing from exchange theory, Gelles (1983) notes that violence and abuse are used when the rewards are higher than the costs. Drawing from social control theories of delinquency, he proposes that the private nature of the family, the reluctance of social institutions and agencies to intervene, and the low risk of other interventions reduce the costs of abuse and violence. The cultural approval of violence as both expressive and instrumental behavior raises the potential rewards for violence.

The patriarchy theory's central thesis is that economic and social processes operate directly and indirectly to support a patriarchal (male-dominated) social order and family structure. The central theoretical argument is that patriarchy leads to the subordination and oppression of women and causes the historical pattern of systematic violence directed against wives (Dobash and Dobash 1979; Pagelow 1984; Yllo 1983, 1993). The patriarchy theory finds the source of family violence in society at large and how it is organized, as opposed to within individual families or communities.

See also: CONFLICT: COUPLE RELATIONSHIPS; CONFLICT: FAMILY RELATIONSHIPS; FAMILY SYSTEMS THEORY; INTERPARENTAL VIOLENCE—EFFECTS ON CHILDREN; MARITAL QUALITY; POSTTRAUMATIC STRESS DISORDER (PTSD); POWER: FAMILY RELATIONSHIPS; POWER: MARITAL RELATIONSHIPS; RAPE; RESOURCE MANAGEMENT; SOCIAL EXCHANGE THEORY; STRESS; THERAPY: COUPLE RELATIONSHIPS

Bibliography

Dobash, R. E., and Dobash, R. (1979). *Violence Against Wives.* New York: Free Press.

Gelles, R. J. (1983). "An Exchange/Social Control Theory." In *The Dark Side of Families: Current Family Violence Research,* ed. D. Finkelhor, R. Gelles, M. Straus, and G. Hotaling. Newbury Park, CA: Sage.

Giles-Sims, J. (1983). *Wife-Beating: A Systems Theory Approach.* New York: Guilford.

Goode, W. (1971). "Force and Violence in the Family." *Journal of Marriage and the Family* 33:624–636.

Pagelow, M. (1984). *Family Violence.* New York: Praeger.

Straus, M. A. (1973). "A General Systems Theory Approach to a Theory of Violence Between Family Members." *Social Science Information* 12:105–125.

Straus, M. A.; Gelles, R. J.; and Steinmetz, S. K. (1980). *Behind Closed Doors: Violence in the American Family.* New York: Doubleday/Anchor.

Yllo, K. (1983). "Using a Feminist Approach in Quantitative Research." In *The Dark Side of Families: Current Family Violence Research,* ed. D. Finkelhor, R. Gelles, M. Straus, and G. Hotaling. Newbury Park, CA: Sage.

Yllo, K. (1993). "Through a Feminist Lens: Gender, Power, and Violence." In *Current Controversies on Family Violence,* ed. R. Gelles and D. Loseke. Newbury Park, CA: Sage.

RICHARD J. GELLES (1995)

STEPFAMILIES

Stepfamilies consist of at least one minor child who is living with a biological parent and that parent's spouse—a stepparent—who is not the child's other biological parent. According to Larry Bumpass, James Sweet, and Teresa Castro Martin (1990), approximately one-half of all marriages are a remarriage for at least one partner. In 1992, 15 percent of all children in the United States lived with a mother and a stepfather (U.S. Bureau of the Census 1995). An estimated one-third of U.S. children will live in a stepfamily household before they reach adulthood. Although the remarriage rates are lower, similar prevalence rates have been reported in Canada and Europe. The large number of parents and children who live in stepfamilies has prompted researchers to study how well family members adjust to living in a stepfamily.

Parenting Roles

A parenting role can be defined as a set of beliefs pertaining to how parents should behave. The beliefs included in a parenting role are reflected in how a parent behaves toward the children. Two types of parenting behaviors that are a part of the parenting role—control and warmth—have been identified as being particularly important for child development. *Control* refers to the degree to which parents set and enforce limits and monitor their children's activities. *Warmth* refers to the extent to which parents communicate with, show caring toward, and support their children. Empirical evidence has consistently shown that the more parents exhibit both control and warmth (referred to as an *authoritative* parenting style), the more positive is children's adjustment (Steinberg, El-men, and Mounts 1989). However, there is an important caveat to consider. Some evidence suggests that authoritative parenting may not be the ideal approach among certain ethnic groups, such as African- and Asian-Americans. For some children in these groups, an *authoritarian* parenting style (consisting of lower levels of warmth and high levels of control) may be most conducive to positive growth and development.

The Stepparent Role

Research has suggested that the stepparent role, according to the beliefs, reported behaviors, and observed behaviors of stepparents, is a less active one than is the role of the biological parent. Mark Fine and Lawrence Kurdek (1994) found that stepparents believe they are less active—and should be less active—as parents than are biological parents. These differences were present in both the warmth and control aspects of the parenting role, although they were strongest in the warmth dimension. However, there also appear to be differences among members of stepfamilies in how actively they believe the stepparent should parent. According to a study by Mark Fine, Marilyn Coleman, and Lawrence Ganong (1998), stepchildren reported that stepparents should be less active as parents than was reported by stepparents and parents in their stepfamilies. In addition, stepchildren were more likely than parents and stepparents to report that the stepparent should play the role of "friend" rather than "parent" or "stepparent." Based on these results and others, Fine, Coleman, and Ganong concluded that "stepparents generally believe that they should play a more active role in parenting than do their stepchildren and, on some dimensions, than their spouses" (1999, p. 290). Because most parents and stepparents report believing that stepparents should function as parents, these authors suggested that the adults in stepfamilies often attempt to recreate their families in the image of a first-marriage, intact family.

When stepparents are asked how they actually behave, not just what their beliefs are, they also report being less active as parents than do biological parents. In a sample of stepfamilies included in the National Survey of Families and Households (Fine, Voydanoff, and Donnelly 1993), stepfathers reported behaving less positively and less negatively toward their stepchildren than did fathers, indicating that they refrain from becoming involved with their stepchildren. However, stepmothers reported responding as positively to their stepchildren as did biological mothers in stepfamilies, although they responded less negatively. This suggests that stepfathers may be less active in demonstrating warmth to children than are fathers, but that stepmothers show as much warmth to children as biological mothers. Moreover, these findings suggest that stepmothers may be more active in parenting than stepfathers, which may partially explain the commonly noted observation that stepmothers have greater adjustment difficulties than stepfathers (Coleman, Ganong, and Fine 2000; McBride 2001).

Finally, in some studies, observers have rated the actual parenting behaviors of stepparents and biological parents. Most of these studies have assessed stepfathers and not stepmothers. As is consistent with the previously discussed studies, these investigations indicate that stepfathers are less active as parents than are biological fathers. In these studies, stepfathers, compared with biological fathers, were less involved with, showed less awareness of, and exerted less discipline over their stepchildren (Hetherington and Clingempeel 1992). When stepfathers in newly formed stepfamilies tried to establish a positive relationship with the stepchild by talking and sharing activities, these efforts were often met with resistance, particularly when the stepchild was an adolescent. Despite this resistance, many stepfathers continued to try to remain involved in the lives of their stepchildren. Over time, however, because of continued resistance or distancing behaviors on the part of the stepchild, most of these stepfathers stopped trying to establish close stepfather-stepchild relationships. There is some evidence, however, that it pays off for stepfathers to be persistent. According to Ganong and his colleagues

(1999), those stepfathers who made consistent and repeated attempts to elicit liking from their stepchildren were rewarded with more enriching and satisfying stepparent-stepchild relationships.

Clarity of the Stepparent Role

There is considerable evidence that the parenting role of the stepparent is ambiguous or unclear (Coleman, Ganong, and Fine 2000). The lack of clarity of the stepparent role is reflected in the notion that there are several plausible ways that the role of the stepparent can be filled. The following are some, but not all, of these possible ways to fill the stepparent role: to act "just like" a parent to the stepchild; to act like a supportive friend to the stepchild; to support the disciplinary policies of the biological parent without independently establishing and enforcing rules of one's own; and to not become involved in the stepchild's life. In the absence of clear social norms, stepparents may not know which of these ways, or others, is the most desirable way for them to fill the stepparent role. In fact, although stepparents understandably experience the most ambiguity about the role of the stepparent (Fine, Coleman, and Ganong 1998), biological parents and stepchildren also may not be sure how they think the stepparent should act. Further, as noted earlier, there often are also disagreements within stepfamilies about the appropriate stepparent role, as parents and stepparents believe that the stepparent should serve as a parenting figure, whereas stepchildren are more likely to believe that the stepparent should try to be a "friend" to them (Fine, Coleman, and Ganong 1998).

Adjustment in Stepfamilies

There has been a great deal of scholarly attention devoted to the issue of how well family members adjust to living in a stepfamily. Most of this research has focused on stepchildren. Children living in stepfamilies, on average, do more poorly than children living in first-marriage families (and similarly to children in single-parent families) in the areas of academic achievement (e.g., grades), psychological well-being (e.g., depression), and behavior problems (Coleman, Ganong, and Fine 2000). However, as Coleman and her colleagues suggest, the differences in adjustment between children in stepfamilies and those in first-marriage families are relatively small and it is possible that the differences are due to a variety of factors in addition to or instead of living in a stepfamily. For example, stepchildren tend to leave home earlier than do children from first marriage families, which may explain their higher school drop-out rate. Further, despite group differences between stepchildren and children living in first-marriage families, most stepchildren do well in school, are psychologically well-adjusted, and have few behavior problems.

How well do stepchildren fare as adults? Recent research has yielded somewhat mixed findings, but most studies, including a major one conducted in the United Kingdom (Rodgers 1994), have found that having parents who remarried is not related to adjustment and the development of emotional problems in adulthood (Coleman, Ganong, and Fine 2000).

Remarriage does not appear to have clear and straightforward effects on the adjustment of adults. There is some evidence that remarried adults have higher levels of depression than adults in first marriages, but other studies have reported that remarried individuals are *less* distressed than those who are divorced and that remarriage is not related to psychological well-being, including a study in the United Kingdom (Richards, Hardy, and Wadsworth 1997). These mixed results suggest that a variety of factors appear to have more influence on adults' well-being and psychological adjustment than does remarriage per se.

There has been very little research into how well members of ethnic and racial minority families adjust to living in a stepfamily; the limited evidence suggests that African-American members of stepfather families may be slightly, but significantly, more depressed than their white counterparts, perhaps because stepfamilies are relatively less common in the African-American community and because extensive kin networks may complicate the successful integration of a new adult into African-American families (Fine, McKenry, Donnelly, and Voydanoff 1992).

Stepparent Role and Adjustment

There is evidence that the stepparent role and the extent to which the role is clear are related to the adjustment of members of stepfamilies. In terms of the nature of the stepparent role, children's adjustment is facilitated when stepparents, at least initially, do not take an active role in discipline. James H. Bray (1999) found that stepparent-stepchild relations and child adjustment were most positive when stepfathers did not actively discipline their stepchildren, but rather supported the disciplinary practices of the child's biological parent. However, over time, stepparents may assume a more active and a more effective parenting role. In Bray's study, after two and one-half years in the stepfamily, stepparents were able to play key parental roles and authoritative parenting behaviors were related to positive child adjustment.

With respect to clarity regarding the stepparent role, there is evidence that greater stepparent role clarity is associated with some dimensions of adjustment. For example, Kurdek and Fine (1991) found that high levels of stepparent role clarity were related to mothers' reports of family/marital/personal life satisfaction and stepfathers' reports of parenting satisfaction. This may indicate that parenting is a more vulnerable and less comfortable area than personal life satisfaction for stepfathers, and the reverse may be true for mothers. Similarly, Fine, Kurdek, and Lorraine Hennigen (1992) found that adolescents who were not clear about their stepmother's role tended to see themselves as low in self-competence. Finally, Fine, Coleman, and Ganong (1998) extended these earlier findings by showing that, when the parent and stepparent were more confident in their views about how the stepparent should behave, their marital, (step)parent-(step)child, and family relationships were more satisfying. How confident stepchildren were about how the stepparent should behave was not related to how satisfied they were with their family relationships or to their individual adjustment.

Interactions Within Stepfamilies

Because the differences in adjustment between members of stepfamilies and members of other types of families are generally small in magnitude, researchers have turned their attention to factors that are associated with positive adjustment in stepfamilies. Several researchers have found that interaction patterns in stepfamilies are similar to those in first-marriage families. In particular, many long-term stepfamilies function quite similarly to first-marriage families (Coleman, Ganong, and Fine 2000). In contrast, several studies have found that members of stepfamilies report that their families are more stressful, less cohesive and adaptable, and have less positive relations between stepparents and stepchildren. These contrasting findings may be explained by the length of time that the stepfamily has been in existence. Newly formed stepfamilies may have more problematic interaction patterns than do first-marriage families; however, if the stepfamily remains intact for several years, interaction patterns may become similar to those in first-marriage families.

In what ways are interactions within stepfamilies related to the adjustment of stepfamily members? Most studies have found that the same types of family interaction patterns that are conducive to positive adjustment in first-marriage families also facilitate well-being in stepfamilies. For example, Fine and Kurdek (1992) found that the adjustment of young adolescents in stepfamilies was more positive to the extent that they characterized their families (and not just their parents) as providing high levels of supervision, warmth, and order, and low levels of conflict. However, there is also some indication that, particularly in recently formed stepfamilies, family members' adjustment is facilitated by somewhat less cohesiveness than is the case in first-marriage families (Waldren et al. 1990), indicating that the lower levels of cohesiveness in stepfamilies relative to first-marriage families may be adaptive.

Stepfamilies and the Law

Although there has been very little study of this issue, it is possible that interaction patterns in stepfamilies are affected by the legal circumstances facing them. Unfortunately, stepparents and stepchildren have an ambiguous legal relationship to one another, because existing laws do not dictate what a stepparent's responsibilities and rights are with respect to his or her stepchild. The only way that a stepparent can be guaranteed to have the rights and responsibilities associated with being a parent is to adopt the stepchild, but this usually requires that the child's biological parent relinquish parental rights. Thus, U.S. law assumes that a child should only have concurrent legal relationships with two adults. By contrast, in the United Kingdom, according to the Children Act 1989, a stepparent (and selected other third parties) has the option of applying for a "residence order," which gives him or her almost the same rights as a parent. Thus, within this system, a stepchild can have legal relationships with three adults (or even more) at one time. Very little research has examined the impact of this British law, but it seems plausible that stepchildren and stepparents, particularly those who have a close relationship, might have an advantage with a secure and clear legal tie to one another.

Conclusion

Stepfamilies have become an increasingly common feature of the family landscape. Stepparents seem to be less involved with their stepchildren than biological parents are with their children, and the role of the stepparent seems to be less clear than the role of the biological parent. In addition, there is evidence that stepchildren fare somewhat more poorly on most adjustment dimensions than do their counterparts from first-marriage families, although the small magnitude of the differences suggests that a host of other factors play a more prominent role in determining children's well-being than the type of family the child lives in. Furthermore, there is growing evidence that the adjustment of stepfamily members is related to beliefs about the stepparent role and the extent to which the stepparent role is clear. However, to be most helpful to stepfamily members, a great deal of additional research is needed on the roles that stepparents play, how these roles affect the well-being of stepfamily members, and how a variety of family-related factors (such as family interaction patterns and not just the type of family the child lives in) are related to the adjustment of stepfamily members.

See also: CHILD CUSTODY; COMMUNICATION: FAMILY RELATIONSHIPS; CONFLICT: COUPLE RELATIONSHIPS; CONFLICT: FAMILY RELATIONSHIPS; CONFLICT: PARENT-CHILD RELATIONSHIPS; DISCIPLINE; DIVORCE: EFFECTS ON CHILDREN; PARENTING STYLES; REMARRIAGE

Bibliography

Bray, J. H. (1999). "From Marriage to Remarriage and Beyond: Findings from the Developmental Issues in Stepfamilies Research Project." In *Coping with Divorce, Single Parenting, and Remarriage: A Risk and Resiliency Perspective,* ed. E. M. Hetherington. Mahwah, NJ: Erlbaum.

Bumpass, L. L.; Sweet, J. A.; and Cherlin, A. (1991). "The Role of Cohabitation in Declining Rates of Marriage." *Journal of Marriage and the Family* 52:747–756.

Coleman, M.; Ganong, L.; and Fine, M. (2000). "Reinvestigating Remarriage: Another Decade of Progress." *Journal of Marriage and the Family* 62:1288–1307.

Fine, M. A.; Coleman, M.; and Ganong, L. H. (1998). "Consistency in Perceptions of the Step-Parent Role among Stepparents, Parents, and Stepchildren." *Journal of Social and Personal Relationships* 15:811–829.

Fine, M. A.; Ganong, L. H.; and Coleman, M. (1999). "A Social Constructionist Multi-Method Approach to Understanding the Stepparent Role." In *Coping With Divorce, Single-Parenthood and Remarriage: A Risk and Resiliency Perspective,* ed. E. M. Hetherington. Mahwah, NJ: Erlbaum.

Fine, M. A., and Kurdek, L. A. (1992). "The Adjustment of Adolescents in Stepfather and Stepmother Families." *Journal of Marriage and the Family* 54:725–736.

Fine, M. A., and Kurdek, L. A. (1994). "Parenting Cognitions in Stepfamilies: Differences Between Parents and Stepparents and Relations to Parenting Satisfaction." *Journal of Social and Personal Relationships* 11:95–112.

Fine, M. A.; Kurdek, L. A.; and Hennigen, L. (1992). "Perceived Self-Competence and Its Relations to Stepfamily Myths and (Step)Parent Role Ambiguity in Adolescents from Stepfather and Stepmother Families." *Journal of Family Psychology* 6:69–76.

Fine, M. A.; McKenry, P. C.; Donnelly, B. W.; and Voydanoff, P. (1992). "Perceived Adjustment of Parents and Children: Variations by Family Structure, Race, and Gender." *Journal of Marriage and the Family* 54:118–127.

Fine, M. A.; Voydanoff, P.; and Donnelly, B. W. (1993). "Relations between Parental Control and Warmth and Child Well-Being in Stepfamilies." *Journal of Family Psychology* 7:222–232.

Ganong, L. H.; Coleman, M.; Fine, M. A.; and Martin, P. (1999). "Stepparents' Affinity-Seeking and Affinity-Maintaining Strategies in Stepfamilies." *Journal of Family Issues* 20:299–327.

Hetherington, E. M., and Clingempeel, W. G. (1992). "Coping with Marital Transitions: A Family Systems Perspective." *Monographs of the Society for Research in Child Development* 57(2–3):Serial no. 227.

Kurdek, L. A., and Fine, M. A. (1991). "Cognitive Correlates of Adjustment for Mothers and Stepfathers in

Stepfather Families." *Journal of Marriage and the Family* 53:565–572.

McBride, J. (2001). *Encouraging Words for New Stepmothers*. Ft. Collins, CO: CDR Press.

Richards, M.; Hardy, R.; and Wadsworth, M. (1997). "The Effects of Divorce and Separation on Mental Health in a National UK Birth Cohort." *Psychological Medicine* 27:1121–1128.

Rodgers, B. (1994). "Pathways between Parental Divorce and Adult Depression." *Journal of Child Psychology and Psychiatry* 35:1289–1294.

Steinberg, L.; El-men, J. D.; and Mounts, N. S. (1989). "Authoritative Parenting, Psychological Maturity, and Academic Success among Adolescents." *Child Development* 60:1424–1436.

U. S. Bureau of the Census (1995). *Statistical Abstract of the United States: 1995*. 115th edition. Washington, DC: U. S. Government Printing Office.

Waldren, T.; Bell, N.; Peek, C.; and Sorell, G. (1990). "Cohesion and Adaptability in Post-Divorce Remarried and First-Married Families: Relationships with Family Stress and Coping Styles." *Journal of Divorce and Remarriage* 14:13–28.

MARK A. FINE
JEAN A. MCBRIDE

STRESS

Stress research includes attention to events or conditions that may cause harm and to the responses aroused by those stressful events or conditions. These outcomes include felt distress, disrupted interaction, and poorer health. The overall *stress process* includes both stressful agents and stress outcomes (see Pearlin et al. 1981). This process also includes two other major sets of variables: social factors that influence *exposure* to stressful conditions, and individual and group *resources* that shape efforts to cope with stressors.

Although early stress research focused on unpleasant *physical stressors* (Selye 1982), social scientists studying families have been particularly interested in *social stressors*—events or conditions that are linked to individuals' and families' social characteristics, positions, and roles.

The concept of social stress calls attention to both environmental/social demands and individual/family capacities or resources; stress occurs when there is a discrepancy between these capacities and demands. Such stressors can come from external demands on families and family members, or they can arise within family roles themselves. Theoretically, a discrepancy can be in either direction: demands could be greater than a person's capacities, or demands could be far below individual capacities. Thus, restricted opportunities can be at least as stressful as high demands: Carol Aneshensel (1999; see also Wheaton 1999) calls attention to stressors that occur when aspects of the social environment obstruct an individual's ability to attain sought-after ends.

One early and influential approach to studying social stressors focused on change per se as stressful. Thomas A. Holmes and Richard H. Rahe (1967) developed a checklist of stressful life events aimed at capturing the set of events that had happened to an individual. These checklist approaches to the measurement of social stress were based on two key assumptions. First, they assumed that one could calculate a standard estimate of the amount of change demanded by a specific event, such as divorce or the birth of a child, and that this amount would be generally the same for all who experienced that event. Second, they assumed that one could capture the effects of the accumulation of several events in a short period of time by summing the amount of change implied by each, and that this total amount of change was the critical dimension linked to stress outcomes.

Subsequent research, however, has cast doubt on each of these assumptions. Change per se does not seem to be the key dimension producing negative outcomes: changes that are undesired, involuntary, unexpected, and involve role losses generally have more negative effects than other changes. Nor is it the case that the same event has uniform effects on different people. Consistent with the concept of stress as a discrepancy between demands and capacities, much depends on the resources and coping repertoires that individuals and families possess.

In addition, the impact of transitions and eventful changes depends in part on the circumstances prevailing prior to a specific life event. A notable example is marital termination: although the end of a marriage is generally viewed as a stressful event, termination of a conflict-filled or unsatisfying relationship may actually improve well-being. And because spouses may differ in how satisfied they are, this example also suggests that the same family event will not necessarily affect all members of a family in the same way. In an influential analysis, Blair Wheaton (1990) has shown that in the case of role exits, including retirement, widowhood, divorce, and a child's move away from home, the more stressful prior conditions in that role, the less the impact on mental health. Similarly, Susan Jekielek (1998) finds that children's response to parental divorce is less adverse when there has been more marital conflict.

Effects of specific life events also depend in part on the subsequent level of chronic problems. It is largely because major life events typically result in an enduring alteration in social circumstances, thereby increasing chronic problems, that they affect individual and family outcomes.

Chronic problems in any given role can also lead to other stressors, in a process that Leonard Pearlin and his colleagues describe as *stress proliferation*—the tendency of stressors to beget other stressors (Pearlin, Aneshensel, and LeBlanc 1997). They illustrate this process in a study of informal caregivers to people with acquired immunodeficiency syndrome (AIDS). As the illness progresses, the difficulties faced in the role of caregiver expand, straining one's capacities to manage those demands. Moreover, these strains affect the caregiver's ability to enjoy the opportunities, and manage the stressors, embedded in other roles such as work roles and social and leisure activities. Once these are affected, the altered conditions in these other roles can have an additional, independent effect on the caregiver's health and well-being.

Thus, the concept of social stressors reaches beyond the notion of discrete life events to include chronic or persisting circumstances, such as low income, unpleasant working conditions, role strains, and conflicts among multiple social roles, as well as the resources that individuals and families are able to bring to bear in their efforts to deal with their circumstances. Because both those circumstances and resources are likely to be linked to social position—as indicated by one's race, gender, marital status, and economic position—this broad definition of social stress brings stress research closer to traditional sociological topics such as social stratification and race and gender discrimination. It offers a more comprehensive way of thinking about the way that social circumstances, including normatively structured family and occupational social roles, shape individual opportunities, individual distress, and family well-being.

Research analyzing the connection between social contexts and stress outcomes for individuals and families has examined several key links. First, research has examined how stressors originating outside the family can affect individual family members' emotional well-being (see, for example, Windell and Dumenci 1999). Second, researchers have investigated how each individual's emotional well-being in turn affects family interaction; these studies find that individuals who are struggling with emotional turmoil or depression are less available for satisfying interaction and more prone to become aggressive and argumentative (Elder 1974). Third, studies also examine how and whether one family member's emotional state can be transmitted to other family members (Larson and Almeida 1999); initial results from these studies suggest that fathers' negative emotions aroused in the workplace "spill over" and affect both spouses and children, but mothers' work-linked emotions are less apt to adversely affect other family members. In turn, of course, negative emotions aroused by difficult family conditions can spill over and affect workplace interaction and performance.

Exposure and Responses to Stressors

As family stress researchers study the resourceful ways in which individuals and families resist stressors, they have also called attention to the ways that social and economic factors shape both their exposure to stressors and their abilities to respond.

In considering the relationship between stressful circumstances on the one hand and family members' individual well-being and overall family functioning on the other, research has tended to focus on two main questions: How can variations in *exposure* to social stressors explain variations in individual and family outcomes? How, in a group of individuals or families who have been exposed to the same stressor, can variations in individual and family capacities, resources, and coping efforts explain variations in outcomes?

Exposure to social stressors. An example of the former is the investigation conducted by Pearlin and his colleagues (1981) into the effect of occupational disruptions on emotional distress. They compared those who had faced recent disruptions with respondents who had not, with statistical controls for other variables known to affect both the likelihood of disruption and the levels of emotional distress, and traced the effects of disruption through diminished self-esteem and compromised sense of mastery to increased distress. Similarly, early family stress research examined exposure to stressors linked to social organization and societal crises, such as widespread male unemployment and extended separations brought on by World War II (see Hill 1949).

These early studies focused on men's unemployment as a social stressor for themselves and their families. As women's employment increased, studies began to examine whether women's holding multiple social roles—both family roles as spouse and mother and work roles as employee—operated as a social stressor, with adverse consequences for themselves and other family members, particularly children. This research has generally been inconclusive: simple cross-sectional contrasts between employed and not-employed mothers have found, if anything, an average benefit of employment for women and little significant differences in their children's outcomes. Ingrid Waldron and her colleagues (1998) provide an example of this line of research, as well as an overview of theoretical arguments regarding how combinations of marriage, mothering, and employment may affect women's health. They find little evidence that combining employment and mothering has adverse effects on physical health. They suggest that marriage and employment each provide similar resources to women, namely income and social supports, and that they can substitute for one another in having a beneficial impact on health. Conversely, these findings suggest that the absence of *both* marriage and employment will be associated with more negative outcomes.

In extensions of this line of research, researchers have argued that the effects of having a particular role or role combination are not uniform, but depend on the role conditions one encounters. For example, research in this tradition focused on employment emphasizes that for men as well as for women, employment in occupations that are free from close supervision and provide opportunities for substantively complex and self-directed work will yield benefits, whereas employment in dull, repetitive, and closely supervised work will not (Kohn and Schooler 1983; Menaghan 1991). Similarly, all marriages are not equal in their costs and benefits, with high-conflict, hostile, or distant relationships more distressing than their counterparts. In support of these arguments, Elizabeth Menaghan and her colleagues (1997) show that the quality of mothers' employment, as well as the quality of their marital relationships, affect mother-child interaction and adolescent children's academic and behavior outcomes.

Social stressors like low income, unemployment, divorce, single parenthood, and family conflict can beget additional stressors, such as applying for welfare, as this woman is doing. STEPHEN FERRY/GAMMA LIAISON NETWORK

Variations in response to stressors as a function of resources. An example of the latter question is Glen Elder's (1974) study of families who faced serious economic decline during the Great Depression. Elder investigated whether couples with more cohesive marital bonds at a prior point were better able to respond to the economic difficulties they faced. Here, the cohesion of marital bonds is conceptualized as a family-level resource that accounted for a difference in outcomes among couples all facing the same economic stressor. In general, family stress researchers have conceptualized stressful outcomes as a function of three major factors: the stressor, family resources, and appraisal or interpretation (Hill 1949). Extending this model, Yoav Lavee and his colleagues emphasized potential changes over time in each of these factors (see

Lavee, McCubbin, and Patterson 1985). Work by Pauline Boss (1999) calls attention to the critical role of appraisal in influencing family members' responses to ambiguous or incomplete losses, including family members who are missing, suffering from dementia, or geographically or emotionally distant.

These same factors are also central to studies of stress at the individual level. Pearlin and his colleagues (1981) stress how material, social, and psychosocial resources, including optimistic appraisals, help to account for variations in the individual distress aroused by stressful circumstances in normative adult roles such as marriage, employment, and parenting. In both literatures, economic resources, social supports from others, coping strategies, and individual levels of self-esteem and mastery are viewed as central resources that can reduce the negative impact of social stressors (Mirowsky and Ross 1986; Turner 1999).

One of the pathways by which social stressors may create adverse impacts is by reducing resources themselves. For example, a period of involuntary unemployment may have a less disastrous impact on families with greater savings. If the period of unemployment is prolonged, however, or if unemployment recurs, families may literally "spend down" their resources. This is probably easiest to measure in terms of tangible resources like savings, but the general argument holds as well for more subtle resources like a sense of mastery over one's circumstances. At any single time point, having more optimistic and internal attitudes may help one to manage potential stressors. But over time, exposure to stressors may cumulatively reduce those feelings of control. Thus, current levels of resources may partially reflect the cumulative history of encounters with social stressors.

Who is exposed to social stressors? To fully understand the processes by which stressors affect families, we also need to consider how social stressors are distributed in populations. Exposure to difficult life events or constraining social circumstances is not a random process, and it is important to view variations in exposure to stressors as a phenomenon that itself needs to be explained. For example, Jay Turner and colleagues (1995) study what they call the *epidemiology of social stress*. They find that the distribution of exposure to social stressors varies significantly by age, gender, marital status, and occupational status, and this distribution parallels the distribution of depressive symptoms and major depressive disorder across the same factors. Catherine Ross and Marieke Van Willigen (1997) also point to educational attainment as a crucial resource that shapes subsequent exposure to more or less stressful circumstances.

Turner and Lloyd (1999) extend this analysis, and find that exposure to social stressors, as well as levels of personal resources and social supports, can explain, on the one hand, observed links between age, gender, marital status, and socioeconomic status, and mental health outcomes on the other. In particular, the linkage between lower socioeconomic status and higher depressive symptoms is completely accounted for by the greater exposure to stressors and fewer resources and social supports of those with lower educations, occupations, and incomes.

Effects of Economic Stressors on Marital Behaviors

Social stress research has repeatedly identified low income and income loss as a major social stressor (see for example, Elder 1974; McLloyd 1990). Given the importance of family income, and its links to both employment and family composition, researchers in the United States have sought to understand how economic circumstances and family formation and stability are linked. As Scott South and Kim Lloyd (1992) have documented, higher rates of male nonemployment have been shown to be associated with reduced marriage rates and higher rates of births to unmarried women for both African-American and white population groups. Women's economic resources also matter: Diane McLaughlin and Daniel Lichter (1999) comment that marriage can provide a route out of poverty for some, but find that poor women, especially those who do not hold jobs, are less likely to marry than are more advantaged women.

Marriages stressed by economic uncertainties have also been more likely to be disrupted. When financial pressures are high, husbands and wives treat each other more negatively, quarrel more, and feel increasingly distant; thoughts of divorce become more common. And as wives' greater employment and earnings prompt them to question disproportionate female responsibility for housework and childcare, conflict between partners is apt to increase. Donald Hernandez (1993) has found that married-couple families below the poverty level are more likely to disrupt their marriages than are couples who have greater economic resources. Among married couples, husbands' nonemployment increases the likelihood of marital disruption (South and Spitze 1986). This occurs in part because men react to employment loss and associated economic hardship with anger, irritability, and withdrawal from interaction (Conger et al. 1990).

Lower likelihood of marital formation and higher rates of marital disruption clearly affect children's life chances as well. In the absence of marriage or after its end, U.S. fathers have been relatively unlikely to share income or time with their biological children, and single-mother families are most vulnerable to economic problems.

Societal Differences, Demographic Factors, and Family Stressors

Much social stress research has focused on differences in exposure and response to social stressors within a single nation, typically the United States. We can gain additional insights if we broaden our perspective to consider differences between nations around the globe. One example is the link between single mothering and low income just noted. In the United States, children living with never-married and formerly married parents, particularly mothers, are disproportionately likely to have low incomes. But in a comparative perspective, it becomes clear that this is not an inevitable consequence of single-mothering: the proportion in poverty varies dramatically across the developed countries, with U.S. rates much higher than in such countries as France or the Netherlands (see Lichter 1997). Lynne Casper and colleagues' (1994) examination of poverty among men and women across Western industrialized countries suggests that much of the explanation lies in differing national policies regarding income transfers and income floors for all citizens, as well as differing supports for employment. Thus, how employment affects families, and how family composition affects family income, varies across nations.

An international perspective also suggests other demographic factors that figure importantly into the kinds of social stressors that families encounter. For example, both within the United States and across the globe, race and ethnic groups vary in their social advantage/disadvantage, exposure to social stressors, and access to resources. These studies suggest that when economic problems become pervasive in a community, overall community levels of family violence and child abuse rise. To the extent that discriminatory labor-market practices compromise minority members' access to income, job security, and occupational quality, racially segregated communities will lack the resources families need to resist stress, and the families living with them may be exposed to greater social stressors as well (see, for example, McLloyd 1990).

As nations and regions become increasingly interconnected, migration across communities, states, and national borders presents an increasingly common social stressor for individuals and families. Min Zhou (1997) summarizes the family and intergenerational stressors that immigrants to the United States face, as family ties are stretched across national borders, and suggests that the success of various family adaptations strategies varies depending on the socioeconomic and ethnic composition of the communities into which they move. Samuel Noh and William Avison (1996) study the experiences of Korean immigrants to Canada, and link increases in depression over time to more undesirable life events, more chronic stressors, and less mastery and sense of support.

Migration may be permanent or temporary, and may involve whole families or individual members. The consequences of migration are likely to vary depending on the circumstances one is leaving behind, the extent of family resources that can be retained, and the conditions faced in one's new environment. Much migration is intentional, as individuals and families seek to improve their circumstances. But war, ethnic violence, crop failures and economic conditions also combine to create huge flows of political and economic refugees; these streams are apt to have fewer resources and greater difficulties.

Changing mortality patterns across populations and across the world also suggest new sources of social stress for families, particularly in the direction and duration of caregiving across generations. In the developed world, increasing life spans may present increased demands for caregiving by adult family members to their elders. In sharp contrast, in many areas of Africa and Asia, increases in sexually transmitted diseases, particularly AIDS-related diseases, have resulted in declining average life expectancies and the deaths of parents in early adulthood. These new mortality patterns create a generation of orphans and present increased demands for caregiving by elder family members and others.

Finally, studies of stress in families, and gender differences in average levels of well-being, call attention to differences in stress processes within families. Societies differ significantly in the extent to which male dominance and female subordination are accepted as part of the normative order. To the extent that male and female family members have strikingly different rights, freedoms, and responsibilities, it is reasonable to expect that they will be exposed to differing stressors, have differing access to social resources, and be differently affected by stressors. Thus, the study of stress in families, both within and across nations, must encompass both individual and family stressors and individual and family outcomes, without assuming that stressors affect male and female family members, or members of different societies, equally.

Conclusion

The study of social stressors affecting families draws attention to the linkages between social factors such as race, gender, education, occupation, and income, and how they shape both exposure to stressors and the possession of resources with which to deal with them. We have noted that greater levels of resources can keep potential social stressors from exerting adverse effects, but over time resources themselves can be whittled away by chronic or recurring exposure to social stressors. Despite much popular concern about role conflicts, particularly between work and family roles for women, studies suggest that more and less stressful conditions within roles may be more consequential than the simple presence or absence of a particular social role. This review of social stress research draws heavily on research conducted in the United States, but it suggests that the stress paradigm can provide a conceptual lens through which one can begin to explore variations in stressful exposure and outcomes across nations as well.

See also: ACQUIRED IMMUNODEFICIENCY SYNDROME (AIDS); BOUNDARY AMBIGUITY; CAREGIVING: INFORMAL; CHRONIC ILLNESS; CONFLICT: FAMILY RELATIONSHIPS; CONFLICT: MARITAL RELATIONSHIPS; CONFLICT: PARENT-CHILD RELATIONSHIPS; DEATH AND DYING; DEPRESSION: ADULTS; DEPRESSION: CHILDREN AND ADOLESCENTS; DISABILITIES; DIVORCE: EFFECTS ON CHILDREN; DIVORCE: EFFECTS ON COUPLES; DIVORCE: EFFECTS ON PARENTS; ELDER ABUSE; FAMILY DEVELOPMENT THEORY; FAMILY ROLES; FAMILY STRENGTHS; FATHERHOOD; GENDER; HEALTH AND FAMILIES; MARITAL QUALITY; MIGRATION; MOTHERHOOD; POVERTY; POWER: MARITAL RELATIONSHIPS; RESOURCE MANAGEMENT; RETIREMENT; SINGLE-PARENT FAMILIES; SOCIAL NETWORKS; SPOUSE ABUSE; THEORETICAL EXPLANATIONS; TRANSITION TO PARENTHOOD; UNEMPLOYMENT; WAR/POLITICAL VIOLENCE; WIDOWHOOD; WORK AND FAMILY

Bibliography

Aneshensel, C. (1999). "Outcomes of the Stress Process." In *A Handbook for the Study of Mental Health: Social Contexts, Theories, and Systems,* ed. A. V. Horwitz and T. L. Scheid. Cambridge, UK: Cambridge University Press.

Boss, P. (1999). *Ambiguous Loss.* Cambridge, MA: Harvard University Press.

Casper, L. M.; McLanahan, S. S.; and Garfinkel, I. (1994). "The Gender-Poverty Gap: What We Can Learn from Other Countries." *American Sociological Review* 59: 594–605.

Conger, R. D.; Elder, G. H., Jr.; Lorenz, F. O.; Conger, K. J.; Simons, R. L.; Whitbeck, L. B.; Huck, S.; and Melby, J. N. (1990). "Linking Economic Hardship to Marital Quality and Instability." *Journal of Marriage and the Family* 52:643–656.

Elder, G. H., Jr. (1974). *Children of the Great Depression.* Chicago: University of Chicago Press.

Hernandez, D. (1993). *America's Children: Resources from Family, Government, and the Economy.* New York: Russell Sage Foundation Press.

Hill, R. (1949). *Families under Stress.* New York: Harper and Row.

Holmes, T. A., and Rahe, R. H. (1967). "The Social Readjustment Rating Scale." *Journal of Psychosomatic Research* 11:213–218.

Jekielek, S. M. (1998). "Parental Conflict, Marital Disruption, Children's Emotional Well-Being." *Social Forces* 76:905–935.

Kohn, M. L., and Schooler, C. (1983). *Work and Personality.* Norwood, NJ: Ablex.

Larson, R. W., and Almeida, D. M. (1999). "Emotional Transmission in the Daily Lives of Families: A New

Paradigm for Studying Family Process." *Journal of Marriage and the Family* 61:5–20.

Lavee, Y.; McCubbin, H. I.; and Patterson, J. M. (1985). "The Double ABCX of Family Stress and Adaptation: An Empirical Test by Analysis of Structural Equations with Latent Variables." *Journal of Marriage and the Family* 47:811–825.

Lichter, D. T. (1997). "Poverty and Inequality among Children." *Annual Review of Sociology* 23:121–145

McLaughlin, D. K., and Lichter, D. T. (1999). "Poverty and the Marital Behavior of Young Women." *Journal of Marriage and the Family* 59:582–594.

McLloyd, V. C. (1990). "The Impact of Economic Hardship on Black Families and Children: Psychological Distress, Parenting, and Socioemotional Development." *Child Development* 61:311–346.

Menaghan, E. G. (1991). "Work Experiences and Family Interaction Processes: The Long Reach of the Job?" *Annual Review of Sociology* 17:419–444.

Menaghan, E. G.; Kowaleski-Jones, L.; and Mott, F. L. (1997). "The Intergenerational Costs of Parental Social Stressors: Academic and Social Difficulties in Early Adolescence for Children of Young Mothers." *Journal of Health and Social Behavior* 38:72–86.

Mirowsky, J., and Ross, C. E. (1986). "Social Patterns of Distress." *Annual Review of Sociology* 12:23–45.

Noh, S., and Avison, W. R. (1996). "Asian Immigrants and the Stress Process: A Study of Koreans in Canada." *Journal of Health and Social Behavior* 37:192–206.

Pearlin, L. I.; Aneshensel, C. S.; and LeBlanc, A. J. (1997). "The Forms and Mechanisms of Stress Proliferation: The Case of AIDS Caregivers." *Journal of Health and Social Behavior* 38:223–236.

Pearlin, L. I.; Lieberman, M. A.; Menaghan, E. G.; and Mullan, J. T. (1981). "The Stress Process." *Journal of Health and Social Behavior* 22:337–356.

Ross, C. E., and Van Willigen, M. (1997). "Education and the Subjective Quality of Life." *Journal of Health and Social Behavior* 38:275–297.

Selye, H. (1982). "History and Present Status of the Stress Concept." In *Handbook of Stress,* ed. L. Goldberger and S. Breznitz. New York: Free Press.

South, S. J., and Lloyd, K. M. (1992). "Marriage Opportunities and Family Formation: Further Implications of Imbalanced Sex Ratios." *Journal of Marriage and the Family* 54:440–451.

South, S. J., and Spitze, G. (1986). "Determinants of Divorce over the Marital Life Course." *American Sociological Review* 51:583–590.

Turner, R. J. (1999). "Social Support and Coping." In *A Handbook for the Study of Mental Health: Social Contexts, Theories, and Systems,* ed. A. V. Horwitz and T. L. Scheid. Cambridge, UK: Cambridge University Press.

Turner, R. J., and Lloyd, D. A. (1999). "The Stress Process and the Social Distribution of Depression." *Journal of Health and Social Behavior* 40:374–404.

Turner, R. J.; Wheaton, B.; and Lloyd, D. A. (1995) "The Epidemiology of Social Stress." *American Sociological Review* 60:104–125.

Waldron, I.; Weiss, C. C.; and Hughes, M. E. (1998). "Interacting Effects of Multiple Roles on Women's Health." *Journal of Health and Social Behavior* 39:216–236.

Wheaton, B. (1990). "Life Transitions, Role Histories, and Mental Health." *American Sociological Review* 55: 209–223.

Wheaton, B. (1999). "The Nature of Stressors." In *A Handbook for the Study of Mental Health: Social Contexts, Theories, and Systems,* ed. A. V. Horwitz and T. L. Scheid. Cambridge, UK: Cambridge University Press.

Windell, M., and Dumenci, L. (1999). "Parental and Occupational Stress as Predictors of Depressive Symptoms among Dual-Earner Couples: A Multilevel Modeling Approach." *Journal of Marriage and the Family* 59: 625–634.

Zhou, M. (1997). "Growing Up American: The Challenge Confronting Immigrant Children and Children of Immigrants." *Annual Review of Sociology* 23:63–95.

ELIZABETH G. MENAGHAN

STRUCTURAL-FUNCTIONAL THEORY

Jennie McIntyre (1966) was the first scholar to discern the curious paradox of structural functionalism (SF) within the realm of research and theory about families. Although only a relatively few researchers in the 1960s labeled themselves as SF-types, the great bulk of published work in the study of families was, she noted, shaped by SF assumptions, perspectives, and views of the social world. She did not, however, attempt to account for that contradiction and, in any case, by the 1970s, functionalist theory was overtly abandoned throughout the social sciences. Subsequently, in today's articles and books about families, the *explicit* use of functionalist jargon has largely vanished. Nevertheless, the fact that by the early twenty-first century SF was formally eradicated in no way diminished its potency. Its continuing influence on the ways research and teaching are carried out, and its impact on public policies for families, are as robust as ever before. Indeed, there is no other single theoretical perspective that seriously rivals it. Despite the range of theories that ostensibly replaced it (Doherty 1999; Vargus 1999), SF remains tenaciously in place. Although virtually no one today would call her or himself a functionalist, SF stands unchallenged in terms of sway it holds over the realm of research and theory about families.

To be sure, like other ancient life forms that have managed to survive, SF has mutated over time. And like those other primordial life forms, its survival is owed in part to its adaptive capabilities. The forms SF took in the 1950s and 1960s came almost exclusively from the imagination of Talcott Parsons (1955); these forms were elaborated by his students (Bell and Vogel 1960; Pitts 1964). Parsons reasoned that the post–World War II isolated nuclear family style was the final culmination of a long journey—the end point of an evolutionary process that had been occurring for several hundred years. He called the process *structural differentiation,* and it coincided with the process of industrialization in the West. Just as the West had evolved from the agricultural to the industrial age, Parsons reasoned that the post–World War II family style had evolved from *extended* into what he called *isolated nuclear.*

The extended style referred to an array of husband-wife households linked both by blood and a network of mutual support. Often, though not always, the households were situated in relative proximity and were frequently (although not always) engaged in shared agricultural pursuits. By contrast, the post–World War II isolated nuclear family style was urban-based and, said Parsons, referred to a heterosexual, and parenting, couple only ever married to each other. The husband's principal roles were good provider and instrumental task-leader, and the woman's were good wife/mother and expressive leader (nurturing agent) for her husband and children. In his role as task-leader, the husband held ultimate household authority.

But if households were predominantly husband-wife in both the extended and in the nuclear styles, what momentous evolutionary change had occurred corresponding to the shift from the agricultural to the industrial age? Unfortunately, Parsons used the misleading term *isolated* to capture what in fact was a highly significant difference. He emphasized that, unlike husband-wife households in the agricultural era, the post–World War II husband-wife household was *independent* from the day-to-day control and ultimate authority of its blood kin. Its autonomy was indicated by a high degree of privacy. And because its boundaries were deemed sacrosanct, happenings within the household were concealed from the prying eyes of kin, friends, and neighbors.

The household gained its independence from kin control, he said, owing to the nature of industrial society. Because the husband could obtain financial wherewithal from sources other than his kin, he and his wife and children were no longer dependent on them. Because it was typically in the household's own best interest to declare their independence from their kin, they did so. Furthermore, the booming postwar economy, including its suburban explosion, made this autonomous household style more of a reality for more citizens than ever before. Parsons emphasized it was *not* the wife's place to pursue occupational achievement in the marketplace. Her mission was to provide a haven for her husband, to nurture her children, and, when possible, to be active in her community (Seeley et al. 1955). Parsons' views regarding rigidly divergent gender roles were molded by his acquiescence to Freud's deterministic notions of biology and psychology, including Freud's most famous—"Anatomy determines destiny."

Importantly, Parsons believed the post–World War II isolated family style represented the summit of social evolution in the same manner that "American society has reached the maximum level of industrialization" (Pitts 1964, p. 88). He took it for granted that family evolution had come to a halt, and he regarded its outcome as the *normal* or *standard* family—the definitive gauge against which all other forms of families were measured and, invariably, found wanting (Parsons 1965). He could not imagine that the postwar isolated family style might not be the end of the line. He did not envision the social evolution of families as a never-ending process. For functionalists of that era, the proposition that there could be a transition from industrial to postindustrial societies, and the thesis that there might be an accompanying transition from industrial to postindustrial families, seemed equally preposterous. The corollary to this position was that development would have uniform effects for all families regardless of culture.

Structural functionalism got backed into the absurd position of calling a halt to social change in part because of the flawed way in which it conceived of social evolution. Owing to its roots in nineteenth-century organicism (Turner 2001), SF believed that social changes come about mainly via economic, political, demographic, and technological forces over which individuals have virtually no volition or control. Those several forces were seen as the analogue of chance genetic mutation and natural selection found in biological evolution. Accordingly, the post–World War II isolated family style evolved quite apart from the choices of citizens. Their only viable option was to conform to that style.

Indeed, Parsons had a profound suspicion of individuals making any choices other than to conform to cultural guidelines. He believed that without clear norms to guide them, men and women would behave in a *utilitarian* or self-interested manner, that is, one that would be dysfunctional for both children and society. Parsons argued that Western societies possessed an exemplary culture consisting of a set of "dominant values" and norms to which people should conform. Men and women, for example, who conform to the norms prescribed above for their instrumental and expressive roles, respectively, produce healthy children. In essence, conformity is the root of social order, as indicated by healthy families and a healthy society. Conversely, failure to conform, or deviance, results in social pathology.

There seems little doubt that the sharpest contrast between SF and the theoretical perspectives that in the 1970s formally replaced it is their take on people's choices, that is, the issue of *human agency.* As one of Parsons' critics put it,

> In Parsons' writing there is no true embrace of the idea that structure is being continuously opened up and reconstructed by the problem-solving behavior of individuals responding to concrete situations. (Selznick 1961, p. 934)

The quagmire that SF got into owing to Parsons's wariness of human agency was made even worse because of its other set of historic roots in philosophical realism (Turner 2001). Parsons and his students *reified* the post–World War II isolated nuclear family style. They assigned a corporeal or material reality to a set of social patterns—a mere sociological abstraction. Furthermore, Parsons was convinced there was an ideal fit between this reified family entity and the industrial society of his day. Hence, because he could not see beyond the industrial epoch, he was blinded to anything beyond his reified family style.

However, when women and men in the 1960s and 1970s began in earnest to make choices about sexuality, abortion, labor force participation, children, marriage, divorce, cohabitation, homosexuality, and so on, that ran counter to the prescribed norms above, SF found itself in a entirely untenable position. Because SF had no theoretical insights explaining how persons could create or invent new norms via creative problem solving, SF was left with nothing to do but to mark the behaviors of growing numbers of people as "deviant." But that sterile label went nowhere, and throughout the social sciences, SF was spurned in large part for the reason Selznick implied—it had no compelling mechanism to account for the complex interplay of social change and social order.

After SF got its decent burial, researchers in the 1970s turned their attention to the new and innovative ways women and men were creating relationships and families (Sussman 1972; Sussman and Cogswell 1972; Macklin and Rubin 1983; Scanzoni 1972, 2001b). And for awhile, it looked as though SF might remain extinct. The old SF question, "How do we get people to conform to prescribed values and norms?" was gradually being overtaken and replaced by a new theoretical question: "How do people and groups go about inventing different ways of doing relationships, families, and parenting?" The long-term process of social change that Parsons erroneously believed had terminated in the 1950s was in fact ongoing, and researchers were eager to study it.

But, strangely enough, a funny thing happened in pursuit of their new question. The counterrevolution that Margaret Mead (1967) predicted came to pass. In the United States, religious, social, and political conservatives joined forces in the 1970s and

1980s for the purpose, first of all, of successfully derailing the Equal Rights Amendment (ERA). The basis for their success was functionalist to the core—the ERA, they charged, would result in innumerable social pathologies. Quite apart from the ERA, the New Right highlighted sharply increasing divorce rates and alleged widespread sexual promiscuity as evidence that the changes begun in the "corrosive 60s," combined with what they saw as the "narcissism" of the 1970s, were taking a heavy toll on the "standard family" (Scanzoni 1989, 1991). However, in Scandinavia and other parts of northern Europe, no counter-revolution has occurred. Owing perhaps to the absence of the U.S.-type coalition of conservative forces, SF remained moribund. European researchers continued to examine the ways in which persons were creating innovative ways of doing families (Gravenhorst 1988; Horelli and Vespa 1994; Scanzoni 2000).

At the same time (1980s and 1990s), U.S. researchers began to shy away from investigating the conditions of innovation and turned instead to examining the correlates of deviation from established norms. They were warned in ominous terms that heterosexual cohabitation, for example, was associated with marital instability. Even gloomier was the assertion that children from one-parent families, and children with employed mothers, might be liable to innumerable defects of one sort or another. Those alleged conclusions, alongside other kinds of allegations, fed on each other so that now that style of work—the dysfunctions of deviance—has almost entirely trumped research questions about innovation.

Parsons' ghost lives in our midst. Many researchers today are, inadvertently to be sure and without calling it SF, utilizing a functionalist agenda. For all too brief a period, the most exciting research question in the field was "How are people or groups—*within a milieu that either enables or constrains them*—able or not to bring about changes in families" (Giddens 1984)? Now, however, efforts to explore the ways in which families might continue to evolve away from the uniformity of the post–World War II isolated nuclear style toward arrangements characterized by diversity (variety of arrangements within the household alongside external household connectedness) are in the distinct minority (Scanzoni 2000, 2001a, in press). Although contemporary researchers throughout the world seldom use Parsons' terminology, they are nonetheless quite busy documenting the dysfunctions of deviance from appropriate norms.

Some researchers, like David Popenoe (1996), are more radical in their agenda. He seems intent on overtly restoring SF to the pinnacle of theories about families. Unlike most other writers, his 1996 essay makes generous use of functionalist jargon and is almost totally governed by SF logic. To be sure, he manages a few slight concessions to the changes of recent decades. For example, although he proposes a *neo*-standard family, it is in almost every important aspect merely a rehashing of Parsons' standard family (Scanzoni 2001b). Popenoe simply disregards the prevailing theories in social science today, most of which consider human agency to be a vital element in explaining social reality (Scanzoni and Marsiglio 1993). Instead, he tends to reify his neo-standard family and, like Parsons, to argue that deviation from culturally appropriate values and norms spawns social pathology.

Although Popenoe is unlikely to succeed in his quest at overt SF restoration, he and many others are responsible for reinvigorating SF's latest influence. But the question remains—why have SF-type research issues gotten so popular? In the 1950s, SF critics charged that it was imbued with a conservative social, economic, and political ideology (Merton 1957). The critics said there was a natural affinity between conservative public policy aimed maintaining the status quo, and a social theory that could not explain social change. The affinity between SF and conservative ideology was made even more apparent, said the critics, when SF labeled change as deviance and viewed it as a catalyst for social pathology.

Today, religious, social, and political conservatives have joined forces not simply to maintain the status quo when it comes to families. Instead, they want to turn back the clock to an earlier time when there were no viable alternatives to the standard family (Council on Families in America 1995). Popenoe, although he does not explicitly endorse the idea of going back, comes awfully close by saying that his reader would probably agree with the statement that, "In many ways, 'things are not as good as they were when I was growing up'" (Popenoe 1996, p. 254).

Idealizing the past is a core conservative theme, and the question is—although it cannot be answered here—does conservative ideology describe a certain proportion of those who teach, study, and write about families? And does that same ideology characterize a ratio of those who make policy recommendations for families? Presuming there is an affinity between conservative ideology and SF offers one possible explanation for the remarkable tenacity of SF in the field of studies about families. Moreover, such an affinity illustrates once again that the scholar's own beliefs and values play a major role in influencing the scientific research questions she or he asks.

Order and innovation exist, obviously, on a continuum. Conservatives are found to its center and right, believing that individual and social well-being are enhanced by a blend of order and innovation that favors that former. Scholars who believe in that formula would feel quite at home with SF even though they never use its jargon. On the other hand, scholars (to the center and left of the continuum) who believe that individual and social well-being are advanced by a formula favoring innovation over order do not feel the least bit comfortable with SF. They are instead much more at home with theories about families in which human agency plays a pivotal role. Research questions about the conditions of order/disorder are in the ascendance. The degree to which—if at all—that situation might change in future to one in which questions about innovation become at least as prominent would likely depend in part on the ideology of researchers now in the field, and of those recruited to it.

See also: FAMILY THEORY

Bibliography

Bell, N. W., and Vogel, E. F. (1960). "Toward a Framework for Functional Analysis of Family Behavior." In *A Modern Introduction to the Family,* ed. N. W. Bell and E. F. Vogel. New York: The Free Press.

Council on Families in America. (1995). "Marriage in America." New York: The Institute for American Values.

Doherty, W. J. (1999). "Postmodernism and Family Theory." In *Handbook of Marriage and the Family,* 2nd edition, ed. M. B. Sussman, S. K. Steinmetz, and G. W. Peterson. New York: Plenum.

Giddens, A. (1984). *The Constitution of Society: Outline of the Theory of Constructionism.* Berkeley: University of California Press.

Gravenhorst, L. (1988). "A Feminist Look at Family Development Theory." In *Social Stress and Family Development,* ed. D. Klein and J. Aldous. New York: Guilford.

Horelli, L., and Vespa, K. (1994). "In Search of Supportive Structures for Everyday Life." In *Women and the Environment,* ed. I. Altman and A. Churchman. New York: Plenum.

Macklin, E. D., and Rubin, R. H., eds. (1983). *Contemporary Families and Alternative Lifestyles.* Beverly Hills, CA: Sage.

McIntyre, J. (1966). "The Structural-Functional Approach to Family Study." In *Emerging Conceptual Frameworks in Family Analysis,* ed. F. I. Nye. New York: Macmillan.

Mead, M. (1967). "The Life Cycle and its Variations: The Division of Roles." *Daedalus* 96:871–875.

Merton, R. K. (1957). *Social Theory and Social Structure.* New York: The Free Press.

Parsons, T. (1955). "The American Family: Its Relations to Personality and to the Social Structure." In *Family, Socialization, and Interaction Process,* ed. T. Parsons and R. F. Bales. New York: Free Press.

Parsons, T. (1965). "The Normal American Family." In *Man and Civilization: The Family's Search for Survival,* ed. S. M. Farber, P. Mustacchi, and R. H. L. Wilson. New York: McGraw-Hill.

Pitts, J. R. (1964). "The Structural-Functional Approach." In *Handbook of Marriage and the Family,* ed. H. T. Christensen. Chicago: Rand McNally.

Popenoe, D. (1996). "Modern Marriage: Revising the Cultural Script." In *Promises To Keep: Decline and Renewal of Marriage in America,* ed. D. Popenoe, J. B. Elshtain, and D. Blankenhorn. Lanham, MD: Rowman and Littlefield.

Scanzoni, J. (1972). *Sexual Bargaining: Power Politics in American Marriage.* Englewood Cliffs, NJ: Prentice-Hall. Rev. 1982. Chicago: University of Chicago Press.

Scanzoni, J. (1989). "Alternative Images For Public Policy: Family Structure Versus Families Struggling." *Policy Studies Review.* 8:599–609.

Scanzoni, J. (1991). "Balancing the Policy Interests of Children and Adults." In *The Reconstruction of Family Policy,* ed. E. A. Anderson and R. C. Hula. New York: Greenwood.

Scanzoni, J. (2000). *Designing Families: The Search for Self and Community in the Information Age.* Thousand Oaks, CA: Pine Forge/Sage.

Scanzoni, J. (2001a). "Reconnecting Household and Community: An Alternative Strategy for Theory and Policy." *Journal of Family Issues* 22:243–264.

Scanzoni, J. (2001b). "From the Normal Family to Alternate Families to the Quest for Diversity with Interdependence." *Journal of Family Issues* 22:688–710.

Scanzoni, J. (In press). "Household Diversity—The Starting Point For Healthy Families In The New Century." In *The Handbook of Contemporary Families: Considering the Past, Contemplating the Future,* ed. M. Coleman and L. Ganong. Thousand Oaks, CA: Sage.

Scanzoni, J., and Marsiglio, W. (1993). "New Action Theory and Contemporary Families." *Journal of Family Issues* 14:105–132.

Seeley, J. R.; Sim, R. A.; and Loosley, E. W. (1956). *Crestwood Heights*. New York: Basic Books.

Selznick, P. (1961). "Review Article: The Social Theories of Talcott Parsons." *American Sociological Review* 26:930–952.

Sussman, M. B. (1972). "Preface." In *Non-Traditional Family Forms in the 1970s,* ed. M. B. Sussman. Minneapolis, MN: National Council on Family Relations.

Sussman, M. B., and Cogswell, B. E. (1972). "The Meaning of Variant and Experimental Marriage Styles and Family Forms." In *Non-Traditional Family Forms in the 1970s,* ed. M. B. Sussman. Minneapolis, MN: National Council on Family Relations.

Turner, J. H., ed. (2001). *Handbook of Sociological Theory*. New York: Kluwer Academic/Plenum.

Vargus, B. S. (1999). "Classical Social Theory and Family Studies: The Triumph of Reactionary Thought in Contemporary Family Studies." In *Handbook of Marriage and the Family,* 2nd edition, ed. M. B. Sussman, S. K. Steinmetz, and G. W. Peterson. New York: Plenum.

JOHN SCANZONI
NANCY KINGSBURY

SUBSTANCE ABUSE

Substance abuse has a substantial and reciprocal impact upon families. There are many definitions of substance abuse and dependence but two authoritative sources are the fourth edition of the *Diagnostic and Statistical Manual* (DSM-IV-TR) (American Psychiatric Association 1994), commonly used in the United States, and the tenth edition of the *International Classification of Diseases* (ICD-10) (World Health Organization 1992). The criteria for alcohol abuse in the DSM-IV-TR include drinking despite recurrent and significant adverse consequences due to alcohol use. A diagnosis of alcohol dependence emphasizes a set of psychological symptoms (e.g., craving); physiological signs (e.g., tolerance and withdrawal); and behavioral indicators (e.g., use of alcohol to relieve discomfort due to withdrawal). Unlike the DSM-IV-TR, the ICD-10 does not include a category *alcohol abuse,* but rather uses the term *harmful use,* created so that problems related to alcohol use would not be underreported. Harmful use implies use that causes physical or mental damage in the absence of dependence (National Institute on Alcohol Abuse and Alcoholism 1995).

One of the limitations of these classifications (particularly with the DSM-IV-TR) is the lack of attention to cultural variations in the diagnosis of substance abuse (Tang and Bigby 1996). Around the world, substance use and abuse take on different meaning and importance. For example, there are different cultural norms about the legal drinking age. The legal age for purchasing alcohol in many European countries is sixteen years (in Denmark it is fifteen) (Eurocare 2001). Among indigenous groups, alcohol and other drugs may be integrated parts of tribal and community existence (Charles et al. 1994) where conventional definitions of abuse and dependence may be not be held. The definitions of substance abuse used in this entry tend to reflect the conventions of the nonindigenous cultures of North America because most of the research cited tends to use the DSM in its various editions. However, to maximize a cross-cultural perspective, multicultural and international studies are also referenced.

The emphasis in this entry is on reporting the evidence base for understanding substance abuse and the family. Popular but evidence-limited notions of the cause, effect, or treatment of substance abuse will not be included.

Prevalence and Incidence

International data suggest widespread and serious substance use and abuse. Within the United States, the annual National Household Survey on Drug Abuse (NHSDA) collects data on substance use patterns and trends among the general population. According to the 2001 NHSDA, 6.3 percent (14 million) of the U.S. population reported current use of illicit drugs (i.e., used an illicit drug at least once during the thirty days before the interview) (Substance Abuse and Mental Health Services Administration 2001). Among major racial/ethnic groups, the current rates for illicit drug use were 6.4 percent each for whites and African Americans and 5.3 percent for Hispanics/Latinos. The rate was highest among American Indian/Alaska Natives (12.6%), with Asians reporting the lowest rate (2.7%). Almost half (46.6%, approximately 104 million) of the U.S. population reported current use of alcohol. Almost 6 percent of the population (5.6%, 12.6 million) were heavy drinkers, consuming five or more drinks on one occasion in five or more days during the thirty days prior to interview.

Although trends in the United States and in other developing countries indicate either flat or declining alcohol use, rates are rising in many developing countries and in Central and Eastern Europe (World Health Organization 2001). One source has noted that "dangerous patterns of heavy drinking exist in most countries" (World Health Organization 2001, p. 1). With respect to illicit drug use, estimates for 1999 indicate 3 percent (180 million people) of the world's population consumed illicit substances (United Nations Office for Drug Control and Crime Prevention 2001). The most commonly consumed substance was cannabis, used by 2.4 percent (144 million people) of the world's population.

Because of the widespread abuse of substances among the world's population, there are likely to be substantial family effects. The next section reviews some of these findings.

Effects of Substance Abuse on Families

The effects of substances on couple and family relationships are both direct and indirect—and substantial. Due to limitations of the research designs, many findings are correlational and not causal. Thus, although many effects are associated with substance use, it is sometimes unclear whether the substance use is the cause or the effect.

Financial effects on families. Substance abuse by family members can have a substantial negative effect on the financial viability of caregivers. Substance-abusing caregivers may spend money allocated for food or clothing for children. Substance abusers may divert money from rent or mortgages to buy substances. Noncustodial parents who abuse alcohol are less likely to provide financial support for their children (Dion et al. 1997). In Yemen and Somalia, users may spend as much on khat (a type of stimulant) as they spend on food (Abdul Ghani et al. 1987). Additionally, families are often unwitting accomplices to their relative's substance abuse as the substance use is often financed by immediate family members (Gearon et al. 2001).

Fetal exposure to alcohol and other drugs. There is considerable evidence for the effects of maternal substance use on the development of the fetus. Specifically, childhood developmental problems have been associated with maternal substance use. For example, prenatal alcohol exposure can lead to mental retardation, behavioral and neurological problems that may lead to poor academic performance, and legal and employment problems in youth and adulthood (National Institute on Alcohol Abuse and Alcoholism 2000). However, researchers do not know how much alcohol produces adverse fetal consequences. Thus, experts recommend that pregnant women should not consume alcohol (National Institute on Alcohol Abuse and Alcoholism 2000).

Early family environment. In addition to the direct effects of substances on the unborn child, the early social environment of children with substance-abusing parents adds potential risks. A high percentage of children in contact with the child welfare system have substance-abusing parents (Jones-Harden 1998). Reviews have consistently documented the association between parental substance abuse and poor parenting skills (Jones-Harden 1998). The type of child maltreatment often associated with these cases includes physical, medical, and emotional neglect (Hawley et al. 1995; Jones-Harden 1998). Research in Israel documented the ill effects of severe environmental deprivation when both parents are heroin-addicted and noted that the early home environment has a greater influence than in-utero exposure on developmental outcomes, as long as there is no significant neurological damage (Ornoy et al. 1996). Other research has found that a positive postnatal caregiving environment can attenuate some of the negative effects of prenatal exposure to substances (Jones-Harden 1998; McNichol and Tash 2001).

Child and adolescent problems. Children with family histories of substance abuse differ from children without such histories in higher levels of aggression, delinquency, sensation-seeking, hyperactivity, impulsivity, negative affectivity (Dore et al.

Children born to alcoholic mothers may have fetal alcohol syndrome (FAS), a condition marked by facial abnormalities and problems with growth and development. Expecting mothers are advised to avoid alcohol entirely during pregnancy. Here, a young adopted boy with fetal alcohol syndrome sits with his disabled father. DAVID H. WELLS/ CORBIS

1996; Giancola and Parker 2001), anxiety, and lower levels of differentiation of self (Maynard 1997). Family history of alcohol dependence, through a moderating influence of adolescent drug dependence, has predicted poor adolescent neuropsychological functioning (i.e., language and attention functioning) (Tapert and Brown 2000). On the other hand, youth without family histories of alcohol dependence seemed to be protected from poorer neuropsychological functioning (Tapert and Brown 2000).

Relational distress, partner and family violence. A nationwide study of married and cohabiting couples found that partners tend to share similar drinking patterns and when there are differences in the amounts of alcohol consumed, couples tend to have serious relationship problems including alcohol-related arguments and physical violence (Leadley, Clark, and Caetano 2000). Alcohol frequently plays a role in intimate partner violence. National surveys in the United States have reported that 30 to 40 percent of men and 27 to 34 percent of women who perpetrated partner violence were drinking at the time (Caetano, Schafer, and Cunradi 2001). The study also revealed that alcohol-related problems were related to partner violence among African Americans and whites, but not among Hispanics/Latinos.

In sum, there appear to be substantial effects of substance abuse on family and couple relationships. The next section reviews the evidence for factors that contribute to or protect from the risk for substance abuse.

Family Factors Contributing to Risk and Resiliency

Substance abuse is the result of a complex interaction of individual, family, peer, community, and societal factors (United Nations Office for Drug Control and Crime Prevention 2000). A consistent global finding is that substance abuse runs in families. A family history of drug abuse and dependence substantially increases the risk for such problems among members (Madianos et al. 1995; Westermeyer and Neider 1994; Wu et al. 1996). The same pattern occurs with alcohol abuse and dependence (Curran et al. 1999; Jauhar and Watson 1995). Although genetics plays a substantial role in both alcohol (Bierut, Dinwiddie, and Regleiter 1998) and drug dependence (Tsuang et al. 1996), the family environment plays a role in both promoting and protecting from substance abuse and dependence. This section reviews some of these factors. Due to the limitations of the research designs, many of these findings are correlational and not causal.

Child physical and sexual abuse. Although much of the research is limited in design (e.g., retrospective designs, clinical samples), childhood abuse appears to be a risk factor for substance abuse. Women who were physically or sexually abused as children are at risk for alcohol abuse as adults (Langeland and Hartgers 1998; Rice et al. 2001) but the evidence for males is contradictory (e.g., contrast Galaif et al. 2001 and Langeland and Hartgers 1998). Childhood sexual abuse may also increase the risk for adolescent drug abuse among females (Jarvis, Copeland, and Walton 1998). Tracey Jarvis and colleagues speculated that the use of drugs might be an effort to self-medicate the emotional pain associated with the abuse.

Family attitudes and practices about substance abuse. Although peer influences are important in explaining substance use among youth (Lane et al. 2001), family attitudes and practices are also significant. Among Hispanic/Latino youth in particular, parents have been more influential than peers

(Coombs, Paulson, and Richardson 1991). Family members' attitudes about and use of substances influence youth substance use. For example, an analysis of the 1997 household survey on substance use found that youth ages twelve to seventeen who perceived that their parents would be "very upset" with marijuana, cigarettes, and binge drinking reported the lowest prevalence of use of these substances in the past year (Lane et al. 2001). Similarly, the protective influence of strong family sanctions against alcohol use reduced the use of that substance among girls in Hungary (Swaim, Nemeth, and Oetting 1995). The level of influence seems to extend to siblings. In one household study in Canada, older sibling drug use, more than parental drug use, was the dominant influence of substance use among youth (Boyle et al. 2001).

Problematic family and partner relations. Family and partner conflict tends to increase risk for substance abuse. The national household survey in the United States found that adolescents who argued with their parents at least several times a week were more likely to have used marijuana in the past year than those who argued with their parents only once a week to once a month (Lane et al. 2001). Internationally, family conflict and lower perceived family caring increases the risk for adolescent substance abuse (Al-Umran, Mahgoub, and Qurashi 1993; Nappo, Galduroz, and Noto 1996; Swaim, Nemeth, and Oetting 1995).

Marital and family conflict appear to increase risk for alcoholism among women in Zagreb (Breitenfeld et al. 1998). Over three-quarters of 100 males admitted for alcohol abuse in Scotland ascribed their marital breakdown or family neglect to their drinking (Jauhar and Watson 1995).

Family structure. Studies of family structure around the world have found that youth who live with both biological parents are significantly less likely to use substances, or to report problems with their use, than those who do not live with both parents (Challier et al. 2000; Johnson, Hoffman, and Gerstein 1996). However, family structure alone does not appear to explain substance abuse. The characteristics of these family structures offer some clues. For example, boys who are in care of their mothers and whose fathers are drug abusers are at increased risk for drug abuse but this is due to the genetic transmission of risk and lack of resources for effective parenting for single mothers (Tarter et al. 2001). Studies in Brazil and Saudi Arabia have noted that the quality of family relationships was more important than structure in explaining substance use (Al-Umran, Mahgoub, and Qurashi 1993; Carvalho et al. 1995).

Disruptions in the family life cycle seem to characterize these single-parent households. An unstable family environment (i.e., father absence, one or both parents who had immigrated, or death of parents) was associated with substance abuse among a nationwide sample of youth in Greece (Madianos et al. 1995). White non-Hispanics/Latinos and African Americans in changed families (e.g., those that changed from two parents to single parents during the study) had the highest rates of substance initiation (Gil, Vega, and Biafora 1998). Moreover, deteriorating family environments were stronger influences of drug initiation among Hispanic/Latino immigrants than nonimmigrants to the United States. Among African Americans, family structure and environment had the weakest effect on substance use and African-American youth in the care of their mothers or other adult family members, had the lowest proportion of drug onset (Gil, Vega, and Biafora 1998).

Thus, family structure along with characteristics of these families seems to account for substance abuse. More research is needed on the quality of the relationships within these family structures and on the time-order of the onset of substance use among youth with different family structures (Johnson, Hoffman, and Gerstein 1996).

Protective family factors that mitigate risk for substance abuse. Although they may place members at risk of substance abuse, family factors may also be protective. As noted above, two-parent households appear protective. High levels of perceived support from family members seems to protect against youth alcohol use (Foxcroft and Lowe 1991) and drug use among Hispanics/Latinos (Frauenglass et al. 1997) and African Americans (Sullivan and Farrell 1999). Researchers have found that effective family relationships (e.g., family involvement and communication, proactive family management, or attachment to family) protect against adolescent substance abuse across racial and cultural groups (Carvalho et al. 1995; Stronski et al. 2000; Williams et al. 1999). Further, the positive effects of family support during adolescence seem long lasting. Greater family support and bonding during adolescence has predicted less problem alcohol use in adulthood (Galaif et al. 2001).

In families with substance-abusing parents, there may be influences that protect from abuse. Preliminary research has suggested that a factor that provides some protection for children in homes with substance-abusing parents is the availability of a stable, nurturing relative such as grandmothers or aunts (Jones-Harden 1998). In research in Colombia, the adverse effects of parental substance abuse were buffered by effective parent-child rearing practices (Brook et al. 2001).

Protection extends beyond parents to siblings. One study reported that older brother abstinence from drugs, as well as strong attachment to parents, explained reduced drug use among younger brothers (Brook, Brook, and Whiteman 1999).

In sum, the risk and protective factors suggest that family relationships have a significant impact on substance abuse and dependence. However, the research is not sufficiently developed to indicate which or how much of these protective factors are necessary to reduce risk. There are variations across groups and in timing in their importance for preventing or reducing risk (Gil, Vega, and Biafora 1998). Further, the risk and protective factors at other levels, such as community or societal, may mitigate or attenuate risk.

Treatment for Substance Abuse

A common reason for seeking treatment for substance abuse is a problem with interpersonal relationships (Tucker and Gladsojo 1993). Given the evidence showing the influence of family and social relationships on substance abuse, cited above, treatment attempts to improve the quality of interpersonal relationships and to teach problem solving skills to couples and families with a substance-abusing member. Interactions between family members are important in the etiology and maintenance of substance use. Family interactions are interdependent and, over time, become patterns of behavior that the family maintains. Family interventions focus on identifying and changing the patterns that support the problematic substance use. Some family-based interventions also acknowledge that the family system is maintained in a broader context of peers, work, school, and neighborhood and attempt to engage elements from these systems in therapy. Although there are different models of family-based interventions, the common focus is on changing the patterns of interaction within the family (Robbins and Szapocznik 2001).

Reviews of the substance abuse treatment literature in the mid-1990s noted that modest benefits could be ascribed to family-based interventions (Edwards and Steinglass 1995; Liddle and Dakof 1995). The reviews concluded that although the research at that time indicated the promise of family-based interventions, there were not enough randomized clinical trials to warrant an endorsement of efficacy, defined as a high degree of confidence that the intervention reduced or eliminated substance abuse.

Treatment of alcohol abuse and alcohol dependency. Three interventions that effectively reduce alcohol abuse and dependency among adults are Behavioral Couples (or marital) Therapy (BCT), Behavioral Family Therapy (BFT), and the Community Reinforcement Approach (CRA). BCT is highly structured and guided by a treatment manual principally developed by Timothy O'Farrell, Barbara McCrady, and their colleagues (Fals-Stewart, Birchler, and O'Farrell 1996; McCrady 2000; O'Farrell, Van Hutton, and Murphy 1999). Early sessions focus on helping the couple to increase positive verbal exchanges and behaviors. Later sessions build skills at positive marital communication and problem solving. Sessions include review of disulfiram (an alcohol antagonist) contracts, homework assignments, and the client's drinking or urges to drink. Sessions continue with the introduction of new material, modeling of new skills by the therapist, and rehearsal of the skills by the couple. To complement the approach, a module of fifteen sessions is used to establish and maintain a relapse prevention plan that includes how to identify and manage warning signs of lapses.

BFT, an efficacious and promising intervention across groups and substances (Azrin et al. 1996; Edwards and Steinglass 1995; Stanton and Shadish 1997), is based on the assumption that behaviors are maintained by consequences. Change is unlikely to occur unless more rewarding consequences result from different behaviors. For example, parent skills training, a feature of BFT, teaches parents to increase reward for positive behaviors and ignore negative behaviors to produce change.

Patients in a temporary heroin detox clinic attempt to quit using the drug. A behavioral approach to the treatment of heroin abuse can be especially effective when combined with medications such as methadone. ED KASHI/CORBIS

A strategy often used is to improve communication between the parents and the adolescent.

CRA is an efficacious and comprehensive intervention that involves spouses, family members, and others in the drinker's social network to change the marital, familial, and social reinforcers that support the drinker's behavior (Kirby et al. 1999; Miller, Meyers, and Hiller Sturmhoefel 1999). Beginning with a functional analysis of the drinking behavior (i.e., a review of persons, places, and contexts that act as triggers for substance use behavior), significant others are trained to help the drinker to engage in treatment and to remove positive reinforcers during drinking episodes. Drink refusal skills, relaxation, control of drinking urges, and methods to deal with risky social situations are taught. Often disulfiram contracts are included.

Two other interventions that show promise in reducing alcohol abuse and dependency are Functional Family Therapy (FFT) and Multi Systemic Family Therapy (MSFT). FFT is a manually guided intervention involving eight to thirty sessions spread over a three-month period (Stanton and Shadish 1997; Weinberg et al. 1998). The approach evolved from the need to serve at-risk adolescents and their families with few resources or who were difficult to treat. FFT has phases that consist of *engagement and motivation, behavior change,* and *generalization.* Each phase involves assessment and intervention. For example, in the engagement and motivation phase, assessment focuses on the level of negativity and blaming in family exchanges. The intervention in this phase would target the development of behaviors and communication that reduce negativity and blaming. Similarly, in the generalization phase, assessment identifies the range of situations to which the family can apply new behaviors. The objective of intervention in this phase would be to maximize the functional range of the family's new behavior(s).

MSFT views substance abuse as antisocial behavior that develops from a complex network of interconnected systems: the individual, the family, and extrafamilial factors such as peers, school, and neighborhood (Henggeler, Pickrel, and Brondino 1999; Schoenwald et al. 1996). The intervention is primarily targeted to adolescents. MSFT attempts to alter parenting skills and resources as well as improve the adolescent's coping skills. The intervention integrates strategic family therapy, structural family therapy, behavioral parent training, and cognitive-behavioral therapy. The home-based intervention is designed to reduce service barriers, increase family retention in treatment, allow for the provision of intensive therapy, and enhance treatment gains. MSFT is designed for approximately sixty hours of contact with the family, but family needs determine the frequency and duration of contact.

Treatment of drug abuse and drug dependency. Although some of the interventions described above are useful in treating drug abuse and dependency, Brief Strategic Family Therapy (BSFT), Multidimensional Family Therapy (MDFT) and the Matrix model (MM) are also promising. BSFT and MDFT target adolescent drug abuse. BSFT is a short-term, problem-focused intervention based partly on classical and operant conditioning (Stanton and Shadish 1997; Szapocznik and Williams 2000). Substance abuse is viewed as the result of problematic family interactions that are rewarding based on familiarity and habit. The focus of the intervention is on improving family interactions so that new behaviors are rewarded and replace the substance abuse by the family member. The techniques used in this process are *joining* (engaging and entering the family system), *diagnosing* (identifying the maladaptive interactions as well as the family strengths), and *restructuring* (transforming maladaptive family interactions). BSFT is delivered in twelve to fifteen sessions over three months.

BFST was developed for application with inner city Hispanic/Latino and African-American families. Therapists are trained to assess and facilitate healthy family interactions based on the cultural norms of the family.

MDFT views the development of adolescent drug use as the result of individual, family, peer, and community influences (Liddle and Dakof 1995; Schmidt, Liddle, and Dakof 1996). Reducing unwanted behavior and increasing desirable behavior occurs in multiple ways and within different settings (e.g., in the home, school, and community). MDFT interventions typically include individual sessions held in parallel with family sessions. In the individual sessions, adolescents learn effective decision making, negotiation, and problem-solving skills. In the family sessions, parents identify their parenting style and learn positive developmentally appropriate skills to influence their child's behavior.

The MM recognizes the important influence of the family on the development, maintenance and consequences of drug abuse (Rawson et al. 1995; Shoptaw et al. 1994). The intervention includes family education groups to assist families in understanding the effects of the drug abuse of the member. The intervention requires therapists to use nonconfrontational methods to promote the individual's self-esteem, dignity, and self-worth. Sessions include early recovery skills groups, conjoint sessions, family education groups, twelve-step programs, relapse analysis, and social support groups.

Conclusion

Much progress has been made in understanding the relationship between substance abuse and the family. Family factors have an important role in explaining the onset, development, and amelioration of substance abuse. Encouraging gains have been made in treating couples and families with substance abuse problems. More research is needed involving diverse and international populations, but efficacious treatments are growing in type and number that bodes well for improving the lives of millions worldwide.

See also: CHILD ABUSE: PHYSICAL ABUSE AND NEGLECT; CHILD ABUSE: SEXUAL ABUSE; CHILDHOOD, STAGES OF: ADOLESCENCE; CHILDREN OF ALCOHOLICS; CHRONIC ILLNESS; CODEPENDENCY; CONDUCT DISORDER; DEVELOPMENTAL PSYCHOPATHOLOGY; FAMILY RITUALS; HEALTH AND FAMILIES; HOMELESS FAMILIES; JUVENILE DELINQUENCY; THERAPY: COUPLE RELATIONSHIPS

Bibliography

Abdul Ghani, N.; Eriksson, M.; Kristiansson, B.; and Qirbi, A. (1987). "The Influence of Khat-Chewing on Birth-Weight in Full-Term Infants." *Social Science and Medicine* 24(7):625–627.

Al-Umran, K.; Mahgoub, O.; and Qurashi, N. (1993). "Volatile Substance Abuse among School Students of Eastern Saudi Arabia." *Annals of Saudi Medicine* 13(6):520–524.

American Psychiatric Association. (2000). *Diagnostic and Statistical Manual of Mental Disorders: DSM-IV-TR,* 4th edition. Washington, DC: Author.

Azrin, N. H.; Acierno, R.; Kogan, E. S.; Donohue, B.; Besalel, V. A.; and McMahon, P. T. (1996). "Follow-Up Results of Supportive versus Behavioral Therapy for Illicit Drug Use." *Behavior Research and Therapy* 34(1): 41–46.

Bierut, L.; Dinwiddie, S.; and Regleiter, H. (1998). "Familial Transmission of Substance Dependence: Alcohol, Marijuana, and Cocaine and Habitual Smoking: A Report from the Collaborative Study on the Genetics of Alcoholism." *Archives of General Psychiatry* 55(11):982–988.

Boyle, M. H.; Sanford, M.; Szatmari, P.; Merikangas, K.; and Offord, D. R. (2001). "Familial Influences on Substance Use by Adolescents and Young Adults." *Canadian Journal of Public Health/Revue Canadienne de Sante Publique* 92(3):206–209.

Breitenfeld, D.; Lang, B.; Thaller, V.; Breitenfeld, T.; De Syo, D.; and Jagetic, N. (1998). "Psycho-Social Characteristics of Female Alcoholics." *Collegium Anthropologicum* 22:613–619.

Brook, J.; Brook, D.; De La Rosa, M.; Whiteman, M.; Johnson, E.; and Montoya, I. (2001). "Adolescent Illegal Drug Use: The Impact of Personality, Family, and Environmental Factors." *Journal of Behavioral Medicine* 24(2):183–204.

Brook, J.; Brook, D.; and Whiteman, M. (1999). "Older Sibling Correlates of Younger Sibling Drug Use in the Context of Parent-Child Relations." *Genetic, Social, and General Psychology Monographs* 125(4):451–468.

Caetano, R.; Schafer, J.; and Cunradi, C. B. (2001). "Alcohol-Related Intimate Partner Violence among White, Black, and Hispanic Couples in the United States." *Alcohol Research and Health* 25(1):58–65.

Carvalho, V.; Pinsky, I.; De Souza E Silva, R.; and Carlini-Cotrim, B. (1995). "Drug and Alcohol Use and Characteristics: A Study among Brazilian High School Students." *Addiction* 90:65–72.

Challier, B.; Chau, N.; Predine, R.; Choquet, M.; and Legras, B. (2000). "Associations of Family Environment and Individual Factors with Tobacco, Alcohol, and Illicit Drug Use in Adolescents." *European Journal of Epidemiology* 16:33–42.

Coombs, R. H.; Paulson, M. J.; and Richardson, M. A. (1991). "Peer vs. Parental Influence in Substance Use among Hispanic and Anglo Children and Adolescents." *Journal of Youth and Adolescence* 20:73–88.

Curran, G.; Stoltenberg, S.; Hill, E.; Mudd, S.; Blow, F.; and Zucker, R. (1999). "Gender Differences in the Relationships among SES, Family History of Alcohol Disorders and Alcohol Dependence." *Journal of Studies on Alcohol* 60(6):825–832.

Dion, M.; Braver, S.; Wolchick, S.; and Sandler, I. (1997). "Alcohol Abuse and Psychopathic Deviance in Noncustodial Parents as Predictors of Child-Support Payment and Visitation." *American Journal of Orthopsychiatry* 67(1):70–79.

Dore, M. M.; Kauffman, E.; Nelson-Zlupko, L.; and Granfort, E. (1996). "Psychosocial Functioning and Treatment Needs of Latency-Age Children from Drug-Involved Families." *Families in Society* 77(10):595–604.

Edwards, M. E., and Steinglass, P. (1995). "Family Therapy Treatment Outcomes for Alcoholism." *Journal of Marital and Family Therapy* 21(4):475–509.

Fals-Stewart, W.; Birchler, G. R.; and O'Farrell, T. J. (1996). "Behavioral Couples Therapy for Male Substance-Abusing Patients: Effects on Relationship Adjustment and Drug-Using Behavior." *Journal of Consulting and Clinical Psychology* 64:959–972.

Foxcroft, D. R., and Lowe, G. (1991). "Adolescent Drinking Behaviour and Family Socialization Factors: A Meta-Analysis." *Journal of Adolescence* 14(3):255–273.

Frauenglass, S.; Routh, D. K.; Pantin, H. M.; and Mason, C. A. (1997). "Family Support Decreases Influence of Deviant Peers on Hispanic Adolescents' Substance Use." *Journal of Clinical Child Psychology* 26(1): 15–23.

Galaif, E. R.; Stein, J. A.; Newcomb, M. D.; and Bernstein, D. P. (2001). "Gender Differences in the Prediction of Problem Alcohol Use in Adulthood: Exploring the Influence of Family Factors and Childhood Maltreatment." *Journal of Studies on Alcohol* 62(4):486–493.

Gearon, J. S.; Bellack, A. S.; Rachbeisel, J.; and Dixon, L. (2001). "Drug-Use Behavior and Correlates in People with Schizophrenia." *Addictive Behaviors* 26(1):51–61.

Giancola, P., and Parker, A. (2001). "A Six-Year Prospective Study of Pathways toward Drug Use in Adolescent Boys with and without a Family History of a Substance Use Disorder." *Journal of Studies on Alcohol* 62(2):166–178.

Gil, A.; Vega, W.; and Biafora, F. (1998). "Temporal Influences of Family Structure and Family Risk Factors on Drug Use Initiation in a Multiethnic Sample of Adolescent Boys." *Journal of Youth and Adolescence* 27(3):373–393.

Hawley, T.; Halle, T.; Drasin, R.; and Thomas, N. (1995). "Children of Addicted Mothers: Effects of the 'Crack Epidemic' on the Caregiving Environment and the Development of Preschoolers." *American Journal of Orthopsychiatry* 65(3):364–379.

Henggeler, S. W.; Pickrel, S. G.; and Brondino, M. J. (1999). "Multisystemic Treatment of Substance-Abusing and Dependent Delinquents: Outcomes, Treatment Fidelity, and Transportability." *Mental Health Services Research* 1(3):171–184.

Jarvis, T.; Copeland, J.; and Walton, L. (1998). "Exploring the Nature of the Relationship between Child Sexual Abuse and Substance Use among Women." *Addiction* 93(3):865–875.

Jauhar, P., and Watson, A. (1995). "Severity of Alcohol Dependence in the East End of Glasgow." *Alcohol and Alcoholism* 30(1):67–70.

Johnson, R.; Hoffman, J.; and Gerstein, D. (1996). *The Relationship between Family Structure and Adolescent Substance Use.* Rockville, MD: Substance Abuse and Mental Health Services Administration.

Jones-Harden, B. (1998). "Building Bridges for Children: Addressing the Consequences of Exposure to Drugs and to the Child Welfare System." In *Substance Abuse, Family Violence, and Child Welfare: Bridging Perspectives,* ed. R. L. Hampton, V. Senatore, and T. P. Gullota. Thousand Oaks, CA: Sage.

Kirby, K. C.; Marlowe, D. B.; Festinger, D. S.; Garvey, K. A.; and La Monaca, V. (1999). "Community Reinforcement Training for Family and Significant Others of Drug Abusers: A Unilateral Intervention to Increase Treatment Entry of Drug Users." *Drug and Alcohol Dependence* 56(1):85–96.

Langeland, W., and Hartgers, C. (1998). "Child Sexual and Physical Abuse and Alcoholism: A Review." *Journal of Studies on Alcohol* 59(3):336–348.

Leadley, K.; Clark, C.; and Caetano, R. (2000). "Couples Drinking Patterns, Intimate Partner Violence, and Alcohol-Related Partnership Problems." *Journal of Substance Abuse* 11(3):253–263.

Liddle, H. A., and Dakof, G. A. (1995). "Efficacy of Family Therapy for Drug Abuse: Promising but Not Definitive." *Journal of Marital and Family Therapy* 21(4):511–543.

Madianos, M.; Gefou-Madianou, D.; Richardson, C.; and Stefanis, C. (1995). "Factors Affecting Illicit and Licit Drug Use among Adolescents and Young Adults in Greece." *Acta Psychiatrica Scandinavica* 91(4):258–264.

Maynard, S. (1997). "Growing Up in an Alcoholic Family System: The Effect on Anxiety and Differentiation of Self." *Journal of Substance Abuse* 9:161–170.

McCrady, B. S. (2000). "Alcohol Use Disorders and the Division 12 Task Force of the American Psychological Association." *Psychology of Addictive Behaviors* 14(3):267–276.

McNichol, T., and Tash, C. (2001). "Parental Substance Abuse and the Development of Children in Family Foster Care." *Child Welfare* 80(2):239–256.

Miller, W. R.; Meyers, R. J.; and Hiller Sturmhoefel, S. (1999). "The Community-Reinforcement Approach." *Alcohol Research and Health* 23(2):116–120.

Nappo, S. A.; Galduroz, J. C.; and Noto, A. R. (1996). "Crack Use in Sao Paulo." *Substance Use and Misuse* 31(5):565–579.

National Institute on Alcohol Abuse and Alcoholism. (1995). "Diagnostic Criteria for Alcohol Abuse and Dependence." *Alcohol Alert* 30.

National Institute on Alcohol Abuse and Alcoholism. (2000). "Fetal Alcohol Exposure and the Brain." *Alcohol Alert* 50.

O'Farrell, T. J.; Van Hutton, V.; and Murphy, C. M. (1999). "Domestic Violence before and after Alcoholism Treatment: A Two-Year Longitudinal Study." *Journal of Studies on Alcohol* 60(3):317–321.

Ornoy, A.; Michailevskaya, V.; Lukashov, I.; Bar-Hamburger, R.; and Harel, S. (1996). "The Developmental Outcome of Children Born to Heroin-Dependent Mothers, Raised at Home or Adopted." *Child Abuse and Neglect* 20(5):385–396.

Rawson, R. A.; Shoptaw, S. J.; Obert, J. L.; McCann, M. J.; Hasson, A. L.; Marinelli-Casey, P. J.; Brethen, P. R.; and Ling, W. (1995). "An Intensive Outpatient Approach for Cocaine Abuse Treatment: The Matrix Model." *Journal of Substance Abuse Treatment* 12(2):117–127.

Rice, C.; Mohr, C. D.; Del Boca, F. K.; Mattson, M. E.; Young, L.; Brady, K.; and Nickless, C. (2001). "Self-Reports of Physical, Sexual and Emotional Abuse in an Alcoholism Treatment Sample." *Journal of Studies on Alcohol* 62(1):114–123.

Robbins, M. S., and Szapocznik, J. (2001). "Family Systems Therapy with Children and Adolescents." In *Children and Adolescents Clinical Formulation and Treatment,* ed. T. Ollendick. New York: Elsevier Science.

Schmidt, S. E.; Liddle, H. A.; and Dakof, G. A. (1996). "Changes in Parenting Practices and Adolescent Drug Abuse during Multidimensional Family Therapy." *Journal of Family Psychology* 10(1):12–27.

Schoenwald, S. K.; Ward, D. M.; Henggeler, S. W.; Pickrel, S. G.; and Patel, H. (1996). "Multisystemic Therapy Treatment of Substance Abusing or Dependent Adolescent Offenders: Costs of Reducing Incarceration, Inpatient, and Residential Placement." *Journal of Adolescence* 19(1):47–61.

Shoptaw, S.; Rawson, R. A.; McCann, M. J.; and Obert, J. L. (1994). "The Matrix Model of Outpatient Stimulant Abuse Treatment: Evidence of Efficacy." *Journal of Addictive Diseases* 13(4):129–141.

Stanton, M. D., and Shadish, W. R. (1997). "Outcome, Attrition, and Family-Couples Treatment for Drug Abuse: A Meta-Analysis and Review of the Controlled, Comparative Studies." *Psychological Bulletin* 122(2):170–191.

Stronski, S.; Ireland, M.; Michaud, P.; Narring, F.; and Resnick, M. (2000). "Protective Correlates of Stages in Adolescent Substance Use: A Swiss National Study." *Journal of Adolescent Health* 26:420–427.

Substance Abuse and Mental Health Services Administration. (2001). *Summary of Findings from the 2000 National Household Survey on Drug Abuse.* Rockville, MD: Author.

Sullivan, T., and Farrell, A. (1999). "Identification and Impact of Risk and Protective Factors for Drug Use among Urban African American Adolescents." *Journal of Clinical Child Psychology* 28(2):122–136.

Swaim, R.; Nemeth, J.; and Oetting, E. (1995). "Alcohol Use and Socialization Characteristics among Hungarian Adolescents: Path Models." *Drugs and Society* 8(3/4):47–63.

Szapocznik, J., and Williams, R. A. (2000). "Brief Strategic Family Therapy: Twenty-Five Years of Interplay among Theory, Research, and Practice in Adolescent

Behavior Problems and Drug Abuse." *Clinical Child and Family Psychology Review* 3(2):117–134.

Tang, W. H., and Bigby, J. (1996). "Cultural Perspectives on Substance Abuse." In *Source Book of Substance Abuse and Addiction,* ed. L. Friedman, N. F. Fleming, D. H. Roberts, and S. E. Hyman. Baltimore, MD: Williams and Wilkins.

Tapert, S., and Brown, S. (2000). "Substance Dependence, Family History of Alcohol Dependence and Neuropsychological Functioning in Adolescence." *Addiction* 95(7):1043–1053.

Tarter, R.; Schultz, K.; Kerisci, L.; and Dunn, M. (2001). "Does Living with a Substance Abusing Father Increase Substance Abuse Risk in Male Offspring? Impact on Individual, Family, School, and Peer Vulnerability Factors." *Journal of Child and Adolescent Substance Abuse* 10(3):59–71.

Tsuang, M.; Lyons, M.; Eisen, S.; Goldberg, J.; True, W.; Lin, N.; Meyer, J.; Toomey, R.; Faraone, S.; and Eaves, L. (1996). "Genetic Influences on DSM III-R Drug Abuse and Dependence: A Study of 3,372 Twin Pairs." *American Journal of Genetics* 67(5):473–477.

Tucker, J. A., and Gladsojo, J. A. (1993). "Help-Seeking and Recovery by Problem Drinkers: Characteristics of Drinkers Who Attend Alcoholics Anonymous or Formal Treatment or Who Recovered without Assistance." *Addictive Behaviors* 18(5):529–542.

United Nations Office for Drug Control and Crime Prevention. (2000). *World Drug Report 2000.* New York: United Nations Publications.

United Nations Office for Drug Control and Crime Prevention. (2001). *Global Illicit Drug Trends: 2001.* New York: United Nations Publications.

Weinberg, N. Z.; Rahdert, E.; Colliver, J. D.; and Glantz, M. D. (1998). "Adolescent Substance Abuse: A Review of the Past 10 Years." *Journal of the American Academy of Child and Adolescent Psychiatry* 37(3):252–261.

Westermeyer, J., and Neider, J. (1994). "Substance Disorder among 100 American Indians versus 200 Other Patients." *Alcoholism, Clinical and Experimental Research* 18(3):692–694.

Williams, J. H.; Ayers, C. D.; Abbott, R. D.; Hawkins, J. D.; and Catalano, R. F. (1999). "Racial Differences in Risk Factors for Delinquency and Substance Abuse among Adolescents." *Social Work Research* 23(4):241–256.

World Health Organization. (1992). *International Statistical Classification of Diseases and Related Health Problems,* 10th rev. edition. Geneva, Switzerland: Author.

World Health Organization. (2001). *A Summary of Global Status Report on Alcohol.* Geneva, Switzerland: Author.

Wu, Z.; Detels, R.; Zhang, J.; Duan, S.; Cheng, H.; Li, Z.; Dong, L.; Huang, S.; Jia, M.; and Bi, X. (1996). "Risk Factors for Intravenous Drug Use and Sharing Equipment among Male Drug Users in Longchuan County, South-West China." *AIDS* 10(9):1017–1024.

Other Resources

Charles, M.; Masihi, H. Y.; Siddiqui, S. V.; Jogarao, H.; D'Lima, H.; Mehta, U.; and Britto, G. (1994). "Culture, Drug Abuse, and Some Reflections on the Family." United Nations Office for Drug Control and Crime Prevention. Available from http://www.undcp.org/bulletin/bulletin_1994-01-01_1_page006.html#s010.

Eurocare. (2001). *Eurocare Country Profiles.* Available from www.eurocare.org.

Lane, J.; Gerstein, D.; Huang, L.; and Wright, D. (2001). "Risk and Protective Factors for Adolescent Drug Use: Findings from the 1997 National Household Survey on Drug Abuse." Substance Abuse and Mental Health Services Administration. Available from http://www.samhsa.gov/oas/nhsda/NAC97/report.htm#3.2.

MARK J. MACGOWAN
CHRISTOPHER P. RICE

SUBSTITUTE CAREGIVERS

Increases in the employment of mothers of young children have focused attention on the issue of substitute care (sometimes called *nonmaternal* care) of young children. In the United States, nearly 60 percent of all women with infants are in the paid labor force (Bachu and O'Connell 2000), and the majority of these children begin nonmaternal care prior to the age of four months for an average of thirty hours per week (NICHD Early Child Care Research Network 1997).

Who cares for these children while their mothers are at work? Substitute caregivers can be broadly grouped into two categories. *Familial* caregivers are related to the child. They include fathers—who in the United States are the primary care providers for about one-fifth of the children of employed mothers (Casper 1997)—grandparents, older siblings, aunts and uncles, and other relatives. Combined, almost half of all children of working mothers are cared for by some family member while the mother works (Smith 2000).

Nonfamilial caregivers are those who are not related to the child, and include group arrangements (preschool, nurseries, day care centers), in-home care (nannies, who care for about 9% of the children of employed mothers), and family day homes. Family day home providers are persons who care for a small number of children (usually fewer than six) in the provider's home. The family day home provider is not necessarily related to the child; the term *family day home* comes from the assumption that care provided in a small-group arrangement in a private home more nearly approximates the type of care the child would receive in his/her own home. Family day homes are often not licensed or regulated by government agencies. Such arrangements account for about one-fifth of all caregiver arrangements.

Although most concern about substitute care has been focused on group arrangements, only about 30 percent of children of employed mothers are cared for in group centers, preschools, and nurseries. In the United States, group centers are generally licensed by state agencies, which set regulations concerning such matters as safety, sanitation, and caregiver/child ratios. Such centers vary greatly in quality, caregiver training, physical facilities, and use of developmental and educational programs.

Effects of Substitute Care on Child Outcomes

There is an extensive literature examining the effects of early maternal employment and nonmaternal care on child cognitive outcomes. Results of these studies are mixed, but they generally suggest that there are no overall effects of maternal employment or nonmaternal care per se on child cognitive functioning (Greenstein 1995; NICHD Early Child Care Research Network 1997). However, the positive effects of early intervention programs on the cognitive functioning of economically disadvantaged children are well documented (Caughy et al. 1994).

Many researchers have studied the possible effects of substitute forms of child care on social development and behavioral problems (Clarke-Stewart 1989). It has been suggested that substitute care—particularly when these substitute forms are of low quality (Phillips et al. 1987; Howes 1990)—may be responsible for impairing social development or creating undesirable behavior such as aggression and noncompliance.

Research by social scientists in this area has centered on effects on emotional insecurity, sociability, and aggression. In particular, the emotional insecurity of children cared for in nonmaternal settings has been the focus of a hotly contested debate. Some researchers have found that infants of full-time employed mothers are more likely to be classified as insecurely attached than are infants of nonemployed mothers or mothers working part-time (see Belsky 1988 and Thompson 1991 for reviews; see Clarke-Stewart 1989 for a critique and meta-analysis). Jay Belsky (1988, p. 235), for example, has argued that "some nonmaternal care arrangements in the first year for more than 20 hours per week may be a risk factor in the emergence of developmental difficulties."

Many clinical studies suggest that children who had extensive nonmaternal care experiences as infants tend to be less compliant with their parents and more aggressive with their peers (Haskins 1985; Vaughn, Deane, and Waters 1985). However, Allison Clarke-Stewart (1989) suggests that these findings may simply reflect the fact that children in substitute care arrangements

> . . . think for themselves and that they want their own way. They are not willing to comply with adults' arbitrary rules. . . . Children who have spent time in day care, then, may be more demanding and independent, more disobedient and more aggressive, more bossy and bratty than children who stay at home because they want their own way and do not have the skills to achieve it smoothly, rather than because they are maladjusted. (p. 269)

There have been a number of studies investigating this issue both in Europe and in North America. In a study of Swedish first-borns, Margarita Prodromidis and colleagues (1995) concluded that child care arrangements were not associated with aggression or noncompliance. Anne I. H. Borge and Edward C. Melhuish's (1995) study of Norwegian children suggested that, based on parental perceptions, day care center experience was associated with a lower level of behavior problems. In Switzerland, Blaise Pierrehumbert and her colleagues (1996) found that the effect of nonparental care on behavior problems was mediated by the pattern of attachment to the mother, and that behavior problems were minimized when the child had extensive nonparental care, or when the care was provided by other family members.

In the United States, there have been a number of large-scale studies of the effects of maternal employment during early childhood and substitute care experiences on child emotional and cognitive outcomes. Summarizing his analyses of one- to four-year-olds from the National Longitudinal Survey of Youth (NLSY), Frank Mott (1991, p. 147) concluded that "extensive use of infant nonmaternal care did not either substantially enhance or negatively influence subsequent scores" on the *Memory for Location and Motor and Social Development* instruments. His analyses of effects on the *Peabody Picture Vocabulary Test,* however, suggest that use of group care arrangements during infancy may enhance cognitive abilities, especially among healthy female infants. Male infants, on the other hand, do not exhibit effects of care arrangement on this cognitive dimension.

Nazli Baydar and Jeanne Brooks-Gunn (1991) studied cognitive and behavioral outcomes for children who were three to four years of age. Some of their analyses show a small but significant negative effect of maternal employment during infancy, and suggest that different types of substitute care may affect boys differently from the way they affect girls.

Jay Belsky and David Eggebeen's (1991) study of two- to six-year-old children suggests that children whose mothers were employed during infancy may be less compliant than other children. Theodore Greenstein (1993) summarized his study of 1,657 NLSY children by concluding that "early and extensive maternal employment does not seem to have generally adverse effects on the behavior of 4- and 5-year-old children" (p. 349). In the National Institute of Child Health and Human Development (NICHD) study, which looked at 1,300 children at ten research sites across the United States, extensive time spent in nonmaternal care was associated with heightened behavioral problems at fourteen and fifty-four months of age (NICHD Early Child Care Research Network 2000, 2001).

In general, it appears that nonmaternal or substitute care in early childhood probably does not have a large effect on child development. In those studies in which differences between children cared for at home by their mothers and children with extensive nonmaternal care experiences are observed, the differences tend to be small. The determining factor seems to be the *quality* of the care received by the child; children who receive high-quality care and high levels of emotional support are likely to be well-adjusted, regardless of who the caregiver is. Conversely, children who are neglected or receive little emotional support will probably demonstrate problems of emotional adjustment.

See also: ANXIETY DISORDERS; ATTACHMENT: PARENT-CHILD RELATIONSHIPS; CAREGIVING: FORMAL; CAREGIVING: INFORMAL; CHILDCARE; CHRONIC ILLNESS; CONDUCT DISORDERS; COPARENTING; DEVELOPMENT: COGNITIVE; DEVELOPMENT: EMOTIONAL; ELDER ABUSE; FATHERHOOD; GRANDPARENTS' RIGHTS; HOSPICE; LATER LIFE FAMILIES; MOTHERHOOD; OPPOSITIONALITY; RESPITE CARE: ADULT; RESPITE CARE: CHILD; WORK AND FAMILY

Bibliography

Ainsworth, M.; Blehar, M.; Waters, E.; and Wall, S. (1988). *Patterns of Attachment: Observations in the Strange Situation and at Home.* Hillsdale, NJ: Erlbaum.

Bachu, A., and O'Connell, M. (2000). *Fertility of American Women: June 1998.* Washington, DC: U.S. Census Bureau.

Baydar, N., and Brooks-Gunn, J. (1991). "Effects of Maternal Employment and Child-Care Arrangements on Preschoolers' Cognitive and Behavioral Outcomes: Evidence from the Children of the National Longitudinal Survey of Youth." *Developmental Psychology* 27:932–945.

Belsky, J. (1988). "The 'Effects' of Infant Day Care Reconsidered." *Early Childhood Research Quarterly* 3:235–272.

Belsky, J. (1992). "Developmental Risks Associated with Infant Day Care: Attachment Insecurity, Noncompliance, and Aggression?" In *Psychosocial Issues In Day Care,* ed. S. S. Chehrazi. Washington, DC: American Psychiatric Press.

Belsky, J., and Eggebeen, D. (1991). "Early and Extensive Maternal Employment and Young Children's Socioemotional Development: Children of the National Longitudinal Survey of Youth." *Journal of Marriage and the Family* 53:1083–1110.

Borge, A. I. H., and Melhuish, E. C. (1995). "A Longitudinal Study of Childhood Behaviour Problems, Maternal Employment, and Day Care in a Rural Norwegian Community." *International Journal of Behavioral Development* 18:23–42.

Casper, L. M. (1997). *My Daddy Takes Care of Me! Fathers as Care Providers*. Washington, DC: U.S. Census Bureau.

Caughy, M. O'B.; DiPietro, J. A.; and Strobino, D. M. (1994). "Day-Care Participation as a Protective Factor in the Cognitive Development of Low-Income Children." *Child Development* 65:457–471.

Clarke-Stewart, K. A. (1989). "Infant Day Care: Maligned or Malignant?" *American Psychologist* 44:266–273.

Desai, S.; Chase-Lansdale, P. L.; and Michael, R. T. (1989). "Mother or Market? Effects of Maternal Employment on the Intellectual Ability of 4-Year-Old Children." *Demography* 26:545–561.

Greenstein, T. N. (1993). "Maternal Employment and Child Behavioral Outcomes: A Household Economics Analysis." *Journal of Family Issues* 14:323–354.

Greenstein, T. N. (1995). "Are the 'Most-Advantaged' Children Truly Disadvantaged by Early Maternal Employment?" *Journal of Family Issues* 16:149–169.

Haskins, R. (1985). "Public School Aggression among Children with Varying Day-Care Experience." *Child Development* 56:689–703.

Howes, C. (1990). "Can the Age of Entry and the Quality of Infant Child Care Predict Behaviors in Kindergarten?" *Developmental Psychology* 26:292–303.

Mott, F. L. (1991). "Developmental Effects of Infant Care: the Mediating Role of Gender and Health." *Journal of Social Issues* 47:139–158.

NICHD Early Child Care Research Network. (1997). "Mother-Child Interaction and Cognitive Outcomes Associated with Early Child Care: Results of the NICHD Study." Paper presented at the biennial meeting of the Society for Research on Child Development, Washington, DC.

NICHD Early Child Care Research Network. (2000). "Childcare in the First Year of Life." *Merrill-Palmer Quarterly* 43:340–360.

NICHD Early Child Care Research Network. (2001). "Early Childcare and Children's Development Prior to School Entry." Paper presented at the biennial meeting of the Society for Research in Child Development, Minneapolis, MN.

Phillips, D.; McCartney, K.; Scarr, S.; and Howes, C. (1987). "Selective Review of Infant Day Care Research: a Cause for Concern!" *Zero to Three* 7:18–21.

Pierrehumbert, B.; Ramstein, T.; Karmaniola, A.; and Halfon, O. (1996). "Child Care in the Preschool Years: Attachment, Behavior Problems, and Cognitive Development." *European Journal of Psychology of Education* 11:201–214.

Prodromidis, M.; Lamb, M. E.; Sternberg, K. J.; Hwang, C. P.; and Broberg, A. G. (1995). "Aggression and Noncompliance among Swedish Children in Center-Based Care, Family Day-Care, and Home Care." *International Journal of Behavioral Development* 18:43–62.

Smith, K. (2000). *Who's Minding the Kids? Child Care Arrangements, Fall 1995*. Washington, DC: U.S. Census Bureau.

Thompson, R. A. (1991). "Infant Day Care: Concerns, Controversies, Choices." In *Employed Mothers and Their Children,* ed. J. V. Lerner and N. L. Galambos. New York: Garland.

Vaughn, B.; Deane, K.; and Waters, E. (1985). "The Impact of Out-Of-Home Care on Child-Mother Attachment Quality: Another Look at Some Enduring Questions." *Monographs of the Society for Research in Child Development* 50:(1–2, Serial No. 209).

THEODORE N. GREENSTEIN

SUDDEN INFANT DEATH SYNDROME (SIDS)

Sudden Infant Death Syndrome (SIDS) was first defined in 1969 as "The sudden death of any infant or young child, which is unexpected by history, and in which a thorough post mortem examination fails to demonstrate an adequate cause for death" (Beckwith 1970, p. 18). New definitions have since been suggested, but they have not been internationally accepted (Guntheroth 1995; Byard 2001). The definition of SIDS has served to focus the attention of the world upon a largely unrecognized problem, to stimulate scientific research, and to increase support for the victims' families.

Current Knowledge of SIDS

It has been suggested that SIDS victims have some inherent weakness due to fetal influences or genetic make-up, which may only become obvious when he or she is subjected to stress during a vulnerable developmental period (Rognum 1995). Many consider SIDS to be due to many factors, not a specific disease process, but a lethal situation in which an infant succumbs from the additive effects of several factors (Byard 2001).

SIDS is an entity with no pathological findings at autopsy, that is, a diagnosis by exclusion. A few similarities are often found at autopsy, but these findings do not provide an explanation for death (Guntheroth 1995; Byard 2001). Externally, the infant appears well developed, and all the pathologist may find is a small amount of mucoid, watery, or bloody fluid in the nostrils. Internally, minute hemorrhagic spots (petecchiae) are seen on the surface of the thymus, lungs, and heart in approximately 75 percent of the cases. There is often evidence of a slight infection in the upper airways, as well as increased amounts of fluid (congestion and edema) and numerous cells (macrophages) in the air sacks of the lungs. Several conditions involving all organ systems may be responsible for sudden death in infants and small children that appear reasonably well prior to death. In investigating cases of suspected SIDS, the possibility of underlying illness, accident, or even homicide must be considered. If an adequate postmortem examination, including a review of the history and circumstances is not performed, the possibility of determining other causes of death may be lost.

In the 1990s, researchers have focused on the role of the immune system in SIDS. Many SIDS victims have shown signs of a slight infection prior to death, and there is often evidence of a subacute infection in the upper airways, or a slight cold. This has led to several studies of the involvement of infections and regulatory immune mechanisms in SIDS. The immune system undergoes rapid development during the first weeks and months of life and can trigger a reduction of oxygen to the blood (hypoxemia), resulting in a self-amplifying vicious circle that can result in death. A possible biochemical marker for hypoxic (insufficient oxygen reaching the infant) episodes prior to death from SIDS, hypoxanthine, has previously been identified (Rognum 1995).

The pathophysiology of SIDS remains unknown. Several studies have suggested possible abnormalities, such as respiratory pattern, arousal responses, temperature regulation, cardiac control, and autonomic function. Abnormalities in the way the nervous system regulates cardiorespiratory control or other autonomic functions provide perhaps the most compelling hypothesis (Hauck 2000).

Epidemiological research has shown modifiable and nonmodifiable factors to be associated with increased or decreased SIDS risk (Guntheroth 1995; Rognum 1995; Byard 2001). From the middle of the 1980s, several studies began to report an increased risk of SIDS attributed to prone sleeping (sleeping on the stomach). *Back to sleep* campaigns were launched in several countries, including Australia, the United States, Germany, France, and Italy, resulting in an immediate decrease in the SIDS rate. Prone sleeping is still a major risk factor for SIDS, as is side sleeping. Other sleep environment factors, such as soft bedding and the use of pillows, covering of the head or face, the use of duvets, and overheating, have also, alone or together with prone sleeping, been associated with increased risk of SIDS. At the beginning of the 1990s there was an increase reported in the risk of SIDS associated with bedsharing or co-sleeping with an adult. Such an association is still controversial.

Sociodemographic factors, such as lower socioeconomic status (measured by low income, unemployment, low education, and young maternal age) have consistently been shown to be associated with greater risk of SIDS. Risk differences are found among different races, with African Americans and indigenous populations in the United States, Australia, and New Zealand having the highest rates, and most Asian communities around the world the lowest. An age peak has been seen between two to four months of age; more males than females are affected;, and SIDS has been more common during the colder months of the year. Factors related to pregnancy have been shown to increase the risk of SIDS, such as higher birth order, lower birth weight, and short gestation period. Maternal smoking during pregnancy is consistently associated with risk of SIDS, often showing a dose-response effect; that is, the more a mother smokes, the greater the risk of SIDS for her infant. Smoking is perhaps the most important maternal risk factor and is viewed as the most important modifiable risk factor of SIDS altogether, after the reduction in prone sleeping. The use of illegal drugs is associated with a somewhat increased risk.

Several epidemiological studies into possible risk and/or protective factors of SIDS have concluded that pacifier use may protect against SIDS. As to the role of breastfeeding as a potential preventive measure against SIDS, studies have been inconclusive. At the end of the 1990s however, comparison of epidemiological characteristics before and after the decline in SIDS rate due to "back-to-sleep" campaigns disclosed significant changes in variables such as a reduction in the two to four month age peak and in the winter peak as well as increased risk with young maternal age, low socioeconomic status, and maternal smoking during pregnancy (Byard 2001). Understanding these changes, coupled with the effects of reducing modifiable factors, will probably reduce the SIDS rate further, and, it is hoped, eventually lead to an understanding of both the etiology and pathogenesis of SIDS.

Genetic factors have also been thought to play a role in SIDS with findings of a modest, but significantly increased, recurrence rate of SIDS in families (Guntheroth 1995; Hauck 2000; Byard 2001). Death from inherited metabolic disorders has been proposed as the cause of death in a small number of SIDS cases. The long-QT syndrome, a cardiac arrhythmia that can cause sudden death, is another inherited disorder proposed as the cause of death in some cases of SIDS.

How SIDS Affects the Family

Suddenness of a loss is particularly stressful to survivors and may lead to long-lasting family crisis. The suddenness of the death of an apparently well infant leaves the family with no opportunity to gradually accept the loss (Guntheroth 1995). Studies have shown that grief in SIDS decreases over time, but a considerable number of parents are still actively dealing with the loss throughout the first year. Men and women grieve differently, and the loss can have an effect on the marriage; some are strengthened, and some end in divorce. Other family members and siblings are affected by the loss. According to SIDS parents, their lives are never the same, and this may be reflected through changes in educational or vocational paths. Many have gotten involved in local, national, or international SIDS organizations in an effort to bring support to recently bereaved families and to promote education and awareness of SIDS to the general public. When a loss such as SIDS occurs, the bereaved frequently search for meaning in the event and for the cause. And in pursuit of the cause, self-accusation is frequent. Although research results can, for some, increase this feeling of guilt, most enthusiastically support research through personal donations or fundraising efforts. It is a way to keep the memory alive and to help find an answer to the SIDS enigma (Byard 2001).

See also: CHILDHOOD, STAGES OF: INFANCY; DEATH AND DYING; GRIEF, LOSS, AND BEREAVEMENT

Bibliography

Beckwith, J. B. (1970). "Discussion of Terminology and Definition of the Sudden Infant Death Syndrome." In *Sudden Infant Death Dyndrome. Proceedings of the Second International Conference on the Causes of Sudden Death in Infants,* ed. A. B. Bergman, J. B. Beckwith, and C. G. Ray. Seattle: University of Washington Press.

Byard, R. W., and Krous, H. F. (2001). *Sudden Infant Death Syndrome: Problems, Progress and Possibilities.* London: Arnold.

Hauck, F. R., and Hunt, C. E. (2000). "Sudden Infant Death Syndrome in 2000." *Current Problems in Pediatrics* 30(8):237–261.

Guntheroth, W. G. (1995). *Crib Death: The Sudden Infant Death Syndrome.* 3rd edition. Armonk, NY: Futura Publishing.

Rognum, T. O. (1995). *Sudden Infant Death Syndrome. New Trends in the Nineties.* Oslo: Scandinavian University Press.

Other Resources

SIDS International. Available from http://www.sidsinternational.minerva.com.au.

MARIANNE ARNESTAD

SUICIDE

The word *suicide* covers a wide range of behaviors, including (1) *completed suicide;* in which the individual dies as a result of the self-destructive act; (2) *attempted suicide,* in which the individual survives the act; and (3) *suicidal ideation,* which refers to the individual thinking about and planning suicidal behavior, but not putting these thoughts into action.

A controversy exists over the term *attempted suicide.* Because many of the individuals who survive a suicidal action did not intend to die (for example, they may have intentionally taken only half of a lethal dose of a medication), some scholars object to the term. Europeans suggested *parasuicide* as an alternative, especially for suicide attempts of low lethality, but in recent years the terms *self-injury* and *self-poisoning* have become popular.

The Epidemiology of Suicide

Completed suicide rates vary widely by nation. According to the latest figures available from the

World Health Organization, rates in the 1990s ranged from thirty to forty per 100,000 per year for Belarus, Estonia, Hungary, Kazakhstan, Latvia, Lithuania, Russia, Slovenia, and the Ukraine to zero to five per 100,000 per year for Armenia, Greece, and Thailand. National rates of attempted suicide are not available, but it is estimated that there may be eight to ten attempts at suicide for every completed suicide.

Completed suicide rates are higher in men than in women in every country except for mainland China, where the female suicide rate exceeds the male suicide rate (Phillips, Liu, and Zhang 1999). However, in every nation, female rates of attempted suicide exceed those for men in the small samples that have been studied.

Completed suicide rates rise with age in men, but in women the peak age for suicide varies with the level of economic development in the nation. Female suicide rates peak in middle age in the most developed nations, but in young women in the least developed nations (Girard 1993). In general, attempted suicides are younger than completed suicides.

In the United States, whites and American Indians have the highest completed suicide rates, whereas Filipino Americans have the lowest rates. African Americans, Chinese Americans and Japanese Americans have intermediate rates (Lester 1998). These ethnic differences in the United States match those in other nations. For example, in Zimbabwe and South Africa, whites have higher completed suicide rates than blacks, and Philippine suicide rates are lower than the rates in China and Japan.

Theories of Suicide

Research into why individuals become suicidal has identified psychiatric disturbance as the strongest predictor of future suicidality. In particular, *depression,* both unipolar and bipolar, is associated with the greatest suicidal risk, and even in schizophrenics and substances abusers, both groups with high rates of suicide, depression is the strongest predictor of which individuals in those groups will complete suicide (Maris, Berman, and Silverman 2000). Among the components of depression, the cognitive component, which has been called *pessimism* and *hopelessness* by Aaron Beck and his colleagues (1979), is a more powerful predictor than the somatic components of depression (such as loss of appetite) or the mood symptoms (such as guilt).

Suicidal individuals are found to have experienced a high level of stress for a long period of time, and often have an increasing level in the time leading up to their suicidal action. In addition, suicidal individuals are found to have few resources, and the resources that they have are often unavailable (Lester 2000). For example, the people available to turn to for help may be resented by the suicidal person, or the resources may be hostile toward the suicidal person.

The family plays a critical role in each of these factors. Physiological and psychological theories of psychiatric disorder stress the role of the parents, either in passing on the genes for the disorder (in physiological theories) or in creating a pathological home environment (in psychological theories) (Maris, Berman, Silverman 2000). Family members are often the cause of much of the stress that suicidal individuals experience, and they are the resources that may be unavailable to the suicidal individual.

Sociological theories of suicide attempt to explain the suicide rates of cultures or regions. They have focused on the role of social disorganization (*social integration* and *social regulation* in Durkheim's theory—see below) or in the opportunity to blame others for one's misfortunes rather than oneself (Henry and Short 1954). For example, African Americans have been oppressed by the racism in U.S. society and so have a clear source of blame for their misery, whereas white Euro Americans have been the oppressors. African Americans have higher murder rates whereas whites have higher suicide rates, in line with this argument.

Marital Status and the Family

Marital status has a strong association with rates of completed suicide. Suicide rates are higher in the divorced and widowed than in single people, who in turn have higher suicide rates than married people. This protective effect of marriage on suicide is stronger for men than for women, although it is found for both men and women (Gove 1972).

The strong association of divorce with suicide is found at the societal level as well as at the individual level. For example, nations with higher divorce rates have higher suicide rates, U.S. states with higher divorce rates have higher suicide rates and, within nations, years with higher divorce rates have higher suicide rates. This association is probably the most robust association found in suicidology. The associations between marriage rates and suicide rates and between birth rates and suicide rates are not as consistent, although they do tend to be negative associations more often than positive associations.

These associations fit well with the classic sociological theory of suicide proposed by Emile Durkheim (1897). Durkheim proposed that suicide would be common where the level of social integration—the extent to which the members of a society are bound together in social networks—was high (leading to *altruistic suicide*) or low (leading to *egoistic suicide*), and where the level of social regulation—the extent to which the behaviors and desires of the members of the society conform to social rules and norms—was high (leading to *fatalistic suicide*) or low (leading to *anomic suicide*).

Modern sociologists have argued that altruistic and fatalistic suicide are rare in modern societies and that it is hard to measure social integration separately from social regulation (Johnson 1965). Thus, they propose that suicide varies inversely with the level of social integration/regulation.

The association between divorce rates and suicide rates has two interpretations. *Composition theory* argues that because suicide rates are higher in divorced individuals, societies with a greater proportion of divorced people will necessarily have a higher suicide rate.

However, looking at the United States, divorce rates are strongly associated over the states with interstate migration rates, alcohol consumption, and low church attendance. Thus, these variables form a cluster of related social indicators, and they perhaps tap some broad, abstract quality of society: perhaps *social disorganization* is an appropriate term. This broad social characteristic has an effect on all of the members of the society, not just the divorced, the alcohol abusers, or the migrants.

Christopher Cantor and Penelope Slater (1995) found that the suicide rate in Queensland, Australia, was highest for men who were separated, as opposed to men who were single, married, divorced, or widowed. For women, the divorced had the highest suicide rate. The increase in the suicide rate in separated men was greater in those who were younger (age 15–19) than in those who were older (over the age of 55). These results suggest that the time during the breakdown in the marriage may be more stressful for men than for women, whereas the state of divorce may be stressful for both men and women.

The higher rate of suicide in widows as compared to those married of the same may be because bereavement increases the risk of suicide or because widows and widowers who are prone to suicide are less likely to get remarried. Some old data from Brian MacMahon and Thomas Pugh (1965) indicate that it is bereavement—and not differential remarriage rates—that is the factor responsible. However, research (for example, a study by Arne Mastekaasa [1993] in Norway) also indicates that, once age is taken into account, the higher suicide rate in the widowed as compared to the divorced is no longer found.

Even though those who are married have lower suicide rates than those in other marital statuses, Walter Gove (1972) has documented that marriage is more beneficial for men than for women, in that the reduction in the suicide rate (and also in rates of psychiatric disturbance) is greater for married men than for married women.

The Protective Effect of Children

The presence of children appears to have a protective effect with regard to suicide. In a study of a large sample of women in Norway, Georg Hoyer and Eiliv Lund (1993) obtained a sample of almost one million single and married women in Norway in 1970 and identified which of them had completed suicide by 1985. They found that unmarried women had a higher suicide rate than married women without children for those aged twenty-five to sixty-four, but not for those over the age of sixty-four. Thus, marriage appeared to reduce the suicide rate in women.

Hoyer and Lund also found that married women with children had lower suicide rates than married women with no children for all age groups. Thus, the presence of children further reduces the risk of suicide in women above and beyond the protective impact of marriage per se. Furthermore, the more children, the lower the suicide rate of the married women.

This study is the best study on the topic reported hitherto, but it confirms the results of earlier studies on smaller samples and without such detailed analyses. For example, in Portugal women with children were found to have a lower suicide rate than childless women, and those with more than five children had the lowest suicide rate (de Castro and Martins 1987).

There is also some evidence that the presence of children reduces the severity of suicidality in suicidal women, for example, making attempted suicide relatively less common and suicidal ideation relatively more common.

The Disturbing Effects of Families

Although the presence of children may protect their parents from suicide, the parents may increase the risk of suicide in the children. Even sibling position may play a role, as Alfred Adler (1958) suggested, with completed suicide being less common in last-borns and attempted suicide less common in first borns (Lester 2000).

Although in general, having a spouse and children reduces the risk of suicide, family members can play a role in precipitating suicide. For example, often family members feel and express a great deal of hostility toward one another. In *psychic homicide,* an individual commits suicide in response to the conscious or unconscious murderous impulses for them (Meerloo 1962). The role of murderous desires of parents toward their offspring may play a greater role in adolescent suicides than in the suicides of older adults. Transactional analysis has proposed that suicidal individuals had parents who experienced these desires (such as "I wish you had never been born") during the baby's first year of life.

It is difficult to show these effects with research, but the hostility has been observed at the time of the suicidal behavior. For example, Milton Rosenbaum and Joseph Richman (1970) in their study of attempted suicides reported a mother's first statement to her 24-year-old son in the hospital, "Next time pick a higher bridge." Or a wife whose 70-year-old husband said to her, "If I had a gun, I'd shoot myself," replied, "I'll buy you a gun." He used pills a few days later instead. A father said to his 17-year-old daughter, "We'd all be better off if you were dead. At least we'd know where you are."

There are many features of family life that impact on suicidal behavior. Abuse of children, both physically and sexually, appears to result in an increase in later suicidal behavior as well as other psychiatric disorders and symptoms.

Loss of parents during childhood, especially between the ages of six and sixteen, increases the risk of suicide. David Lester (1989) found that exactly half of a sample of famous suicides, for whom detailed biographies were available, had experienced such loss, such as the poet Sylvia Plath whose father died of natural causes when she was eight. If the parent dies from suicide, then suicide is even more likely in the children.

In general, research finds that married couples in which one partner attempts suicide have poorer communication between each other and more destructive conflicts (such as avoiding discussion and fleeing the home), and that the suicidal partner is more psychiatrically disturbed (Lester 2000).

Suicidal behavior in family members increases the risk of suicide in other family members, perhaps because this indicates a greater acceptance of suicidal behavior as a solution to problems in that family, or perhaps because the occurrence of suicide in many family members indicates the presence of an inherited psychiatric disorder. In the Hemingway family, for example, Ernest's father completed suicide, and so did three of his six children (including Ernest, of course). It is likely that an affective disorder was passed down in this family, but also completing suicide in middle age when suffering from severe medical problems appears to have become a learned strategy in the family.

However, this *copycat* (or *contagion*) effect is also found in social groups. A suicide in an adolescent is occasionally followed by "imitation" suicides among his or her peers (Maris, Berman, and Silverman 2000), and in these cases inheritance does not play a role.

Helping Suicidal Individuals

The most common tactic for suicidal individuals is to treat the underlying psychiatric disturbance using medication and psychotherapy. In recent years, the increasing prescribing of antidepressants appears to have resulted in a decline in suicide rates (Isacsson 2000). In addition, effective psychotherapies have been devised for suicidal individuals (Linehan 1993), and many countries now have networks of telephone crisis centers, functioning twenty-four hours a day, seven days a week, for individuals to call during times when they are most distressed (Mishara and Daigle 2001).

However, because interpersonal factors are often involved in precipitating and maintaining the suicidality of people, family therapy is perhaps the most appropriate format for psychotherapy for suicidal individuals. Joseph Richman (1986) has been the leading advocate of this approach.

Problems for Survivors

Those who experience the suicide of a significant other are known as *survivors*. Survivors have great difficulty coping with the death, perhaps more so than those whose significant others die of natural causes. In some cases, it is the family members who discover the body of the suicide, often greatly disfigured by the suicide. For example, Leicester Hemingway, Ernest's brother, was only thirteen when he found his father dead from a firearm wound. Leicester was one of the three children who later completed suicide.

Furthermore, the grieving process after a suicide is different in significant ways from the grieving after natural deaths. There is more anger felt toward the suicide and guilt over what the survivors might have done to prevent the suicide. Group therapy is particularly helpful for survivors whether led by peers or by professionals (Farberow 2001).

In recent years, survivors have banded together to form organizations to help one another and to work for the prevention of suicide in general. There are survivor groups in many countries and, in some countries, in every region. In the United States, the *American Association of Suicidology* maintains a directory of these services and, internationally, *Befrienders International* has services (usually under the name *The Samaritans*) in more than forty countries.

Many countries have networks of telephone crisis centers, such as this one, staffed by volunteers. The crisis centers function twenty-four hours a day, seven days a week, for individuals to call during times when they are most distressed. MARY KATE DENNY/PHOTO EDIT

See also: CHILDHOOD, STAGES OF: ADOLESCENCE; DEATH AND DYING; DEPRESSION: ADULTS; DEPRESSION: CHILDREN AND ADOLESCENTS; EUTHANASIA; GRIEF, LOSS, AND BEREAVEMENT; RAPE; SELF-ESTEEM; WIDOWHOOD

Bibliography

Adler, A. (1958). "Suicide." *Journal of Individual Psychology* 14:57–61.

Beck, A. T.; Rush, A. J.; Shaw, B. F.; and Emery, G. (1979). *Cognitive Therapy of Depression*. New York: Guilford.

Cantor, C. H., and Slater, P. J. (1995). "Marital Breakdown, Parenthood, and Suicide." *Journal of Family Studies* 1:91–102.

de Castro, E. F., and Martins, I. (1987). "The Role of Female Autonomy in Suicide among Portuguese Women." *Acta Psychiatrica Scandinavica* 75:337–343.

Durkheim, E. (1897). *Le Suicide*. Paris: Felix Alcan.

Farberow, N. L. (2001). "Helping Suicide Survivors." In *Suicide Prevention: Resources for the Millennium,* ed. D. Lester. Philadelphia: Brunner-Routledge.

Girard, C. (1993). "Age, Gender, and Suicide." *American Sociological Review* 58:553–574.

Gove, W. (1972). "Sex, Marital Status and Suicide." *Journal of Health and Social Behavior* 13:204–213.

Henry, A. F., and Short, J. F. (1954). *Suicide and Homicide*. New York: Free Press.

Hoyer, G., and Lund, E. (1993). "Suicide among Women Related to Number of Children in Marriage." *Archives of General Psychiatry* 50:134–137.

Isacsson, G. (2000). "Suicide Prevention: A Medical Breakthrough?" *Acta Psychiatrica Scandinavica* 102: 113–117.

Johnson, B. D. (1965). "Durkheim's One Cause of Suicide." *American Sociological Review* 30:875–886.

Lester, D. (1989). "Experience of Personal Loss and Later Suicide." *Acta Psychiatrica Scandinavica* 79:450–452.

Lester, D. (1998). *Suicide in African Americans.* Commack, NY: Nova Science.

Lester, D. (2000). *Why People Kill Themselves,* 4th edition. Springfield, IL: Charles C. Thomas.

Linehan, M. M. (1993). *Cognitive-Behavioral Therapy of Borderline Personality Disorder.* New York: Guilford.

MacMahon, B., and Pugh, T. F. (1965). "Suicide in the Widowed." *American Journal of Epidemiology* 81:23–31.

Maris, R. W.; Berman, A. L.; and Silverman, M. M. (2000). *Comprehensive Textbook of Suicidology.* New York: Guilford.

Mastekaasa, A. (1993). "Marital Status and Subjective Well-Being." *Social Indicators Research* 29:249–276.

Meerloo, J. A. M. (1962). *Suicide and Mass Suicide.* New York: Grune and Stratton.

Mishara, B., and Daigle, M. (2001). "Helplines and Crisis Intervention Services." In *Suicide Prevention: Resources for the Millennium,* ed. D. Lester. Philadelphia: Brunner-Routledge.

Phillips, M. R.; Liu, H. Q.; and Zhang, Y. P. (1999). Suicide and Social Change in China. *Culture, Medicine and Psychiatry* 23:25–50.

Richman, J. (1986). *Family Therapy for Suicidal People.* New York: Springer.

Rosenbaum, M., and Richman, J. (1970). "Suicide: The Role of Hostility and Death Wishes from the Family and Significant Others." *American Journal of Psychiatry* 126:1652–1655.

Other Resources

American Association of Suicidology. (2002). Available from http://www.suicidology.org.

World Health Organization. (2002). Available from www.who.int.

DAVID LESTER

SURROGACY

Surrogate motherhood is one of many currently available forms of Assisted Reproductive Technologies (ARTs) that have developed in response to the increasing number of individuals/couples who find themselves unable to conceive a child on their own. Surrogate motherhood involves the services of a woman who agrees to carry/gestate a child for the express purpose of surrendering that child to the intending/commissioning couple upon the birth of the child. The demand for surrogate motherhood is created by a diagnosis of female infertility, although a woman need not be infertile in order to employ the services of a surrogate. Factors that have contributed to the popularization of surrogate motherhood and other reproductive technologies are both medical and social in nature. In the United States there are reportedly two to three million infertile couples (Office of Technology Assessment 1988). A diagnosis of infertility is defined as the inability of a heterosexual couple to produce a pregnancy after one year of regular intercourse, that is, unprotected intercourse (Stangel 1979). The social factors that have contributed to the rise in the rates of infertility and that have resulted in an increase in the demand for reproductive technologies are the trend toward later marriages and the tendency for growing numbers of women to delay having children until later in their reproductive years. With advances in reproductive medicine, couples who would not have been able to reproduce in the past are now able to have children who are completely or partially genetically related to them.

Approximately 35 percent of couples who choose surrogacy have either attempted or considered *adoption* (Ragoné 1994). The majority of those who eventually choose surrogacy view the adoption process as one that is riddled with problems and that has been, in most cases, unable to provide them with a suitable child (Ragoné 2000). For example, in 1983, 50,000 adoptions were completed in the United States, but an estimated two million couples were still seeking to adopt (Office of Technology Assessment 1988).

Historically, there have been three profound shifts in the Western conceptualization of the categories of conception, reproduction, and parenthood. The first occurred in response to the separation of intercourse from reproduction through birth control methods. A second shift occurred in response to the emergence of assisted reproductive technologies and to the subsequent fragmentation of the unity of reproduction, when it became possible for pregnancy to occur without necessarily having been "preceded by sexual intercourse" (Snowden, Snowden, and Snowden 1983). The third shift occurred in response to further advances in reproductive medicine that called into question the "organic unity of fetus and mother" (Martin 1987). It was not, however, until the emergence of reproductive medicine that the fragmentation of motherhood become a reality; with that historical change, what was once the "single figure of the mother is dispersed among, several potential figures, as the functions of maternal procreation—aspects of her physical parenthood—become dispersed" (Strathern 1991). It is now possible for five separate individuals to claim parenthood in a given situation: the woman who contributes an ovum (*genetic mother*), the woman who gestates the child (*gestational mother*), the intending mother (the *social mother*/the woman who will raise the child and may also gestate the child), the sperm donor (*genetic father*) and the intending father (the *social father*/the man who will raise the child).

During the early 1980s, all surrogate motherhood arrangements (*traditional surrogacy,* in which the child was genetically related to the husband only) involved the union of the husband's sperm and the surrogate's ovum. Since 1994, however, over 50 percent of all surrogates are *gestational,* in other words, the surrogate gestates the couples' embryos (providing them with a child that may be genetically related to both wife and husband). However, one should not assume that it is the intending father's sperm or the intending mother's ovum that creates the embryo; the ovum may have been procured through ovum donation then mixed with the husband's sperm. Should a couple use the intending father's sperm, donor ova, and a gestational surrogate, the couple will have the same genetic relationship to the child as that provided by traditional surrogacy (i.e., a genetic tie for the father only). However, one of the reasons cited for choosing gestational surrogacy is consumer choice; specifically, couples who choose the route of donor ova plus gestational surrogacy rather than traditional surrogacy have a significantly greater number of ovum donors from which to choose.

Contexualizing Surrogacy

Many individuals view surrogate motherhood as a positive addition to the ever-expanding range of technologies now available as remedies for infertility. Others, however, view it as symptomatic of the dissolution of the traditional/nuclear U.S. family and the sanctity of motherhood, as something structurally akin to prostitution that reduces or assigns women to a breeder class (Dworkin 1978), or as a form of commercial baby selling (Annas 1988; Neuhaus 1988).

The opinion among both scholars and the general population that surrogates are motivated primarily by financial gain has tended to result in oversimplified analyses of surrogate motivations. In surrogate mother programs surrogates receive on average between $10,000 and $15,000 (for three to four months of insemination and nine months of pregnancy), a fee that has changed only nominally since the early 1980s. Although surrogates do accept (and appreciate/value to varying degrees) monetary compensation for their reproductive work, the role of this compensation is a multifaceted one. The surrogate pregnancy, unlike a traditional pregnancy, is viewed by the surrogate and her family as work, and surrogates rarely spend the money they earn on themselves. The majority spend the money on their children, for example, as a contribution to their college education funds, whereas others spend it on home improvement, gifts for their husbands, a family vacation, or simply to pay off family debts.

One of the principal reasons that most surrogates do not spend the money they earn on themselves alone appears to stem from the fact that the money serves as a buffer against and/or reward to their families, in particular to their husbands who must make a number of compromises as a result of the surrogate arrangement. One of these compromises is obligatory abstention from sexual intercourse from the time insemination begins until a pregnancy has been confirmed (a period of time that is an average of three to four months in length, but that may be extended for as long as one year). Surrogates embrace the *gift formulation,* which holds particular appeal because it reinforces the idea that having a child for someone is an act that cannot be compensated monetarily (Ragoné 1994, 1996, 1999, 2000).

Cultural/Legal Implications

The United States is unquestionably the world's leader in availability of surrogacy arrangements. Britain, for example, implemented a ban against *commercial surrogacy*—in other words, any arrangement in which a surrogate receives payment for her services. On the other hand, Israel permits commercial surrogacy but the *Embryo*

Carrying Agreements Law (1996) advances the position that a "severe effort" be made to permit only unmarried women to serve as surrogates because it is reasoned that allowing married women to serve as surrogates would violate culturally prescribed definitions and norms about kinship, the status of the child that is born, and family (Kahn 2000). This position stands in contrast to U.S. arrangements in which established surrogate mother programs typically insist that their surrogates be either married or in a committed relationship. They also require surrogates to have children of their own in order to discourage them from wanting to keep the child. Programs reason that an unmarried woman who has never had children is much more likely to want to keep a child produced through surrogacy than a married woman with children of her own (see Ragoné 1994, 1996, 1998).

From the couple's perspective, surrogacy is conceptualized not as a radical departure from tradition but as an attempt to achieve a traditional and acceptable end: to have a child who is biologically related to at least one of them—that is, traditional surrogacy. In the gestational surrogacy arrangement, the child may be related to both the mother and father. This idea is consistent with the emphasis on the primacy of the blood tie in EuroAmerican kinship ideology and the importance of family. One of the most interesting aspects of a surrogate's perception of the fetus she is carrying is that it is not her child. This belief holds true whether the child is produced with her genetic contribution (50% in traditional surrogacy and, of course, in a traditional pregnancy) or not genetically related to her at all, as in gestational surrogacy. It will be interesting to learn whether the Israeli policy, which allows only unmarried women to serve as surrogates, will result in an increase in the number of surrogates wanting to keep the child(ren) they produce.

Because of the liberal policies and efficient programs available in the United States, couples routinely travel from abroad to participate in surrogate motherhood arrangements. The growing prevalence of gestational surrogacy has introduced a host of new legal and social questions, especially concerning a recent legal precedent in which a surrogate who does not contribute an ovum toward the creation of a child has a significantly reduced possibility of being awarded custody of the child.

But not all gestational surrogacy arrangements involve the couple's embryos; numerous cases involve the combination of donor ova and the intending father's semen. Why, then, do couples pursue gestational surrogacy when traditional surrogacy (with the surrogate providing the ova) provides them with the same degree of genetic linkage to the child, has a higher likelihood of being successful, and costs less? Several reasons were cited by members of the staff of the largest surrogate mother program in the world, the primary one being that many more women are willing to donate ova than are willing to serve as traditional surrogate mothers.

The second reason, as previously mentioned, is that the U.S. courts would, in theory, be less likely to award custody to a gestational surrogate. The growing prevalence of gestational surrogacy is, in part, guided by recent legal precedents in which a surrogate who does not contribute an ovum toward the creation of the child has a significantly reduced possibility of being awarded custody in the event that she reneges on her contract and attempts to retain custody of the child. However, although legal factors have certainly contributed to the meteoric rise in the rates of gestational surrogacy, it should be remembered that for couples the ability to create a child genetically related to both parents is the primary reason that gestational surrogacy continues to grow in popularity.

In June 1993, in a precedent-setting decision, the California Supreme Court upheld lower and appellate court decisions with respect to a gestational surrogacy contract. In *Anna Johnson v. Mark and Crispina Calvert* (SO 23721), a case involving an African-American gestational surrogate, a Filipina-American mother, and a EuroAmerican father, the gestational surrogate and commissioning couple both filed custody suits. Under California law, both of the women could, however, claim maternal rights: Johnson, by virtue of being the woman who gave birth to the child, and Calvert, who donated the ovum, because she is the child's genetic mother. In rendering its decision, however, the court circumvented the issue of relatedness, instead emphasizing the *intent* of the parties as the ultimate and decisive factor in any determination of parenthood. The court concluded that if the genetic and birth mother are not one and the same person, then "she who intended to procreate the child—that is, she who intended to bring about the birth of a child that she intended to raise as her own—is the natural mother under California law."

Perhaps most important, when commissioning couples choose to use donor ova and gestational surrogacy, they sever the surrogate's genetic link to and/or claim to the child, whereas in the traditional surrogacy arrangement the adoptive mother must emphasize the importance of nurturance and social parenthood while the surrogate mother deemphasizes her biological and genetic ties to the child in order to strengthen the adoptive mother's relationship to the child.

An additional reason for choosing gestational surrogacy, and one that is of critical importance, is that couples from certain racial, ethnic, and religious groups (such as Japanese, Taiwanese, and Jewish couples) in the past often experienced great difficulty locating surrogates from their own groups. They were, however, able to find suitable ovum donors. Thus, couples from various ethnic/cultural, racial, or religious groups who are seeking donors from those groups often pursue ovum donation and gestational surrogacy. Gestational surrogates reason that they (unlike traditional surrogates and ovum donors) do not part with any genetic material, and they are thus able to deny that the child(ren) they produce are related to them. Ovum donors however do not perceive their donation of genetic material as problematic. Why women from different cultural groups are willing to donate ova but not serve as surrogates is a subject deserving of further study.

In conclusion, it can be said that all the participants involved in the surrogacy process wish to attain traditional ends, and are therefore willing to set aside their reservations about the means by which parenthood is attained. Placing surrogacy inside of tradition, they attempt to circumvent some of the more difficult issues raised by the surrogacy process. In this way, programs and participants pick and choose among U.S. cultural values about family, parenthood, and reproduction, now choosing biological relatedness, now nurture, according to their needs.

See also: ASSISTED REPRODUCTIVE TECHNOLOGIES; FATHERHOOD; FERTILITY; GAY PARENTS; LESBIAN PARENTS; MOTHERHOOD

Bibliography

Annas, G. (1988). "Fairy Tales Surrogate Mothers Tell." In *Surrogate Motherhood: Politics and Privacy,* ed. L. Gostin. Bloomington: Indiana University Press.

Dworkin, A. (1978). *Right Wing Women.* New York: Perigee Books.

Kahn, S. (2000). *Reproducing Jews: A Cultural Account of Assisted Conception in Israel.* Durham, NC: Duke University Press.

Martin, E. (1987). *The Woman in the Body: A Cultural Analysis of Reproduction.* Boston: Beacon Press.

Neuhaus, R. (1988). "Renting Women, Buying Babies and Class Struggles." *Society* 25(3):8–10.

Office of Technology Assessment. (1988). *Infertility: Medical and Social Choices.* Washington, DC: Government Printing Office.

Ragoné, H. (1994). *Surrogate Motherhood: Conception in the Heart.* Boulder, CO: Westview Press.

Ragoné, H. (1996). "Chasing the Blood Tie: Surrogate Mothers, Adoptive Mothers and Fathers." *American Ethnologist* 23(2):352–365.

Ragoné, H. (1998). "Incontestable Motivations." In *Reproducing Reproduction: Kinship, Power, and Technological Innovation,* ed. S. Franklin and H. Ragoné. Philadelphia: University of Pennsylvania Press.

Ragoné, H. (1999). "The Gift of Life: Surrogate Motherhood, Gamete Donations and Constructions of Altruism." In *Transformative Mothering: On Giving and Getting in a Consumer Culture,* ed. L. Layne. New York: New York University Press.

Ragoné, H. (2000). "Of Likeness and Difference: How Race is Being Transfigured by Gestational Surrogacy." In *Ideologies and Technologies of Motherhood: Race, Class, Sexuality and Nationalism,* ed. H. Ragoné and F. W. Twine. New York: Routledge.

Snowden, R. G.; Snowden, M.; and Snowden, E. (1983). *Artificial Reproduction: A Social Investigation.* London: Allen and Unwin.

Stangel, J. (1979). *The New Fertility and Conception.* New York: Plume Books.

Strathern, M. (1991). "The Pursuit of Certainty: Investigating Kinship in the Late Twentieth Century." Paper presented at the American Anthropological Association meeting, Chicago.

HELÉNA RAGONÉ

SWEDEN

See SCANDINAVIA

SWITZERLAND

Switzerland is a highly *segmented society*. Marital behavior, divorce, and fertility have varied significantly by language regions and religious denomination. In addition, regional differences in family law and social policies, which are strong due to the far-reaching autonomy of the cantons (administrative and geographic units analogous to states or provinces), have played an important role in this respect (Sommer and Höpflinger 1989; Fux 2002a).

Switzerland can be characterized by its early modernization of family and household structures as well as of marital and reproductive behavior. Socioeconomic and cultural factors favored the early demographic shift to the nuclear family. The same conditions probably influenced the early diffusion of contraception (Fux 2002a). *Marriage rates* were significantly lower than they were in most other European countries from the nineteenth century up to the 1980s. Since then, first marriage rates have tended to converge with those of the other European countries.

Switzerland has always had comparatively high ages at marriage and high proportions of people remaining single. Differences among countries in men's and women's ages at first marriage and mother's age at first birth have grown in recent years. In 1999, the mean age of women at first marriage was 27.7 years. The divorce rate in the past was continuously higher than the European average, possibly because of comparatively liberal divorce law. Since the 1970s, Switzerland's divorce rates have tended to become more like those of other European countries. However, a total divorce rate of 50 per 100 initial marriages in 1999 is still one of the highest in Europe.

The rise and fall of marital birth rates in Switzerland follows the European average very closely (Lüscher and Engstler 1991; Fux 1994). Total fertility rates fluctuated at 1.5 (1999). In 1999, the age at first birth stood at 28.5 years and the mean age at childbearing (any child) at 29.7 years. By contrast, out-of-wedlock births have remained constant at a comparatively low level. No more than 10 out of 100 births were registered as extramarital. The number of couples remaining childless, however, is rapidly increasing. Among all (married and unmarried) women born in 1963, 27.9 percent remain childless. This is one of the highest rates in Europe (Fux and Baumgartner 2000).

Pragmatic accommodation strategies rather than fundamentally conservative behavior and beliefs reflect what might appear to be conflicting trends: Families in Switzerland were early adopters of modern family and household structure but also retained traditional values and attitudes. Switzerland's particular characteristics are influenced by several factors. First, couples have to accommodate barriers produced by a lean welfare state that force them to find individual solutions for the organization of family life (Coenen-Huther et al. 1994; Fux 1997, 2001b; Fux and Baumgartner 2002). The welfare state also influences the low rate of out-of-wedlock births and the comparatively high and increasing age at marriage and at first births, as well as the increasing celibacy and proportion of couples remaining childless.

Households and Families

Families in Switzerland are confronted with a changing temporal organization of the life course. Under current conditions, people, particularly those between the ages of twenty and thirty, decide more or less on their own in what order they will make important changes in their lives, such as leaving the parental home, starting a partnership or marriage, or becoming a parent. This is related to the emergence of new phases in the life course, such as singlehood or the premarital stage. Consequently, the proportion of one-person households doubled from 14.2 percent in 1960 to 32.4 percent in 1990.

A rapid spread of new living arrangements has also become evident. In particular, unmarried cohabitation became very popular. In 1995, cohabitation rates stood as follows: 25 percent of people between the ages of twenty and twenty-four were cohabiting; 20 percent of people between twenty-five and twenty-nine; 11 percent of people between the ages of thirty and thirty-four; and 7 percent of the group between the ages of thirty-five and thirty-nine. In international comparisons, Switzerland is ranked in the upper quartile out of a sample of nineteen countries. However, few couples with children cohabitant. Parenthood is still a strong motivation to marry. For birth cohorts from 1955 onwards, unmarried cohabitation is the first step in partnership formation for more than 60 percent of the population (Fux and Baumgartner 1998).

Single parenthood is rare (in 1960, 6.2 percent, and 1990, 5.1 percent of all private households; census data in Switzerland), and did not increase, in contrast to many other countries. The rapid increase in childlessness has already been discussed. This increase is influenced by problems in reconciling employment and the family. Women's labor force participation among the population of Swiss origin was very low until the late 1970s, but then started to rise continuously. However, analyzing the pattern in the division of labor between spouses, the traditional breadwinner/homemaker model is still dominant. Evidence indicates that 40 to 50 percent of the population believes that the model "no job, if children are young" is the best strategy, and only 5 to 10 percent favor "no job, if a person has children" as the best solution (Fux 1997, 1998).

Deficiencies in the family policy system (e.g., scarcity of public childcare arrangements, barriers to female labor force participation, insufficient recognition of family achievements) enforce a polarization between the married and nonmarried, and the family (couples with children) and the nonfamily sector, respectively. These trends are linked with relevant changes in the meaning of the components that constitute a family. Adaptations in the patterns of intergenerational solidarity and the functions of the kinship networks are reflected in the much longer time that young adults remain in the parental household. The mean age at leaving the parental home increased from 20.4 and 19.2 for men and women, respectively, who were born between 1945 and 1949 to 21.7 and 19.9 for men and women born between 1965 and 1969 (Gabadinho and Wanner 1999). Furthermore, quasi-simultaneous transitions (i.e., an interval of less than six months between leaving home and marrying) from living in the parental home to a marital union is rapidly decreasing. Also, the meaning of marriage is changing towards a pragmatic interpretation (in the sense of a bilateral contract rather than as an institution). Marital functioning of families is changing. Types of family functioning based on companionship and a weak association between the partners have become very popular, in contrast to other types that are characterized by a strong hierarchy between spouses, or by a traditional form in the division of labor (Coenen-Huther et al. 1994; Kellerhals 1992; Kellerhals et al. 1991).

Parenthood, too, is showing shifts in its meaning and function. Premodern societies were characterized by rigid religious and ethical norms that dictated a close coupling between sexuality and procreation. This connection has become weaker during the past decades. Sexuality has become a commonly accepted part of an individual's way of life. Biological reproduction, by contrast, has to compete more and more with other values, aims, and interests of a person or couple. It becomes therefore an object of rational planning. The postponement of the age at marriage, the age at birth of a first child, as well as the gravitation towards smaller family sizes all depend on such a rationalization of reproductive behavior.

Attitudes

Different traditions influence attitudinal change in Switzerland. Liberalism favored the spread of a concept of privacy in which the family was seen as largely autonomous and able to provide for itself. Liberalism (predominant in the traditionally Protestant cantons and cities) is positively associated with the acceptance of divorce, abortion, and the spread of new living arrangements. A more conservative ideology dominates in central Switzerland and some of the French-speaking cantons. It is linked with Catholicism and anti-etatism (opposition to state intervention). Conservatives view the family as a fundamental institution and children as essential elements. From this point of view, the value of children is high, and divorce and abortion are less accepted. Social democratic and feminist ideologies are more common in the urban and economic centers and are often linked with postmaterialist orientations (i.e., having interests in things other than consumption—for example, personal autonomy, self-fulfilment, environmental quality, community, conviviality, etc.); thus family and children are not major issues. It seems that leftist ideas are associated with a higher propensity to accept abortion and new living arrangements.

The first representative polls on family attitudes were conducted around 1990 (Melich et al. 1991; Fux et al. 1997; Dorbritz and Fux 1997; Fux and Pfeiffer 1999; Gabadinho and Wanner 1999; Fux and Baumgartner 1998). In 1992, a huge majority of the Swiss population aged eighteen and older was not in favor of the increase in divorce (84 percent) (Fux et al. 1997; Dorbritz and Fux

1997; Fux and Pfeiffer 1999). "The partner does not love me any longer" (73%), disharmony between spouses (59%), and infidelity (56%), however, are widely accepted grounds for divorce (Gabadinho and Wanner 1999; Fux and Baumgartner 1998). Ninety-one percent of the Swiss population considered the well-being of the mother and 61 percent the risk of bearing a handicapped child as legitimate reasons for abortion. About one out of four respondents mentioned that abortion is justified if the woman (26%) or the couple (24%) does not want a child, or if the mother is unmarried (15%). According to this source, 47 percent of respondents had no objections to single women wanting to raise their own children alone. One in three respondents (31%) mentioned that parents should always "sacrifice for the sake of their children." In contrast, 75 percent of all respondents agreed with the statement "parents must always be loved and respected by their children," rather than the alternative, "one cannot demand that children are always obedient to their parents."

Beat Fux's research allows international comparisons because similar surveys were conducted also in eight other European countries (Fux et al. 1997). Many Swiss people accept recent demographic trends (decrease in marriages and births, increase in divorce) and the spread of new living arrangements (unmarried cohabitation, childlessness, single parenthood, singlehood, and out-of-wedlock births). The degree of tolerance towards these trends (Switzerland, mean: 7.2) is lower than in the Netherlands (mean: 9.5), but significantly higher than in the former Czechoslovakia (mean: 5.3), Austria (mean: 6.5), and Italy (mean: 6.6). Within Switzerland, French-speaking and Italian-speaking people accept these trends to a lesser degree than do German-speaking people. However, intranational variation is smaller than international variation in this respect.

A similar pattern can be found regarding the belief in the value of children. Along with the Netherlands, Switzerland belongs to the countries that place a comparatively low value on children, while respondents in former socialist countries, in the south of Europe, and in Germany, give significantly higher value to children. Again, a marked variation is observed within Switzerland. In the French- and Italian-speaking parts of the country, children seem to be more valued than in the German-speaking regions. By contrast, attitudes and value orientations related to the family show only a small variation, both among countries and within Switzerland. In all of the countries under observation, the family remains an important institution.

Switzerland is characterized by a comparatively high tolerance towards various family-related trends, though such openness to new family forms does not preclude a high appreciation for the family institution. The internal divisions within Swiss society markedly influence individual attitudes. In the French-speaking regions and urban centers, and among those with no religious affiliation, acceptance of divorce and abortion is higher than in the German- and Italian-speaking areas. Regarding the spread of new living arrangements, the German-speaking areas seem to be more tolerant, while intergenerational relations and children are more valued in the Latin areas than in the German regions. Catholics and Protestants, however, show only minor differences. In an international perspective, Switzerland is more similar to the Netherlands than to Austria, Germany, or Italy.

Conclusion

Changes related to the family and the household composition in Switzerland remain moderate. Many of the relevant shifts in behavior and attitudes are comparable with experiences in other European countries. However, Switzerland is distinctive in some notable ways. On the one hand, Switzerland was an early adopter of modern lifestyles (e.g., demographic transition, decline of fertility, nuclearization, increase in divorce, and in unmarried cohabitation). On the other, what also remain are more traditional aspects, such as the low proportions of extramarital births and few single parents, as well as women's comparatively slow entrance into the labor force, and the persistence of such values and attitudes as a high appreciation of marriage and parenting.

These diverging trends highlight differences between liberal and more conservative forces within the country. Explanations for this polarization are twofold. First, Switzerland is a highly segmented society (in terms of its economic, cultural, religious, and linguistic conditions). Second, Swiss families are confronted with comparatively high thresholds due to important deficiencies in the country's family policy. The latter cause influences the strong postponement in the age of marriage and first births, and the increase in childlessness.

See also: GERMANY

Bibliography

Coenen-Huther, J.; Kellerhals, J.; and von Allmen, Malik. (1994). *Les réseaux de solidarité dans la famille.* Lausanne: Réalités sociales.

Dorbritz, J., and Fux, B., eds. (1997). *Einstellungen zur Familienpolitik in Europa. Ergebnisse eines vergleichenden Surveys in den Ländern des "European Comparative Survey on Population Policy Acceptance" (PPA).* Schriftenreihe des Bundesinstituts für Bevölkerungsforschung Bd. 24. München: Harald Boldt Verlag im R. Oldenbourg Verlag.

Fux, B. (1994). *Der familienpolitische Diskurs. Eine theoretische und empirische Untersuchung über das Zusammenwirken und den Wandel von Familienpolitik, Fertilität und Familie.* Sozialpolitische Schriften, Heft 64. Berlin: Duncker and Humblot.

Fux, B. (1997). "Switzerland: The Family Neglected by the State." In *Family Life and Family Policies in Europe,* Vol. 1: *Structures and Trends in the 1980s,* ed. F.-X. Kaufmann, A. Kuijsten, H.-J. Schulze, and K. P. Strohmeier. Oxford: Clarendon Press.

Fux, B. (2002a). "Family Change and Family Policy in Switzerland." In *Family Change and Family Policies in Consociational Democracies: Belgium, Switzerland, and the Netherlands,* Vol. 2, ed. P. Flora. Oxford: Clarendon Press.

Fux, B. (2002b). "Which Models of the Family are En- or Discouraged by Different Family Policies?" In *Family Life and Family Policies in Europe,* Vol. 2: *Comparative Analyses,* ed. F.-X. Kaufmann, H.-J. Schulze, et al. Oxford: Clarendon Press.

Fux, B., and Baumgartner, A. D. (1998). *Wandel von familialen Lebensformen: Lebensverläufe—Lebensentwürfe.* Materialienband 3. Zürich: Schlussbericht an den schweizerischen Nationalfonds.

Fux, B., and Baumgartner, A.D. (2000). "Ein Baby? Eher nicht. Die neue Kinderlosigkeit—ein gesellschaftlicher Trend und dessen Hintergründe." *Neue Zürcher Zeitung* 123(27/28):101–102.

Fux, B., and Baumgartner, A. D. (2002). "Impact of Population Related Policies on Selected Living Arrangements. Comparative Analyses on Regional Level in Belgium, the Netherlands, and Switzerland." In *Comparative Analyses on the Basis of Family and Fertility Surveys (FFS),* Vol. 2, ed. UN-ECE, Genf 2001.

Fux, B.; Bösch, A.; Gisler, P.; and Baumgartner, A. D. (1997). *Bevölkerung-und eine Prise Politik. Die schweizerische Migrations-, Familien- und Alterspolitik im Fadenkreuz von Einstellungen und Bewertungen.* Zürich: Seismo Verlag.

Fux, B., and Pfeiffer, C. (1999). "Ehe, Familie, Kinderzahl: Gesellschaftliche Normen und individuelle Zielvorstellungen." In *Bericht über die Situation der Familie in Österreich 1999,* ed. Bundesministerium für Umwelt, Jugend und Familie. Wien: BMUJF.

Gabadinho, A., and Wanner, P. (1999). *Fertility and Family Surveys in Countries of the ECE Region, Standard Country Report: Switzerland.* Geneva: UN-ECE.

Hoffmann-Nowotny, H.-J.; Höhn, C.; and Fux, B. (1992). *Kinderzahl und Familienpolitik im Drei-Länder-Vergleich.* Schriftenreihe des Bundesinstituts für Bevölkerungsforschung. Boppard a.Rh.: Boldt Verlag.

Hoffmann-Nowotny, H.-J.; Höpflinger, F.; et al. (1984). *Planspiel Familie. Familie, Kinderwunsch und Familienplanung in der Schweiz.* Diessenhofen: Rüegger.

Höpflinger, F., and Erni-Schneuwly, D., eds. (1989). *Weichenstellungen - Lebensformen im Wandel und Lebenslage junger Frauen.* Bern: Haupt.

Kellerhals, J. (1992). *Microsociologie de la famille.* 2nd edition. Paris: PUF.

Kellerhals, J., and Montandon, C. (1991). *Les stratégies éducatives des familles : milieu social, dynamique familiale et éducation des pré-adolescents.* Lausanne et Neuch,tel: Delachaux et Niestlé.

Lüscher, K., and Engstler, H. (1991). *Formen der Familiengründung in der Schweiz.* Bern: Bundesamt für Statistik.

Melich, Anna, et al., eds. (1991). *Les valeurs des Suisses.* Bern: Lang.

Sommer, J. H., and Höpflinger, F. (1989). *Wandel der Lebensformen und soziale Sicherheit. Forschungsstand und Wissenslücken.* Chur: Rüegger.

BEAT FUX

SYMBOLIC INTERACTIONISM

Symbolic interactionism is a sociological perspective on self and society based on the ideas of George H. Mead (1934), Charles H. Cooley (1902), W. I. Thomas (1931), and other pragmatists associated, primarily, with the University of Chicago in the early twentieth century. The central theme of symbolic interactionism is that human life is lived in the symbolic domain. Symbols are culturally derived social objects having shared meanings that are created and maintained in social interaction. Through language and communication, symbols provide the means by which reality is constructed. Reality is primarily a social product, and all that is humanly consequential—self, mind, society, culture—emerges from and is dependent on symbolic interactions for its existence. Even the physical environment is relevant to human conduct *mainly* as it is interpreted through symbolic systems.

Importance of Meanings

The label *symbolic interactionism* was coined by Herbert Blumer (1969), one of Mead's students. Blumer, who did much to shape this perspective, specified its three basic premises: (1) Humans act toward things on the basis of the meanings that things have for them; (2) the meanings of things derive from social interaction; and (3) these meanings are dependent on, and modified by, an interpretive process of the people who interact with one another. The focus here is on meaning, which is defined in terms of action and its consequences (reflecting the influence of pragmatism). The meaning of a thing resides in the action that it elicits. For example, the meaning of "grass" is food to a cow, shelter to a fox, and the like. In the case of symbols, meanings also depend on a degree of consensual responses between two or more people. The meaning of the word *husband,* for example, depends on the consensual responses of those who use it. If most of those who use it agree, the meaning of a symbol is clear; if consensus is low, the meaning is ambiguous, and communication is problematic. Within a culture, a general consensus prevails on the meanings associated with various words or symbols. However, in practice, the meanings of things are highly variable and depend on processes of interpretation and negotiation of the interactants.

The interpretive process entails what Blumer refers to as *role-taking,* the cognitive ability to take the perspective of another. It is a critical process in communication because it enables actors to interpret one another's responses, thereby bringing about greater consensus on the meanings of the symbols used. The determination of meanings also depends on negotiation—that is, on mutual adjustments and accommodations of those who are interacting. In short, meaning is emergent, problematic, and dependent on processes of role-taking and negotiation. Most concepts of symbolic interactionism are related to the concept of meaning.

Situational Definitions

The importance of meanings is reflected in Thomas's (1931) famous dictum: If situations are defined as real, they are real in their consequences. The definition of the situation emphasizes that people act in situations on the basis of how they are defined. Definitions, even when at variance with "objective" reality, have real consequences for people's actions and events.

The definitional process involves the determination of relevant identities and attributes of interactants. If, for example, a teacher defines a student as a slow learner (based on inaccurate information), her discriminatory behavior (e.g., less attention and lower expectations) may have a negative effect on the student's intellectual development, resulting in a self-fulfilling prophecy. This process, in combination with interactionist ideas about self-concept formation, is the basis of the *labeling theory* of deviance. Labeling theory proposes that a key factor in the development of deviants is the negative label of identity imposed on the person (e.g., "criminal," "pervert") who engages in deviant behavior (Becker 1963).

Defining a situation is not a static process. An initial definition, based on past experiences or cultural expectations, may be revised in the course of interaction. Much of the negotiation in social situations entails an attempt to present the self in a favorable light or to defend a valued identity. Erving Goffman's (1959) insightful analyses of impression management and the use of deference and demeanor, as well as Marvin Scott and Stanford Lyman's (1968) examination of the use of excuses, justifications, and accounts, speak to the intricacies involved in situational definitions. Where power or status disparities exist, the dominant interactant's definition of the situation likely prevails.

Self-Concept Formation

Along with symbols, meaning, and interaction, the *self* is a basic concept in symbolic interactionism.

The essential feature of the self is that it is a reflexive phenomenon. Reflexivity enables humans to act toward themselves as objects, or to reflect on themselves, argue with themselves, evaluate themselves, and so forth. This human attribute (although dolphins and the great apes show some evidence of a self as well), based on the social character of human language and the ability to role-take, enables individuals to see themselves from the perspective of another and thereby to form a conception of themselves, a self-concept.

Two types of *others* are critical in the development of the self. The *significant other* refers to people who are important to an individual, whose opinions matter. The *generalized other* refers to a conception of the community, group, or any organized system of roles (e.g., a baseball team) that are used as a point of reference from which to view the self.

The importance of others in the formation of self-concepts is captured in Cooley's (1902) influential concept, the *looking-glass self.* Cooley proposed that to some extent individuals see themselves as they think others see them. Self-conceptions and self-feelings (e.g., pride or shame) are a consequence of how people imagine others perceive and evaluate them. Within contemporary symbolic interactionism, this process is called *reflected appraisals* and is the main process emphasized in the development of the self.

The self is considered a social product in other ways, too. The content of self-concepts reflects the content and organization of society. This is evident with regard to the roles that are internalized as role-identities (e.g., father, student). Roles, as behavioral expectations associated with a status within a set of relationships, constitute a major link between social and personal organization. Sheldon Stryker (1980) proposes that differential commitment to various role-identities provides much of the structure and organization of self-concepts. To the extent that individuals are committed to a particular role identity, they are motivated to act according to their conception of the identity and to maintain and protect it, because their role performance implicates their self-esteem. Much of socialization, particularly during childhood, involves learning social roles and associated values, attitudes, and beliefs. Initially this takes place in the family, then in larger arenas (e.g., peer groups, school, work settings) of the individual's social world. The role identities formed early in life, such as gender and filial identities, remain some of the most important throughout life. Yet socialization is lifelong, and individuals assume various role identities throughout their life course.

Socialization is not a passive process of learning roles and conforming to other's expectations. The self is highly active and selective, having a major influence on its environment and itself. When people play roles, role-making often is as evident as is learning roles. In role-making, individuals actively construct, interpret, and uniquely express their roles. When they perceive an incongruity between a role imposed on them and some valued aspect of their self-conception, they may distance themselves from a role, which is the disassociation of self from role. A pervasive theme in this literature is that the self actively engages in its own development, a process that may be unpredictable.

Divisions Within Symbolic Interactionism

Symbolic interactionism is not a homogeneous theoretical perspective. Although interactionists agree that humans rely on shared symbols to construct their realities and on the methodological requirement of understanding behavior by "getting inside" the reality of the actor, substantial divisions remain within this perspective. The main division is between those who emphasize process and those who emphasize structure in studying human realities. The former, associated with Blumer (1969) and known as the Chicago School, advocates the use of qualitative methods in studying the process of reality construction within natural social settings. The latter, associated with Manfurd Kuhn (1964) and labeled the Iowa School, advocates the use of quantitative methods in studying the products of social interaction, especially self-concepts. The differences between these two schools of symbolic interactionism reflect the fundamental division in the social sciences between humanistic/interpretive orientations, which align with history and the humanities, and positivistic orientations, which align with the physical sciences. Both of these orientations to symbolic interactionism are evident in marriage and family studies, although the structural orientation predominates.

Symbolic Interactionism and Family Studies

Symbolic interactionism has been an important theoretical perspective in family studies since its early development in the 1920s and 1930s (LaRossa and Reitzes 1993). William Thomas and Florian Znaniecki's (1918–1920) monumental study, *The Polish Peasant in Europe and America,* was an early application of some of the main themes and concepts of the perspective. This study focused on the adjustments and transformations in personality and family patterns in the Polish peasant community in the course of immigration to the United States during the early 1900s. Processes of socialization, adaptation, definition formation, role-making, and self-concept development were major themes in their analysis.

Ernest Burgess, however, was the first to call for the systematic application of "processual" symbolic interactionism to family studies. He proposed that the family can be viewed as "a unity of interacting personalities" (Burgess 1926), a little universe of communication in which roles and selves are shaped and each personality affects every other personality. Unfortunately, few heeded Burgess's call to study the dynamic interactions of whole families (for an exception, see Hess and Handel 1959). It is impractical for most family researchers to study whole family dynamics over time. Burgess's own empirical studies mostly used conventional survey methods and measurements in studying marital adjustment (Burgess and Cottrell 1939), and reflect a more *structural interactionism* (i.e., emphasis on social structure rather than process) characteristic of the Iowa school.

Another pioneer in the symbolic interactionist approach to family research was Willard Waller (1937, 1938). Waller used qualitative methods (e.g., case studies and novels) to study family dynamics, particularly processes of interpersonal conflict, bargaining, and exploitation. His *principle of least interest* suggests that the person least interested in or committed to the marital or dating relationship has the most power in that relationship and frequently exploits the other. The theme of conflict and exploitation was prominent in his analysis of college dating patterns in the 1930s. Reuben Hill, who shaped much of the contemporary research on the family, reworked Waller's treatise by shifting the focus from a conflict and process orientation to a relatively structured developmental perspective emphasizing family roles and a more harmonious view of family life (Waller and Hill 1951).

Much contemporary family research from a symbolic interactionist perspective deals with some type of role analysis, such as how the roles of husband and wife are defined during stages of family life; how gender role conceptions affect the definitions of spousal roles; how the arrival of children and the transition to parental roles change role constellations and interaction patterns; how external events (e.g., parental employment, natural disasters, migration) and internal events (e.g., births, deaths, divorces) affect role definitions, performance, stress, or conflict; and how these role-specific variables affect the attitudes, dispositions, and self-conceptions of family members (Hutter 1985). The concept of role is also important for most of the major sociological perspectives (e.g., structural functionalism, social exchange theory, and even conflict theory). The symbolic interactionist perspective emphasizes the processes of role-making, role definition, role negotiation, and role identity within the family (Hochschild 1989).

A large area of symbolic interactionist research deals with socialization—the processes through which personalities and self-concepts are formed, values and attitudes are transmitted, and the culture of one generation is passed to the next. The socialization of children is one of the few remaining (and the most critical) functions of the family in modern societies. It has received considerable attention from researchers. A symbolic interactionist perspective on child socialization encompasses a broad range of processes and outcomes involved in integrating the newborn into its family and society. Most of the socialization research has focused on the development of some aspect of the self (e.g., self-esteem, gender, and filial identities). The research indicates that positive reflected appraisals from parents along with parental support and the use of inductive control have positive socialization outcomes for the children's self-concept (Gecas and Schwalbe 1986; Peterson and Rollins 1987).

The socialization process is highly reciprocal; parents and children affect one anothers' self-concepts. The high levels of reciprocity characteristic of family socialization processes (and a hallmark of symbolic interactionism) are rarely reflected in family research, although researchers are increasingly sensitive to it. A focus on reciprocity is more evident in research where identity negotiation is problematic, as in the case of lesbian motherhood (Hequembourg and Farrell 1999) or in the case of immigrant families where parents and children must renegotiate their roles in unfamiliar cultural contexts (Hyman and Vu 2000).

In addition to pursuing traditional interests in family studies, mostly in the United States, symbolic interactionists are increasingly pursuing cross-cultural and international research. In the area of self and identity, for example, Steve Derne (1999) shows how male filmgoers in India use their interpretations of Western films to both maintain and enhance their sense of male privilege. This research demonstrates how, when exposed to cultural perspectives that may threaten their own self-concepts or ethnic identities, people engage in interpretive processes that serve to incorporate these ideas into existing self-structures. Research in Nigeria (Rotini 1986) has shown how car ownership, an influential status symbol, shapes personal interactions among the owners of different types of cars and how the infiltration of new technologies into cultures can alter role-relations in social institutions such as the family, law, and religion.

Cross-cultural research also explores how family relations are conducted within specific ethnic domains, and how the cultural contexts in which communication occurs shape family interactions and identity negotiations (Luo and Wiseman 2000). Mzobanzi Mboya (1993), for example, offers a compelling study of the ways that the self-concepts of South African adolescent schoolchildren are related to their perceptions of parental behavior. Simon Cheng's (2000) research on the child socialization mechanisms used by Chinese families who have immigrated to the United States demonstrates how ethnic identities are socially constructed, negotiated, and maintained through parent-child interactions that occur in heterogeneous cultural milieus.

Broadly speaking, social movements, national dilemmas, international conflict, and the flow of international immigrants frame the symbolic domains in which families live. Immigrant families and children encountering cultures and lifestyles that are vastly different from their own struggle to realize new opportunities and to maintain their own ethnic identities and integrity (Zhou 1997). Global social movements such as the women's movement offer opportunities for women to reconstruct their identities and, in doing so, to reconstruct the institution of the family itself (Ray and Korteweg 1999).

Conclusion

Many areas of family research reflect symbolic interactionist ideas, often in diffuse and diluted form. For instance, in much of the research on marital satisfaction, marital quality, patterns of dating and mating, and various family-relevant attitudes (e.g., premarital sex, abortion), symbolic interactionist ideas are likely to be *implicitly* rather than explicitly stated and tested. Although this may hinder the development and refinement of symbolic interactionism, it can also be viewed as an indication of the success of this theoretical perspective—that many of its concepts and ideas have become a part of the common wisdom of family studies. The theory's use in family research across cultural domains also points to the broad applicability of its fundamental premises and constructs.

See also: FAMILY ROLES; FAMILY THEORY; GENDER IDENTITY; RELATIONSHIP THEORIES—SELF-OTHER RELATIONSHIP; ROLE THEORY; SELF-ESTEEM; SOCIALIZATION; TRANSITION TO PARENTHOOD

Bibliography

Becker, H. S. (1963). *Outsiders: Studies in the Sociology of Deviance.* New York: Free Press.

Blumer, H. (1969). *Symbolic Interactionism: Perspective and Method.* Englewood Cliffs, NJ: Prentice Hall.

Bohannon, J. R., and Blanton, P. W. (1999). "Gender Role Attitudes of American Mothers and Daughters Over Time." *Journal of Social Psychology* 139:173–179.

Burgess, E. W. (1926). "The Family as a Unity of Interacting Personalities." *Family* 7:3–9.

Burgess, E. W., and Cottrell, L. S., Jr. (1939). *Predicting Success or Failure in Marriage.* New York: Prentice Hall.

Charon, J. (1989). *Symbolic Interactionism,* 3rd edition. Englewood Cliffs, NJ: Prentice Hall.

Cheng, S. H., and W. H. Kuo. (2000). "Family Socialization of Ethnic Identity among Chinese American Pre-Adolescents." *Journal of Comparative Family Studies* 31:463–484.

Cooley, C. H. (1902). *Human Nature and the Social Order.* New York: Scribner.

Derne, S. (1999). "Handling Ambivalence toward 'Western' Ways: Transnational Cultural Flows and Men's Identity in India." *Studies in Symbolic Interaction* 22:17–45.

Gecas, V., and Schwalbe, M. L. (1986). "Parental Behavior and Adolescent Self-Esteem." *Journal of Marriage and the Family* 48:37–46.

Goffman, E. (1959). *The Presentations of Self in Everyday Life.* New York: Doubleday.

Gordon, M. (1977). "Kinship Boundaries and Kinship Knowledge in Urban Ireland." *International Journal of Sociology of the Family.* 7:1–14.

Hequembourg, A. L., and Farrell, M. P. (1999). "Lesbian Motherhood: Negotiating Marginal-Mainstream Identities." *Gender & Society* 13:540–557.

Hess, R. D., and Handel, G. (1959). *Family Worlds.* Chicago: University of Chicago Press.

Hochschild, A. R. (1989). *The Second Shift: Working Parents and the Revolution at Home.* New York: Viking.

Hutter, M. (1985). "Symbolic Interaction and the Study of the Family." In *Foundations of Interpretive Sociology: Studies in Symbolic Interaction,* ed. H. A. Farberman and R. S. Perinbanayagam. Greenwich, CT: JAI Press.

Hyman, I.; Vu, N.; and Beiser, M. "Post-Migration Stresses among Southeast Asian Refugee Youth in Canada: A Research Note." *Journal of Comparative Family Studies* 31:281–293.

Kuhn, M. H. (1964). "Major Trends In Symbolic Interaction Theory in the Past Twenty-Five Years." *Sociological Quarterly* 5:61–84.

LaRossa, R., and Reitzes, D. C. (1993). "Symbolic Interactionism and Family Studies." In *Sourcebook of Family Theories and Methods,* ed. P. G. Boss; W. J. Doherty; R. LaRossa; W. R. Schumm; and S. K. Steinmetz. New York: Plenum.

Luo, S. H., and Wiseman, R. L. (2000). "Ethnic Language Maintenance among Chinese Immigrant Children in the United States." *International Journal of Intercultural Relations* 24:307–324.

Mboya, M. M. (1993). "Parental Behavior and African Adolescents' Self-Concepts." *School Psychology International* 14:317–326.

Mead, G. H. (1934). *Mind, Self, and Society.* Chicago: University of Chicago Press.

Peterson, G. W., and Rollins, B. C. (1987). "Parent-Child Socialization." In *Handbook of Marriage and the Family,* ed. M. B. Sussman and S. K. Steinmetz. New York: Plenum.

Ray, R., and Kortweweg, A. C. (1999). "Women's Movements in the Third World: Identity, Mobilization, and Autonomy." *Annual Review of Sociology* 25:47–71.

Rotini, A. (1986). "Retrospective Participant Observation on Driving and Car Ownership in Nigeria." *International Review of Modern Sociology* 16:395–406.

Scott, M. E., and Lyman, S. M. (1968). "Accounts." *American Sociological Review* 33:46–62.

Stryker, S. (1980). *Symbolic Interactionism.* Menlo Park, CA: Benjamin/Cummings.

Thomas, W. I. (1931). *The Unadjusted Girl.* Boston: Little, Brown.

Thomas, W. I., and Znaniecki, F. (1918–1920). *The Polish Peasant in Europe and America,* 5 Vols. Boston: Badger.

Waller, W. (1937). "The Rating-Dating Complex." *American Sociological Review* 2:727–734.

Waller, W. (1938). *The Family: A Dynamic Interpretation.* New York: Dryden.

Waller, W., and Hill, R. (1951). *The Family: A Dynamic Interpretation,* rev. edition. New York: Dryden.

Zhou, M. (1997). "Growing Up American: The Challenge Confronting Immigrant Children and Children of Immigrants." *Annual Review of Sociology* 23:63–95.

VIKTOR GECAS
TERESA TSUSHIMA

T

TELEVISION AND FAMILY

Television has long been like a member of the family. In some countries televisions occupy almost every room, and family members are exposed to it from infancy. It baby-sits, educates, gives comfort, and tells us what family life should be like. Even though most people do not consider television a major part of their lives, it is an inescapable part of modern culture.

Television itself is not easily defined. The images on a television screen can be broadcast, or can come from cable, videotape, or even a computer. Similarly, one can watch streaming video on a computer monitor, as well as calling up Web sites closely tied to what might be on the television screen. Media are converging, and simple distinctions no longer apply.

The Portrayal of Family on Television

How television has portrayed the family is important because television is a source for learning about family: what families look like, what an ideal family is, how spouses are supposed to behave, how parents are expected to treat their children, and how families resolve problems. Most research has focused on capturing rich descriptions of the portrayals of family structure, the presence of diverse portrayals, and types of relational interactions within television facilities. Because U.S. media products have dominated international programming, most analyses of family portrayals have been of U.S. programs.

Family structure and diversity. The portrayal of family varies by type of programming. Situation comedies, family dramas, and soap operas are often about family, and are the subject of most research into the portrayals of family. Programming types such as action adventure are less likely to use family as the core of their program appeal. Some programming reveals real families' dysfunctional structure, communication, and conflict. For example, distorted relationships, fighting, and jealousy among family members are often displayed on daytime television talk shows such as *The Jerry Springer Show*.

The comedies of the 1950s and 1960s started out with diverse families, ranging from *I Love Lucy* to the infamous *Amos 'n Andy* and the Jewish family of *The Goldbergs*. But by the middle of the decade, situation comedies and family dramas presented a traditional family structure—a nuclear family with two biological parents and their children, epitomized by *Leave It to Beaver* and *The Adventures of Ozzie and Harriet*. During the rest of the 1950s and 1960s, white middle-class families dominated programs. The 1960s, however, began to showcase more structural variability, with an increase in families headed by a single widowed parent, such as in *The Andy Griffith Show*. Throughout television history, however, married couples have headed most families and the most common configuration was nuclear.

The 1970s and 1980s saw an increase in racial diversity. Successful shows such as the groundbreaking mini-series *Roots* (1977) and the situation comedy *The Cosby Show* (1984–1992) created an atmosphere in which African-American programs could emerge. *The Cosby Show* is often credited with reviving the domestic situation comedy. With the explosion of programs on cable, the 1990s featured many African-American family programs. The positive and upscale images in *Cosby* contrasted with earlier negative images of African Americans. Historically, the portrayal of minority families has been distorted, with African-American individuals often depicted as irresponsible, lazy, and the target of humor.

Minority families continue to struggle for representation and positive portrayals. Native Americans appear infrequently and are often stereotyped as alcoholics with impoverished, dysfunctional families. Latino families are underrepresented and often portrayed as lawbreakers with little education, but with strong family ties. Asian-American families rarely appear. In the 1990s, unmarried relationships and couples without children were more common than ever on television.

Portrayal of family relationships. Historically, television has promoted a traditional family model with wise parents, little serious conflict, and mostly conforming behavior. Families on television during the 1950s and much of the 1960s talked with each other, and parents always helped their children through adolescence. Although the 1970s had a number of sentimental portrayals, such as *Little House on the Prairie* or the still popular *Brady Bunch,* it also experimented with more conflictual relationship patterns in such favorites as *All in the Family* and *The Jeffersons.* In *All in the Family* family members were likely to ignore, withdraw, and oppose one another, in addition to showing support and caring. During the 1980s, *The Cosby Show* dominated public perceptions of family portrayals with an enviable family. Prime-time soap operas such as *Dallas* and *Dynasty* explored the seamier side of extended families. The end of the 1980s saw a more cynical view of the family in such comedy hits as *Roseanne* and *The Simpsons.* By the 1990s family relationships were again portrayed more positively in terms of psychological health on shows such as *Family Matters* and *Home Improvement* (Bryant and Bryant 2001). Although conflicts in family programs have increased rapidly from the late 1970s, family members almost always successfully resolved the conflicts by way of positive, affiliative, prosocial communication.

In addition to showing how parents behave, television also presents a picture of the relationships among siblings. Like portrayals of parent-child relationships, sibling relationships generally emphasize efforts to resolve conflicts and to maintain positive emotional ties. There is, however, considerable variation depending on the program. *Married with Children* and *Roseanne* feature rather hostile sibling relationships, whereas *The Simpsons* portrays more affiliative and supportive relationships.

The Social Uses and Influence of Television on Families

The relationships between television and the family are not fully explored by asking about the effect of portrayals. Indeed, a significant body of research asks not what television does to families, but how families use television. These perspectives, with particular emphasis on the children within viewing families, can be roughly subdivided into three overlapping areas of research: *family image, parental mediation,* and the *family viewing context.*

Family image. The paradigmatic question asked by researchers within this area is: What is the effect of television content about families on viewers? Research has looked for evidence that television's images of marriage and family life influence the conceptions that children and adults hold about family. *Social learning theory* (Bandura 1977) argues for imitative behavior and learning from television of behaviors seen as rewarding and realistic. It uses both imitation and identification to explain how people learn through observation of others in their environment. The *cultivation perspective* (Gerber and Gross 1976) posits the cultivation of a worldview skewed toward that of televised portrayals among heavy viewers. This worldview, although possibly inaccurate, becomes the social reality of heavy viewers. Both social learning theory and the cultivation perspective provide the theoretical linkage between exposure to content and its consequence.

Evidence suggests that depictions do have consequences. For example, those who watch more television than average, particularly children, tend to hold more traditional notions of gender roles. Television cultivates beliefs in children such as "women are happiest at home raising children" and "men are born with more ambition than women" (Signorielli 1990).

Images of family life itself may also be influenced. Heavy viewers tend to perceive being single as negative, express profamily sentiments, and believe that families in real life show support and concern for each other. On the other hand, heavy soap opera viewers tend to overestimate the number of illegitimate children, happy marriages, divorces, and extramarital affairs (Signorielli 1990). In all, these studies suggest that media portrayals reflect and reinforce views about the nature of the family in society. Changing social norms and television portrayals mean that assessing the impact of portrayals must be an ongoing effort.

Parental mediation. The paradigmatic question for those working within this area is: What is the structure and effect of parental mediation of television viewing? Within this domain researchers ask about the nature and consequences of the efforts made by parents to influence the potential outcomes of exposure. Much of the writing within the area has concentrated on coviewing, rulemaking, and interaction.

Coviewing. Television viewing with family members is common. Reports estimate that 65 to 85 percent of young children's viewing is with family members, with more than half of that viewing with parents (Van Evra 1998). Although early studies equated coviewing with mediation, research soon established coviewing was more coincidental than planned, and most likely had a modeling rather a mediative effect on children (Singer and Singer 2001). Coviewing occurred least often with younger children, who need it most, and reflected similar preferences rather than explicit mentoring. Viewing with siblings clearly influences the younger child: they *watch up* to the older children's preferences, and are the recipient of older siblings' interpretation.

Interaction. A number of studies convincingly demonstrate the *potential* for family interaction to mediate the impact of television. In experimental settings parental or adult comments have been found to aid children's understanding of program content to shape perceptions of families in the real world, to foster critical viewing skills, and to increase recall of information from educational programs (Bryant and Bryant 2001). Despite these potential benefits, little evidence exists to suggest that parents actually engage in these behaviors. Coviewing in a context of limited interaction tends to be the norm, restricting the learning that interaction could promote.

Coviewing between children and their parents can help the children develop critical viewing skills, increase understanding of content, and increase recall of information. Here, a French family watches election coverage together. OWEN FRANKEN/CORBIS

There is a growing body of observational research that describes how interpretation of meaning is accomplished within the family viewing context. Most of the research in this area has focused on the development of children's understanding of the television medium. Empirical observation of interaction is sparse, but the existing research suggests that children as well as adults create television-related interactive sequences. Very young children interact with the television during viewing, including naming or identifying familiar objects, repeating labels, asking questions, and relating television content to the child's experience. The majority of sibling television-related interaction for these young children was interpretive in function. Younger children asked about character identification, problematic visual devices, narrative conventions, and the medium per se (Lindlof 1987).

Interview and observational data reinforce these conclusions. Mothers report frequent use of interpretive or evaluative statements. They describe a variety of interactions in which they tell children about things that could not happen in real life, including drawing complex distinctions between the improbable and the impossible and explaining disturbing images, such as immorality and poverty (Van Evra 1998).

Rulemaking. In many families television gives rise to issues involving control of how much, when, and what is viewed. Control of television viewing has been studied in terms of explicit rules about amount and content of exposure, sometimes called *restrictive mediation.* The most consistent finding is the paucity of rules, with estimates ranging from 19 to 69 percent of families that report any rules, varying due to age of children, class, and by whether mother or child responded (Singer and Singer 2001). Parents commonly report more attempts to control the amount and time of viewing of younger children, and the viewing content of older children. Beyond the explicit rules about television viewing that operate within the family system, it is easy to miss the implicit rules that govern viewing. For example, the television may never be on during weekend days because children have learned that if parents find them "goofing off too much" they will be assigned chores. Although it is doubtful that anyone would describe this as a family rule, such practices have the force of limiting viewing contexts.

The family viewing context. The paradigmatic question within this research frame is: How do families use television within the family system? One important area of research addresses the uses and gratifications tradition that asks about the psychological needs and motivations of viewers and their gratifications from viewing. Thus, researchers in this tradition have explored family uses of media as an aggregate of individual viewing motives and gratifications.

In the late twentieth and early twenty-first centuries, the consumption of media became an increasingly solitary experience. Multiple television sets, as well as video games, computers, and stereos, allow members, particularly older children, to select content based on individual needs. Viewing becomes a social family activity when a special event occurs, such as a special movie rental or a major television event such as the Superbowl.

Family systems-based media research uses a communicative perspective on the role of television in family interaction and begins by examining the family as the context in which viewing is performed and made meaningful. Of the many contexts that influence meaning and behavior, none is more ubiquitous than the family. This *interactionist perspective* from family process research has been modified by communication researchers with a strong symbolic orientation to become the predominant position in the field of communication.

The most frequently used measure of family communication in mass communication research comes from the work of Jack McLeod and Steven Chaffee (1973). Their schema of family communication patterns is based on two communicative dimensions (*socio- and concept-orientation*) in which parents stress harmony and obedience on the one hand, and negotiation and self-reliance on the other. It has been linked with differences in political knowledge, exposure to types of programming, social adaptability, and family rules.

From a *critical/cultural perspective,* researchers have asked about how media and families consuming media are reproducing social structures of power in regard to race, class, and gender. For example, David Morley (1986) examined the construction of gender roles in his observations of the media selection process in homes in the United Kingdom. Steven Klein writes about the political economy of children's television production, and the resulting commercialization of childhood (Klein 1993). Concerns with media literacy are international in scope. Many countries have adopted media literacy programs for children, with strong emphases on understanding the commercial nature of media systems and its possible consequences (Buckingham 1998).

With the emergence of interest in qualitative investigations of how media are used in everyday life, researchers began to observe the nature and consequences of television-related interaction in the home (Lindlof 1987). One major conclusion from this line of research is that television may serve an almost limitless range of diverse uses and functions. Family members can watch television to be together, or to get away from each other; as a basis for talk or to avoid interaction; as a source of conflict, or an escape from it (Lull 1980). Because much of the time that family members spend together is in the presence of television, television at least partially defines the context within which family interaction occurs and therefore helps determine the meaning of that interaction. From this perspective, family themes, roles, or issues are carried out in a variety of contexts, and the television viewing context becomes one in which it is useful to study patterns of family interaction in general. As such, media are implicated in the accomplishment of numerous family functions, including defining role expectations, articulating the nature of relationships, and using economic and relational currencies in the negotiation of intimacy and power.

See also: COMPUTERS AND FAMILY; GLOBAL CITIZENSHIP; HOME; LEISURE; PLAY; TIME USE

Bibliography

Bandura, A. (1977). *Social Learning Theory*. Englewood Cliffs, NJ: Prentice Hall.

Bryant, J., and Bryant, J. A., eds. (2001). *Television and the American Family,* 2nd edition. Mahwah, NJ: Lawrence Erlbaum Associates.

Buckingham, D., ed. (1998). *Teaching Popular Culture*. London: UCL Press.

Gerbner, G., and Gross, L. (1976). "Living with Television: The Violence Profile." *Journal of Communication* 26(2):173–199.

Kline, S. (1993). *Out of the Garden*. London: Verso.

Lindlof, T., ed. (1987). *Natural Audiences: Qualitative Research of Media Uses and Effects*. Norwood, NJ: Ablex.

Lull, J. (1980). "The Social Uses of Television." *Human Communication Research* 6:197–209.

McLeod, J. M., and Chaffee, S. (1973). "Interpersonal Approaches to Communication Research." *American Behavioral Scientist* 16:469–499.

Morley, D. (1986). *Family Television: Cultural Power and Domestic Leisure*. London: Comedia.

Signorielli, N. (1990). *A Sourcebook on Children and Television*. Westport, CT: Greenwood Press.

Singer, J., and Singer, D. (2001). *Handbook of Children and Media*. Thousand Oaks, CA: Sage.

Van Evra, J. P. (1988). *Television and Child Development,* 2nd edition. Mahwah, NJ: Lawrence Erlbaum Associates.

ALISON ALEXANDER
YEORA KIM

TEMPERAMENT

Temperament is defined as biologically based individual differences in emotional and motor reactivity, attention, and self-regulation (Rothbart and Bates 1998). Temperament is an aspect of personality that is seen in human infants and in other animals; it constitutes the core of the developing personality. Temperamental characteristics are dispositions or capacities; temperament is not seen continually, but only in situations that bring out the reaction or the capacity. There has been increasing interest in the possibility that biologically based temperament will affect children's social experiences and personality development. Taking temperament into account emphasizes what the child brings to the family, and the way parenting and child temperament work together to influence the child's social development. Temperament is also related to adult patterns in forming a family and having children.

Measurement of Temperament

Methods of measuring temperament include self-report and caregiver-report questionnaires, laboratory observations, and home observations (Rothbart and Bates 1998). Questionnaires ask parents and other caregivers to report on the behaviors of their children, and the researcher then combines this information across situations and conditions for a measure of temperament. For older children and adults, self-reported feelings and behaviors in specific situations are also assessed. With the exception of reports of sadness, moderate levels of agreement are generally found between children's and parents' reports of the child's temperament.

Strengths of questionnaires as a method for measuring temperament include the broad range of information they can assess and the ease of their administration. Limitations include the possibility that parents may describe their child in a generally positive (or negative) way. Many studies, however, have found significant agreement between questionnaires and other measures of temperament (Rothbart and Bates 1998).

Laboratory studies focus on children's reactions to presentations that are likely to lead to an emotion, action, or focus of attention, comparing one child's reaction with that of other children. The child's behavior in the home has also been observed. Strengths of laboratory methods include the ability to use standard situations to elicit temperament in all children, and to measure heart rate and other psychological reactions. Limitations of the laboratory include high cost and emotional carryover from one measure to another. Use of home observations permits researchers to see the child's temperamental responding in a natural setting, but home observations lack the standardized control of the situation allowed by the laboratory.

The Structure of Temperament

Groundwork was laid for research on temperament in childhood by Alexander Thomas, Stella Chess, and their colleagues in the New York Longitudinal Study (Thomas et al. 1963). They analyzed interviews with parents about behaviors of their two-to-six-month-old infants, and identified nine dimensions of temperament: activity level, approach/withdrawal to new situations, adaptability to the desires of the parent, mood (positive versus negative), threshold, intensity, distractability, rhythmicity, and attention span/persistence.

Major revisions to this list have been proposed, based on factor analytic research on children's temperament. Factor analysis examines correlations among items or variables to determine which items or scales cluster together and which are relatively unrelated. The list of temperament dimensions in infancy and early childhood includes activity level, positive affectivity, fearfulness, anger/frustration, and by early childhood, effortful control (Rothbart and Mauro 1990). Effortful control refers to the capacity to inhibit a dominant response, such as opening a present, in order to perform a less dominant response, such as waiting for the appropriate occasion.

Studies of temperament in childhood have identified three broad factors of individual differences (Rothbart and Bates 1998). The first is *surgency* or *extraversion,* including activity level, high-intensity pleasure (risk seeking), impulsivity, positive excitement, smiling and laughter, and low shyness. The second is *negative emotionality,* including discomfort, sadness, anger/frustration, fear, and low soothability. The third is *effortful control,* including inhibitory control, attention, perceptual sensitivity, and low-intensity pleasure. Data on a large sample of toddlers in the Australian Temperament Project have yielded broad factors of negative emotionality, *self-regulation,* and *sociability* (Prior et al. 1989) that are very similar to negative emotionality, effortful control, and extraversion/surgency.

Typologies

Some psychologists have suggested that there are categories or types of people based on their temperament. Jerome Kagan (1998), for example, has argued that behaviorally inhibited and uninhibited children are two temperament types. Thomas and Chess (1977) described types of children labeled *difficult, easy,* and *slow to warm up.* In their view, difficult children were high on negative mood, withdrawal, adaptability, intensity, and low on rhythmicity, whereas easy children were defined by the opposite pattern. Slow to warm up children were seen as having mild, negative reactions to new stimuli, adapting slowly to the new situations. Because the factor analysis on which their typology was based has not held up in later research, the term *difficult* has not had consistent meanings. There are other problems with typologies: often many children do not fall into any of the categories. In addition, one of the types is often judged as negative, leading to expectations of future negative behavior from the child that may not be justified. John Bates's (1980) view of difficultness as defined by negative emotionality and demandingness has been a helpful contribution to the field, but his definition does not require the use of a typology.

The end of the twentieth century brought additional typologies of temperament (Robins, John, and Caspi 1997) related to Jack and Jeanne Block's (1980) categories of personality. One type, called *overcontrollers,* includes children who appear to be high in control of their impulses, often showing rigid patterns of behavior. *Undercontrollers* include children who are impulsive and who may act aggressively against others. A third type, *resilients,* includes children who respond in a flexible way to the demands of the environment. The expectation would be that overcontrollers would be high on fearfulness, undercontrollers would be high on surgency, low on fear and effortful control, and probably also high on anger/frustration. Resilient children would likely be high on effortful control. Future research may bring typologies and more dimensional approaches together.

Stability and Development of Temperament

Looking at children's temperament across time and development, seven-year-old temperament has been predicted by laboratory measures of fear, anger, and positive affect/surgency in infancy (Rothbart, Derryberry, and Hershey 2000), although attention showed little stability from infancy. This is probably related to the relatively later development of the executive attention system. As this system develops, the child's thoughts, emotions, and behaviors can come increasingly under self-control (Posner and Rothbart 1998). By the age of four, children's ability to delay going after a reward predicts higher achievement and greater emotional control in adolescence. Avshalom Caspi and Phil Silva (1995) found that children who were high on approach or confidence at three to four were also more impulsive at age eighteen, and higher on social potency, that is, taking charge of situations. More fearful children at age three to four were later higher on harm avoidance (avoidance of danger), lower on aggression, and lower on social potency. Children's distress proneness, when combined with lack of attentional control at three to four years, predicted higher distress tendencies at age eighteen.

The same longitudinal study (Caspi et al. 1995) predicted behavior problems at age fifteen from behavior at three to five years. Preschool approach predicted later lower anxiety and withdrawal in boys, and preschool distress combined with lack of attentional control predicted problems such as impulsivity and aggression, in both boys and girls. A number of links have now been identified between temperament and the development of psychopathology (see review by Rothbart and Bates 1998), as well as between temperament and health status, including adolescent substance use (Wills et al. 2002).

Parenting

Temperament, conscience, and discipline. Temperament measures allow study of the way temperament and social experience influence each other in personality development. For example, children's fearful temperament interacts with their treatment by parents in the development of conscience. Grazyna Kochanska (1995) found that more fearful children showed greater early development of conscience than less fearful children. She also found that gentle parenting (without using punishment) predicted conscience development among fearful children, but not among fearless children. In contrast, moral behavior of less fearful and more uninhibited children, but not fearful children, was greater when their mothers were responsive and when the mother/child attachment was secure (Kochanska 1995).

Kochanska's studies suggest that there are different developmental pathways to conscience for children who are temperamentally different. Gentle discipline de-emphasizing power may fit well by not allowing fearful children's arousal to reach such high levels that the child cannot take in parental messages. The use of power and punishment may raise these children's arousal to levels that may interfere with internalizing parent messages. Gentle discipline does not, however, promote morality in fearless children, who appear to be more sensitive to rewards associated with responsive parenting and to a close relationship with their parent.

Temperament and attachment. Attachment refers to thoughts, feelings, and behaviors shown by a child in a close relation to others, most often the mother or other primary caregiver. Although research findings have not been altogether consistent, there are reports of significant relationships between temperament and attachment measures (Rothbart and Bates 1998). One of the most interesting was reported by Dymphna van den Boom (1989). She found that infants who were irritable as newborns were more likely to be insecurely attached to their mothers at the end of the first year than nonirritable newborns. In a second study, van den Boom enrolled irritable newborn infants and their mothers for an intervention study. One group of mothers was taught parenting skills, including how to soothe and play with their babies; another group was not. With intervention, the trained mothers became more responsive to their babies, and more of their infants were identified as secure in their attachment at one year. Continued positive effects of this intervention on children's social behavior have been found for the children up to ages two and three years (van den Boom 1995).

Goodness of fit. Thomas and Chess developed the idea of goodness of fit to think about how temperament and parenting may interact to influence children's adjustment. Goodness of fit was said to result "when the child's capacities, motivations, and temperament are adequate to master the demands, expectations, and opportunities of the environment" (Chess and Thomas 1989, p. 380). The idea behind this concept is that different family situations may be a better fit for some children than others, depending on the child's temperament. Parents may also place different values on temperament-related behaviors. Behaviors seen as negative by parents would be considered a "poor fit." Thus, behaviors of an extraverted child may match one parent's values, but be seen as inappropriate by other parents.

Chess and Thomas (1984) gave as an example of poor fit the case of Roy, a highly distractible child. As an infant, Roy's distractibility allowed parental soothing to be quick and effective. Later, however, the distractibility that had been helpful to the parent in infancy was a problem as Roy became unreliable and forgetful as an older child. His mother nagged him to get things done, and in time, Roy ignored his mother's messages. This, in turn, led Roy's mother to judge him in negative terms. Roy's behavior did not improve, and the mother did not recognize that what had made him a good baby was now leading to unreliable behavior at home and at school that led her to judge him negatively. Although goodness of fit has been difficult to study, there is now some evidence of relations between goodness of fit, higher achievement, and more positive classroom behaviors (Paterson and Sanson 1999).

Additional Influences on Temperament and Parenting

Other factors may influence the relationship between temperament and parenting (Sanson and Rothbart 1995). These include the age and sex of the child, as well as social factors. In studies of mothers' responses to children's temperament, similar behaviors may lead to different responses depending on the child's age. At younger ages in infancy (e.g., six and twelve months), higher distress is related to more mother involvement. At later ages (e.g., eighteen and twenty-four months), the same behavior is related to lower mother involvement (Sanson and Rothbart 1995). Parents may begin by showing greater effort in raising a distress-prone child, but may not be able to sustain the effort over time and development.

Differences have also been found in parents' reactions to similar behaviors depending on the child's sex. More positive response to boys' than girls' irritability and negative emotion has been found, especially from fathers (Sanson and Rothbart 1995). Different beliefs of parents about how acceptable a temperamental attribute is for boys and girls might lead to different parent responses to similar behaviors from girls or boys.

Some studies examining the relationship between socioeconomic status (SES) and temperament have found no relationship. In a study of temperament and parenting in children aged three to four years, however, Margot Prior, Ann Sanson, and their colleagues (1989) found twice as many significant correlations between temperament and parenting measures in a high SES group than in a low SES group. The authors interpreted this as evidence of possible greater sensitivity and accommodation to the individuality of their children among high SES mothers.

Temperament and marriage. Temperament's relevance to marriage and the family involves adults as well as children. For example, temperament is related to age of marriage and of having children. In both U.S. and Swedish samples, childhood shyness was found to be related to later age of marriage and having children for men, but not for women (Kerr, Lambert, and Bem 1996). These findings suggest a tendency of less outgoing men to be less forward in the mating area. For women, these characteristics may be less important.

With data from a longitudinal sample followed for thirty years beginning at ages eight to ten, Avshalom Caspi, Glen Elder, and Daryl Bem (1989) found similar marriage patterns in adults who were shy as children. Men who were shy as children married an average of three years later, became fathers an average of four years later, and entered into a career path an average of three years later than men who were not shy as children. Childhood shyness in females predicted more traditional marriage and career paths, although women who were shy in childhood married at the same age as their nonshy counterparts, they spent fewer years in the workforce than women who were outgoing in childhood (Caspi, Elder, and Bem 1989).

Caspi, Elder, and Bem (1987) also examined the life-course patterns of adults with a history of explosive behaviors as children. Men who were ill-tempered as children (showing frequent and severe tantrums) were more likely to divorce and to have erratic work lives in comparison with men who were not ill-tempered as children. Women with histories of childhood tantrums tended to marry men with lower occupational status, were likely to divorce, and were considered to be ill-tempered as mothers (Caspi, Elder, and Bem 1987).

Differences in marital and family functioning have also been related to child temperament (Stoneman, Brody, and Burke 1989). For both fathers and mothers, consistent ratings of their older girls' temperamental difficulty (defined by Stoneman et al. as active and emotional) was related to decreased marital satisfaction and a less positive family climate in two-child families. Marital and family distresses were also related to having two temperamentally difficult siblings.

Temperament and culture. Numerous studies have found both similarities in the structure of temperament across cultures, and differences in levels of temperament between children of different cultures. A study of children's temperament in the People's Republic of China found lower surgency and higher negative affect than in a U.S. sample, with the two cultures also showing differences in relations among temperament variables (Ahadi; Rothbart; and Ye 1993). In the United States, but not China, children with higher effortful control were reported to have lower negative affectivity (fear, sadness, etc.). In China, but not the United States, higher effortful control was related to lower surgency. Culture may influence behaviors of children seen as worthy of control, and these behaviors can vary across cultures. In the United States, it may be more important to control negative feelings, whereas in China, stress may be placed on controlling one's outgoing and impulsive behaviors.

In an examination of relationships among culture, parental attitudes, and temperament, Xinyin Chen and colleagues (1998) studied two-year-old Chinese children in the People's Republic of China and Caucasian children in Canada. Chinese children were significantly more inhibited than the Canadian children, and inhibition was related to more acceptance and warmth from the Chinese mothers. In Canadian children, inhibition was negatively related to mothers' acceptance and encouragement. Again, there is the suggestion that cultural values may shape temperament by encouraging valued and discouraging de-valued characteristics.

Conclusion

This review has focused on individual differences in temperament and development, including family interaction. However, temperamental individuality among adult partners and its relation to family functioning is worthy of greater research interest. Future research on marriage and family processes should increasingly make use of measures of individual differences in temperament. Results of these studies, in turn, can be applied to marriage and family counseling. A temperament approach adds complexity to our view of childrearing and our thinking about how families function, but it also offers possibilities for increased understanding that would not be possible with simple, one-directional views of how parents influence children.

See also: ATTENTION DEFICIT/HYPERACTIVITY DISORDER (ADHD); CHILDHOOD, STAGES OF: INFANCY; CONDUCT DISORDER; DEVELOPMENTAL PSYCHOPATHOLOGY; DISCIPLINE; JUVENILE DELINQUENCY; OPPOSITIONALITY; PARENTING STYLES; SHYNESS

Bibliography

Ahadi, S. A.; Rothbart, M. K.; and Ye, R. M. (1993). "Children's Temperament in the U.S. and China: Similarities and Differences." *European Journal of Personality* 7:359–377.

Bates, J. E. (1980). "The Concept of Difficult Temperament." *Merrill Palmer Quarterly* 26:299–319.

Block, J. H., and Block, J. (1980). "The role of ego-control and ego-resiliency in the organization of behavior." In *Minnesota Symposium on Child Psychology,* ed. W. A. Collins. Hillsdale, NJ: Erlbaum.

Caspi, A.; Elder, G. H.; and Bem, D. J. (1987). "Moving Against the World: Life-Course Patterns of Explosive Children." *Developmental Psychology* 23:308–313.

Caspi, A.; Elder, G. H.; and Bem, D. J. (1989). "Moving Away From the World: Life-Course Patterns of Shy Children." In *Annual Progress in Child Psychiatry and Development,* ed. S. Chess and M. E. Hertzig. New York: Brunner/Mazel.

Caspi, A., and Silva, P. A. (1995). "Temperamental Qualities at Age Three Predict Personality Traits in Young Adulthood." *Child Development* 66:486–498.

Caspi, A.; Henry, B.; McGee, R. O.; Moffitt, T. E.; and Silva, P. A. (1995). "Temperamental Origins of Child and Adolescent Behavior Problems: From Age Three to Fifteen." *Child Development* 66:55–68.

Chen, X.; Hastings, P.D.; Rubin, K.H.; Chen, H.; Cen, G.; and Stewart, S.L. (1998). "Child-Rearing Attitudes and Behavioral Inhibition in Chinese and Canadian Toddlers: A Cross-Cultural Study." *Developmental Psychology* 34:677–686.

Chess, S., and Thomas, A. (1984). *Origins and Evolution of Behavior Disorders.* New York: Brunner/Mazel.

Chess, S., and Thomas, A. (1989). "Issues in the Clinical Application of Temperament." In *Temperament in Childhood,* ed. G. A. Kohnstamm, J. E. Bates, and M. K. Rothbart. Chichester, UK: John Wiley and Sons.

Kagan, J. (1998). "Biology and the Child." In *Handbook of Child Psychology: Vol. 3. Social, Emotional, and Personality Development,* 5th edition, series ed. W. Damon and volume ed. N. Eisenberg. New York: John Wiley and Sons.

Kerr, M.; Lambert, W. W.; and Bem, D. J. (1996). "Life Course Sequelae of Childhood Shyness in Sweden: Comparison with the United States." *Developmental Psychology* 32:1100–1105.

Kochanska, G. (1995). Children's Temperament, Mothers' Discipline, and Security of Attachment: Multiple Pathways to Emerging Internalization. *Child Development.* 66:597–615.

Paterson, G., and Sanson, A. (1999). "The Association of Behavioural Adjustment to Temperament, Parenting, and Family Characteristics among 5-Year-Old Children." *Social Development* 8:293–309.

Posner, M. I., and Rothbart, M. K. (1998). "Attention, Self-Regulation and Consciousness." *Philosophical Transactions of the Royal Society of London* B 353:1915–1927.

Prior, M.; Sanson, A.; Carroll, R.; and Oberklaid, F. (1989). "Social Class Differences in Temperament Ratings of Pre-School Children." *Merrill-Palmer Quarterly* 35:239–248.

Robins, R. W.; John, O. P.; and Caspi, A. (1997). "The Typological Approach to Studying Personality." In *Methods and Models for Studying the Individual,* ed. R. B. Cairns, L. R. Bergman, and J. Kagan. Thousand Oaks, CA: Sage.

Rothbart, M. K., and Bates, J. E. (1998). "Temperament." In *Handbook of Child Psychology,* Vol. 3: *Social, Emotional, and Personality Development,* 5th edition, series ed. W. Damon and volume ed. N. Eisenberg. New York: John Wiley and Sons.

Rothbart, M. K.; Derryberry, D.; and Hershey, K. (2000). "Stability of Temperament in Childhood: Laboratory Infant Assessment to Parent Report at Seven Years." In *Temperament and Personality Development Across the Life Span,* ed. V. J. Molfese and D. L. Molfese. Hillsdale, NJ: Erlbaum.

Rothbart, M. K., and Mauro, J. A. (1990). "Questionnaire Approaches to the Study of Infant Temperament." In *Individual Differences in Infancy: Reliability, Stability and Prediction,* ed. J. W. Fagen and J. Colombo. Hillsdale, NJ: Erlbaum.

Sanson, A., and Rothbart, M. K. (1995). "Child Temperament and Parenting." In *Parenting,* ed. M. Bornstein. Hillsdale, NJ: Erlbaum.

Stoneman, Z.; Brody, G. H.; and Burke, M. (1989). "Sibling Temperament and Maternal and Paternal Perceptions of Marital, Family, and Personal Functioning." *Journal of Marriage and Family* 51:99–113.

Thomas, A., and Chess, S. (1977). *Temperament and Development.* New York: Brunner/Mazel.

Thomas, A.; Chess, S.; Birch, H. G.; Hertzig, M. E.; and Korn, S. (1963). *Behavioral Individuality in Early Childhood.* New York: New York University Press.

van den Boom, D. (1989). "Neonatal Irritability and the Development of Attachment." In *Temperament in Childhood,* ed. G. A. Kohnstamm, J. E. Bates, and M. K. Rothbart. Chichester, UK: John Wiley and Sons.

van den Boom, D. (1995). "Do First-Year Intervention Effects Endure? Follow-Up During Toddlerhood of a Sample of Dutch Irritable Infants." *Child Development* 66:1798–1816.

Wills, T. A.; Cleary, S. D.; Shinar, O.; and Filer, M. (2002). "Temperament Dimensions and Health Behavior: A Developmental Model." In *Health and Behavior in Childhood and Adolescence,* ed. L. L. Hayman, M. M. Mahon, and J. R. Turner. New York: Springer.

MARY K. ROTHBART
JENNIFER SIMONDS

THERAPY

COUPLE RELATIONSHIPS

Contemporary couples therapy has its origins in several counseling movements. According to Carlfred Broderick and Sandra Schrader's (1991) history of marital and family therapy, couples therapy initially grew out of the marriage-counseling and sex therapy movements of the early twentieth century. Social workers recognized the need to work with the family and marital systems, as well as the individual, long before the growing fields of psychology and psychoanalysis. In addition, burgeoning interest in human sexuality and sex therapy, which grew out of the work of Havelock Ellis in Great Britain and Magnus Hirschfeld in Germany shortly after World War I, influenced the growing emphasis on the couple dyad. Marriage counseling, however, was not truly considered a profession until the 1960s and 1970s, when it developed a professional organization, journals, and standards. It was somewhat eclipsed by the more popular family therapy movement in the 1970s, though the two eventually became strongly linked, with shared journals, organizations, and practitioners. Today, although there are distinct theories and practices of marital and family therapy, there continue to be many shared links.

Models of Couples Therapy

In general, couples therapy has been shown in dozens of studies to be more effective than no treatment (for meta-analyses of these studies, see Baucom et al. 1998 and Shadish et al. 1993). Although most couples are helped by therapy, less than half end up in the nondistressed range (Shadish et al. 1993). At the beginning of the twenty-first century, the therapies with the most support are *behavioral couples therapy, cognitive behavioral couples therapy,* and *emotionally focused therapy* (Christensen and Heavey 1999). A new model in the field, *integrative behavioral couples therapy* (Jacobson and Christensen 1996; Christensen and Jacobson 2000), also has empirical support. In addition to these, there are several less researched, but promising, models of couples therapy, including *family systems therapy* and *problem-* and *solution-focused therapies.*

Behavioral Couples Therapy

Behavioral couples therapy (BCT) is the most widely researched and well-validated model of couple therapy (Christensen and Heavey 1999). Like individual behavioral therapy, BCT is derived from social learning and social exchange theories, which emphasize the influence of the environment and its behavioral and emotional rewards and costs. Behavioral couples therapy is built upon the idea that couple satisfaction is determined, in large part, by the positive and negative nature of spouses' interactions with each other.

Many distressed couples report feeling unable to communicate with each other or solve problems when they arise, which leads them to feel unhappy and frustrated with each other. According to behavioral theory, these negative interactions decrease the rewards couples gain from their relationship. In response to this reward reduction, BCT focuses on increasing the ratio of positive to negative behaviors for couples in distress and teaching them effective communication behaviors so that they may handle difficulties when they arise.

Several kinds of skills-oriented therapeutic techniques are used in BCT. First, therapists often work with couples to increase the number of positive behaviors that partners do for each other. For example, the therapist may guide partners in generating a list of positive actions that they could do for the other, such as complimenting the other or fixing the other breakfast. The therapist may then encourage partners to enact the behaviors on the list. Norman Epstein, Donald Baucom, and Anthony Daiuto (1997) suggest, however, that these interventions may be most effective if they address an area of concern for the couple. For example, a couple in conflict over parenting might be asked engage in positive behaviors in the domain of parenting, such as sharing diaper-changing duties.

The other main focus of BCT is improving communication skills and teaching problem-solving strategies. Communication skills that therapists may teach couples include the use of "I statements" that express feelings without blaming the partner, the use of verbal and nonverbal cues in listening, moderation of negative statements with the inclusion of positive feelings, and reflecting back of what each partner has said (Epstein, Baucom, and Daiuto 1997). Problem-solving training typically involves helping the couple to define a problem clearly, generate alternative solutions, compromise on a solution, implement it, and evaluate its effectiveness (Christensen and Heavey 1999).

Cognitive Behavioral Couples Therapy

Cognitive behavioral couples therapy (CBCT) includes the ideas and techniques of its predecessor, BCT, with an added cognitive component. In

Couples seek counseling for many reasons, ranging from difficulty communicating with each other to disagreements on parenting. Emotional outpouring, as shown here, is a common and expected part of the therapy. PHOTOEDIT

CBCT, several kinds of cognitions may be targeted, including assumptions about the partner, relationship standards, attributions of past partner behavior, expectations regarding how partners will behave, and selective attention to some aspects of partner behavior and not others (Epstein, Baucom, and Daiuto 1997). Cognitive behavioral couples therapy intervention techniques involve the use of cognitive restructuring, a process of evaluating cognitions systematically, determining their accuracy, and changing those that are unrealistic or inaccurate. For unrealistic attributions, assumptions, standards, and expectations, the therapist and partners work together to generate alternative explanations that are more accurate and lead to greater positive feelings between partners.

Integrative Behavioral Couples Therapy

Integrative behavioral couples therapy (Jacobson and Christensen 1996) is an adaptation of BCT that focuses not only on behavioral change, but also includes an emphasis on acceptance of problems that are difficult or impossible to change. In order to promote acceptance, therapists may help couples reformulate problems as differences, rather than deficiencies; promote the expression of the vulnerable feelings that often lie behind aversive behavior; encourage an objective analysis of the problematic patterns couples experience; or engage in reenactment of aversive behavior in ways that promote increased tolerance. Not only are these strategies designed to promote acceptance, but they may indirectly foster change in the problematic behavior and increase emotional closeness between the pair.

Emotionally Focused Therapy

In contrast to more behavioral therapies, *emotionally focused therapy* (EFT) explains relationship distress in terms of attachment theory, rather than behavioral exchange. Emotionally focused therapy, developed by Leslie Greenberg and Susan Johnson (1988), involves the identification of problematic interaction cycles between partners and the emotions underlying them. Relationship distress is believed to arise when attachment bonds are disrupted or have not been fully formed, leading partners to engage in rigid interactional patterns that prevent emotional closeness (Christensen and Heavey 1999). Emotionally focused therapy works to help couples recognize their emotional experience in the relationship and restructure their interactions in order to create a more satisfying relationship. The therapist and couple work together to reprocess and redefine the relationship in such a way that it provides a more secure attachment base for both partners.

Family Systems

The *family systems* approach to couple therapy emerged as part of the field of family systems research, with the couple seen as the central and most influential subunit of a larger family system (Fraenkel 1997). The foundation of systemic couple theory is that all problems, including couple problems, occur in a multilevel context, which ranges in specificity from the just the two members of the couple to their immediate environment (i.e., family, work, or school) to their larger society or culture.

For couples, intervention techniques vary widely, as a function of the specific type of systems theory from which they are derived (examples of different types include *structural, strategic,* and *experiental*). However, Peter Fraenkel (1997) notes a variety of common goals of systems therapy, including focusing on strengths and resources, attending to the therapeutic environment as a "system," and identifying, stopping, and changing problematic interaction patterns. Family systems therapists may ensure that the therapy is of a brief duration to save time and energy and avoid dependence upon the therapist. The therapist may also model important concepts, including teaching how different family members may emotionally respond to each other and how partners may maintain their separate identities and perspectives while still working together as a couple (Papero 1995).

Problem- and Solution-Focused Therapy

Problem- and *solution-focused therapies* are approaches that focus on expedient problem resolution for couples, rather than on protracted work toward personal growth, underlying emotional issues, or general communication skills (Shoham, Rohrbaugh, and Patterson 1995). These therapies focus not only on how partners behave in the situation of conflict, but also how they view the problem. The two therapies, problem and solution focused, differ somewhat in their balance of behavioral versus cognitive change and their manner of reinforcing change, but they are quite similar in their focus on parsimonious therapeutic work toward single problem resolution (Shoham, Rohrbaugh, and Patterson 1995).

What Brings Couples to Therapy

Couples seek help from therapists for many reasons, ranging from difficulty communicating and dissatisfaction with their sex life to problems in coparenting or wanting to prevent divorce or separation. Other common reasons include a lack of emotional affection, divorce/separation concerns, infidelity, and domestic violence. Couples may come to therapy for any issue that they must face together, which can also include individual problems, such as mental illness, or family difficulties, such as a child's problems in school. The role of the therapist is to help them cope with these difficulties together, solve them when possible, and, as discussed above, accept them when no solution can be found.

Specific Issues

Couples frequently come to therapy to seek help in dealing with children and parenting. This is particularly true in the case of blended families, in which one partner is a stepparent to the other's child or children. Anne Bernstein (2000) notes that stepchildren are often a source of conflict, as the couple must try to develop their relationship without the freedom to focus solely on their own needs, which newly married couples without children may have. Other issues that can surface in this area include disagreements about parenting, conflicts with a particular child, or marital conflicts expressed through parent-child difficulties. Often, parent-training or family therapy are also appropriate treatments for these difficulties.

Sexual difficulties are one of the more common problems that couples bring to therapy. Couples may disagree on when, where, or how often they have sex, as well as what activities they engage in. This can be complicated by the emotional meaning sex has for each member of the couple, as when one member wants to use sex to make up after a fight and the other can't have sex until they've made up.

Infidelity is one of the most emotionally laden problems that couples bring to therapy. Shirley Glass and Thomas Wright (1997) discuss the many issues infidelity raises, including how and when discovery of an affair is made, how long the affair went on and with whom, and whether the involved spouse is willing to give up the affair. A major issue is whether the couple will remain together. If they stay together they must discuss what information about the affair the betrayed spouse needs or wants to know, how they can understand the affair, and how they can rebuild trust.

Finally, domestic violence is a serious problem in relationships. As Richard Heyman and Peter Neidig (1997) note, all couples therapists treat couples dealing with violence, whether they know it or not. Although couples may fail to identify violence as a problem in their relationship, its effects can still be quite damaging and therapists need to be vigilant in assessing for violence among couples. If violence is present, the therapist must decide whether or not it is appropriate to treat the couple together. Some researchers and clinicians contend that if violence is present, couples therapy should not be attempted, as it may exacerbate conflicts that put the abused partner at risk. Others suggest that, under certain specific conditions, a couples therapy that is designed to treat violence may be appropriate (e.g., Heyman and Neidig 1997).

Specific Groups

Any couple can face some or all of the problems listed above, but some couples bring other specific issues to therapy, such as unmarried couples, same-sex couples, aging couples, couples of lower socioeconomic status, and interracial or intercultural couples.

Unmarried couples range from dating couples to committed cohabiting couples who have either chosen to remain unmarried or are not permitted to marry (such as lesbian and gay couples). These couples may be more likely to bring in issues concerning whether or not to commit to a long-term relationship, or they may want help in resolving certain problems before making such a commitment. They are less likely to have conflicts over childrearing, though they may disagree about whether to have children. They may also need help in dealing with the stigma for cohabiting without marriage or with pressure from family members to get married (or not to marry).

Same-sex couples face many of the same issues that opposite-sex couples do, but may also carry the additional burdens of homophobia and heterosexism. This can manifest in couple difficulties in a number of ways, including stress related to family disapproval, conflicts over how "out" to be, and distress over not being able to legally commit to one another. Same-sex couples may also have difficulties surrounding differences in identity development. One partner may be more comfortable with his/her sexuality and put pressure on the other to be more "out" than he/she can be at their personal stage of development. Conversely, they may feel held back or forced to remain closeted by a partner who is still coming to terms with their sexuality (Okun 1996).

Aging couples face a number of difficulties they may bring to therapy, including the transition to retirement, dealing with adult children and grandchildren, coping with illness, and learning to be alone when their partner dies. As the population ages, couples will have a longer period of time together in the "empty nest" and presumably a greater need for couple therapy (Rosowsky 1999).

Couples of lower socioeconomic status may face a number of financial tensions and stressors as they attempt to support their families on a low income. This may be particularly problematic if one member of the couple comes from a wealthier family, resulting in tensions over "marrying down" (Ross 1995). Low-income couples may also face difficulties over whether they can afford therapy and how severe problems must be to warrant seeking outside help.

Finally, interracial or intercultural couples face a number of specific challenges in their relationships, which can result in relationship distress. These couples must often deal with the racism and prejudices faced by all people of color, but may also have to cope with the merging of two cultures and two sets of expectations about relationships. It is the task of the couples therapist to be sensitive to the cultural differences and needs of each member, and to help each member of the couple understand how these factors might affect them individually and as a couple (Okun 1996).

Couples Therapy and Individual Issues

In addition to being effective for relationship problems, couples therapy has been repeatedly shown to be effective for individual problems. Studies of couples treatment for individual psychopathology have varied in several ways, including the individual disorder studied, the satisfaction of the couple, and the extent to which the therapy focuses on relationship problems versus an individual spouse's difficulties. Therapies with more minimal involvement of one spouse and a strong focus on an individual issue are often termed *spouse-aided* rather than *couple therapy*. The three domains in which couples treatment have been most studied (and appear most efficacious) are *depression, anxiety,* and *substance abuse*.

Although causal links between depression and marital discord are unknown, the odds of being depressed increase tenfold for both partners if they are distressed in their relationship (O'Leary, Christian, and Mendell 1994). There is growing support in the literature for couples treatment for depression, and marital therapy used to treat individual depression in a maritally distressed couple has been found to be significantly more effective than no treatment both in increasing marital satisfaction and reducing depressive symptoms (Beach, Fincham, and Katz 1998). Furthermore, several studies have found BCT to be as effective as individual cognitive therapy for reducing depressive symptoms and somewhat more effective than individual therapy for improving marital functioning (see Jacobson et al. 1991 and Beach and O'Leary 1992). Not surprisingly, couples therapy does not appear to be as helpful for depression in the absence of marital distress (Gotlib and Hammen 1992; Beach, Fincham, and Katz 1998).

The most efficacious couples treatments for depression seem to focus on enhancing communication and intimacy and improving interpersonal interactions. This focus may help to improve both the relationship and individual symptomology, although this has not been tested on severely depressed or hospitalized patients. (Beach and O'Leary 1992). However, couples therapy may be contraindicated if one partner is so severely depressed that he or she needs to be the sole focus of treatment or the depression is psychotic or bipolar, all of which would limit that person's ability to focus on the relationship.

Spouse-aided treatment for *anxiety spectrum disorders* also appears to be efficacious, particularly for *agoraphobia* and *generalized anxiety disorder*. W. Kim Halford and Ruth Bouma (1997) note that the relationship between marital difficulties and anxiety is moderated by gender, type of anxiety, and whether both spouses have anxiety disorders. As in the case of depression, research suggests that couples treatment for anxiety may be most effective in the presence of marital distress, although if a spouse reinforces or helps to perpetuate anxiety symptoms (for instance, if a spouse facilitates avoidance behavior), then spouse-aided therapy may also be helpful. Some outcome studies suggest that *in vivo* treatment for agoraphobia including a focus on couple functioning is more effective at follow-up than *in vivo* treatment without the couple focus (Epstein, Baucom, and Daiuto 1997). However, other studies have found spouse-aided therapy to be neither more nor less effective than individual therapy for agoraphobia (Emmelkamp et al. 1992).

Substance abuse in a marital relationship may be among the most destructive of comorbid disorders due to its many potential relationship and individual consequences, including poor physical health, unemployment, abdication of household and other responsibilities, and potential for violence. Couples therapy for individual substance abuse shows promise, although research on this topic has varied widely in models of substance abuse, methodology, and level of spousal involvement. Most couples therapy research on substance abuse has focused on alcoholism, and therapy goals typically involve eliminating drinking or supporting the drinker's efforts to stop, altering marital interactions to create an environment that encourages sobriety, preventing relapse, and dealing with more general marital issues (O'Farrell and Rotunda 1997).

Interventions are likely to focus on the urge to drink or do drugs, important events in the last week relating to substance use, helping couples identify behaviors in themselves and each other that may trigger substance use, strategies to increase positive nonalcohol-related behaviors between spouses, and teaching communication and problem-solving skills. Timothy O'Farrell and William Fals-Stewart's (2000) application of behavioral couples therapy for alcoholism and drug abuse found that it was more effective than individual treatment for producing abstinence and fewer substance-related problems, higher relationship satisfaction, decreased domestic violence, and lower risk for marital separation.

Culture, Ethnicity, and Couples Therapy

Culture and ethnicity have been increasingly recognized as important factors in therapy. It is also increasingly evident that therapists can make serious mistakes when they fail to recognize cultural explanations for behaviors or problems and then over- or under-pathologize patients on that basis. This can be a problem in couples therapy, as an uninformed therapist may label a behavior that is acceptable and adaptive from the couple's point of view as problematic because it does not fit his/her cultural standards for a healthy relationship. There are several solutions to this potential problem, including obtaining knowledge about the cultural background of the couple, becoming aware of one's own cultural background, and becoming a culturally sensitive therapist.

The first step, obtaining knowledge about the cultural background of the couple, is similar to researching any issue that might affect the effectiveness of therapy. The greater the therapist's understanding of each member's cultural background, the more likely that they will be able offer interpretations and suggestions that fit the couple's schema. The most important and best source of this information is the couple itself. Although obtaining information on specific ethnic or cultural groups might be useful, it is important to remember that such information may not apply to specific individuals. Rather, a culturally sensitive therapist recognizes that the members of the couple are the best experts on how their cultural backgrounds affect their lives and experiences.

According to Monica McGoldrick and Joe Giordano (1996), it is just as important for the therapist to become aware of his/her own cultural background and influences. Culturally sensitive therapists recognize that their own values and expectations, as well as those of their clients, stem from culture, rather than assuming that such ideas are universal. For example, a therapist may think that it is a universal rule that communicating clearly and openly about one's emotions is healthy, failing to recognize that the idea is, in fact, culturally determined, and that there are many cultures in which straightforward communication about emotions is considered immature or rude.

In other words, a culturally sensitive therapist is one who, as defined by Steven Lopez (1997), is able to recognize the different cultural "lenses" that clients and therapists bring to therapy. According to Lopez, every person views the world through the lens of culture, and it is the therapist's job to learn about their client's lens and find a way to work together in a way that is compatible with both views. This is especially important in couples therapy, as each member of the couple brings a separate lens. The lenses may be vastly different in the case of an interracial or intercultural couple, or they may be only slightly discrepant, in the case of a couple in which both members are from the same culture.

It is extremely important to maintain an awareness of the impact of racism, prejudice, and discrimination. Therapists of the dominant culture may have unconscious or unacknowledged negative attitudes towards people of other cultures. These feelings can emerge in subtle ways that denigrate or ignore the cultural needs and characteristics of a couple. Similarly, a therapist who is not of the dominant culture may have to deal with such negative attitudes from clients of the dominant culture. Even when therapists and couples match in ethnicity or culture, they may find that they have different ideas about what it means to be a member of that culture. Couples in which one or both members are not from the dominant culture may face prejudice and discrimination in the society they live in. This experience can place strain on the health of the relationship, as well as that of the individual. Couples may experience conflict over how and when to confront racism and prejudice and over determining the best ways to cope (Okun 1996).

Conclusion

Since its origins in the marriage-counseling movement, couples therapy has grown and diversified. There are many models of couples therapy, which share the goal of improved relationship functioning. These therapies, however, may differ significantly in the techniques they use, from teaching new skills to focusing on emotions and acceptance.

Moreover, the couples entering therapy may differ in the problems that bring them to therapy from communication, to sex, to children, to violence between partners. There is increasing evidence indicating that couples therapy may be useful for treating individual problems as well, including depression, anxiety, and substance abuse.

Couples therapists are also becoming more sensitive to their own and their clients' sociocultural backgrounds, needs, and interests. This trend is important, as there is no single type of couple that may benefit from couples therapy, and couples may vary tremendously in their levels of commitment and the relationship issues with which they are dealing. Further research should address how to differentiate between couples who will improve in therapy and those who will not, what kinds of problems couples therapists are best prepared to help, and how to generalize our treatments so that they work for couples of all ages and backgrounds. Fortunately, with the variety of models, approaches, and techniques available as well as the creativity and careful work of researchers and clinicians, the future looks bright for couples therapy.

See also: ANXIETY DISORDERS; ATTACHMENT: COUPLE RELATIONSHIPS; ATTRIBUTION IN RELATIONSHIPS; CODEPENDENCY; COMMUNICATION: COUPLE RELATIONSHIPS; CONFLICT: COUPLE RELATIONSHIPS; COPARENTING; DEPRESSION: ADULTS; FAMILY SYSTEMS THEORY; FORGIVENESS; INFIDELITY; JEALOUSY; MARITAL QUALITY; MARITAL SEX; MARITAL TYPOLOGIES; MARRIAGE ENRICHMENT; POWER: MARITAL RELATIONSHIPS; PROBLEM SOLVING; SEXUAL COMMUNICATION: COUPLE RELATIONSHIPS; SEXUAL DYSFUNCTION; THERAPY: FAMILY RELATIONSHIPS; SOCIAL EXCHANGE THEORY; SPOUSE ABUSE: PREVALENCE; SPOUSE ABUSE: THEORETICAL EXPLANATIONS; SUBSTANCE ABUSE; TRANSITION TO PARENTHOOD

Bibliography

Baucom, D. H.; Shoham, V.; Meuser, K. T.; Daiuto, A.; and Stickle, T. R. (1998). "Empirically Supported Couple and Family Interventions for Marital Distress and Adult Mental Health Problems." *Journal of Counseling and Clinical Psychology* 66:53–88.

Beach, S. R.; Fincham, F. D.; and Katz, J. (1998). "Marital Therapy in the Treatment of Depression: Toward a Third Generation of Therapy and Research." *Clinical Psychology Review* 18:635–661.

Beach, S. R., and O'Leary K. D. (1992). "Treating Depression in the Context of Marital Discord: Outcome and Predictors of Response for Marital Therapy vs. Cognitive Therapy." *Behavior Therapy* 23:507–528.

Bernstein, A. C. (2000). "Remarriage: Redesigning Couplehood." In *Couples on the Fault Line: New Directions for Therapists,* ed. P. Papp. New York: Guilford Press.

Broderick, C. B., and Schrader, S. S. (1991). "The History of Professional Marriage and Family Therapy." In *Handbook of Family Therapy,* Vol. 2, ed. A. S. Gurman and D. P. Kniskern. New York: Brunner/Mazel.

Christensen, A., and Heavey, C. L. (1999). "Interventions for Couples." *Annual Review of Psychology* 50:165–190.

Christensen A., and Jacobson, N. S. (2000). *Reconcilable Differences.* New York: Guilford Press.

Emmelkamp, P. M.; Van Dyck, R.; Bitter, M.; Heins, R.; Onstein, E. J.; and Eisen, B. (1992). "Spouse-Aided Therapy with Agoraphobics." *British Journal of Psychiatry* 160:51–56.

Epstein, N. H.; Baucom, D. H.; and Daiuto, A. (1997). "Cognitive-Behavioral Couples Therapy." In *Clinical Handbook of Marriage and Couples Interventions,* ed. W. K. Halford and H. Markman. New York: Wiley.

Fraenkel, P. (1997). "Systems Approaches to Couple Therapy." In *Clinical Handbook of Marriage and Couples Interventions,* ed. W. K. Halford and H. Markman. New York: Wiley.

Glass, S. P., and Wright, T. L. (1997). "Reconstructing Marriages after the Trauma of Infidelity." In *Clinical Handbook of Marriage and Couples Interventions,* ed. W. K. Halford and H. Markman. New York: Wiley.

Greenberg, L. S., and Johnson, S. M. (1988). *Emotionally Focused Therapy for Couples.* New York: Guilford Press.

Gotlib, I. H., and Hammen, C. L. (1992). *Psychological Aspects of Depression: Toward a Cognitive-Interpersonal Integration.* New York: Wiley.

Halford, W. K., and Bouma, R. (1997). "Individual Psychopathology and Marital Distress." In *Clinical Handbook of Marriage and Couples Interventions,* ed. W. K. Halford and H. Markman. New York: Wiley.

Heyman, R. E., and Neidig, P. H. (1997). "Physical Aggression Couples Treatment." In *Clinical Handbook of Marriage and Couples Interventions,* ed. W. K. Halford and H. Markman. New York: Wiley.

Jacobson, N. S., and Christensen, A. (1996) *Integrative Couple Therapy.* New York: Norton.

Jacobson, N. S.; Dobson, K.; Fruzetti, A. E.; Schmaling, K. B.; and Salusky, S. (1991). "Marital Therapy As a Treatment for Depression." *Journal of Consulting and Clinical Psychology* 59:547–557.

Lopez, S. R. (1997). "Cultural Competence in Psychotherapy: A Guide for Clinicians and Their Supervisors." In *Handbook of Psychotherapy Supervision,* ed. C. E. Watkins, Jr. New York: Wiley.

McGoldrick, M., and Giordano, J. (1996). "Overview: Ethnicity and Family Therapy." In *Ethnicity and Family Therapy,* 2nd edition, ed. M. McGoldrick, J. Giordano, and J. K. Pearce. New York: Guilford Press.

O'Farrell, T. J., and Fals-Stewart, W. (2000). "Behavioral Couples Therapy for Alcoholism and Drug Abuse." *Journal of Substance Abuse Treatment* 18:51–54.

O'Farrell, T. J., and Rotunda, R. J. (1997). "Couples Interventions and Alcohol Abuse." In *Clinical Handbook of Marriage and Couples Interventions,* ed. W. K. Halford and H. Markman. New York: Wiley.

Okun, B. F. (1996). *Understanding Diverse Families: What Practitioners Need to Know.* New York: Guilford Press.

O'Leary, K. D.; Christian, J. L.; and Mendell, N. R. (1994). "A Closer Look at the Link between Marital Discord and Depressive Symptomatology." *Journal of Social and Clinical Psychology* 13:33–41.

Papero, D. V. (1995). "Bowen Family Systems and Marriage." In *Clinical Handbook of Couple Therapy,* ed. N. S. Jacobson and A. S. Gurman. New York: Guilford Press.

Rosowsky, E. (1999). "Couple Therapy with Long-Married Older Adults." In *Handbook of Counseling and Psychotherapy with Older Adults,* ed. M. Duffy. New York: Wiley.

Ross, J. L. (1995). "Social Class Tensions within Families." *American Journal of Family Therapy* 23(4):338–350.

Shadish, W. R.; Montgomery, L. M.; Wilson, P.; Wilson, M. R.; Bright, I.; and Okwumabua, T. (1993). "Effects of Family and Marital Psychotherapies: A Meta-Analysis." *Journal of Consulting and Clinical Psychology* 61:992–1002.

Shoham, V.; Rohrbaugh, M.; and Patterson, J. (1995). "Problem- and Solution-Focused Therapies: The MRI and Milwaukee Models." In *Clinical Handbook of Couple Therapy,* ed. N. S. Jacobson and A. S. Gurman. New York: Guilford Press.

LORELEI E. SIMPSON
KRISTA S. GATTIS
ANDREW CHRISTENSEN

FAMILY RELATIONSHIPS

Models of family therapy were developing in many different countries during the 1950s, but in the United States, it was a twin birth, with one branch of family therapy being developed on the West Coast (with Gregory Bateson and Don Jackson) and another on the East Coast (with Nathan Ackerman). The field has since grown like an onion, one development layering upon another in a way that makes each development independently useful and still part of an increasingly complex system of interventions. Therapists are always reaching back to older techniques and theories as they also evolve new concepts and interventions.

The First Generation of Family Therapy

Gregory Bateson (an anthropologist) and Don Jackson (a psychiatrist) developed a systemic approach to schizophrenia while working at the Palo Alto Veterans Hospital (Bateson 1973; Jackson, 1961, 1973). The Bateson Project stressed that problems do not exist in any one person—relationship problems and/or dysfunctional interaction styles cause distress in individual family members. The dysfunction resides not in the "identified patient" but in the verbal and non-verbal communications that occur between family members. For example, if a father tells his son (the identified patient) to "be independent" one day and "obey your father" on the next day, he is putting the child in a position where the son will be emotionally conflicted and lose no matter what he does. The child cannot escape the relationship, his desire to please his parent, or his inability to be both "obedient" and "independent" at the same time. Jackson called this a *double bind* and thought that it was related to the etiology of schizophrenia. While Jackson was wrong in assuming that family communication patterns "cause" schizophrenia, his work on dysfunctional communications in the family was the seed of the second-generation "family systems" therapies.

Nathan Ackerman (1958), a clinician working in New York City, realized that when parents brought their children into the clinic, they were often blind to how their roles as parents and spouses were inciting and exacerbating the children's problems. Ackerman was the leader in reorienting treatment for children referred to child guidance centers to include the entire family. Ackerman came from a psychodynamic background but he understood that individuals are shaped by current family circumstances as well as their intrapsychic issues. He postulated that many problems in adolescence and adulthood are due to family conflicts over how the family should be organized and how it should carry out essential family functions. For example, should the mother work a second job so her children can buy expensive sneakers? Should the children be allowed to determine their own bedtime? Families inevitably confront many such issues due to changes in their children or themselves. As the family matures and changes, all the members must adapt and change. When family members do not want to change or do not know how to change, conflict characterizes family interaction, and individual members start showing psychological symptoms of distress. Ackerman also focused on the complementary interactions between the family and the individual—how each needs the other's affection and protection to survive.

Second-Generation Family Therapies

As the family approach became more popular, the theories and techniques began to multiply. Most could be grouped under one of the following six headings: Psychodynamic, Structural, Strategic, Conjoint/Humanistic, Cognitive/Behavioral, and Solution-Focused (see Figure 1).

Psychodynamic/transgenerational family therapy. This approach was developed by Murray Bowen, Ivan Boszormenyi-Nagy, and James Framo (Bowen 1978; Boszormenyi-Nagy 1973; Framo 1982). Family members who enter psychodynamic Bowian therapy spend a lot of time thinking about the childhood forces that shape their personalities (Papero 1990). Often, a person will be in individual therapy alone. What makes this family therapy instead of psychodynamic therapy is that the emphasis is not uni-directional, analyzing only what parents did to their children, but rather on what clients really want to do in their lives and how the family has made it difficult for them to move towards their desired goals. They then have to confront their parents as adults, whenever possible, so that instead of being emotionally dependent on the parents for approval, they become interdependent with them as adults. Indeed, Framo (1982) has focused on creating family-of-origin sessions, so that adult children can confront their parents and learn to communicate on a more open, adult, and caring level.

Bowen was highly theoretical in his approach, and many of his concepts are so popular and endemic that they are considered to be the core concepts of the entire field. The five major concepts are as follows (Bowen 1978):

- *Differentiation of self.* This is the ability to distinguish intellectual from emotional needs, desires, and responses. Young adults who feel guilty leaving their parents' homes are not even going to think about applying to a school 1,000 miles away if they have a low level of differentation. With a high level of differentiation, they will be able to consider the pros and cons of schools both near and far.
- *Triangles.* When two people have difficulty communicating with one another, it becomes much easier for both to focus on a third person and triangulate them into the relationship. Sometimes the third person has divided loyalties and must shift from side to side (as children in many divorce situations do); sometimes the third person simply aligns himself or herself with one person (e.g., when mother and daughter are on one side and father is alone on the other). There are also many triangles where the two parties who are at odds (usually the parents) decide to focus on and micro-manage the problems of a third person (usually one of the children) to have some interactions that do not touch the most explosive areas of the relationship.
- *Family projection process.* Not all children in the family are treated similarly by the parents. The child who is most emotionally involved with the parents and the least likely to differentiate from them is the object of the family projection process.
- *Emotional cutoff.* When children have trouble successfully differentiating they sometime resort to avoiding any real psychological intimacy or self-disclosure with their parents. Sometimes, they will physically move to another state or continent to avoid contact.
- *Multigenerational transmission process.* Family functioning is passed on like many genetic traits. Psychological functioning is passed down through the generations by two mechanisms. First, individuals tend to marry someone at the same level of differentiation as themselves, so that poorly differentiated

FIGURE 1

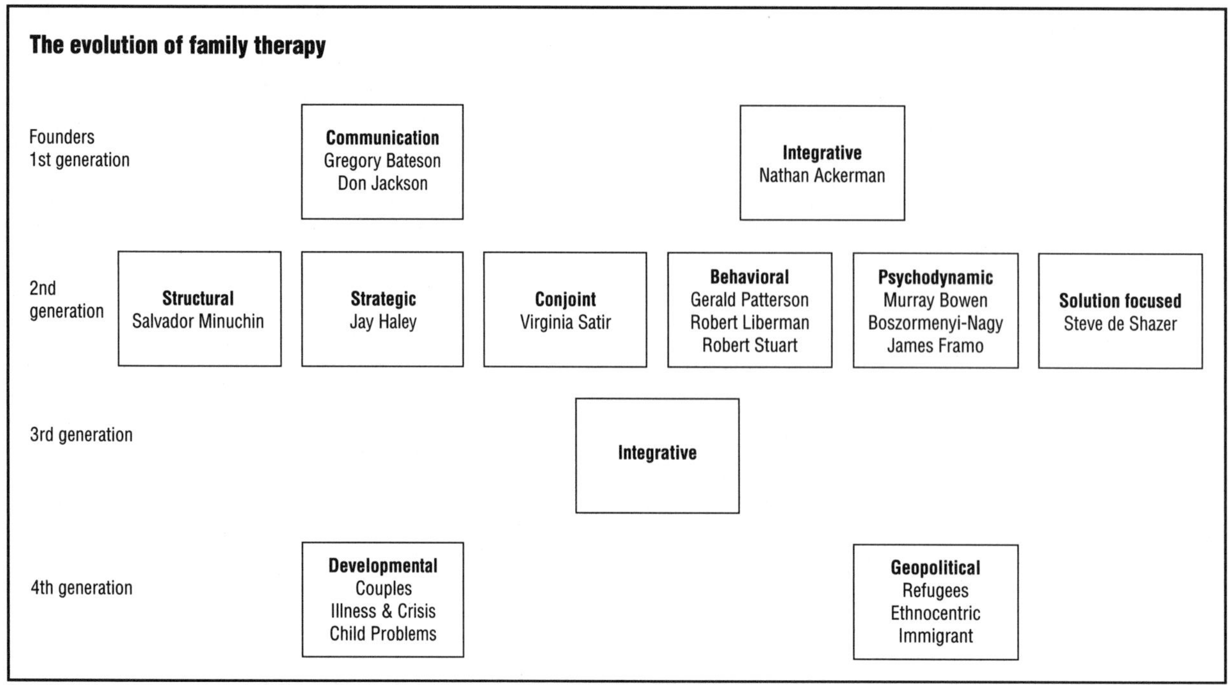

people marry one another and cannot really relate as independent adults. Then, through the family projection process, at least one of the children is pulled into their emotional neediness circle and can function even less as an independent adult.

The goal is to help each person achieve maximum self-differentiation. The therapist stays removed and de-triangulated from the family, acting as a coach to help the family do research into its own family functioning. Remaining emotionally neutral, the therapist helps each person in the family realize the part that he or she is playing in maintaining the problem. Each person talks to the therapist (instead of each other) as each tries to communicate true thoughts and feelings. The therapist builds a mini-relationship with each person in the family, modeling how each should focus on self-disclosure and respectfully listening instead of talking about a third person. Openly expressing one's thoughts is promoted so that the family hears one another's perspectives. The therapist often works with the most psychologically healthy person in the family, with the idea that he or she will be able to differentiate most successfully and serve as a model for the rest of the family.

The most widely used of Bowen's techniques is the *family genogram,* where the structure and characteristics of family members are mapped over at least three generations to look for multigenerational influences. Other psychodynamic family therapists have focused on how the children become indebted to their parents and help them find ways to "balance the ledger" (Boszormenyi-Nagy 1973).

Structural family therapy. A family who enters structural family therapy, an approach developed by Salvador Minuchin (1974), will talk about the past as well as the present, since the family's current problems are seen as a carry over from earlier transactional patterns. The therapist looks for transactional boundaries defining the communication rules in the family by watching who talks to whom and how the family breaks up into sub-groups for support and problem solving. They look for triangles, where two family members resolve tensions between themselves by focusing on a third person in the family (Minuchin 1974; Minuchin and Fishman 1981).

The therapist's goal is to restructure family interactions between the family members, so they can more effectively solve their problems. Once dysfunctional transaction patterns are replaced with new, adaptive patterns the relationship loses its toxic nature and individuals no longer need to express their distress or dissatisfaction in an aberrant way.

Structural therapists use five hallmark techniques. They actively try to get the family to be comfortable with them as a person—it is said they *join* with the family. This is accomplished by *maintenance* (verbally supporting and reinforcing the family's behaviors and verbalizations), *tracking* (asking for clarification and amplification of statements to show interest), and *mimesis* (mimicking the affective tone, communication style, and level of formality that the family portrays in an effort to show that the therapist is "one of them"). A second technique is *structured mapping,* where the therapist diagrams which interactions in the family are healthy and which are characterized by over-involvement, distance, or anger. Entire families can be described as *enmeshed* (if they are over-involved) or *disengaged* (if they are too distant from one another). Other assessment techniques used to discern the structure of the family are *enactments* (where the family is asked to re-enact an everyday routine or the crisis situation) and *actualizing family transactional patterns* (where the therapist does not engage in the conversation or choose the topic but simply watches the family as they naturally communicate with one another and sees who communicates with whom under what conditions).

The fifth and most important technique involves various forms of *restructuring the family.* It may involve actively moving the family's seating arrangements within the therapy session, to help facilitate the restructuring of family communication patterns. It may involve assigning tasks so that individuals who usually do not interact with one another are joined in a purposeful activity. The therapist may help the family mark boundaries by setting up new rules or negotiating old rules.

Structural therapists must learn how culture affects family interactions so that they are not simply projecting their own idea of normal functioning onto their clients. For example, Hispanic families often give more authority to the father than Jewish families do. Structural therapists evaluate the family interaction pattern to determine if it is maintaining a specific problem, not simply judging the pattern. Structural family therapy seems to work especially well with families who have out-of-control or over-controlled teenagers.

Strategic family therapy. A family who enters Strategic Family Therapy, developed by Jay Haley (1963, 1987), talks almost exclusively about what is going on in the present. This therapy assumes that problems are the result of the current dysfunctional interactions taking place in the family. The therapist looks at the presenting symptom as a communication towards the other family members. Perhaps the child's morning stomachache is communicating that the child is sick for mother, who is traveling during the week. Perhaps the marijuana abuse of a teenager is a way to communicate to his mother that he feels out-of-touch with a new stepfather in the house (Haley 1963, 1987; Madanes 1981). The therapist's goal is to be the most powerful person in the therapy room so that the suggested interventions will be carried out and help restructure the power relations within the family.

The most well-known technique used by structural family therapists is *problem focused prescriptions that are paradoxical.* This involves telling the client to continue doing the very behavior that is labeled "the problem." If the problem is bedwetting, for example, the child is told to try to wet the bed every night. If the problem is an angry husband, he is instructed not to smile or act cordially to anyone in the family during the entire next week. If the symptom is communicating something important, when the client engages in the symptomatic behavior to comply with the therapist, it loses its communication value within the family. In the above prescription it is unclear after therapy what the husband is communicating by not smiling. Is he communicating compliance with the therapist or disdain with his home life? One has to be unsure. This opens the possibility that the client will choose a new and healthier way to communicate his or her needs (after all, the symptom by this time has become a habit that has trapped the person into responding to the family in a particular, defensive way). For problem-focused prescriptions to work, they need to be accompanied by a very plausible explanation. For example, the bedwetters might be told that it is bad for their bladder to try to keep dry; it is more important for their bladder to void during the night, and everyone will just have to learn to live with the bedwetting. Whenever possible, the therapist gives the family a chance to do a small version of the task in the session (e.g., instructing the father on how to keep a straight face), in order to make the assignment more likely to be carried out in the home.

Another famous strategic technique is *reframing.* With reframing, a person learns how to look at the cup of family virtues as "half full" instead of "half empty." A family may learn that the "immaturity" label that they have given to their son's shy behaviors can also be labeled as "social sensitivity."

Strategic family therapy is usually used with families who have not responded to other types of treatment. Empirical research on the effectiveness of strategic techniques is mixed, and some shy away from this technique, in part, because of the ethical issues of deception that surround the technique (paradoxically telling clients to do *A* when you really want them to do *not A*).

Conjoint family therapy. Conjoint family therapy was developed by Virginia Satir, the first major female family therapist, and the founder of the first formal training program in family therapy (Satir 1967, 1972). She combined the historical approaches of the psychodynamic theorists with the here-and-now emphasis found in the structural and strategic approaches. Satir believed that each person in the family was trying to keep the system in balance but that the "price" that each person "paid" was often very inequitable. When people in the family show a maladaptive symptom, it is because their growth is being blocked by the family unit's need for balance. The rules that create balance in a family are the result of how parents go about achieving and maintaining self-esteem. What mothers and fathers do to create an atmosphere that says "I am a worthy person" affects the context in which the children develop their own self-esteem.

Here the family experiences a very warm and emotionally involved therapist who stays in the present or goes into history as the case dictates. For conjoint family therapists the goal is always to help each individual family member build self-esteem. An equally important secondary goal is to expose and correct discrepancies in how the family communicates.

Satir found that under stress, problem families take on rigid communication styles. Each person develops a communication front: The *placator* is always trying to please; the *blamer* is finding fault with everyone; the *super-reasonable* person is always trying to intellectually analyze what is happening; and the *irrelevant* person acts in a distracting way, not wanting to relate to anything going on in the family. Conjoint family therapy tries to teach the *congruent style* of communication where people are honest, vulnerable, caring, and responsible for sending clear messages.

One of Satir's most famous techniques is the *family life chronology,* where the therapist initiates treatment by understanding the family's history through the various life stages and how they want to experience their current family life. This is a therapeutic system that greatly respects the rights of children to be heard, to be loved, and to be respected.

Conjoint family therapy works on eight different levels: physical, intellectual, emotional, sensual, interactional, contextual, nutritional, and spiritual. Sometimes a child needs to be hugged in the session (physical/interactional), for example, and sometimes it is best to cry along with a father grieving for his lost son (spiritual/emotional). The art of conjoint family therapy is learning to work on different levels simultaneously in a natural manner that resonates with the family's needs at the time of the session.

Conjoint family therapy is like solution-focused therapy in that both assume that people have the resources within them to flourish. They both encourage people to take risks and take control of their lives in a very direct and open manner. Also, they both stylistically rely on a very down to earth, approachable manner in the therapist.

Cognitive/behavioral family therapy. Cognitive/behavioral family therapy was developed by Gerald Patterson, Robert Liberman and Robert Stuart in the 1970s. It was a natural outgrowth of applying academic principles of learning and behavior change to the family situation (Liberman et al. 1980; Patterson 1971; Stuart 1980).

A family who enters cognitive/behavioral family therapy spends the first few sessions undergoing a careful functional assessment devoted towards defining exactly what the problem behaviors, attitudes, and interactions are in the family and under what conditions these troublesome symptoms appear. Cognitive/behavioral family therapists focus on dyadic interactions (e.g., husband-wife, parent-child) much more than those in other schools of therapy. The therapist's goal is to teach how one's behavior can influence the others in the family and how controlling one's own thoughts can control how one feels.

The range of techniques used in cognitive-behavioral family therapy is multidimensional. The basic learning principles of *positive reinforcement, negative reinforcement, extinction,* and *modeling* are used, as well as more complex clinical procedures such as *contingency contracting* (where each person writes down their obligations in the relationship and the privileges or rewards they expect to get from the relationship). A very popular technique developed by Stuart (1980) in his work with couples is to have *caring days*. In this technique, each partner writes down what behaviors he or she wants the other to exhibit. Then each partner promises to carry out eight to twenty of the requests made by the other partner during the week. There is no quid pro quo here. Each person engages in the behavior to become a "reinforcing object" for the other.

Cognitive-behavioral family therapy is successful with a very wide range of problems including marital problems, sexual problems, dealing with children who are diagnosed with conduct disorder or oppositional disorder, coping with mental or physical illness in the family, and dealing with children with anxiety disorders. There is more empirical evidence to support the efficaciousness of cognitive-behavioral family therapy than any other modality.

Solution-focused family therapy. A family who enters solution-focused family therapy, developed by Steven deShazer (1982, 1985, 1994), spends their time talking about the present and the future. All of the techniques are driven by the therapist's goal to use minimal interventions to help the family rediscover what will help them solve their problem.

The therapist's goal is to stay in the here and now and help the family re-discover resources that have helped them solve difficult problems in the past. The focus is always on what is possible and changeable. The prior solutions are labeled as the "problem" and the presenting problem is often left backstage as new solutions are highlighted. The therapist is very active and directive, and like the strategic family therapist, accepts responsibility for the family's outcome. The treatment is brief; sometimes it can consist of only one session. The therapist is looking for behavioral changes and when these occur, the case is closed.

The first and most popular technique is geared towards helping the family define what they want to be the goal of therapy. The family is quickly able to supply these goals by asking *the miracle question*. The question is posed to the family in the following way: "Suppose you were to wake up tomorrow morning and your problems were solved by some miracle. How would you know that a miracle had occurred? What would be different?" For a depressed mother the answer may be, "I would wake and smile at my daughter and fix her a good, nutritious breakfast. After she went off to school, I would spend the morning looking for a job." Once the therapist helps clients achieve these realistic goals, they feel empowered to create additional changes (deShazer 1982, 1985, 1994).

Another popular technique is *scaling,* where the family members rate the family well-being on a scale of one to ten, with one being the worst and ten being the best. By frequently asking for ratings the therapist gets feedback on the different perceptions of the family members and the effects of the intervention, and can give the family the expectation for change.

There are four types of conversations fostered during the therapy session: (1) *competence talk* (focusing on the strengths of individual family members and their collective strengths a family); (2) *exception talk* (searching for instances in the past where they have dealt with the problem or a similar problem in a successful way); (3) *context-changing talk* (focusing on how they act differently in different situations); and (4) *deconstructing the problem* (helping the family see how the problem makes changes inevitable and possible).

While solution-focused therapy has many similarities with strategic therapy (they are both brief and centered in the here and now and have active directive therapists), the big difference is that in solution-focused therapy the therapist is looking for clients to come up with new solutions that can work for them, and in strategic therapy the therapist is coming up with directives that seduce the family into trying a new set of behaviors.

Third-Generation Family Therapies

By the mid 1980s, a number of therapists had written books about the need to integrate the different schools of family therapy. Eclectic family therapy became the "buzz." The two hallmarks of eclectic approaches are: (1) they attempt to respect and utilize cultural attitudes, values, rituals, and social structures, and (2) they borrow theory and technique from a variety of schools to assess the family and develop a treatment plan.

Eclectic therapies do not assume that everyone wants to individuate from their families of origin. Indeed, they acknowledge that for many minority cultures in America the greatest value is placed on interdependence of family members and sacrifice of individual goals for the good of the family (Sue and Sue 1990). The eclectic therapist is expected to learn about different cultures and master the art of understanding cultural norms, avoiding stereotypes, and respecting individual differences.

The eclectic therapies often offer a guidebook to help therapists choose from the buffet table of techniques and theories available to them. The essential point is to realize that solution-focused therapy is not for everyone, nor is structural family therapy. The goal of a successful family therapist is to learn to use the right assessment tools to find the right intervention strategy for a particular type of family with a particular type of problem. A depressed eight-year-old female living with her grandmother in the inner city needs a different combination of family assessments and interventions than a depressed sixteen-year-old boy with a twin sister who is being brought up by his mother and her lesbian partner.

The most influential eclectic family therapy approaches are Larry Feldman's (1992) integrative multilevel family therapy, William Walsh's (1991) integrative family therapy, William Nichol's (1988) integrative approach to marital therapy, and David Will and Robert Wrate's (1985) problem-centered psychodynamic family therapy.

Fourth-Generation Family Therapies: Developmental, Positive, and Ethno-Political Approaches

Experience and research with the eclectic approach revealed that certain technique combinations do consistently work with certain populations. Family therapy is becoming specialized according to the presenting problem and the goals of therapy. For example, often therapists dealing with eating disorders start with a core of behavioral/cognitive interventions and then use structural techniques, as needed, on a case-by-case basis. In addition, empirical research has led to at least two new broad portals that define fourth generation family therapies at the beginning of the twenty-first century.

Developmental family therapies are therapies helping families deal with developmental crises that arise at each stage of the family life cycle—e.g., infertility, dual careers, death, disability, chronic illness, stepfamilies. Specific theories about the nature and trauma of each event guide the family therapist in a highly tailored assessment process and intervention strategy (Carter and McGoldrick 1989). These specialized approaches have been around since the early 1960s but their acceptance, popularity, and common philosophy define them as a twenty-first-century force in the field. The most empirically validated therapies in this category include medical family therapy programs (McDaniel, Helpworth, and Doherty 1992), sexual dysfunction therapies (Leiblum and Rosen 2000), and family programs for severe mental illness (Marsh, Dickens, and Torrey 1998).

Ethno-political family therapies take a transcultural perspective and help resolve problems families have interfacing across cultures and different political regimes. These therapists are involved in helping refugees adjust to their new countries, victims of political unrest and war cope with new family demands, and governments and agencies develop programs based on economic and political analyses of family stressors. For example, when working with refugees who migrate to the United States, therapists first need to learn about the premigration stressors. Was the family fleeing from a war or a famine? Were they trying to reunite with family in the United States? Did they have a comfortable life style in their country of origin? Then, therapists need to assess post-migration stressors. Do the refugees know how to speak English well? Are they embarrassed by their accents? Are they able to find a job commensurate with their level of education? What is there visa status? Are they worried about family left behind? Do they have a financial responsibility to send money home? Third, the therapist must assess the social support system. Who are they looking to for help and for emotional support in this country? In which social institutions are they comfortable (e.g., school, church, community center), and which are threatening to them? Finally, do they think of their visit here as "temporary" and wait for the opportunity to return home, or do they want to become U.S.

citizens? Interventions then vary by need and cultural considerations. For example, interventions designed to support Hispanic women who are the major breadwinners may help empower their husbands and make the pair comfortable in developing a new, more balanced relationship to fit the new social demands of the situation. Interventions for a Russian Jewish family where the parents feel isolated may concentrate on helping them establish ties with the wider Jewish-American community.

In this portal, therapists are developing approaches for families to deal with racism (Boyd-Franklin 1993), culturally pluralistic environments (Szapocznik et al. 1994), and oppression (Sue 1994). Most ethno-political therapists have followed and elaborated on Minuchin's structural approach, making it more relevant to diverse ethnic groups and cultural milieus.

Family Therapy and Ethics

A wide assortment of mental health professionals practice family therapy including psychologists, psychiatrists, psychiatric social workers, psychiatric nurses, and pastoral counselors. While all family therapists must follow the ethical guidelines established in their discipline, there are ethical issues unique to family therapy. Thus, special ethical guidelines have been established by the American Association of Family Therapists. Two of the thorniest issues concern defining who is the client (Is it the parent who brings the child, the child, or both of them? Is it the wife, the husband, or the couple?) and confidentiality (If the child tells you he is smoking marijuana do you have to keep confidentiality or do you have to break confidentiality and tell the parent?) (Gladding, Remley, and Huber 2000).

See also: BOUNDARY DISSOLUTION; CODEPENDENCY; CONFLICT: FAMILY RELATIONSHIPS; EATING DISORDERS; FAMILY ASSESSMENT; FAMILY DIAGNOSIS/DSM-IV; FAMILY RITUALS; FAMILY SCIENCE; FAMILY SYSTEMS THEORY; FORGIVENESS; MUNCHAUSEN SYNDROME BY PROXY; RELATIONSHIP METAPHORS; SELF-ESTEEM; SEPARATION ANXIETY; THERAPY: COUPLE RELATIONSHIPS; THERAPY: PARENT-CHILD RELATIONSHIPS; TRIANGULATION

Bibliography

Ackerman, N. (1958). *The Psychodynamics of Family Life.* New York: Basic Books.

Bateson, G. (1973). *Steps to an Ecology of Mind.* New York: Ballantine.

Berg-Cross, L. (2001). *Couples Therapy,* 2nd edition. New York: Haworth Press.

Boszormenyi-Nagy, I. (1973). *Intensive Family Therapy: Theoretical and Practical Aspects.* New York: Harper-Collins.

Bowen, M. (1978). *Family Therapy in Clinical Practice.* New York: Jason Aronson.

Boyd-Franklin, N. (1993). "The Invisibility Syndrome." *Family Networker* (July/August):33–39.

Briesmeister, J. M., and Schaefer, C. E. (1998). *Handbook of Parent Training: Parents as Co-Therapists for Children's Behavior Problems.* New York: Wiley.

Carter, B., and McGoldrick, M. (1989). *The Changing Family Life-Cycle.* Needham Heights, MA: Allyn and Bacon.

deShazer, S. (1982). *Patterns of Brief Family Therapy: An Ecosystemic Approach.* New York: Guilford Press.

deShazer, S. (1985). *Keys to Solutions in Brief Psychotherapy.* New York: W. W. Norton.

deShazer, S. (1994). *Words Were Originally Magic.* New York: W. W. Norton.

Feldman, L. (1992). *Integrating Individual and Family Therapy.* New York: Brunner/Mazel.

Framo, J. (1982). *Explorations in Marital and Family Therapy.* New York: Springer Publishing.

Gladding, S.; Remley, T.; and Huber, C. (2000). *Ethical, Legal, and Professional Issues in the Practice of Marital and Family Therapy.* New York: Prentice Hall Computer Books.

Haley, J. (1963). *Strategies of Psychotherapy.* New York: Grune and Stratton.

Haley, J. (1987). *Problem-Solving Therapy,* 2nd edition. San Francisco: Jossey-Boss.

Jackson, D. D. (1961). "Interactional Psychotherapy." In *Contemporary Psychotherapies,* ed. M. Stein. Glencoe, IL: The Free Press.

Jackson, D. D. (1973). *Therapy, Communication, and Change.* Palo Alto: Science and Behavior Books.

Leiblum, S. and Rosen, R. (2000). *Principles and Practice of Sex Therapy.* New York: Guilford Press.

Liberman, R.; Wheeler, E.; de Visser, L.; Kuehnel, J.; and Kuehnel, T. (1980). *Handbook of Marital Therapy: A Positive Approach to Helping Troubled Relationships.* New York: Plenum.

Madanes, C. (1981). *Strategic Family Therapy.* San Francisco: Jossey-Bass.

Marsh, D.; Dickens, R.; and Torrey, F. (1998). *How to Cope with Mental Illness in Your Family: A Self Care Guide for Siblings, Parents, and Offspring*. New York: J. P. Tarcher.

McDaniel, S. H.; Hepworth, J.; and Doherty, W. (1992). *Medical Family Therapy: A Biopsychosocial Approach to Families with Health Problems*. New York: Basic Books.

Minuchin, S. (1974). *Families and Family Therapy*. Cambridge, MA: Harvard University Press.

Minuchin, S., and Fishman, C. (1981). *Family Therapy Techniques*. Cambridge, MA: Harvard University Press.

Nichols, W. 1988. *Marital Therapy. An Integrative Approach*. New York: Guilford.

Olson, D. H.; Fournier, D. G.; and Druckman, J. M. 1992. *PREPARE/ENRICH Counselors Manual,* rev. edition. Minneapolis, MN: PREPARE/ENRICH.

Papero, D. V. (1990). *Bowen Family Systems Theory*. Boston: Allyn and Bacon.

Patterson, G. R. (1971). *Families: Application of Social Learning to Family Life*. Champaign, IL: Research Press.

Satir, V. M. (1967). *Conjoint Family Therapy,* rev. edition. Palo Alto, CA: Science and Behavior Books.

Satir, V. M. (1972). *Peoplemaking*. Palo Alto, CA: Science and Behavior Books.

Selvini-Palazzoli, M. (1978). *Self-Starvation*. Northvale, NJ: Jason Aronson.

Selvini-Palazzoli, M., and Viaro, M. (1988). "The Anorectic Process in the Family: A Six-Stage Model as Guide for Individual Therapy." *Family Process* 27:129–148.

Sue, D. (1994). "Incorporating Cultural Diversity in Family Therapy." *The Family Psychologist* 10(2):19–21.

Sue, D. W., and Sue, D. (1990). *Counseling the Culturally Different: Theory and Practice*. New York: John Wiley and Sons.

Szapocznik, J.; Scopetta, M. A.; Ceballos, A.; and Santisteban, D. (1994). "Understanding, Supporting and Empowering Families: From Microanalysis to Macrointervention." *Family Psychologist* 10(2):23–27.

Stuart, R. B. (1980). *Helping Couples Change: A Social Learning Approach to Marital Therapy*. Champaign, IL: Research Press.

Walsh, W. (1991). *Case Studies in Family Therapy: An Integrated Approach*. Boston: Allyn and Bacon.

Webster-Stratton, C., and Hancock, L. (1998). "Training for Parents of Young Children with Conduct Problems: Content, Methods and Therapeutic Processes." In *Handbook of Parent Training: Parents as Co-Therapists for Children's Behavior Problems,* ed. J. M. Briesmeister and C. E. Schaefer. New York: Wiley.

Will, D., and Wrate, R. (1985). *Integrated Family Therapy: A Problem-Centered Psychodynamic Approach*. London: Tavistock.

LINDA BERG-CROSS
MICHELLE MORALES
CHRISTI MOORE

PARENT-CHILD RELATIONSHIPS

Preventive and therapeutic interventions in infancy and early childhood are often directed at the parents' sensitivity. *Sensitivity* refers to parents' ability to perceive their children's signals and needs accurately and to respond to these signals promptly and adequately (Ainsworth et al. 1978). Enhanced parental sensitivity stimulates the children's socioemotional development, in particular their attachment security. The theory of *attachment* was developed by John Bowlby (1982, 1988) to explain the nature of a child's emotional tie to his or her parent, and the attachment relationship with the parent is one of the child's first and most important developmental milestones. Children who are securely attached to their parent seek support from their parent in times of stress and distress, and are able to explore the world and mature in a healthy way. If the attachment relationship is insecure, children do not have a sense of a secure base, and the development of normal behaviors such as exploration, play, and social interactions is impaired. Attachment experiences become internalized as a working model of attachment. Long-term research suggests that children who, as infants, were securely attached have more optimal social and emotional functioning. Therefore, preventive and therapeutic interventions often aim at enhancing parental sensitivity and children's attachment security. Although most of these interventions take place in industrialized Western countries, they are based on fundamental research conducted in various parts of the world, which supports the cross-cultural validity of the basic assumptions (van IJzendoorn and Sagi 1999). It should be noted that several intervention studies have been implemented with cultural minority samples.

Types of Interventions

Byron Egeland and his colleagues (2000) identified three types of intervention: (1) programs directed at the parent's sensitive behavior; (2) programs that focus on the parent's working model (or mental representation) of attachment and parenting; and (3) intervention efforts that attempt to stimulate or provide social support for parents (for a narrative review of the studies, see Juffer, Bakermans-Kranenburg, and Van IJzendoorn, in press).

The first type of intervention, focusing on *sensitivity,* often starts by teaching parents observational skills in order to make them better *perceivers.* This goal can be reached in several ways: for example through stimulating parents to complete a workbook about the behavior of their child, or by encouraging parents to engage in "speaking for the baby" through verbalizing their child's behavior (Carter, Osofsky, and Hann 1991). The therapist may also encourage the parent to perceive the child's behavior in a more correct, objective way, in other words, without distortions, by explaining salient issues about the child's development. Many interventions that focus on parental sensitivity concentrate on prompt and adequate responding, for example through discussing parenting brochures or by modeling the desired behaviors. Another strategy to enhance sensitivity is by reinforcing sensitive and responsive behaviors that the parents already show to their child, for example with video feedback (e.g., Bakermans-Kranenburg, Juffer, and Van IJzendoorn 1998; Seifer, Clark, and Sameroff 1991).

In the second type of intervention efforts are directed towards the parent's mental *representation,* and the focus of change is the parent's working model or representation of his or her own attachment experiences (Bowlby 1982). Many of these intervention programs base their approach on the work of Selma Fraiberg (Fraiberg, Adelson, and Shapiro 1975). Fraiberg realized that parents are apt to "re-enact" or repeat the parenting behavior of their own parents, even unconsciously and involuntarily. Her famous metaphor of "ghosts in the nursery" has inspired interventions that are typically insight-oriented, therapeutic, and lengthy. The idea is that maladaptive parenting behavior may be changed by changing the mental representations or inner working models of the parents. In this type of intervention parents are involved in discussions about their past and present attachment experiences and feelings in child-parent psychotherapy or in psychodynamic therapy. Often these interventions take a long time, for example, fifty sessions, although some interventions attempt to pursue their goal in a shorter period of time, for example, four to ten sessions.

Nancy Cohen and her colleagues (1999) describe two examples of interventions focusing on the parent's representation. One of the two treatments evaluated in this study was *Psychodynamic Psychotherapy* (PPT), a parent-infant therapy for clinically referred infants. During center-based sessions mother and infant are invited to play. The mother and therapist talk together, but they also try to attend to the infant's activities. In this representational approach the therapist makes use of psychodynamic transference, repetition of the past, reexperiencing of affect, and interpretation. In the second treatment, *Watch, Wait, and Wonder* (WWW), a representational approach is combined with a behavioral approach. The authors describe WWW as infant-led psychotherapy: Mothers are given the opportunity to explore with the therapist intergenerational (*representational*) issues, although a specific and ultimate goal of WWW is to enable the mother to follow her infant's lead (*behavioral approach*). For half of each session the mother is instructed to get down on the floor, to observe her infant, and to interact only at her child's initiative. According to the authors, this method places the mother in the position of being more sensitive and responsive. After about fifteen sessions both PPT and WWW were successful in reducing infant-presenting problems and in reducing maternal intrusiveness. The infants in the WWW group showed a greater shift towards secure attachment, and their emotion regulation improved more than in the PPT group.

The third type of intervention aims at stimulating or providing *social support* to parents. The importance of practical and emotional support from relatives or friends for the parent's functioning and subsequently the child's developmental outcome has been supported by ample empirical evidence. Several interventions make use of social support primarily, sometimes by giving practical help and advice, by offering individualized services, by providing information about community services, or by stimulating the parents to extend their social network.

Social support may be more influential at particular times in the parent's development. The transition to parenthood, as a period of considerable change in routines, expectations, and behaviors, requires numerous physical and emotional adjustments. In such a transition period parents may not only need more help, but may also be more receptive for support from others. An intervention program that is illustrative of this line of reasoning is the *preventive intervention* for couples becoming parents. In groups that extend from pregnancy through three months postpartum, expectant parents receive support from the group leaders (a married couple) and from the other group members by sharing hopes, feelings, and worrisome thoughts (Cowan and Cowan 1987).

Other interventions combine the provision or enhancement of support with promoting sensitive parenting. Finally, the provision of social support can be combined with both a behaviorally focused intervention and a representational approach. For example, in project STEEP (Steps Toward Effective and Enjoyable Parenting) (Egeland et al. 2000), mothers not only receive practical support and advice, but also video feedback, in order to increase sensitive parenting, and help to examine and discuss their own childhood experiences.

Effectiveness of Interventions

Are family interventions effective in enhancing parental sensitivity and children's attachment security? A meta-analysis of seventy published papers reporting on eighty-eight interventions with effects on sensitivity (81 studies with a total of 7,636 participants) and/or attachment (29 studies with 1,503 participants) revealed that interventions are significantly but only modestly effective in enhancing maternal sensitivity. The effect on attachment was even smaller. Intervention that focused on sensitivity only showed the largest combined effect on sensitivity, meaning that interventions with a relatively "narrow" focus tend to be more effective than "broadband" interventions (see also Van IJzendoorn, Juffer, and Duyvesteyn 1995). With respect to attachment, interventions that focused solely on enhancing maternal sensitivity also showed a positive effect on infant attachment security, and these interventions were more effective than the others. In fact, it was the only type of intervention yielding a significant combined effect size. Unexpectedly, a large effect on sensitivity was found in a small subset of three studies that did not use personal contact in the intervention, but a soft baby carrier, a videotape, or a parenting brochure. However, because this set of studies was small, this finding does not allow for strong conclusions.

Somewhat puzzling was the finding that studies with *fewer* intervention sessions were more effective in changing maternal sensitivity than studies with *more* intervention sessions. Interventions with fewer than five sessions were as effective as interventions with five to sixteen sessions, but both were more effective than interventions with more than sixteen sessions. Jennifer MacLeod and Geoffrey Nelson (2000) came to a similar conclusion in their meta-analysis of the reported effects of programs for the promotion of family wellness and child maltreatment. Contrary to their hypothesis, effect sizes were highest for interventions with one to twelve visits, lowest for those with thirteen to fifty visits, and in-between for those with more than fifty visits. Less seems more, at least in the area of preventive and therapeutic family interventions.

The interventions that were directed at families at risk (e.g., poverty, depression, lack of support, or adolescent mothers) showed as much improvement on attachment security as interventions that approached families without risks. Interventions in samples with a higher percentage of insecure children in the control group reached relatively large effects on attachment. In samples with more security in the group to which the intervention group is compared, it is difficult to reach an even higher percentage of security as an effect of the intervention. Surprisingly, however, at-risk samples were comparable to other samples in their response to different types of interventions, and more intensive interventions do not seem to be more effective in groups with more serious problems.

Conclusion

The study of early intervention in the service of children's socioemotional development involves thousands of families with multiple problems. Enhanced parental sensitivity and a secure attachment relationship are at the heart of the interventions. Other theoretical frameworks have inspired parent-management training programs for parents of children with conduct problems or disruptive behaviors (e.g., Foote, Schuhmann, Jones, and Eyberg 1998). Huge investments to accomplish these goals are made by intervenors, using a wide array of intervention methods. Nevertheless, interventions appear to have a varying degree of success in reaching their goals. Behaviorally focused interventions with a modest number of sessions appear most efficient. From a population health perspective, society should profit from the insights of successful early intervention programs, as childhood experiences may affect subsequent health status in profound and long-lasting ways.

See also: ATTACHMENT: PARENT-CHILD RELATIONSHIPS; BOUNDARY DISSOLUTION; CONFLICT: PARENT-CHILD RELATIONSHIPS; DISCIPLINE; EATING DISORDERS; FAMILY ASSESSMENT; PARENTING EDUCATION; PARENTING STYLES; SEPARATION ANXIETY; THERAPY: FAMILY RELATIONSHIPS; TRIANGULATION

Bibliography

Ainsworth, M. D. S.; Blehar, M. C.; Waters, E.; and Wall, S. (1978). *Patterns of Attachment: A Psychological Study of the Strange Situation*. Hillsdale, NJ: Lawrence Erlbaum Associates.

Bakermans-Kranenburg, M. J.; Juffer, F.; and van IJzendoorn, M. H. (1998). "Interventions with Video Feedback and Attachment Discussions: Does Type of Maternal Insecurity Make a Difference?" *Infant Mental Health Journal* 19:202–219.

Bowlby, J. (1982). *Attachment,* 2nd edition, Vol. 1: *Attachment and Loss*. New York: Basic Books.

Bowlby, J. (1988). *A Secure Base: Clinical Applications of Attachment Theory*. London: Routledge.

Carter, S. L.; Osofsky, J. D.; and Hann, D. M. (1991). "Speaking for the Baby: A Therapeutic Intervention with Adolescent Mothers and Their Infants." *Infant Mental Health Journal* 12:291–301.

Cohen, N. J.; Muir, E.; Parker, C. J.; Brown, M.; Lojkasek, M.; Muir, R.; and Barwick, M. (1999). "Watch, Wait, and Wonder: Testing the Effectiveness of a New Approach to Mother-Infant Psychotherapy." *Infant Mental Health Journal* 20:429–451.

Cowan, C. P., and Cowan, P. A. (1987). "A Preventive Intervention for Couples Becoming Parents." In *Research on Support for Parents and Infants in the Postnatal Period,* ed. C. F. Z. Boukydis. Norwood, NJ: Ablex.

Egeland, B.; Weinfield, N. S.; Bosquet, M.; and Cheng, V. K. (2000). "Remembering, Repeating, and Working Through: Lessons from Attachment-Based Interventions." In *Handbook of Infant Mental Health,* Vol. 4: *Infant Mental Health in Groups at High Risk,* ed. J. D. Osofsky and H. E. Fitzgerald. World Association for Infant Mental Health. New York: Wiley.

Foote, R. C.; Schuhmann, E. M.; Jones, M. L.; and Eyberg, S. M. (1998). "Parent-Child Interaction Therapy: A Guide for Clinicians." *Clinical Child Psychology and Psychiatry* 3:361–373.

Fraiberg, S.; Adelson, E.; and Shapiro, V. (1975). "Ghosts in the Nursery: A Psychoanalytic Approach to the Problems of Impaired Infant-Mother Relationships." *Journal of the American Academy of Child Psychiatry* 14:387–422.

Juffer, F.; Bakermans-Kranenburg, M. J.; and van IJzendoorn, M. H. (in press). "Enhancing Children's Socio-Emotional Development: A Review of Intervention Studies." In *Handbook of Research Methods in Developmental Psychology,* ed. D. M. Teti. New York: Blackwell.

MacLeod, J., and Nelson, G. (2000). "Programs for the Promotion of Family Wellness and the Prevention of Child Maltreatment: A Meta-Analytic Review." *Child Abuse and Neglect* 24:1127–1149.

Seifer, R.; Clark, G. N.; and Sameroff, A. J. (1991). "Positive Effects of Interaction Coaching on Infants with Developmental Disabilities and Their Mothers." *American Journal on Mental Retardation* 96:1–11.

van IJzendoorn, M. H.; Juffer, F.; and Duyvesteyn, M. G. C. (1995). "Breaking the Intergenerational Cycle of Insecure Attachment: A Review of the Effects of Attachment-Based Interventions on Maternal Sensitivity and Infant Security." *Journal of Child Psychology and Psychiatry* 36:225–248.

van IJzendoorn, M. H., and Sagi, A. (1999). "Cross-Cultural Patterns of Attachment: Universal and Contextual Dimensions." In *Handbook of Attachment,* ed. J. Cassidy and P. R. Shaver. New York: Guilford Press.

MARIAN J. BAKERMANS-KRANENBURG
MARINUS H. VAN IJZENDOORN
FEMMIE JUFFER

TIME USE

Family scholars have traditionally been interested in the role of time in shaping the organization of family experience. Anthropologists who studied families in preindustrial cultures were interested in the way that families lived their lives according to the temporal rhythms of nature, with the tides, the seasons, and the movement of the sun giving structure to everyday life. Although different time devices such as sundials and water clocks have been used throughout the ages to measure time, it was only in the thirteenth century that the mechanical clock came into being as a more precise measure of time. Mechanical clocks were first developed in medieval monasteries as an aid to the discipline of monastic life (Whitrow 1988). Over the course of the fourteenth century clocks became more numerous on church steeples and in the main town belfry. These public clocks, which began with only an hour hand (because people then did not have the same concern with precision as we currently have) were central to community organization, bringing citizens together to defend, celebrate, or mourn. During this time, families had much less privacy, and the temporal routine of everyday life was shaped more by community activity. In contrast with the tendency to think of current nuclear families as very private and determining their own daily schedules, families during this period were more likely to be defined as households with boarders and a regular flow of guests that contributed to a much looser, and in some ways a more chaotic, everyday routine. Celebrations that we now typically associate with being special family time such as Christmas, weddings, or funerals were more likely to be treated as community, rather than family, celebrations (Gillis 1996). Although *family time* has become increasingly important among dual-earner families today, this is a concept that had no meaning until it was introduced in the mid-nineteenth century by the Protestant middle classes during the Victorian era. Prior to this, families experienced their leisure time through participation in community fairs, games, and festivals. During the Victorian period, families became more focused on and invested in children. As a result, family times such as Christmas, Easter, Chanukah, birthdays, graduations, confirmations, and bar and bat mitzvahs played an increasingly important role in marking family time as special and unique. It was also during this time that Sunday became the archetypal day for family time and the family dinner, the living room parlor and children's bedtimes took on importance as part of family rituals.

Mechanical clocks also had a profound impact on the way that time was valued and controlled. With the rise of the money economy in the fourteenth century, the value of time began to rise (Whitrow 1988). As money circulated, time came to be associated with commercial value because the activities used to generate money or profit could now be weighed in terms of how much time it took to ready a product for sale. It was during the period of industrialization and the rise of the factory system (eighteenth and nineteenth centuries) that clocks more firmly established the close association between time and money. Karl Marx wrote about the clock as a being a precise measure of labor activity that was the basis for increasing the efficiency of labor power, which was so important for generating a profit in capitalist industries. In the late 1800s, Fredrick Taylor (i.e., the Taylorization of the workplace) introduced time and motion studies to the shop floor with the intention of making the manufacturing process more precise, calculated, efficient, and profitable.

These economic changes had important implications for the organization of time in family life. Capitalism created a split between *wage labor,* now taking place in the factory, and the forms of production that were previously taking place in the family and the community. The separation of work and family during the onset of industrial capitalism played a key role in bracketing free time and family time as different from work time. In addition, it gave a different meaning to the work carried out by men and women. Because men were the first to be called on for jobs in the factory, their time came to be more highly valued because it received a wage and was connected with the production of profit in the company. By contrast, women's work became private labor in the home and was undervalued because of its disconnection with commercial activity. Continuing disparities in the value of women and men's time have their roots in these economic developments.

Dramatic changes in the patterns of women and men's work since World War II have had an enormous impact on the way that time is organized in families. Following the war years when women were recruited to work in the factories to support the war effort, governments created policies that restricted women from working in many occupations and encouraged women to stay at home and care for families. This was short-lived. The rise of feminism in the 1960s and 1970s resulted in a dramatic return of women to the paid labor force. Buoyed by developments in birth control, equal pay policies, and the rise of day care, women moved into the labor force in massive numbers such that the majority of women in families are now in the paid labor force (see *Trends* below). This had profound implications for the organization of time in these families. Whereas single breadwinner families had schedules that involved a clear division of labor and tended to be dominated by the work schedules of the husband, dual-earner families were faced with a convoluted division of labor and a much more challenging set of negotiations for working out the everyday family schedule. Competing schedules and organizing day care coverage for preschool children, as well as reallocating household responsibilities, were central to the creation of the daily routine. During this same period, family structures also changed dramatically, due in large part to the rise of divorce. As a result, stepparenting, single parenting, and custody arrangements created different challenges for planning, coordinating, and organizing time in families.

Although the mean number of paid working hours for individual women and men did not increase dramatically in the United States between 1970 and 1997 (Robinson and Godbey 1997), there are three factors that have contributed to a growing feeling of time urgency in families (Jacobs and Gerson 1998). First, the dramatic increase in the number of wives and mothers in the paid labor force has reduced the amount of unpaid familial support in the home. Second, there have been increases in the number of hours (ten hours per couple between 1970 and 1997) that husbands and wives combine to spend in the labor market, again resulting in a net drain on family time. Third, there has been an escalation of overwork (working fifty or more hours per week) among the well educated in managerial and professional positions. Canadian data from the 1998 General Social Survey indicate that those between the ages of twenty-five and forty-four who were married parents and employed full-time faced the biggest time stresses: overall men worked an average of 48.6 hours and women 38.8 hours of paid work activities (Statistics Canada 1999).

Globalization has also had an impact on the experience of time in families. During the time when community life was organized around the main town clock, there was no coordination of time from one town to another. Time was local, and the clock was set according to local standards. The sophistication of travel through the use of trains in the late nineteenth century created a demand for the coordination of these local times. Watches and personal clocks also became more accessible during this time and added to the pressure to find a system for standardizing time. These efforts culminated in the creation of uniform system of world time called *Greenwich time* at the International Conference on Time in Paris in 1912.

Since then, the development of sophisticated computer technology and the breakdown of international trade barriers have given rise to the globalization of the world economy. These developments have taken time from the town belfry and put it at the center of a highly sophisticated world system of trade and communication. Globalization has broken down the boundaries of space and in so doing has delocalized time and loosened it from its moorings in the community environment. The Internet gives access to a world that never sleeps. Globalization has created new time pressures, new anxieties about time that go well beyond the traditional anxiety associated with getting to work on time. Faxes, conference calls, electronic mail, and the interdependence of global stock markets require a temporal coordination that extends beyond one's immediate geographical context. For families, vigilance to the multiple demands of *world time* results in constant sensitivity of time, a hurried pace of life, an expectation of growing possibilities in the efficient use of time, and the potential for more competing demands in the individual use of time within families.

Technology plays a major role in reshaping the meaning of family time. Devices such as cellular phones and home computers have made the boundary between work time and family time much more permeable than it ever was. By opening a hole in the fence that surrounds private family time, technology keeps families in a state of interruption. At the same time, the availability of technology within the home also appears to be playing a role in keeping the family closer to home. The increasing availability of VCRs, compact disks, home computers, and home exercise machines means an increase in the opportunities for leisure at home. Devices such as pagers, once used only for business purposes, are now commonly used for family reasons with children and aging parents. Similarly, electronic mail, phone mail, fax machines, and computer networks create an opportunity for family members to do their paid work at home. Television, too, with its expanding band of cable channels, continues to draw families around the electronic hearth. Television represents one of the main uses of free time in the United States. For example, people with grade-school educations spend more than half of their free time watching television compared with just over one-third for college graduates (Robinson and Godbey 1997).

Forces such as industrialization, information technology, and the globalization of the world economy have given rise to a perception that the pace of life has accelerated dramatically. The values of speed and efficiency have come to dominate daily life. As the world puts on pace with respect to the exchange of information and commercial goods, so too have families put on pace as a way of adapting to these changes (Daly 1996). Our language of time is revealing: we talk of time famine, time compression, multitasking, and time scarcity. One of the ways that families cope with the demands of speed and efficiency is through *time-deepening* whereby they plan activities with a precise regard to time, carry out more than one activity at a time, or substitute a faster leisure activity for one that takes a long time (Robinson and Godbey 1997).

Conceptions of Time in Families

Our dominant approach for studying time in families has been to examine, through time diary studies, how much time family members devote to the activities of paid work, unpaid work in the home, leisure activity, and time for personal care. National time diary studies offer insights into the patterns of time use within families and as they change historically (see *Trends* below for a review of key trends). Many other conceptualizations of time, however, have relevance for understanding time in families.

Circular models. Circular models of time are driven by nature. Time is viewed as a cycle of seasons, the cyclical rhythm of day and night, and through the human cycle of birth and death. For families, cyclical patterns of work and rest, planting and harvesting, celebration and mourning, or growth and decay are tied to the cycles of the natural world. Circular models of time continue to dominate the patterns of experience for hunting and gathering and agricultural societies.

Linear models. The past, present, and the future give rise to a conception of time that is organized in a linear fashion. We think of the *arrow of time* or the *march of time* as we move progressively and unidirectionally through time without any return to the past. Individual aging, the progression of families through their developmental stages, and history itself are all linear ways of thinking about time. Families have linear histories marked by a series of events, including birthdays, deaths, and anniversaries. Although some of the rituals that are used to mark these events are repeatable and cyclical, they typically represent the idea of progression through time—a directionality of success (as in marriage anniversaries), maturity (as in birthdays), or accomplishment (as in graduations). In each of these, movement along a time line is the implicit focus of the celebration.

Biology and time. At the root of the individual experience of time is the process of change and development that is part of the aging process. From pimples to wrinkles, bodies provide the tangible signs of individual aging and the passage of time. These developmental changes are also the basis for social evaluations of being *on-time* or *off-time* with respect to family transitions. Becoming pregnant as a teen is therefore deemed early, whereas a pregnancy at forty-seven is considered late. Like all living organisms, human beings experience the rhythm of their own circadian clocks, which regulate a variety of behavioral and physiological rhythms. These are associated with twenty-four-hour cycles of temperature and light and include sleep-wake cycles, feeding cycles, body temperature cycles, and a variety of hormonal and metabolic oscillations. Illnesses also precipitate a reordering of time in families to accommodate doctor's visits and reallocate tasks left undone as a result of the illness.

Social organization of time. Although clocks are a relatively recent invention in the history of humankind, they are now central to the organization of complex societies. As a result, children are socialized from early on to pay attention to schedules and to learn the social value of punctuality and the organization of time. Whereas families were once more likely to live and work together, they now require sophisticated time scheduling tools to manage the intersection of many independent schedules. Families routinely disperse into their own temporal schedules, which not only requires that children be equipped with time skills early on, but that the family be diligent about managing their time together and apart.

As part of social organization, time is expressed through explicit rules and informal norms that govern social life. Hence, work organizations have rules about the hours of work, businesses dictate the hours of commerce, and schools have rules about attendance and punctuality. These formal time rules provide a structure for everyday life. Families also create time rules having to do with curfew, being home for meals, or TV time. Although these may be formal, they are more often a part of a web of social expectations that are understood but not explicitly stated. Informal time norms get expressed through social expectations such as promptness, not wasting time, or the tendency to think of work before play.

Culture and time. Cross-cultural lenses can play a useful part in contrasting the values currently associated with time in our own culture. For example, while punctuality in North America means that you must arrive within minutes of the appointed hour in order to be on time, in many Latin American countries one usually has the flexibility of an hour or two before being considered late (Levine 1988). Ethnic groups within a larger culture also have different temporal norms and practices about when childbearing and rearing should begin and end, the timing of marriage, or the relative importance of work and leisure. Some countries, most notably in Europe, are much more deliberate about actively discouraging overwork. For example, France and Italy have taken the lead in legislating the thirty-five-hour work week supported by tax incentives and fines. Most European countries have twice the amount of vacation that is usually granted in the United States. (Robinson and Godbey 1997).

Controlling time. As time is perceived to be more scarce, more conflicts arise about time control, allocation, and entitlement. This happens both within families and between families and the social organizations they participate in. Within families, the control of time is manifested in a variety of ways: tag-team parents negotiate who will be home for the children after school and who will do the pick ups and drop-offs; separated and divorced parents negotiate custody schedules; and siblings negotiate TV times. Controlling time within families has been a central part of gender politics with women and men struggling to work out responsibilities for childcare, housework, and a fair entitlement to free time.

The struggle to control time between families and the organizations of which they are a part is most apparent in the challenge that families have in trying to balance work and family. Work represents a dominant obligation for families. Work organizations take precedence with the consequence that people (especially men) in Western cultures overperform in occupations and underperform in other roles. Because people have much less control over their work lives than over their family lives, their family lives tend to adjust to their work schedules rather than the reverse. Work organizations have begun to develop family-responsive policies that shift the control balance towards more control of time for family members. Flexible scheduling or working from home, for example, allow men and women more discretion in the way that they set up their daily or weekly schedule so that they can avoid conflicts with family and household responsibilities.

Since Victorian times, family gatherings on holidays such as Christmas, Chanukah (pictured), birthdays, graduations, confirmations, and bar and bat mitzvahs have played an important role in marking family time as special and unique. A/P WIDE WORLD PHOTOS

Major Trends in Time Use in Families

Although the way that families allocate their time to various activities is subject to multiple measurement challenges, several key trends offer insight into the way time is used in North American families.

Paid work. Based on U.S. data, the overall employment rate for married women between the ages of sixteen and sixty-four has risen from three out of ten in 1960 to six out of ten in 1997. For married men, there has been a decline from 90 percent in 1960 to 78 percent in 1997 (Teachman, Tedrow, and Crowder 2000). Sixty-four percent of women with children under the age of six and 78 percent of women with children between the ages six and seventeen were employed. (Jenkins, Repetti, and Crouter 2000).

In spite of the dramatic increase in the number of women in the paid labor force, men spend more time in paid work than do women. According to the most recent time diary data (collected in 1985), employed men spend an average of forty hours per week in paid work compared to just over thirty hours for women (Robinson and Godbey 1997).

Unpaid work. When all unpaid activities in the home are taken together, women appear to devote twice as much time as men (Robinson and Godbey 1997). When the focus is on childcare activities only, significant disparities remain, but the overall trend is toward convergence. Based on an extensive review of the parental involvement literature, Pleck (1997) reports that whereas men spent only about one-third the amount of time that women did being engaged with their children in the 1960s and 1970s, that figure has risen to approximately 44 percent in the 1990s. Furthermore, as higher numbers of women continue with paid employment after having children, women are doing less housework, and men are doing slightly more (Coltrane 2000).

Leisure time. In general, women have less leisure time than men (Robinson and Godbey 1997). However, employment status is an important factor. In a national study of time use in Canada, full-time employed married mothers and full-time employed single mothers have the least amount of leisure time (3.6 hours a day each). By comparison, mothers who worked part-time had 4.5 hours a day, and nonemployed mothers had 5.0 hours a day. Full-time employed fathers (25–44) have more leisure (4.2 hours per day) than full-time employed mothers or single mothers (3.6 hours each) but less than mothers who work part-time (4.5 hours per day) or nonemployed mothers (5.0 hours per day) (Statistics Canada 1999).

Family time. A national survey of the changing workforce in the United States indicates that 70 percent of employed mothers and fathers feel that they do not have enough time to spend with their children (Bond, Galinsky, and Swanberg 1998). Among Canadians, the 1998 General Social Survey indicates that approximately eight out of ten full-time employed married women and men with at least one child at home felt that weekdays were too short to accomplish what they wanted to do, with more than one-half indicating that they would want to spend more time with their family and friends if they had more time (Statistics Canada 1999). By contrast, a recent study indicates that children are much less likely to report having too little time with their parents—approximately 30 percent (Galinsky 1999). In spite of parents' desire to spend more time with their families, indications are that parents are spending as much or slightly more time with their children compared to twenty years ago (Bond et al. 1998).

Children's use of time. Based on U.S. national data collected in 1997, 55 percent of an average child's week was spent eating, sleeping, or in personal care (Hofferth and Sandberg 2001). Fifteen percent of their time was spent in school or day care. The remaining 30 percent of the child's time was discretionary. Of this discretionary time, 29 percent was used for free play, 24 percent for television viewing, and 18 percent in structured activities. The remainder of their time was used for art or education-related activities, housework, or conversation.

See also: CHILDCARE; COMPUTERS AND FAMILY; DIVISION OF LABOR; DUAL-EARNER FAMILIES; FAMILY LIFE EDUCATION; FAMILY RITUALS; FAMILY ROLES; FAMILY STRENGTHS; GLOBAL CITIZENSHIP; HOUSEWORK; INDUSTRIALIZATION; LEISURE; LIFE COURSE THEORY; PLAY; RESOURCE MANAGEMENT; RETIREMENT; TELEVISION AND FAMILY; WORK AND FAMILY

Bibliography

Bond, James T.; Galinsky, E.; and Swanberg, J. E. (1998). *The 1997 National Study of the Changing Workforce.* New York: The Families and Work Institute.

Coltrane, S. (2000). "Research on Household Labour: Modeling and Measuring the Social Embeddedness of Routine Family Work." *Journal of Marriage and the Family.* 62:1208–1233.

Daly, K. J. (1996). *Families and Time: Keeping Pace in a Hurried Culture.* Thousand Oaks CA: Sage.

Galinsky, E. (1999). *Ask the Children: What America's Children Really Think about Working Parents.* New York: William Morrow.

Gillis, J. (1996). *A World of Their Own Making: Myth, Ritual and the Quest for Family Values.* New York: Basic Books.

Jacobs, J. and Gerson, K. (1998). "Who Are the Overworked Americans?" *Review of Social Economy* 4:442–459.

Hofferth, S. L., and Sandberg, J. F. (2001). "How American Children Spend their Time." *Journal of Marriage and the Family.* 63:295–308.

Levine, R. V. (1988). "The Pace of Life Across Cultures." In *The Social Psychology of Time: New Perspectives,* ed. J. E. McGrath. Newbury Park CA: Sage.

Perry-Jenkins, M.: Repetti, R. L.: and Crouter, A. (2000). "Work and Family in the 1990's." *Journal of Marriage and the Family* 62:981–998.

Pleck, J. (1997). "Paternal Involvement: Levels, Sources, and Consequences." In *The Role of the Father in Child Development,* ed. M. E. Lamb. New York: John Wiley and Sons.

Robinson, J. P., and Godbey, G. (1997). *Time for Life: The Surprising Ways Americans Use Their Time.* University Park, PA: The Pennsylvania State University Press.

Statistics Canada. (1999). *Overview of the Time Use of Canadians in 1998.* Ottawa. Catalogue no. 12F0080XIE.

Teachman, J. D.; Tedrow, L. M.; and Crowder, K. D. (2000). "The Changing Demography of America's Families." *Journal of Marriage and the Family* 62:1234–1246.

Whitrow, G. J. (1988). *Time in History.* Oxford: Oxford University Press.

KERRY J. DALY

TOGO

In Togo, a West African nation that lies between Ghana and Benin, the term *family* is broadly defined. A family is more than a husband, a wife, and children. Blood relatives of both spouses are considered part of the family, and the extended family embraces all relatives, living or dead. There is a strong cultural belief that ancestors, also called the living dead, are spiritually in contact with the souls of the living. Families often show reverence to their ancestors during ceremonies marking major life-cycle events and achievements, such as the birth of a child, marriage, death of a family member, or a professional achievement. Traditional social and cultural beliefs have regulated marriage and family behavior for many centuries. The social organization of most ethnic groups was based on a patrilineal system of descent, where sons were given inheritance over daughters (Fiawoo 1984). Some features have changed because of contact with Western civilization. However, instead of a convergence to the Western nuclear family model, the family has adapted traditional features to contemporary contexts and constraints.

Traditional Features of Marriage and Family

Within the traditional model of the family, marriage is virtually universal and closely associated with reproduction. It is an alliance between two lineages, beyond the realm of two individuals.

Traditionally, senior family members have watched closely over the mate selection process to ensure that social rules and beliefs were respected. Only elder members of the extended family were invested with authority to handle marriage negotiations. The blood relatives of both prospective spouses carefully studied the alliance of marriage to determine whether it was possible and worthy. Some types of marriages were prohibited, and others were preferred. Marriages of men inside their parents' minimal lineages and marriages with two living sisters were prohibited. The reasons invoked for these prohibitions were mainly supranatural and genetic disorders. The preferred marriage was between cross-cousins and, specifically, between second cousins. The groom's elder family members paid several visits to the lineage members of the bride to sort out concerns and determine whether the marriage was feasible. They also negotiated the amount and composition of the bride-wealth, or bride-price.

Marriage ceremonies used to last many days. They were opportunities for the extended families to get together. The actual marriage ceremonies started with payment of a bride-wealth to the bride's blood relatives. The bride-wealth could be composed of specially prepared food, palm wine, clothing, jewelry, and money (Manoukian 1952). During the ceremony the bride was handed over to the lineage members of the groom. This was followed by the consummation rituals, which included the verification of the bride's virginity. The bride was required to be virgin at marriage; this was an indication that she was raised in a respectable family. The amount of the bride-wealth was revised down if the bride was found not to be virgin (Nukunya 1969).

Polygamy, the marriage of a man with more than one woman, was an important aspect of marriage. Traditionally, men could take additional wives to increase the size of their family line. Farming was rudimentary and relied on heavy physical labor. Additional wives and children helped to make the farm more productive. Thus, a large number of relatives was therefore associated with wealth and prestige. This was the philosophy of old men, who were the ones in control of community resources. Their philosophy of life was law in the community.

Customary laws discouraged divorce. Blood kin were active in resolving disputes among spouses, and generally succeeded; it was rare that intermediation by the family did not save the marriage. If the wife initiated the divorce, then her relatives had to pay back the bride-wealth. In the husband initiated the divorce, he could not reclaim the bride-wealth.

When a married man died, customs allowed one of his brothers to inherit his wives. The wives and children then became part of the immediate household of that brother and remained part of the family line. This practice was called the *levirate* and was consistent with the social and economic values attached to wives and children.

Children were raised following strict social rules. They were taught to show respect to all adults in general. Everyone in the community was concerned with their socialization, not only their biological parents. Children were expected to win the trust of adults to gain knowledge. The transfer of knowledge was in the oral tradition, and only well-behaved children could have the knowledge revealed to them. Boys and girls were socialized differently in ways that were consistent with the roles they were expected to play as adults.

Factors in Change of Family Life

Traditional social beliefs have regulated individual behavior for many centuries. They may have altered over time, but few accounts exist to substantiate these changes. Recorded changes can only be traced back to contacts through trade with Europeans (Portuguese, Dutch, Danish, French, and British) initiated in the fifteenth century. Ethnic groups of the coastal region of Togo participated in the trade of humans from the seventeenth century to the first half of the nineteenth century. This tragedy affected families and may have reinforced the strong belief in having many children. Exposure to alternative lifestyles came mostly through missionaries, European colonialism, urbanization, and Western education. From the mid-1980s to the late 1990s, economic hardship and poverty were also important factors changing marriage and family behavior.

The first German missionaries came to Togo in 1847. They were convinced that the people there were living in sin, and they were particularly disturbed by the worship of ancestors and shocked by the practice of polygamy. Missionaries, through Christian education, promoted the benefits and sanctity of the Western nuclear family.

The work of missionaries was made easier with colonization. Togo experienced three colonial administrations: German, British, and French (Decalo 1996). Many aspects of social life, such as names, dress codes, and marriage customs, were subject to new regulations. For example, on November 17, 1924, the French colonial administration passed an ordinance aimed at regulating marriages in Togo. This ordinance was intended to make it mandatory that the bride consent to a marriage, in the expectation that it would reduce arranged marriages and polygamy (Kuczynski 1939; Knoll 1978).

The German and French administrations both built urban centers from which they could coordinate commercial and administrative activities (Nyassogbo 1984). Because key administrative and economic activities were concentrated in one place, many individuals had to move there to participate in the growing wage economy. This migration resulted in the emergence of new needs and aspirations. People from different social backgrounds were leaving communities with their own rules and customs, and they had to recreate a new community at the crossroads of traditional rules and modern ones. In a situation where both partners were able to earn money, and because every marriage could turn polygamous, women opted for separate budgets and their financial independence in marriage.

Western education is perhaps the most powerful among all factors that affected marriage and family behavior. The missionaries virtually controlled the education system (Lange 1991). It was a powerful medium to diffuse Western values and to challenge the customary social order. For the first time in history, children began to question the elderly lineage members' authority by aspiring to different lifestyles. Economic factors also affected families. From the mid-1980s until the end of the 1990s, families found themselves living with severe economic hardship and poverty. Young couples found it more difficult to afford marriage. Families began to find it difficult to meet the basic survival needs. In this environment, couples with children had difficulty enforcing traditional values. Further, the expectation that children succeed in life and help out their parents financially weakened.

Contemporary Marriage and Family Patterns

Another powerful influence on the family in Togo is an awareness of alternative lifestyles. Awareness of these lifestyles is one thing; their adoption is quite another. Togolese families, however, are adopting them, and they are displaying a spectrum of patterns that do not necessarily converge into the Western nuclear family model. Current and emerging marriage and family patterns are the result of an adaptation of traditional values, beliefs, and customs to the realities and constraints of modern life (Locoh 1984; Assogba 1990; Ekouevi 1994).

Especially in urban areas, features of the traditional marriage, such as the strong role of lineage members in marriage decisions, virginity of the bride, and elaborate marriage ceremonies, have altered over time. Social background and socioeconomic status now exert a more powerful influence on the mate selection process. A bride-wealth is still given to the bride's blood relatives as a symbolic gesture.

Three main forms of marriage co-exist in Togo: the traditional marriage, the Christian marriage, and the city hall, or official, marriage. According to the Togolese Family Code, constructed as a compromise between the law of custom and the French Law, a marriage performed by a traditional chief is validated as legal if reported to the municipal government. Under this condition, the traditional marriage is as valid as the civil marriage performed by a government official. The Family Code, however, does not validate a marriage performed by a Christian priest as legal (Pokanam 1982). Couples can perform all three of these forms of marriage either in a relatively short time or throughout the duration of their marriage. Often, the customary marriage is the first one, followed by either a Christian one, a civil one, or both.

The practice of polygamy has persisted over time despite different attempts to eradicate it. However, in urban areas, polygamy has mainly survived because spouses adopt separate living arrangements. A husband in a polygamous union visits his wives; often, he lives with one wife, and in addition, he has another wife in a different area of the city. In 1998 about 34 percent of women between fifteen and forty-nine years of age were in polygamous unions in urban areas and 47 percent in rural areas (Anipah et al. 1999).

A growing number of young men, even if they have university degrees, are finding it difficult to find employment. They cannot afford to marry and start families. One result is a growing number of pseudofamilies, in which the husband lives with his parents and the wife and children live with the wife's parents. The couple stays in this separate living arrangement hoping for better days when they can afford housing and live together. Informal unions exist also with women having a status of a mistress. In difficult economic circumstances, a relationship with a man (usually married) can improve a woman's financial situation and is part of her survival strategy. At the same time, as families face severe economic difficulties, a growing number of unmarried couples are having children.

Another indication of family breakdown is the high number of female heads of households. About 29 percent of households are headed by females in urban areas and 22 percent in rural areas (Anipah et al. 1999). In some cases, women choose to have children and cannot live with their children's fathers, especially if the man is already married. More and more well-educated women and women with successful businesses are finding themselves in this situation. They want to have children, but their pool of prospective husbands is small. They end up settling with a married man, and they have to raise their children by themselves. Most often, however, women are pushed to face the responsibilities of raising children alone because husbands cannot play the role of breadwinner anymore, due to economic difficulties.

Another shift in family behavior is that parents are having a harder time exercising their authority over their children, which is being eroded by hard times and poverty. They are failing to provide their children with basic necessities, and children have to try to meet these needs on their own.

See also: KINSHIP

Bibliography

Anipah, K.; Mboup, G.; Ouro-Gnao, A. M.; Boukpessi, B.; Adade, M. P.; and Salami-Odjo, R. (1999). *Enquête Démographique et de Santé, Togo 1998.* Calverton, MD: Direction de la Statistique et Macro International.

Assogba, M. L. (1990). "Transition du Statut de la Femme, Transition dans les Structures Familiales et Transition de la Fécondité dans le Golfe du Bénin." *Etudes Togolaises de Population* 15:55–105.

Decalo, S. (1996). "Historical Dictionary of Togo." *African Historical Dictionaries,* No. 9, 3rd. ed. Lanham, MD: Scarecrow Press.

Ekouevi, K. (1994). "Family and Reproductive Behavior in a Changing Society: The Case of Urban Togo." *Union for African Population Studies,* No. 7.

Fiawoo, D. K. (1984). "Some Reflections on Ewe Social Organization." In *Peuples du Golfe du Bénin (Aja-Ewe),* ed. F. de Meideros. Paris: Editions Karthala.

Knoll, A. J. (1978). *Togo Under Imperial Germany 1884–1914: A Case Study in Colonial Rule.* Stanford, CA: Hoover Institution Press.

Kuczynski, R. (1939). *The Cameroons and Togoland: A Demographic Study.* Oxford, UK: Oxford University Press.

Lange, M-F. (1991). "Cent Cinquante Ans de Scolarisation au Togo: Bilan et Perpectives." *Dossiers de L'URD.* Unité de Recherche Démographique. Lomé, Togo: Université du Benin.

Locoh, T. (1984). "L'Evolution de la Famille en Afrique de l'Ouest: Le Togo Méridional Contemporain." *Institut National d'Etudes Démographiques Travaux et Documents Cahier* No. 107. Paris: Presses Universitaires de France.

Manoukian, M. (1952). *The Ewe-Speaking People of Togoland and the Gold Coast.* Ethnographic Survey of Africa, Western Africa, part VI. London: International African Institute.

Nukunya, G.K. (1969). "Kinship and Marriage among the Anlo Ewe." *Monographs on Social Anthropology* No. 37. London School of Economics, University of London. London: The Athlone Press.

Nyassogbo, K. (1984). "L'Urbanization et son Evolution au Togo." *Cahier d'Outre-Mer* 37:135–158.

Pokanam, G. (1982). "Quelques Aspects du Code Togolais de la Famille." *Etudes Togolaises de Population* 4:1–40.

KOFFI EKOUEVI

TRANSITION TO PARENTHOOD

Within the family life-cycle literature, the addition of a first child to the marital system is considered one of the stages that a family will likely experience during its developmental lifetime. For the couple experiencing the birth of a first child, this change is one of most unsettling, but most common, examples of change within a marital relationship. Indeed, having a baby has been ranked as high as sixth out of 102 stressful life events (Dohrenwend et al. 1978). It is also one of the more common occurrences for a couple, with over 1,000,000 first-born babies born annually to couples in the United States (Statistical Abstract of the United States 2000). Nora Ephron, in the novel *Heartburn,* sums up the potential impact of a baby on the marital relationship: ". . . Now, of course, I realized something else no one tells you; that a child is a grenade. When you have a baby, you set off an explosion in your marriage, and when the dust settles, your marriage is different from what it was. Not better, necessarily; not worse, necessarily; but different" (1983, p. 158).

Parenthood as Crisis versus Transition to Parenthood

In 1949, Reuben Hill formulated the perspective of a "family crisis" in his landmark book *Families Under Stress.* Hill defined a family crisis as "a situation in which the usual behavior patterns are found to be unrewarding and new ones are called for immediately. Theoretically we know that three variables are present in a situation which determine whether or not a crisis is created: (1) the hardships of the event, (2) the resources of the family to meet the event, and (3) the family's definition of the event" (p. 51).

This notion of crisis created a framework for a pair of studies concluding that the transition to parenthood created a crisis situation for new parents (Dyer 1963; Lemasters 1957); other researchers, however, asserted the opposite—that first time parents had little difficulty in adjusting to parenthood (Hobbs; 1965, 1968). Equally as important, however, to the emerging interest in the effect of a child's birth on the marital relationship was the recommendation to drop the term *crisis* and "to view the addition of the first child to the marriage as a period of transition which is somewhat stressful" (Hobbs 1968, p. 417). The emphasis on "the transition to parenthood" was reiterated by Alice Rossi (1968) in an article of the same name, and since then the research has highlighted the process whereby couples move from the role of spouse to the role of parent through the pregnancy and immediate postpartum period.

Changes in the Marital Relationship

There is little doubt that the birth of a child changes a couple's marriage; the questions are how much and in what areas. One review of the literature on the transition to parenthood concluded that: (1) the changes that occur in parents' lives during the early postpartum period are more negative than positive; and (2) the transition to parenthood is equally disruptive for men, for women, and for the couple (Cowan and Cowan 1988).

One consistent finding is a decrease in marital satisfaction during the transition to parenthood (Cowan and Cowan 1988; Tomlinson 1996). However, while the "average" couple will have a decline in marital satisfaction in the immediate postpartum period, those same couples may have a rebound over time as they adjust to their new family roles. Three factors in particular may impact satisfaction during the transition to parenthood: prebaby expectations, changes in communication, and pre-baby marital strain.

First, the expectations of the prospective parents may impact the postpartum experience. Some of the connections between pre-baby expectations and postpartum experience include: (1) a positive relationship exists between prenatal expectations and ease of transition (Wylie 1979); (2) inaccurate expectations lead to adjustment problems (Kach and McGhee 1982); (3) negative expectations of prospective parents result in negative experiences afterwards (Belsky, Lang, and Rovine 1985); (4) parents whose positive expectations were violated had more negative marital change (Belsky 1985); (5) violated expectations regarding the sharing of both childcare and housekeeping responsibilities contribute to women's marital dissatisfactions (Ruble et al. 1988); and (6) increased complexity in thinking about expectations results in better adjustment for women after the birth of a child (Pancer et al. 2000).

Secondly, communication changes in both quantity and quality post baby. Typically, the amount of communication between spouses decreases during the transition to parenthood, with reduced communication associated with decreased marital satisfaction (Cowan and Cowan 1988). Moreover, the quality of communication may change as well. For example, either more arguments or less openness over childcare or relationship issues can occur. For those couples used to spontaneous and frequent interaction with each other, these changes can be problematic.

Third, and perhaps most important, the largest factor determining dissatisfaction after the baby is born is strain in the marriage prior to the birth (Cowan and Cowan 1992). Couples with better pre-birth problem-solving abilities and conflict strategies show less, if any, decline in marital satisfaction after the birth of the child compared to those couples with less developed conflict tactics (Cox et al. 1999). The old adage for couples that "having a baby will bring us together" may actually have the opposite effect, particularly for those couples whose marriage is already strained. Having a baby may not solve, but exacerbate the problems in the marriage.

Two long-term programs of research by Jay Belsky and his colleagues and Carolyn Cowan and Philip Cowan and their colleagues have focused on the effect of parenthood on a couple's relationship. Both research programs have been concerned with documenting the changes within individuals, as well as in the marital relationship, during the transition to parenthood; both concur that the transition to parenthood is multidimensional in nature; and each deserve mention due to the holistic approach the researchers take in understanding the complicated nature of the transition to parenthood.

For Cowan and Cowan (1992, p. 5), there are five central aspects of family life that are affected when partners become parents. These five domains are:

- "The inner life of both parents and the first child, with special emphasis on each one's sense of self."
- "The quality of the relationship between the husband and wife, with special emphasis on their family roles and patterns of communication."
- "The quality of the relationships among the grandparents, parents, and children."
- "The relationship between the nuclear family members and key individuals or institutions outside the family (work, friends, child care)."
- "The quality of the relationship between each parent and their first child."

What is important from their perspective is how becoming a parent affects each of these important areas of life, and how change in any one area can affect other areas.

Jay Belsky and John Kelly (1994) have also identified five areas related to the transition to parenthood, though their themes are focused on the areas of potential spousal disagreement. For new parents, these include:

- Chores and division of labor;
- Money;
- Work;
- Their relationship; and
- Social life.

Belsky and Kelly assert that these five areas "constitute the raw material of marital change during the transition. Quite simply, couples who manage to resolve these issues in a mutually satisfying way generally become happier with their marriages, whereas those who do not become unhappier" (1994, p. 32).

To cite one example from the list above, Cowan and Cowan (1988) state that the number one issue leading to conflict was the division of labor in the family. Many factors may affect the division of labor issue, with labor inequity affecting wives more than husbands. For example, it is often the wife that aligns her preferences about the division of childcare tasks with her husband's preferences during the transition to parenthood (Johnson and Huston 1998). In addition, during pregnancy, many women became more interested in goals related to motherhood ("to be a good mother") and less interested in achievement-related goals ("to make career decisions") (Salmela-Aro et al. 2000). Finally, motherhood increases wives' hours spent on at-house duties but reduces other employment hours (Sanchez and Thomson 1997). These findings indicate that wives especially may have decreased satisfaction, particularly if they perceive that there is ongoing inequity between themselves and their husbands in the childcare duties.

Theoretical Assumptions

Four general theories have been utilized to explain the transition to parenthood: systems theory, developmental theory, role theory, and dialectical theory.

Systems theory. The examination of a family as a system is a popular theoretical and therapeutic approach. One of the primary dimensions of a family system is the interdependence among the members and how what happens to one member affects the entire system. The addition of a baby makes a dyad (the spousal couple) a triad and therefore adds complexity to the system. That is, prior to the baby's arrival there are three subsystems: each individual person and the relationship between the couple. After the baby is born, seven subsystems exist: each individual person, three possible dyadic relationships (e.g. mother and child, mother and father, father and child), and the relationship between all three together.

For some systems therapists (e.g., Minuchin 1974) the strain felt after a child is born is due to competition between the spousal subsystem and the parental subsystems: that is, the spousal relationship may be compromised through the additional demand of raising a child.

Cowan and Cowan's five dimensions epitomize a systems perspective, as applied to new parents. An example they use to link various areas is offered: "Think, for example, of a man who feels anxious about becoming a new father (inner life) and wants to be more involved with his child than his father was with him (quality of relationships in family of origin) but feels pressured by the demands of his job (stress outside the family). Once the baby is born, he may have difficulty negotiating new family roles and decisions with his wife (quality of the marriage)" (Cowan and Cowan 1992, p. 6). One can see from this example that the myriad areas of one's life are all connected and that a change (the baby) in one area can affect all other areas.

Developmental theory. A theory held by many researchers is a stage model of family development. Rossi (1968), who helped shift the focus from "crisis" to "transition," did so with the understanding that a transition implies a movement from one stage to another, in this case a movement from preparenthood to parenthood. Other researchers have echoed this assumption, including the identification of the transition as a normal developmental event for married adults (Miller and Sollie 1980), the examination of the family life cycle during the transition (Entwisle and Doering 1981), and how pregnancy and parenthood progress from one stage to the next (Feldman and Nash 1984).

The important points to be taken from a developmental approach is that the transition to parenthood may be (1) a normal change involving a move from one stage of life to another and (2) that inhabiting a different life stage may change many aspects of one's life, including relationships and self identity.

Role theory. The third theory used in understanding the transition to parenthood is role theory. The addition of the child is often discussed in terms of the additional, and subsequently strained, role obligations of the marital couple. Cowan and colleagues (1985) have examined role strain during the transition to parenthood using a "pie" analogy. Individual spouses are asked to both list and divide their main roles (on a circle) before and after the birth of their child.

Results from the pie indicate clearly that the roles of partner and lover get smaller while the role of parent gets larger with the advent of parenthood.

The findings from research using a role related approach during the transition to parenthood include:

(1) There is an increase in role segregation, and discrepant perceptions of role performances, by spouses (Cowan et al. 1978);

(2) More traditional roles are enacted during parenthood (McHale and Huston 1985);

(3) Wives who did not see female sex-typed attributes in themselves (relative to those who saw themselves in sex-stereotyped ways) were more apt to evaluate their marriage less favorably after the birth of the child (Belsky, Lang, and Huston 1986);

(4) Role strain is more successfully predicted from both husband and wife measures which "underlines the point that becoming a parent is a couple experience as well as an individual experience" (Feldman 1987, p. 29);

(5) One or both spouses may "feel trapped in the 'foreverness' of the parent role" (Cowan et al. 1985, p. 476); and

(6) Spouses learn to enact and negotiate the role of parent through their ongoing interactions with each other (Stamp 1994).

Dialectical theory. The transition to parenthood can also be examined through dialectical theory, an approach concerned with understanding the inherent contradictions that occur in family life. These contradictions include autonomy versus connectedness, expressive versus instrumental communication, and stability versus change.

The tension between autonomy for self versus connection with other is particularly pronounced after the birth of a child. Nicolina Fedele and her colleagues explain:

> Since parenthood involves negotiating commitments to self and to others, the dialectic between autonomy and affiliation becomes highlighted around the transition to parenthood. The search for the balance between self and other affects the marital relationship and the parent-child relationship. Parenting provides a unique and complex interaction of affiliation and autonomy since each individual in the family unit—mother, father, and child—is in some way negotiating the dilemma, but in reference to one another. (1988, p. 96)

One of the most typical experiences that spouses feel after the birth of a baby is "constrained autonomy" or "the overwhelming feeling that one's sense of independence is severely compromised by factors outside one's control" (Stamp and Banski 1992, p. 285–286). The ways in which the autonomy of a new parent is affected include having less time for oneself, having to restructure activities, and the addition of new and difficult tasks related to childcare.

A second dialectic is the dialectic between expressiveness and instrumentality. Rossi (1968) discussed expressive and instrumental functions in her seminal paper on the transition to parenthood. She concluded that "the role of father, husband, wife, or mother, each has these two independent dimensions of authority and support, instrumentality and expressiveness, work and love" (p. 37) and that role conflict is present whenever these polarities are required.

One of the ways a marriage changes after the birth of a baby is from a relationship primarily focused on emotional expression to one focused on instrumental aspects (Belsky et al. 1983). In addition, marital satisfaction is correlated with this change; marital quality goes down as the relationship becomes more instrumental (Belsky et al. 1983; McHale and Huston 1985).

A third dialectic is between stability and change, which involves the struggle between the couple to maintain the predictable patterns within their relationship while attempting to adapt to the changes within their life due to the pregnancy and new baby. During the transition to parenthood pronounced change is occurring within a formerly stable union.

These three dialectics—autonomy/affiliation, expressiveness/instrumentality, stability/change—are clearly experienced during the transition to parenthood and present dilemmas and opportunities for spouses to solve.

Alternative/Multicultural Findings

In many ways, the findings reported here tend to be fairly narrow in scope, as the focus has been primarily white U.S. subjects in more "traditional" relationships. As such, less is known about how other ethnic groups or other types of couples (or individuals) might experience the transition to parenthood.

For example, if couples who adopt children experience the transition similarly to biological parents is relatively unexplored. One research project did compare the transition experience between adoptive and biological couples (Levy-Shiff, Goldshmidt, and Har-Even 1991). Compared to biological parents, adoptive couples had more positive expectations and more satisfying and positive experiences. One explanation offered for this finding may be that the desire to have a child may be stronger with adoptive parents, leading to an overall more satisfying experience.

Other ethnic groups or non-U.S. couples have also not been studied. Susan Crohan (1996) offers an exception with her comparison of African-American and white couples. Similar experiences were found in both sets of new parents, including decreased satisfaction, more conflict, and more tension after the birth of the child. Across ethnic or cultural groups, there may be more similarity than difference in the transition experience; however, the research has not been extensive enough to draw firm conclusions.

A final group deserving mention are single parents. The overall literature on the transition to parenthood has focused on the impact on the marital couple, or the individual spouses within the marriage. With almost one-third of American births to single mothers (Statistical Abstract of the United States 2000), the experience of these mothers has not been examined. Research needs to be conducted on single parents to see what type of experiences they have, both individually and within their relationships.

Conclusion

The transition to parenthood is one of the most exciting life events a person can experience. Although this entry may paint a rather negative picture, much individual joy and potentially positive marital changes can occur as a result of having a baby. Belsky and Kelly observed that "some marriages decline and others improve during the transition" (1994, p. 17). All individuals and marriages, though, change as a result of a baby.

See also: ADULTHOOD; CHILDCARE; COMMUNICATION: COUPLE RELATIONSHIPS; COMMUNICATION: FAMILY RELATIONSHIPS; CONFLICT: COUPLE RELATIONSHIPS; COPARENTING; DIALECTICAL THEORY; FAMILY DEVELOPMENT THEORY; FAMILY ROLES; FAMILY SYSTEMS THEORY; FATHERHOOD; LIFE COURSE THEORY; MARITAL QUALITY; MOTHERHOOD; PARENTING EDUCATION; RELATIONSHIP MAINTENANCE; ROLE THEORY; SELF-ESTEEM; STRESS; SYMBOLIC INTERACTIONISM; THERAPY: COUPLE RELATIONSHIPS

Bibliography

Belsky, J. (1985). "Exploring Individual Differences in Marital Change Across the Transition to Parenthood: The Role of Violated Expectations." *Journal of Marriage and the Family* 47:1037–1044.

Belsky, J., and Kelly, J. (1994). *The Transition to Parenthood.* New York: Delacorte Press.

Belsky, J.; Lang, M. E.; and Huston, T. L. (1986). "Sex Typing and Division of Labor as Determinants of Marital Change Across the Transition to Parenthood." *Journal of Personality and Social Psychology* 50:517–522.

Belsky, J.; Lang, M. E.; and Rovine, M. (1985). "Stability and Change in Marriage Across the Transition to Parenthood: A Second Study." *Journal of Marriage and the Family* 47:855–865.

Belsky, J.; Spanier, G.; and Rovine, M. (1983). "Stability and Change in Marriage Across the Transition to Parenthood." *Journal of Marriage and the Family* 45:567–577.

Cowan, C. P., and Cowan, P. A. (1992). *When Parents Become Partners: The Big Life Change For Couples.* New York: Basic Books.

Cowan, C. P.; Cowan, P. A.; Coie, L.; and Coie, J. D. (1978). "Becoming a Family: The Impact of a First Child's Birth on the Couple's Relationship." In *The First Child and Family Formation,* eds. W. B. Miller and L. F. Newman. Chapel Hill: Carolina Population Center, University of North Carolina.

Cowan, C. P.; Cowan, P. A.; Heming, G.; Garrett, E.; Coysh, W. S.; Curtis-Boles, H.; and Boles A. J., III. (1985). "Transitions to Parenthood: His, Hers, and Theirs." *Journal of Family Issues* 6:451–482.

Cowan, P. A., and Cowan, C. P. (1988). "Changes in Marriage During the Transition to Parenthood: Must We Blame the Baby?" In *The Transition to Parenthood: Current Theory and Research,* ed. G. Y. Michaels and W. A. Goldberg. New York: Cambridge University Press.

Cox, M.; Paley, B.; Burchinal, M.; and Payne, C. (1999). "Marital Perceptions and Interactions Across the Transition to Parenthood." *Journal of Marriage and the Family* 6:611–625.

Crohan, S. E. (1996). "Marital Quality and Conflict Across the Transition to Parenthood in African American and White Couples." *Journal of Marriage and the Family* 58:933–944.

Dohrenwend, B.; Krasnoff, L.; Askenasy, A.; and Dohrenwend, B. (1978). "Exemplification of a Method for Scaling Life Events." *Journal of Health and Social Behavior* 19:205–229.

Dyer, E. D. (1963). "Parenthood as Crisis: A Re-Study." *Marriage and Family Living* 25:196–201.

Entwisle, D. R., and Doering, S. G. (1981). *The First Birth.* Baltimore, MD: John Hopkins University Press.

Ephron, N. (1983). *Heartburn.* New York: Alfred A. Knopf.

Fedele, N. M.; Golding, E. R.; Grossman, F. K.; and Pollack, W. S. (1988). "Psychological Issues in Adjustment to First Parenthood." In *The Transition to Parenthood: Current Theory and Research,* ed. G. Y. Michaels and W. A. Goldberg. New York: Cambridge University Press.

Feldman, S. S. (1987). "Predicting Strain in Mothers and Fathers of 6-Month Old Infants: A Short Term Longitudinal Study." In *Men's Transitions to Parenthood,* eds. P. Berman and F. Pedersen. Hillsdale, NJ: Erlbaum.

Feldman, S. S., and Nash, S. C. (1984). "The Transition From Expectancy to Parenthood: Impact of the Firstborn Child on Men and Women." *Sex Roles* 11:61–78.

Hill, R. (1949). *Families Under Stress.* New York: Harper and Brothers.

Hobbs, D. F., Jr. (1965). "Parenthood as Crisis: A Third Study." *Journal of Marriage and the Family* 27:367–372.

Hobbs, D. F., Jr. (1968). "Transition to Parenthood: A Replication and an Extension." *Journal of Marriage and the Family* 30:413–417.

Johnson, E. M., and Huston, T. L. (1998). "The Perils of Love, or Why Wives Adapt to Husbands During the Transition to Parenthood." *Journal of Marriage and the Family* 60:195–204.

Kach, J., and McGhee, P. (1982). "Adjustment to Early Parenthood: The Role of Accuracy of Preparenthood Expectations." *Journal of Family Issues* 3:361–374.

Lemasters, E. E. (1957). "Parenthood as Crisis." *Marriage and Family Living* 19:352–355.

Levy-Shiff, R.; Goldshmidt, I.; and Har-Even, D. (1991). "Transition to Parenthood in Adoptive Families." *Developmental Psychology* 27:131–140.

McHale, S. M., and Huston, T. L. (1985). "The Effect of the Transition to Parenthood on the Marriage Relationship: A Longitudinal Study." *Journal of Family Issues* 6:409–433.

Miller, B. C., and Sollie, D. L. (1980). "Normal Stresses During the Transition to Parenthood." *Family Relations* 29:459–465.

Minuchin, S. (1974). *Families and Family Therapy*. Cambridge, MA: Harvard University Press.

Pancer, S.; Pratt, M.; Hunsberger, B.; and Gallant, M. (2000). "Thinking Ahead: Complexity of Expectations and the Transition to Parenthood." *Journal of Personality* 68:253–280.

Rossi, A. S. (1968). "Transition to Parenthood." *Journal of Marriage and the Family* 30:26–39.

Ruble, D.; Fleming, A.; Hackel, L.; and Stangor, C. (1988). "Changes in the Marital Relationship During the Transition to First-Time Motherhood." *Journal of Personality and Social Psychology* 55:78–87.

Salmela-Aro, K.; Nurmi, J.; Saisto, T.; and Halmesmaeki, E. (2000). "Women's and Men's Personal Goals During the Transition to Parenthood." *Journal of Family Psychology* 14:171–186.

Sanchez, L., and Thomson, E. (1997). "Becoming Mothers and Fathers: Parenthood, Gender, and the Division of Labor." *Gender and Society* 11:747–772.

Stamp, G. H. (1994). "The Appropriation of the Parental Role Through Communication During the Transition to Parenthood." *Communication Monographs* 61:89–112.

Stamp, G. H., and Banski, M. A. (1992). "The Communicative Management of Constrained Autonomy During the Transition to Parenthood." *Western Journal of Communication* 56:281–300.

Statistical Abstract of the United States: 2000, 120th edition. Washington, DC: U.S. Census Bureau.

Tomlinson, P. (1996). "Marital Relationship Change in the Transition to Parenthood: A Reexamination as Interpreted Through Transition Theory." *Journal of Family Nursing* 2:286–305.

Wylie, M. L. (1979). "The Effect of Expectations on the Transition to Parenthood." *Sociological Focus* 12:323–329.

GLEN H. STAMP

TRIANGULATION

Since the mid-1960s, there has been increasing appreciation for the importance of the family environment in understanding normative child development and child maladjustment. In their search for theoretically sound and empirically testable hypotheses about family functioning and its impact on children, researchers have found a rich resource in the work of family systems theorists and therapists. As a consequence, concepts from the study and practice of family therapy have slowly been working their way into the lexicon and empirical investigations of diverse disciplines (e.g., psychology, family studies, sociology). At its core, regardless of the specific model being applied, family therapy requires that one think of the family as a dynamic system in which all parts are interdependent (Minuchin 1985).

Systemic and Structural Family Theories

In efforts to describe family processes that extend beyond the dyadic level, the idea of *triangles* within the family, or *triangulation,* is one of the more robust theoretical concepts that has emerged. Triangulation can occur in a variety of ways, but always involves a pair of family members incorporating or rejecting a third family member. Triangulation is seen in the cross-generational coalitions that can develop within families, a concept that many family therapists, including such prominent pioneers as Murray Bowen (see Bowen 1966, 1978; Kerr and Bowen 1988) and Salvador Minuchin (see Minuchin 1974), have linked to the development of maladjustment in children. Although the theoretical models of both of these men extend far beyond the concept of triangulation, their theories were foremost among those that helped establish the construct as an important one.

Bowen. One of the seminal constructs of Bowen's theory is the idea of an *emotional triangle* (Friedman 1991). In Bowenian terms, triangles occur in all families and social groups (Hoffman 1981). They are fluid—rather than static—as all two-person relationships go through cycles of closeness and distance (as dictated by individuals' varying needs for connectedness and autonomy). Drawing in a third party is one way to try and stabilize the relationship. For Bowen, triangles are most likely to develop when a dyad is experiencing stress (Nichols and Schwartz 1995). Triangulating patterns tend to become rigid when created under duress but tend to be more flexible during calmer periods in the family life-cycle (Hoffman 1981). When tension exists between two family members, one of them (most likely the person experiencing the greater level of discomfort) may attempt to "triangle in" a third person either directly or indirectly (e.g., by bringing them up, telling a story about them). For example, in the case of marital triangles, a husband who is upset with his wife might start spending more time with their child or a distressed wife might start confiding about the marital difficulties with their child. Both situations result in a temporary reduction of marital tension though the essential problem remains unresolved. A third party (e.g., child, friend) who is sensitive to one spouse's anxiety or to the conflict between the dyad can also insert themselves into the dyad and thereby create a triangle as they try to offer reassurance, advice, or pleadings to reduce the conflict.

Minuchin. Salvador Minuchin is credited with developing the structural school of family therapy (Minuchin 1974). The term *family structure* refers to the organized patterns in which family members interact. When certain sequences of interaction are repeated, enduring patterns or covert rules can be created that determine how, when, and to whom family members relate (Nicholas and Schwartz 1995). Each individual, like dyads and larger groups, is a subsystem (Minuchin 1974). Individuals and subsystems are demarcated by *interpersonal boundaries*: invisible barriers that surround individuals and subsystems and regulate the amount of contact with others. Boundaries vary from rigid to diffuse and one of their functions is to manage hierarchy within the family.

Detouring and *cross-generational coalitions* are two types of triangulation described by Minuchin (Minuchin 1974). When parents are unable to resolve problems between them, they may direct their focus of concern away from themselves and onto the child, perhaps reinforcing maladaptive behavior in the child. The child may then become identified as the problematic member of the family. Detouring occurs when parents, rather than directing anger or criticism toward each other, focus the negativity on the child and the parent-child conflict thus serves to distract from the tension in the marital subsystem. This type of triangulation also is sometimes referred to as *scapegoating* as the child's well-being is sacrificed in order that the marital conflict might be avoided (Minuchin 1974). Cross-generational coalitions develop when one or both parents trying to enlist the support of the child against the other parent. Cross-generational coalitions also exist when one of the parents responds to the child's needs with excessive concern and devotion (*enmeshment*) while the other parent withdraws and becomes less responsive. In the latter situation, the attention to the child is supportive rather than critical or conflictual. Minuchin believed cross-generational coalitions to be particularly associated with psychosomatic illness (Minuchin, Rosman, and Baker 1978) and recent research also shows associations with marital distress (e.g., Kerig 1995; Lindahl, Clements, and Markman 1997).

Detriangulation

In Bowenian family therapy, it is argued that a conflict between two people will resolve itself in the presence of a third person who can avoid emotional participation with either while relating actively to both (Bowen 1978). Typically, it is the therapist who takes on the *nonanxious* role and forms a triangle with a couple. While remaining emotionally unreactive, the therapist is able to induce change in the relationship that would not have occurred had the same things been said in the absence of the therapist (Friedman 1991). Alternatively, a family system can be *detriangulated* when the therapist insists that one family member take a position on an issue and maintain that position despite opposition from other family members that might occur (Hoffman 1981). This strategy helps establish *differentiation of self* but also, in a three-person emotional system, allows one person to remain detached and unreactive.

An essential element of structural family therapy is introducing challenges to the prevailing maladaptive family structure (Minuchin and Fishman 1981). In the case of triangulating cross-generational coalitions, it is the goal of the therapist to realign subsystem boundaries. For example, if a family is characterized by an overinvolved mother-child dyad and an excluded father, techniques are employed to strengthen the parenting alliance and to increase the father's participation in the parental subsystem. One way to do this is to give the parents a common task (e.g., directing them to support one another's parenting efforts). This type of intervention strengthens the parental subsystem and increases the proximity between the spouses while at the same time increasing the psychological distance between the mother and the child. Family members may be asked to physically change their seating arrangement in order to facilitate proper boundary development. If a child engages in frequent detouring behaviors in the

Couples that are unable to resolve problems between themselves may redirect their concern onto their children. One parent might show excessive concern for the child while the other parent withdraws. LAURA DWIGHT/CORBIS

face of interparental conflict, the therapist may ask the child to sit next to him and instruct the parents to request that their child be quiet while they discuss an area of disagreement.

The Empirical Study of Triangulation

Historically, most investigations of familial interaction have taken a dyadic approach, studying the antecedent-consequent interactions of two family members at a time (e.g., parent criticism followed by child negative affect). Until the end of the twentieth century, there had been surprisingly little empirical research examining whole-family (or any family unit that extends beyond dyads) dynamics and their implications for child development. An implicit assumption seemed to be that triadic or family-level processes had little impact on children's behavior beyond the contributions of dyadic husband-wife and parent-child interactions. However, twenty-first-century researchers began to establish the importance of triangulation (among other triadic processes) for child functioning. For the most part, triangulating processes have been studied in the context of marital conflict and how it may negatively affect other family subsystems.

Marital functioning. Several studies found children to be more likely to be triangulated into marital disputes in families characterized by higher levels of marital conflict. Kristin Lindahl, Mari Clements, and Howard Markman (1997) found marital distress and conflict before the birth of a child to be predictive of the development of cross-generational coalitions and husbands' tendency to triangulate the child into marital disputes five years later. In other words, when couples were ineffective at regulating negativity between them before a child was born, they were more likely to later try to form alliances with the child against the other parent, and fathers were more likely to involve or incorporate the child into ongoing marital conflict years later. Exposure to intense marital conflict, including aggression, has been shown to be related to children's tendency, especially in boys, to make efforts to distract or deflect parents' attention away from ongoing interspousal conflict (Gordis, Margolin, and John 1997).

Using a *pictorial assessment strategy,* Patricia Kerig (1995) asked parents and their children to describe their family structure by pointing to the drawing that best illustrated the level of closeness that existed between the different members in their family. Parents from triangulated families, in which there were cross-generational coalitions between parents and children, rated their marriages as the highest in conflict and maladjustment. Cross-generational coalitions or alliances would seem likely to threaten the relationship the child has with each parent, both the one seeking an alliance with the child as well the one against whom the child is being asked to align. The child may feel anger or resentment at being asked to in essence betray the other parent (Cox, Paley, and Harter 2001). In addition, child triangulation is thought to prolong marital distress and family tension as the original conflict is not resolved.

Child functioning. Triangulating processes have been shown to be linked to higher levels of maladjustment in children in several studies (Jenkins,

Smith, and Graham 1989; O'Brien, Margolin, and John 1995). Children who report coping with interparental discord by becoming involved in the conflict, either through intervention or distraction and acting out, have been found to have higher levels of anxiety and hostility, and lower levels of self-esteem than children who cope by avoidance or self-reliance (O'Brien, Margolin, and John 1995). Children who triangulate themselves may perceive a conflicted parent-child relationship as one that is less threatening and easier to manage than a conflicted marital relationship (Cox, Paley, and Harter 2001). In one of the few empirical investigations to include a clinical sample in the study triangulating processes, Barton Mann and colleagues (1990) examined parent-child coalitions in families with a delinquent adolescent and in families with a well-adjusted adolescent. Cross-generational coalitions, defined by the degree of verbal activity, supportiveness, and conflict-hostility in one parent-child dyad relative to the other, occurred significantly more often in the families with antisocial teenagers. In particular, in the delinquent sample, the adolescents were more often aligned with their mothers (who often perceived their husbands as too harsh) and disengaged from their fathers (who were often punitive and emotionally distant from the child).

Although the majority of the studies examining family processes have focused on middle-class Anglo families, there is evidence to suggest that triangulating processes occur in other ethnic groups as well. Kristin Lindahl and Neena Malik (1999) compared Anglo, Hispanic, and biethnic (Anglo/Hispanic) families and found detouring marital coalitions (spouses' marital conflict was redirected to the child in an attacking and critical manner) to be associated with higher levels of marital conflict and externalizing behavior problems in children across all three ethnic groups. Within a clinical sample of Hispanic families, José Szapocznik and his colleagues (1989) found family therapy to be related to improvements in family functioning (including triangulation).

Conclusion

As suggested by early family therapists such as Bowen and Minuchin, and echoed by empirical researchers such as Robert Emery, Frank Fincham, and Mark Cummings (1992), the family is more complex than a simple collection of dyadic relationships and children's development is intimately intertwined in this web of reciprocal family interactions. Triangulation of children into ongoing marital disputes, whether it be through scapegoating the child, detouring marital conflict through the child, or the establishment of an overly close parent-child alliance that excludes the other parent, has been linked to marital dysfunction as well as child behavioral and emotional problems. Ongoing areas of research and clinical work are focused on better understanding the complex reciprocal nature of family relationships and the development of effective interventions that can reduce the likelihood of triangulation as well as reduce impact of problematic interaction processes (such as triangulation) on child development.

See also: BOUNDARY DISSOLUTION; CONFLICT: COUPLE RELATIONSHIPS; CONFLICT: FAMILY RELATIONSHIPS; CONFLICT: PARENT-CHILD RELATIONSHIPS; COPARENTING; FAMILY, DIAGRAMMATIC ASSESSMENT: GENOGRAM; FAMILY SYSTEMS THEORY; INTERPARENTAL CONFLICT—EFFECTS ON CHILDREN; THERAPY: FAMILY RELATIONSHIPS; THERAPY: PARENT-CHILD RELATIONSHIPS

Bibliography

Bowen, M. (1966). "The Use of Family Theory in Clinical Practice." *Comprehensive Psychiatry* 7:345–374.

Bowen, M. (1978). *Family Therapy in Clinical Practice.* New York: Jason Aronson.

Cox, M. J.; Paley, B.; and Harter, K. (2001). "Interparental Conflict and Parent-Child Relationships." In *Interparental Conflict and Child Development,* ed. J. H. Grych and F. D. Fincham. Cambridge: Cambridge University Press.

Emery, R. E.; Fincham, F. D.; and Cummings, E. M. (1992). "Parenting in Context: Systematic Thinking about Parental Conflict and Its Influence on Children." *Journal of Consulting and Clinical Psychology* 60: 909–912.

Friedman, E. H. (1991). "Bowen Theory and Therapy." In *Handbook of Family Therapy,* Vol. 2, ed. A. S. Gurman and D. P. Kniskern. New York: Brunner/Mazel.

Gordis, E. B.; Margolin, G.; and John, R. S. (1997). "Marital Aggression, Observed Parental Hostility, and Child Behavior during Triadic Family Interaction." *Journal of Family Psychology* 11:76–89.

Hoffman, L. (1981). *Foundations of Family Therapy: A Conceptual Framework for Systems Change.* New York: Basic Books.

Jenkins, J. M.; Smith, M. A.; and Graham, P. J. (1989). "Coping with Parental Quarrels." *Journal of the American Academy of Child and Adolescent Psychiatry* 28:182–189.

Kerig, P. K. (1995). "Triangles in the Family Circle: Effects of Family Structure on Marriage, Parenting, and Child Adjustment." *Journal of Family Psychology* 9:28–43.

Kerr, M., and Bowen, M. (1988). *Family Evaluation.* New York: Norton.

Lindahl, K. M.; Clements, M.; and Markman, H. (1997). "Predicting Marital and Parent Functioning in Dyads and Triads: A Longitudinal Investigation of Marital Processes." *Journal of Family Psychology* 11:139–151.

Lindahl, K. M., and Malik, N. M. (1999). "Marital Conflict, Family Processes, and Boys' Externalizing Behavior in Hispanic American and European American Families." *Journal of Clinical Child Psychology* 28:12–24.

Mann, B. J.; Borduin, C. M.; Henggeler, S. W.; and Blaske, D. M. (1990). "An Investigation of Systemic Conceptualizations of Parent-Child Coalitions and Symptom Change." *Journal of Consulting and Clinical Psychology* 58:336–344.

Minuchin, P. (1985). "Families and Individual Development: Provocations from the Field of Family Therapy." *Child Development* 56:289–302.

Minuchin, S. (1974). *Families and Family therapy.* Cambridge, MA: Harvard University Press.

Minuchin, S., and Fishman, H. C. (1981). *Family Therapy Techniques.* Cambridge, MA: Harvard University Press.

Minuchin, S.; Rosman, B.; and Baker, L. (1978). *Psychosomatic Families: Anorexia Nervosa in Context.* Cambridge, MA: Harvard University Press.

Nichols, M. P., and Schwartz, R. C. (1995). *Family Therapy: Concepts and Methods,* 3rd edition. Boston: Allyn and Bacon.

O'Brien, M.; Margolin, G.; and John, R. S. (1995). "Relation among Marital Conflict, Child Coping, and Child Adjustment." *Journal of Clinical Child Psychology* 24: 346–361.

Szapocznik, J.; Rio, A.; Murray, E.; Cohen, R.; Scopetta, M.; Rivas-Vazquez, A.; Hervis, O.; Posada, V.; and Kurtines, W. (1989). "Structural Family versus Psychodynamic Child Therapy for Problematic Hispanic Boys." *Journal of Consulting and Clinical Psychology* 57:571–578.

KRISTIN LINDAHL

TRUST

Trust in an intimate partner or family member occupies a central place in a rewarding and successful relationship. Consistently, trust is regarded as one of, if not *the,* most important component of a loving relationship (Regan, Kocan, and Whitlock 1998), and international studies have found trust to be a critical factor in the success of long-term marriages (Roizblatt et al. 1999; Sharlin 1996). Indeed, feelings of trust early in a marriage are predictive of marital adjustment two years later. There is no question that trust plays an important role in social interaction. This chapter will specifically examine the development and impact of trust in intimate relationships.

Defining Trust

Trust is a fundamental component of virtually all social interactions. In the context of a close relationship, trust refers to *the level of confidence we have that the other person will act in ways that will fulfill our expectations.* This confidence does not merely reflect an intellectual assessment of the likelihood that a partner will act as anticipated, but also an emotionally experienced sense of security and assurance in the partner's behavior and motives.

The fulfillment of many of our most cherished hopes and dreams requires the active presence and participation of important people in our lives in ways that are frequently beyond our control. Yet how do we characterize the multitude of goals, plans, and expectations that we have for others and ourselves? Trust researchers have offered various systems for organizing these expectations and, despite the differences in these organizational schemes, they tend to share one common theme. In virtually all cases, researchers have related trust to what they consider to be the most important interpersonal goal in a close relationship—the belief that our partner is motivated by feelings of responsiveness and caring towards us.

Robert Larzelere and Ted Huston (1980) have suggested that the most important expectations involve confidence in another person's benevolence and honesty or sincerity. Benevolence involves a genuine concern for the other's welfare and the motivation to maximize positive outcomes. Thus, for Larzelere and Huston, the core issues of trust in a close relationship involve the expectations that the other person cares and can be believed.

Similarly, Cynthia Johnson-George and Walter Swap (1982) developed a measure of *emotional trust* that taps into expectations of a partner's openness, honesty, and concern for the other's welfare. Again, the most important set of expectations involves confidence in a partner's expressions of caring and concern.

This same theme also occurs in the work of John Holmes and John Rempel and their colleagues. For example, Rempel, Holmes, and Mark Zanna (1985) organized expectations along a dimension from specific concrete behaviors to abstract interpersonal motives. *Predictability* is the most concrete dimension and it refers to expectations for specific behaviors. *Dependability* refers to expectations based more on qualities and characteristics such as honesty and reliability that identify the partner as a trustworthy person. Finally, *faith,* the most general and abstract level of expectations, reflects an emotional security that enables people to go beyond the available evidence and feel, with assurance, that their partner will be responsive and caring whatever the future may hold. An emphasis on a partner's motives of love and caring as the central component of trust in a close relationship occurs consistently in other work produced by these authors (e.g., Holmes 1991; Holmes and Rempel 1989).

Thus, the most important aspect of trust in an intimate relationship appears to involve expectations that individuals will be caring and will act in ways that will take the needs and desires of their partner into account, even at a cost to themselves. Confidence in this central belief may translate into a host of more specific goals and expectations unique to each couple.

The Development of Trust

As with many aspects of our lives, there is evidence that the foundation for trust is established in early relationships with primary caregivers. In his influential theory of psychosocial development, Erik Erikson theorized that the critical developmental task or "crisis" that must be confronted during the first year of life is trust versus mistrust. Trust in infancy sets the stage for a lifelong expectation that the world will be a good and pleasant place in which to live.

This idea is echoed in the foundational thinking and research of attachment theorists John Bowlby and Mary Ainsworth and her colleagues. If caregivers are sensitive and responsive to their infant's needs, the infants develop a *secure* attachment—they learn that the world is a safe place where others can be relied on, and they come to feel that they are worthy of being cared for. If caregivers respond inconsistently or are not responsive to their infant's needs, these infants develop an *insecure* attachment—they learn that the world is an unpredictable or hostile place where they cannot rely on others to care for them. Given these beginnings, it is not surprising to find that trust is indicative of secure attachment, not only in children, but also in adults (Mikulincer 1998).

Thus, there is evidence that people's earliest relationships establish a foundation for trust that can set the stage for their adult relationships. Current research suggests that parents shape their children's trust beliefs (Rotenburg 1995) and that feelings of trust in young adults are related to the experience of deep attachment to their parents (Amagai 1999). Indeed, in a longitudinal study, Kristina Moeller and Hakan Stattin (2001) report that adolescents with trustful parental relationships experienced greater satisfaction with their partner relationships in midlife.

The suggestion that the capacity to trust is rooted in the social interactions of infancy may imply that trust is a learned personality characteristic that people develop and subsequently carry from relationship to relationship. Certainly there is evidence to suggest that people do differ in *global trust,* the extent to which they trust other people in general (Rotter 1967). In addition, Laurie Couch and Warren Jones (1997) have suggested that there may be relatively stable individual differences in *network trust,* the extent to which people trust their family and friends.

However, even if people differ in their general tendency to trust others, there is currently no reason to believe that these levels are completely fixed and immovable. Certainly there is anecdotal evidence to suggest that, with time, even individuals who have been badly scarred by their past experiences can learn to put their faith in people who prove themselves to be consistently caring and trustworthy. More importantly, even if people do have a general capacity to trust based on their

A mother cradles her sleeping infant on her shoulder. Because the mother is sensitive and responsive to her infant's needs, the infant develops a secure attachment and trust in the mother. KAREN HUNTT MASON/CORBIS

social history, the distinct features of a unique relationship with a specific individual will ultimately determine how much confidence people are willing to place in that person's motives.

How is it that people develop *relational trust* (Couch and Jones 1997)—trust in a relationship with a specific individual? Currently there are no definitive answers to this question, but scholars generally agree that trust is demonstrated most clearly in situations of risk and vulnerability. As paradoxical as it may sound, people can only learn about how much a partner genuinely cares for them when it is possible for that partner to act in an untrustworthy manner. Only in circumstances where there is a risk of betrayal and disappointment will people be able to confidently regard their partner's behaviors as voluntary actions motivated by feelings of love. Trust in a close relationship develops as each person demonstrates a willingness to respond to the needs and concerns of their partner at some personal cost to themselves.

Although risk-taking fuels the development of trust (Boon 1994), the strength and pattern of interactions involving risk will change as the relationship progresses. The earliest expressions of confidence in a romantic partner may reflect a "blind trust" in an idealized image of the partner constructed from carefully selected fragments of information. Indeed, strong feelings of trust appear to be present even among casually dating couples who have had few opportunities to base their feelings of trust on diagnostic experiences involving risk and vulnerability (Larzelere and Huston 1980). Nonetheless, at some level, newly formed couples seem to realize that their indiscriminate trust is built on a fragile foundation. During the transition from a platonic to a romantic relationship, couples are particularly likely to use social strategies—or "secret tests"—to assess the state of their relationship (Baxter and Wilmot 1984). Furthermore, as intimacy grows, the idealized depictions of the partner are increasingly challenged by evidence from the partner's actual behaviors. Feelings of confidence may be called into question as the lofty images of the partner are replaced with more realistic assessments of the partner's shortcomings (Holmes 1991).

As the relationship progresses there are increasing opportunities for uncertainty to develop, but these same situations also offer opportunities for trust to grow. As the lives of both partners become increasingly intertwined, the possibilities for conflict are intensified. These points of conflict carry with them risks of rejection and harm but, at the same time, they offer opportunities for each partner to demonstrate concern for the relationship and a willingness to take the other's needs into account. If conflict issues are successfully resolved, not only is trust strengthened, but each partner also develops greater confidence that future problems can be solved together.

Thus, trust develops as people demonstrate a willingness to sacrifice their own interests in order to take the needs and concerns of their partner into account. With each successful experience of disclosure or conflict resolution there is further evidence of the partner's commitment to the relationship and greater confidence that the relationship will last and grow stronger.

The Impact of Trust in Established Relationships

Trust is a dynamic process. Even after a solid foundation of trust has been established, feelings of confidence continue to respond to changes and transitions in the relationship. Just as trust has been built up, it can also wear down. The impact that different levels of trust have on the nature of a close relationship has only recently become the subject of study, and much still remains to be learned. However, from the evidence that already exists, it is clear that the relationships of people with higher levels of trust are categorically different from relationships where trust levels are lower. In an important set of longitudinal studies of commitment and trust, Jennifer Wieselquist and her colleagues (1999) have provided evidence that changes in trust are related to the perception of a partner's positive actions. Individuals come to trust their partners when they are committed to them and when they perceive that their partners have acted in positive ways. Additionally, it has been shown that changes in trust must ultimately reflect changes in attributions to the partner's motives (Miller and Rempel 2000). People must not only notice their partner's behavior, they must interpret it differently from how they have in the past. In this respect, trust can act as a "filter" through which new events and experiences are interpreted.

The beliefs of high-trust people are anchored both by positive conclusions about their partner's motives drawn from past evidence and by faith in what the future holds. They expect their partner to act in ways that are motivated by a desire to improve the relationship. Even when faced with events that could potentially challenge their convictions, such as a conflict or disagreement, people in high-trust relationships are unlikely to call their partner's motives into question. Rather, as much as possible, negative events are seen as less significant when compared against the large accumulation of positive experiences. Negative incidents are likely to be explained in less harmful ways, treated as isolated events, or understood to reflect an unfortunate, but less significant component of the relationship. This is not to say that trusting people are unaware of or naïvely ignore the negative events that occur in their relationship. However, unless an incident truly merits suspicion, they tend to place some limits on the negative implications the event could have for their relationship. Thus, a high-trust relationship is one in which partners share openly with each other and give each other the benefit of the doubt.

For many couples, a trusting relationship remains an elusive goal. For some, past experiences with parents or former partners have left them unable to completely set their doubts aside and confidently relinquish control to an intimate partner. Others, who started out with high levels of trust, may have run out of convincing charitable explanations for their partner's negative behaviors. Worn down from the accumulated weight of evidence, they increasingly entertain doubts and concerns about their partner's caring motives.

Whatever the cause, people in medium-trust relationships are uncertain about their partner's intentions and they are alert for signs that indicate further risk. They still have hope for their relationship and they may long to achieve the elusive sense of security. Yet, ironically, despite a desire for positive convictions, people in medium-trust relationships appear to place greater emphasis on negative events in their relationship. Recent studies have shown that medium-trust couples are more likely than high- or low-trust couples to use manipulative and coercive power tactics during a conflict interaction (Rempel, Hiller, and Cocivera 2000). Thus, it seems that medium-trust individuals are hesitant to dismiss warning signs that signal the potential for disappointment. In order to avoid making unwarranted positive attributions for their partner's behavior, and running the greater risk of having their hopes undermined, these individuals protect themselves with a risk-avoidant strategy that leads them to adopt more stringent criteria before inferring positive motives for their partner's positive behaviors (Holmes and Rempel 1989). Thus, medium-trust couples may, paradoxically, overemphasize the diagnostic importance of negative events and underestimate the importance of events that could advance their hopes.

As feelings of confidence continue to diminish, people arrive at the point where they no longer expect the events in their relationship to reflect motives of concern and caring. Instead, they are more likely to expect indifference, or even hostility. Low-trust people cannot, with any confidence, embrace residual hopes that their partner is concerned about them or the relationship. Thus, they are likely to confront positive incidents with skepticism, discounting the encouraging implications such events might have for the future of their relationship. Negative events, on the other hand, serve to confirm the belief that confidence in the partner is not warranted—they represent one more piece of data in support of the conclusion that the partner no longer cares.

The sad irony is that, once trust has been betrayed, it may be doubly difficult to restore. Lurking close to the surface of most low-trust relationships is a history of broken promises, unmet expectations, and emotional disappointments.

Even if the offending partner "turns over a new leaf" and begins to work at the relationship, it is all too easy for these positive events to be explained away. The reluctance of low-trust individuals to accept their partner's positive behaviors is understandable—they have taken risks and lost. To protect themselves from the danger of drawing unwarranted positive conclusions and to minimize the pain of involvement with an unconcerned partner, low-trust people may attempt to reduce emotional investment in their relationship. Indeed, recent studies indicate that low-trust couples act in ways that minimize the potential for conflict (Rempel, Hiller, and Cocivera 2000). Thus, at least when the issues do not demand a confrontation, the interactions of low-trust couples appear to be characterized by indifference and emotional distance. In such a climate, the potential for rebuilding a trusting relationship represents a daunting prospect.

The scenario is not hopeless, of course, but no one should underestimate the difficulty of rebuilding trust once it has been betrayed. For trust to grow after it has been violated people must resist the natural tendency to jump to harsh conclusions about their partner's motives and character in new situations. Furthermore, people must allow their partner the leeway for occasional unintended missteps. The offending partner, in turn, must make a profound effort to live up to his or her promises of change in ways that clearly signal to the offended partner that these risks are worth taking. To be able to trust, people must take the risk of trusting. By giving their partner a second chance to renew trust in the relationship people risk being wrong, but if they do not try they can never be right.

Conclusion

Trust is a central feature of all human relationships. It begins with our earliest social interactions and has powerful implications for our most intimate relationships throughout our lives. There is still much to learn about the origins of trust, the ways in which trust develops in a specific relationship, the consequences for a relationship when trust breaks down, and the ways in which trust can be rebuilt. However, the study of this important topic has already produced valuable insights. As we continue gain knowledge about trust, the things we learn hold great promise for enriching the quality of our most valued intimate relationships.

See also: ATTACHMENT: COUPLE RELATIONSHIPS; ATTACHMENT: PARENT-CHILD RELATIONSHIPS; COMMUTER MARRIAGES; FAMILY STRENGTHS; FRIENDSHIP; INFIDELITY; INTIMACY; LOVE; RELATIONSHIP INITIATION; RELATIONSHIP MAINTENANCE; SOCIAL EXCHANGE THEORY

Bibliography

Amagai, Y. (1999). "Main Experiential Factors Affecting Trust in Regular High School Students and Delinquents." *Japanese Journal of Educational Psychology* 47:229–238.

Baxter, L. A., and Wilmot, W. W. (1984). "'Secret Tests': Social Strategies for Acquiring Information about the State of the Relationship." *Human Communication Research* 11:17–201.

Boon, S. D. (1994). "Dispelling Doubt and Uncertainty: Trust in Romantic Relationships." In *Dynamics of Relationships,* Vol. 4: *Understanding Relationship Processes,* ed. S. Duck. Thousand Oaks, CA: Sage Publications.

Couch, L. L., and Jones, W. H. (1997). "Measuring Levels of Trust." *Journal of Research in Personality* 31:319–336.

Holmes, J. G. (1991). "Trust and the Appraisal Process in Close Relationships." In *Advances in Personal Relationships*, Vol. 2, ed. W. H. Jones and D. Perlman. London: Jessica Kingsley.

Holmes, J. G., and Rempel, J. K. (1989). "Trust in Close Relationships." In *Review of Personality and Social Psychology*, Vol. 10, ed. C. Hendrick. Beverly Hills, CA: Sage Publications.

Johnson-George, C., and Swap, W. (1982). "Measurement of Specific Interpersonal Trust: Construction and Validation of a Scale to Assess Trust in a Specific Order." *Journal of Personality and Social Psychology* 43:1306–1317.

Larzelere, R. E., and Huston, T. L. (1980)."The Dyadic Trust Scale: Toward Understanding Interpersonal Trust in Close Relationships." *Journal of Marriage and the Family* 42:595–604.

Mikulincer, M. (1998). "Attachment Working Models and the Sense of Trust: An Exploration of Interaction Goals and Affect Regulation." *Journal of Personality and Social Psychology* 74:1209–1224.

Miller, P. J., and Rempel, J. K. (2000). "The Development and Decline of Trust in Close Relationships." Manuscript submitted for publication.

Moeller, K., and Stattin, H. (2001). "Are Close Relationships in Adolescence Linked with Partner Relationships in Midlife? A Longitudinal, Prospective Study." *International Journal of Behavioral Development* 25:69–77.

Regan, P. C.; Kocan, E. R.; and Whitlock, T. (1998). "Ain't Love Grand! A Prototype Analysis of the Concept of Romantic Love." *Journal of Social and Personal Relationships* 15:411–420.

Rempel, J. K.; Hiller, C.; and Cocivera, T. (2000). "Power and Trust in Close Relationships." Manuscript submitted for publication.

Rempel, J. K.; Holmes, J. G.; and Zanna, M. P. (1985). "Trust in Close Relationships." *Journal of Personality and Social Psychology* 49:95–112.

Roizblatt, A.; Kaslow, F.; Rivera, S.; Fuchs, T.; Conejero, C.; and Zacharias, A. (1999). "Long Lasting Marriages in Chile." *Contemporary Family Therapy: An International Journal* 21:113–129.

Rotenburg, K. J. (1995). "The Socialization of Trust: Parents' and Children's Interpersonal Trust." *International Journal of Behavioral Development* 18:713–726.

Rotter, J. B. (1967). "A New Scale for the Measurement of Interpersonal Trust." *Journal of Personality* 35:651–665.

Sharlin, S. A. (1996). "Long-Term Successful Marriages in Israel." *Contemporary Family Therapy: An International Journal* 18:225–242.

Wieselquist, J.; Rusbult, C. E.; Foster, C. A.; and Agnew, C. R. (1999). "Commitment, Pro-Relationship Behavior, and Trust in Close Relationships." *Journal of Personality and Social Psychology* 77:942–966.

Zak, A.; Brewer, E.; Clark, K.; DeAngelis, R.; Nielsen, M.; and Turek, C. (2000). "Once Bitten, Twice Shy: The Effects of Past Partner Experiences on Current Love and Trust." *North American Journal of Psychology* 2:71–74.

JOHN K. REMPEL

TURKEY

The family is both the strongest social institution in Turkey and the foundation that supports the twin pillars of tradition and adaptation. The durability of marital unions, coupled with pressures for mutual commitment and obligation, contribute to this family stability. In 2001, for example, Turkey experienced a serious economic crisis, but despite severe levels of unemployment, rampant inflation, and frequent devaluations of the Turkish lira, there were few public protests towards the policies of the government or the World Bank. Many experts have attributed this to the strength of the traditional Turkish family, where members continue to support each other in times of need and crisis, offsetting the negative effects of such economic problems as unemployment. The family thus provides not only a supportive network for individuals, but forms a framework to enforce social controls and acceptable patterns of public behavior.

Situated in Eastern Europe, Turkey has a population of about 68 million (SIS December 2001). Founded in 1924 as a secular republic, Turkey was the last nation-state to be formed out of the geographic entity that once was the Ottoman Empire, which contained many of the modern states of the Middle East, North Africa, the Balkans, and southeastern Europe.

The majority of the population is Muslim (about 99%), most being Sunnis. Shiite Muslims represent about 15 percent of the population, and there are smaller groups of Christians and Jews. Turkey has inherited a complex historical and cultural legacy. Ethnically, the predominant majority are Turks, and there are also groupings of Kurds, Greeks, Armenians, Caucasians, Arabs, and others. The official language of the country is Turkish, a Ural-Altaic language spoken by most citizens.

Family law in Ottoman society was mainly defined by Islamic sharia law. The laws allowed polygamy, with men legally entitled to four wives as long as they could support them all and treat them fairly. Men also had the exclusive right to dissolve their marriages. These laws began to change only in the twentieth century, with, for example, a rule that made it obligatory for a man who wanted to marry a second wife to gain the permission of the first.

After the caliphate was abolished (in 1923), and with the establishment of the Republic of Turkey (in 1924), secular law replaced the sharia. The 1926 Civil Code, modeled on the Swiss Civil Code, abolished polygamy and endorsed compulsory civil marriage for all citizens, regardless of their religious affiliations. The new laws recognized the right of divorce for both partners and accepted egalitarian inheritance laws and the separation of property in marriage. Since then, when the law set itself the task of improving the status of women and making a break with the past, it has

An Ankara family living in the Old Citadel Quarter of Turkey's capital. RICHARD T. NOWITZ/CORBIS

become extremely difficult for a man to obtain a divorce without the consent of the wife.

Geography and Demographics

Turkey occupies about 780 square kilometers. Approximately 97 percent of its land area lies in Asia, on an extended peninsula called Anatolia. The country has seas on three sides: The Black Sea on the north, the Aegean on the west, and the Mediterranean to the south. The straits of the Bosphorous and the Dardanelles, which along with the Sea of Marmara link the Black Sea to the Aegean and Mediterranean Seas, is an important international waterway and is completely under Turkey's control. Turkey borders on Greece and Bulgaria in the west, on the republics of Georgia, Azerbaijan, and Armenia to the north, and Syria, Iran, and Iraq to the east. This significant geographical location places Turkey amid the Balkans, the states of the former Soviet Union, Central Asia, and the Middle East, and has forced Turkey to be an active player in geopolitics.

Over the past fifty years, Turkey has also absorbed waves of immigrants and refugees in large numbers. In this context, recent immigrants have come from the Balkans, as well as those who fled the political turmoil in Iran in the 1980s, the dissolution of the Soviet Union, and Iraq after the Gulf War in 1990. Turkey is the centerpiece of a very unstable region, both geographically and politically, and its institutions have shown remarkable resilience in dealing with an unending series of crises.

Turkey's gross national product (GNP) per capita is estimated to be about $2,986 U.S. (SIS 2000). The economy is based mostly on agriculture, along with the construction industry, mining, textiles, and tourism. Turkey's chief exports include cement, citrus fruits, cotton, figs, hazelnuts, hides and leather goods, minerals, sultana raisins, textiles, and tobacco. Its chief imports are chemicals and related products, natural gas and crude oil, electrical and transportation equipment, rubber, and plastics. The percentage of households below poverty line is estimated to be 14.2 percent (SPO 1997).

About 35 percent of the population lives in rural areas, and 65 percent in urban areas. However, the rate of urbanization has been so rapid that sociologists have defined this process as "the ruralization of towns and cities." The three most populous cities of Turkey are Istanbul, Ankara (the capital), and Izmir. The population of Istanbul rose from about five million in 1965 to over ten million in 2000. There is also a small population of nomadic pastoralists, but their numbers, never high, are decreasing rapidly as animal husbandry loses its economic significance, and urban areas steadily expand. The country has eighty-one provinces and is divided into seven regions that feature significantly different climatic, economic, and social conditions. These are the Marmara, the Aegean, the Mediterranean, Central Anatolia, the Black Sea, Eastern Anatolia, and Southeastern Anatolia. This diversity is also reflected in the dynamics of regional family structures, which adds to the complexities in the rapidly expanding urban configurations.

Family Life and Structure

Turkey has a young age structure: 10 percent of the population is under five years of age and 32 percent below the age of fifteen. The percentage of the population sixty-five and over, however, constitutes only 6 percent of the total. Life expectancy is sixty-six years for men and seventy-one years for women. (TDHS 1998, p. 4). The literacy rate in 1998 was 94 percent for men, and 74 percent for women (UNICEF 2001), but few adults have progressed beyond primary school.

Households. Households in Turkey hold an average of 4.3 persons. In urban areas, this figure drops to an average of four persons; in rural areas, it rises to 4.9. Only 5 percent of Turkish households are single-person households, while two in every five households have five or more members (TDHS 1998:4).

Today, about 70 percent of Turkish households are *nuclear,* with at least one child and both parents, and 20 percent of households are *extended* families, married couple living with other kin, mostly the parent(s) or other relatives of the husband. Even when a household is classified as nuclear, most often close extended family members will be living in very nearby. About 5 percent of households can be defined as *dispersed* families, in which single parents or some kinfolk living together. Polygamous households are statistically negligible, but remain despite their illegality.

Marriage. Since the enactment of the republic's 1926 Civil Code, municipal authorities perform marriages in a secular ceremony. Marriages carried out only by religious authorities are considered legally invalid, so people who want to be united in a religious marriage must do so after their official service. Nevertheless, despite this clear requirement, it is estimated that religious marriages (those not accompanied by civil ceremonies) often take place, especially in the eastern and southeastern parts of Anatolia. Therefore, the number of marriages appears lower than it actually is because religious marriages are not included in official statistics (SIS Marriage Statistics 1997).

Even taking only the official statistics into account, however, marriage is almost universal in Turkey. By the time women have reached their early thirties, 93 percent are or have been married, and by the end of their reproductive years, only 2 percent of women have never married. The 1998 Turkish Demographic and Health Survey found 15 percent of women aged fifteen to nineteen to be married (THDS 1998). Divorce rates are very low. The crude divorce rate of Turkey is less than one per thousand per year, quite low when compared to international divorce rates, and much lower than those of Europe. In 1999, the crude divorce rate was 0.49 per thousand.

The diversity of marriage ceremonies and customs reflect the regional, urban, rural, ethnic, and socioeconomic differences within the country. In rural areas (35%) and small towns (30%), the girl's family receives a dowry from the groom's family. Newcomers to metropolitan areas (25%) are not always able to give a dowry to the bride's family. Among the established population in metropolitan areas (10%), many couples marry later, after they complete their education. Parents give their children substantial presents and may assist them financially, at least in early married life. There are many colorful varieties of weddings, but most couples marry with the bride wearing a white wedding dress, and the groom a dark suit.

Fertility. Turkish families greatly value children, and the desire to have children is universal. Traditionally, families prefer boys over girls. Women at the start of the twenty-first century gave birth to an average of 2.6 children. Childbearing occurs often between the ages of fifteen and nineteen, with the highest fertility rate among women between twenty and twenty-four. There are, however, wide variations in fertility levels among regions, with the highest rate in the east (4.2 children per woman) and lowest in the west (2.0 children). Women living in the east marry nearly two years earlier than those living in the west. Fertility also varies widely with urban and rural residence, with women living in rural areas having an average of almost one child more than those living in urban areas. Education levels affect fertility levels, with those lacking a primary education having an average of almost one child more than women who have primary education, and 2.2 children more than those with at least a secondary-level education (TDHS 1998). Overall, when asked how many children they would choose to have if they could live their lives over, women gave an average ideal family size of 2.5 children, which is very close to actual fertility rates.

Maternal and child health. For many years Turkey has been troubled by infant and child mortality rates that are higher than might be expected, given the economic and demographic figures of the country and other development criteria. The infant mortality rate (a reflection of overall child health in a society) is about forty per thousand, and among children under five, the mortality rate was about forth-eight per thousand in the late 1990s. Infant and child mortality rates declined in the past decade. However, the infant mortality rate in the rural areas is about 1.6 times higher than in urban areas. Infant mortality rates are lower than the national average in the western and southern regions, close to the national average in the central and northern regions, and nearly 1.5 times higher than the national average in the eastern region (TDHS 1998). Among other factors, children's chances of survival are closely related to the parent's levels of education (Gürsoy 1992).

Medical care is another important factor in the reduction of mortality rates, which drop significantly if the mother has received both antenatal and delivery care from health professionals. If she has received neither, under-five mortality can be as high as 116 per thousand and infant mortality as high as 95 per thousand. About three-fourths of births now occur in health facilities, although this figure varies from around 44 percent in the east to 87 percent in the west. About 80 percent of all births are assisted by either a doctor or a qualified midwife-nurse. Infants born less than two years after a sibling have a considerably higher chance of dying. For these children, mortality risks are 2.8 times higher than for children born after an interval of four years or more (TDHS 1998).

Almost all babies are breastfed. The median duration of breastfeeding is twelve months. Most children are also given supplementary foods and liquids at an early age, which medical authorities consider not only unnecessary, but a potential source of infection. Twenty percent of children under age five are short for their age; this is more prevalent in rural areas, in the east, and among children of uneducated mothers (TDHS 1998).

Issues Related To Family Life

Because almost the entire adult population is married, the meaning and quality of marital and family life are extremely important and dominate the social, sexual, economic, and cultural aspects of adult life. No public or private initiative, for example, may be considered without reference to its possible impact on the somewhat idealized environment of the "average" Turkish family. Much of the urban informal economy, for example, relies on home-based work, engages the labor of women, but is conceived in family and kin-terms (White 1994, 2000).

With the lives of most adult Turks defined by their roles and positions in these family systems, their status and worth as individuals are closely linked to the public perception of the family's strengths and extended relationships. This is positive in some ways, in that every person has a place in the family; that the weak, the aged, and the handicapped are seen primarily as family responsibilities and not the sole concern of the state; and that the extended family functions as a single unit in times of stress, whether due to natural disasters (Turkey is located in a highly active earthquake zone), economic instability, medical emergencies, or threats in general from the outside world.

Just as the family protects its individual members, however, so must they unite to protect the family and its honor in terms of both public behavior and popular perception. This duty is an important mark of individual worth. One does not do things that will embarrass the family or tarnish its public image, and this rule is rigidly enforced. For example, female sexual purity, or honor before marriage must be preserved at all costs. In certain regions, honor is preserved in an extreme form of *honor killings,* whereby male kinsmen may kill their errant daughters or sisters. In similar fashion, feuds between families may force individual male family members to take revenge for killings of their own kinfolk or become targets themselves. Both honor killings and feuds are against the law, but given the strength of customs in certain regions, they prevail.

The patriarchal structure of society means girls are subject to a much stricter code of sexual purity, and that in general, they are rarely given the opportunities available to boys. In rural areas, every member of the family works, but girls look after siblings and carry goods to the field, while boys tend animals. In towns, girls help mothers while boys follow fathers to work and coffeehouses. The heads of families arrange most marriages, and girls are trained to be subservient to males in most situations. This pattern was changing, but remained the dominant feature of married life at the start of the twenty-first century.

The children of working families are also viewed as economic contributors from an early age, with schooling a secondary consideration. As the family ascends the ladder of economic well-being, however, this picture changes dramatically, and education becomes much more important. A larger middle class is developing, slowly, and this shift has profound implications for the family structure.

Within a male-dominated society, and one that prizes masculine codes of behavior, the discipline within a family is frequently harsh and may be based on physical punishment. This does not rule out affection, togetherness, or mutual love, but a stern system of respect has a strict code of discipline at its core.

Changes in Family Life

Only a generation ago, the majority of Turkish families lived in rural areas, and every member of the family had a place, a position, and a function. Young children and the elderly were cared for, everyone else contributed what he or she could. With the onset of industrialization and urbanization, however, the extended family network came under great strain. Fewer of the elderly, for example, can now live with their sons or daughters in small urban apartments, and so they must make other arrangements. The urge to acquire more material goods (televisions, automobiles, mobile telephones, etc.) has become more important, and the family may enjoy the benefits of a consumer society only by reducing its contributions to the extended family.

Faced with perceived threats towards the traditional Turkish family in 1990, the Prime Ministry Division for Family Research convened the First National Assembly on the Family (*Aile Surasi*). Attended by selected scholars, social service professionals, civil representatives, politicians, bureaucrats, and the media, the assembly developed multiple policy recommendations in family-related areas of economic life, health and nutrition, and other areas, with resolutions calling for increased child-care services and more public attention to the care of the elderly.

Constant change is a permanent aspect in most Turkish families. Some of this change is reflected in national statistics, but some is not. Change has also rearranged family values and priorities, to the extent that suicides, for example, rose because more people simply could not cope with modern life. Suicides have been uncommon in Turkey, but analysis suggests that the most prevalent reasons in 1998 were related to family and marital life, with 26 percent of suicides attributed to incompatibilities and conflicts within the family. Additionally, 13 percent of suicides were due to emotional relationships or the inability to marry the person of one's choice. These two categories together account for the majority of suicides. Most suicides occur in relatively young age groups (15–34), with women being more prone to suicide (SIS 1998).

As Turkey strives to become a successful member of the European Community, it is also changing its Civil Codes (2002), with profound implications for the rights of the individual, the legal status of women, children's rights, democratic practices, and social services.

Increasingly, the European and American models, through mass media, films, international agreements, more foreign tourists (more than 9 million in 2001), along with the explosive development of the Internet, are influencing the younger generation and providing alternatives to the traditional family structure. Literally, and often painfully, Turkey has, in the words of a former politician "leapt an era" and moved in a lifetime from being an insular, predominantly rural, and conservative society to a prominent player in the larger world, in almost every category of modern development. This change is continuing, with constant reliance on and modifications of traditional family structures throughout Turkey.

See also: ISLAM; KURDISH FAMILIES

Bibliography

Anadan-Unat, N. (1981). *Women in Turkish Society.* Leiden, the Netherlands: E. J. Brill.

Arat, Y. (1989). *The Patriarchal Paradox: Women Politicians in Turkey.* Rutherford, NH: Furleigh Dickinson University Press.

Bultay, T., ed. (2000). *Employment and Training Project Labour Market Information (TOR 6) Informal Sector.* Ankara: State Institute of Statistics Prime Ministry Republic of Turkey.

Delaney, C. (1991). *The Seed and the Soil: Gender and Cosmology in Turkish Village Society.* Berkeley: University of California Press.

Duben, A., ed. (1986). *Family in Turkish Society, Sociological and Legal Studies.* Ankara: Turkish Social Science Association.

Duben, A., and Behar, C. (1991). *Istanbul Households: Marriage, Family and Fertility 1880-1940.* Cambridge, UK: Cambridge University Press.

Gürsoy, A. (1992). "Infant Mortality: A Turkish Puzzle?" *Health Transition Review* 2(2)131–149.

Gürsoy, A. (1994). "Traditional Practices Affecting the Health of Women and Children." In *The Basics of Maternal and Child Health,* ed. O. Neyzi. Istanbul: Institute of Child Health, Istanbul University/UNICEF.

Gürsoy, A. (1995). "Child Mortality and the Changing Discourse on Childhood in Turkey." In *Children in the Muslim Middle East,* ed. E. W. Fernea. Austin: University of Texas Press.

Gürsoy, A. (1996). "Abortion in Turkey: A Matter of State, Family, or Individual Decision." *Social Science & Medicine* 24(4):531–542.

Kagitçibasi, Ç., ed. (1982). *Sex Roles, Family and Community in Turkey.* Bloomington, IN: Indiana University Press.

Kagitçibasi, Ç. (1996). *Family and Human Development Across Cultures—A View from the Other Side.* Mahwah, NJ: Lawrence Erlbaum Associates.

Measure DHS+ Macro International Inc. (1999). *Turkey Demographic and Health Survey 1998 Summary Report.* Ankara: Hacettepe Institute of Population Studies.

Ministry of Health General Directorate of Mother and Child Health and Family Planning, Hacettepe University Institute of Population Studies, Demographic and Health Surveys Macro International Inc., (1995). *Trends in Fertility, Family Planning, and Childhood Mortality in Turkey, Findings from National Demographic Surveys and Population Censuses.* Ankara: Author.

State Institute of Statistics, Prime Ministry, Republic of Turkey. (2001). *Statistical Indicators 1923—1998. Ankara. Census of Population Provisional Results.* Ankara: Author.

State Institute of Statistics, Prime Ministry, Republic of Turkey. (2001). *Suicide Statistics 1998.* Ankara: Author.

State Institute of Statistics, Prime Ministry, Republic of Turkey. (2001). *Divorce Statistics 1999.* Ankara: Author.

State Institute of Statistics, Prime Ministry, Republic of Turkey. (2000). *Household Labour Force Survey Results.* Ankara: Author.

State Institute of Statistics, Prime Ministry, Republic of Turkey. (1999). *Marriage Statistics 1997.* Ankara: Author.

State Institute of Statistics, Prime Ministry, Republic of Turkey. (1995). Women in Statistics 1927–1992. Ankara: Author.

State Institute of Statistics, Prime Ministry, Republic of Turkey, and International Labor Organization. (1997). *Child Labor in Turkey 1999—Türkiye'de Çalişan Çocuklar 1999* (In Turkish).

United Nations Development Programme. (1999). *Human Development Report, Turkey 1999.* Ankara: Author.

UNICEF. (2001). *The State of the World's Children 2001.* New York: Author.

White, J. (1994). *Money Makes Us Relatives, Women's Labor in Urban Turkey.* Austin: University of Texas Press.

White, J. (2000). "Kinship, Reciprocity, and the World Market." In *Dividends of Kinship, Meanings and Uses of Social Relatedness,* ed. P. P. Schweitzer. New York: Routledge.

AKILE GURSOY

TYPOLOGIES

See ARRANGED MARRIAGES; INTERFAITH MARRIAGE; INTERRACIAL MARRIAGE; MARITAL TYPOLOGIES

UNCLE

Like *aunt, uncle* is not a universal kinship term. In Hawaii, for example, there is no uncle term because mothers' and fathers' brothers are included in the same category as father (Keesing 1975). Generally, however, uncle refers to a mother's brother, a father's brother, or the husband of one's aunt. In English-speaking countries, all of these relatives are lumped together under one term, uncle. Neither English nor French distinguishes between the father's sister's husband (a relative by marriage) and the father's brother (a blood relative). Both are uncles (Segalen 1986).

In contrast, the kinship terminology in many non-English-speaking Western societies distinguishes between *consanguineal* (biological) and *affinal* (marital) uncles. In Denmark and Norway, for example, *morbror* refers to a mother's brother (and usually also to the husband of the mother's sister) while *farbror* refers to the father's brother (as well as the husband of the father's sister). Although affinal ties can be broken (as through divorce), consanguineal ties are rarely severed.

In many nonindustrial societies, maternal and paternal uncles typically play a critical kinship role. In patrilineal kinship systems—like China and Korea—where descent and inheritance are vested in males, the father's oldest brother has the authority and responsibility to make decisions affecting the household during the father's absence or after his death (Choi 2000; Lee 1997). In other patrilineal societies, such as the Tswana in Africa, a mother's brother must be consulted in all matters affecting his sister's children. He helps with food, clothes, and other gifts at all their rites of passage; acts as mediator when disputes arise between father and son; and has veto power when the children's marriages are arranged (Schapera 1950).

In matrilineal systems, the men belong to their mother's social group. Although the father begets children, the mother's brother plays an important role in everyday activities. Among some North American Indian tribes (such as the Hopi, Shoshone, and Iroquois) and the Trobriand Islanders of Melanesia, there is a strong bond between brothers and sisters because the children of the sisters are the men's heirs and successors. If, especially, there is a good deal of personal wealth, the mother's brother's power over his maternal nephews is likely to be quite strong (Fox 1967; Weiner 1988). In other matrilineal systems, such as the Ashanti and Bantu in central Africa, the mother's brother has a variety of rights and responsibilities: correcting and otherwise disciplining his sisters' children; helping his maternal nephews by paying for their schooling, setting them up in business, or giving them headships; intervening in the selection of a marital partner; and demanding financial assistance, when necessary (Fortes 1950; Richards 1950).

See also: AUNT; COUSINS; KINSHIP; SIBLING RELATIONSHIPS

Bibliography

Choi, S. H. (2000). "Land is Thicker than Blood: Revisiting 'Kinship Paternalism' in a Peasant Village in South

Korea." *Journal of Anthropological Research* 56:349–363.

Fortes, M. (1950). "Kinship and Marriage among the Ashanti." In *African Systems of Kinship and Marriage,* ed. A. R. Radcliffe-Brown and D. Forde. New York: Oxford University Press.

Fox, R. (1967). *Kinship and Marriage: An Anthropological Perspective.* Harmondsworth, UK: Penguin Books.

Keesing, R. (1975). *Kin Groups and Social Structure.* New York: Holt, Rinehart, and Winston.

Richards, A. I. (1950). "Some Types of Family Structure amongst the Central Bantu." In *African Systems of Kinship and Marriage,* ed. A. R. Radcliffe-Brown and D. Forde. New York: Oxford University Press.

Schapera, I. (1950). "Kinship and Marriage among the Tswana." In *African Systems of Kinship and Marriage,* ed. A. R. Radcliffe-Brown and D. Forde. New York: Oxford University Press.

Segalen, M. (1986). *Historical Anthropology of the Family.* New York: Cambridge University Press.

Weiner, A. B. (1988). *The Trobrianders of Papua New Guinea.* New York: Holt, Rinehart, and Winston.

Other Resources

Lee, G. Y. (1997). "Hmong World View and Social Structure." In *Lao Study Review.* Available at http://www.global.lao.net.

NIJOLE V. BENOKRAITIS

UNEMPLOYMENT

Unemployment is widely regarded as a major social and economic global problem. When referring to someone as unemployed, most people have in mind a state consistent with the International Labour Office's (ILO) definition, namely a person who does not have a job, is available for work, and is actively looking for work (ILO 1998). This is certainly the case for government agencies, like the Bureau of Labor Statistics in the United States, that publish unemployment statistics. These statistics are used in a variety of situations, but mostly as an indication of the underuse of a nation's resources, and to inform on the economic and social hardship associated with the absence of employment. The data listed in Table 1 show that unemployment rates are high for most countries. These high unemployment rates have been extensively studied. See, for example, Richard Jackman (1997a) for OECD countries, Richard Jackman (1997b) for Central and Eastern Europe, Albert Berry, Maria Mendex, and Jaime Tenjo (1997) for Latin America, and Anh Le and Paul Miller (2000) for Australia. The findings from this research indicate that the unemployment experience is now very well documented.

Most of the people who become unemployed remain without work for very short periods. However, there is also a hard core of unemployed who remain without work for long periods of time. The adverse consequences of unemployment are much more acute for this group.

Consequences of Unemployment

Unemployment has obvious and well-documented links to economic disadvantage and has also been connected in some discussion to higher crime rates (Cantor and Land 1985; Ottosen and Thompson 1996), especially among the young (Britt 1994), suicide, and homicide (Yang and Lester 1994; Ottosen and Thompson 1996). Garry Ottosen and Douglas Thompson (1996) broaden the consequences of unemployment, relating it to increases in the incidences of alcoholism, child abuse, family breakdown, psychiatric hospitalization, and a variety of physical complaints and illnesses. Some researchers have emphasized the importance of preventing youth from falling into unemployment traps. Robert Gitter and Markus Scheuer (1997) suggest that unemployment among youth not only causes current hardship, but may also hinder future economic success. This is because unemployed youths are not able to gain experience and on-the-job training and because a history of joblessness signals that the individual may not have the qualities that are valued in the labor market.

Unemployment may impair the functioning of families (see, for example, Liker and Elder 1983; Barling 1990) by affecting the parents' interactions with their children and the interactions between partners. Although it has been shown that unemployed parents spend more time with their children, the quality of these interactions suffers in comparison with those of employed parents. Unemployment, particularly among male partners, is also likely to lead to major role changes in the home. For example, whether it is because they

TABLE 1

Unemployment rates by region, 2000

Region	Unemployment rate	Region	Unemployment rate
North America		**Middle East**	
Canada	6.8	Israel	8.8
United Sates	4.0	Turkey	7.3
South/Central America		United Arab Emirates	2.3
Argentina	15.0	**Africa**	
Chile	8.3	Egypt	8.1
Colombia	20.5	Suriname	14.0
Costa Rica	5.2	Algeria	29.8
Peru	7.4	Tunisia	15.6
Europe		**Asia**	
France	9.6	Korea, Republic of	4.1
Germany	7.9	Japan	4.7
Italy	10.5	Philippines	10.1
Netherlands	3.3	Singapore	4.4
Sweden	4.7	Sri Lanka	8.0
United Kingdom	5.5	Thailand	2.4
Eastern Europe		**Oceania**	
Bulgaria	16.4	Australia	6.6
Czech Republic	8.3	New Zealand	6.0
Hungary	6.4		
Poland	16.1		
Romania	7.1		
Slovakia	18.6		

Note: The unemployment data for South/Central America include those who are aged 10 years and over. The unemployment rates for Egypt, Suriname, and Turkey are for the year 1999.

SOURCE: International Labour Office, http://laborsta.ilo.org/

have more time or they feel that they have to undertake additional household duties when they are no longer the financial provider for the family, unemployed husbands are more likely to increase their participation in domestic activities (e.g., household tasks, shopping, meal preparation). In some circumstances, the loss of financial responsibility among husbands may lead to discontent within the marriage: unemployed husbands are more likely to have disagreements and arguments with their spouses than are employed husbands, and this has the potential to lead to spouse abuse and marriage dissolution.

It is very difficult to place a dollar figure on many of the social costs that unemployment imposes on the individual, his or her family, and society. Given the gravity of the problems created, the cost would seem to be enormous. Attempts have, however, been made to estimate the economic cost associated with unemployment. Ottosen and Thompson (1996, p.5) noted that "the United States loses a little less than one percentage point of potential gross domestic product (GDP) or output for each one percentage point of unemployment. This implies that an unemployment rate of 7 percent costs the United States at least $400 billion annually in foregone output. This is more than $2,000 for every man, woman, and child over 16 years of age." Similarly, in Australia, Peter Kenyon (1998) calculated that the loss of GDP associated with an unemployment rate above the full-employment rate is the equivalent of one year's worth of GDP over the past two decades.

In addition to the loss of GDP, high unemployment increases the burden on social welfare programs. These include unemployment insurance programs and other types of welfare, such as food stamps, Medicaid, Medicare, and Supplemental Security Income (Ottosen and Thompson 1996). There are also intergenerational effects, as unemployment of parents will limit their capacity to finance the schooling of their children. As education is the primary means of social mobility, this intergenerational effect will give rise to an inheritance of inequality.

Problems with the Statistics

Unemployment statistics are used in a variety of situations. Users of these statistics are usually well acquainted with at least some of their deficiencies. The main issue is that the conventional definition of unemployment does not capture some major categories of the underuse of labor. These include visible underemployment (i.e., an employed person who works fewer hours than desired), invisible underemployment (i.e., an employed person whose actual working time is not used to potential), and discouraged workers (i.e., those who no longer seek work due to their perception that suitable jobs are not available). Underemployment is typically a more important issue for developing countries than it is for industrialized countries. Unemployment statistics for developing countries are also difficult to interpret because of varying definitions (see also Berry et al. 1997).

Researchers in several countries have examined some alternative definitions of unemployment that might address these shortcomings of official unemployment statistics. John Bregger and Steven Haugen (1995) discussed alternative unemployment indicators that would allow certain groups to be added to the unemployment statistics, such as involuntary and voluntary part-time workers. Aldrich Finegan (1978) examined the importance of discouraged workers and argued that they represent losses for society and for themselves that are no different from the output foregone and income lost because of unemployment. Adjusting the unemployment statistics for these deficiencies makes a substantial difference. Mark Wooden (1996) quantifies these categories for the Australian labor market, with his estimates for September 1995 revealing that only 48 percent of the underused labor hours were in the "unemployment" category, 17 percent were in the "visible underemployment" category, 28 percent in the "invisible underemployment" category, and 10 percent were in "hidden unemployment." Haugen and William Parks (1990) calculated that if all individuals "who wanted a job" had been included in the definition of unemployment, this would have increased the unemployment rate in the U.S. labor market for the fourth quarter of 1989 from 5.3 percent to 9.1 percent.

Situations where the official unemployment category counts for only around one-half of the total underuse of labor suggest that the official unemployment rate does not reflect the true state of the labor market. It also means that forecasting change in the official unemployment count will be quite difficult. In many periods, the employment effects of increases in economic activity can be absorbed by higher rates of use of the employed, or by flows into the labor market of discouraged job seekers, rather than by reductions in the official unemployment category.

Who Becomes Unemployed?

The statistics show that the burden of unemployment is distributed unevenly across sections of society. To illustrate this point, Table 2 outlines the unemployment rate for various age groups, education levels, ethnic groups, and family status for the U.S. labor market in June 2001.

Age. The Table 2 data indicate that the unemployment rate varies considerably across age groups. The individual's age is generally used as a measure of the accumulation of knowledge of the labor market (best practice with respect to job search processes, information networks) that occurs through labor market activity. Individuals between the ages of sixteen and nineteen have the highest unemployment rate (15.9 percent for males and 12.7 percent for females). In comparison, individuals who are fifty-five years or over have the lowest unemployment rate, around 3 percent. The relatively high unemployment rate experienced by youth is the basis for arguments that they should be given priority in unemployment reduction policies. To the extent that unemployment today diminishes an individual's future job prospects (Le and Miller 2000), there is an additional reason to be concerned over the labor market difficulties encountered by many youth. In such a situation, failure to address the current unemployment problem may leave a large number of youth exposed to a process of cumulative disadvantage in the labor market over much of their working lives.

Education. The formal skills that may affect unemployment outcomes include schooling, qualifications, and language proficiency. Educational attainment is arguably the most important of these. The data in Table 2 indicate a pronounced, inverse association between unemployment and educational attainment. For example, the unemployment

TABLE 2

Distribution of unemployment in the U.S. civilian population, June 2001

Characteristic	Unemployment rate
Age	
Males	4.7
16 to 19 years	15.9
20 to 24 years	9.5
25 to 54 years	3.5
55 years and over	3.0
Females	4.4
16 to 19 years	12.7
20 to 24 years	6.7
25 to 54 years	3.8
55 years and over	2.5
Education[a]	
Less than high school diploma	6.8
High school graduate, no degree	3.9
Less than a bachelors degree	3.2
College graduate	2.2

Characteristic	Unemployment rate
Family status	
Married men, spouse present	2.6
Widowed, divorced, or separated	4.2
Single (never married)	9.5
With own children under 18 years	2.2
With own children 6 to 17 years, none younger	2.1
With own children under 6 years	2.3
Married women, spouse present	3.0
Widowed, divorced, or separated	4.5
Single (never married)	8.5
Women who maintain family	6.3
With own children under 18 years	4.3
With own children 6 to 17 years, none younger	3.4
With own children under 6 years	5.6
Racial group	
White	4.0
16 to 19 years	12.6
Black	8.4
16 to 19 years	28.2
Hispanic	6.6

Note: [a] The figures are for individuals aged 25 years and over.
Unemployment rate represented as a percentage of the labor force.

SOURCE: Bureau of Labor Statistics, labor force statistics from the Current Population Survey and monthly statistics from Employment and Earnings.

rate of those who did not complete a high school diploma is three times higher than that of college graduates. There is also a notable difference between the unemployment rate of a non-high school graduate (7 percent) and one who has graduated (4 percent). The pattern in the data suggests that individuals can enhance their employment prospects considerably by completing high school.

Racial groups. Labor market performances also differ across racial groups. To illustrate this, data for the White, Black, and Hispanic racial groups are included in Table 2. The data show that the unemployment of white Americans (about 4 percent) is around one-half that of blacks and Hispanics (unemployment rates of 8 percent and 7 percent, respectively). Black youths (16–19) appear to be particularly disadvantaged, with an unemployment rate of 28 percent. These unemployment rate differentials paint a picture of disadvantage similar to that which emerges from study of other labor market indicators, such as earnings.

Family status. Most studies of unemployment recognize the importance of marital status as a determinant of labor market outcomes. The data in Table 2 indicate that married men and women with spouse present have the lowest rates of unemployment of the family states distinguished in the table. Individuals who have never married have the highest rate of unemployment, around 9 percent. The unemployment rate of women who maintain a family (spouse absent) is twice that of women who are married with their spouse present.

The Table 2 data illustrate that the presence of children increases the unemployment rate among women, but seems to have minimal impact on the employment outcome of men. This differential in impact presumably is associated with women still having primary responsibility for the care of children, with this responsibility limiting the types of work they obtain. Moreover, there appears to be an inverse relationship between the female unemployment rate and the age of the children. For example, the unemployment rate among women with children under six years is 6 percent compared to only 3 percent for women with children between six and seventeen years. Young children are relatively time-intensive for mothers, whereas older children tend to be more market-goods intensive. In addition, older children can provide

An unemployed auto worker stands in an unemployment line with her two children. Unemployment has been connected to higher crime rates, increases in the incidences of alcoholism, child abuse, family breakdown, psychiatric hospitalization, and a variety of physical complaints and illnesses. BETTMANN/CORBIS

care for younger siblings, enabling their mothers to pursue a greater range of market opportunities.

The characteristics such as a low level of education and membership of ethnic minorities that are associated with disproportionately high unemployment rates are also generally associated with low incomes among the employed and low-status occupations. Job instability will therefore compound the problems of the low-income groups in society. Not only is unemployment spread unevenly across sectors of society, but the burden of joblessness falls most heavily on those groups who do not have adequate resources to cope with the job loss.

Solutions to the Unemployment Problem

Much of the discussion on finding solutions to the unemployment problem has centered on the pivotal role of faster economic growth and cuts in real wages. Faster economic growth is viewed as a means of generating more jobs. Cuts in real wages are a reaction to the view that through their demands for higher wages, some groups of workers have priced themselves out of a job. How much growth and how large a fall in real wages would be required to reduce the size of the unemployment problem both remain matters for debate. Ottosen and Thompson (1996) suggest an overhaul of the National Labor Relations Act in the United States as a way of preventing unions from delivering the monopolistic wages and fringe benefit premiums that raise business costs and lead to unemployment. Such proposals are often very difficult to implement. Simulations by Guy Debelle and James Vickery (1998) for the Australian labor market are suggestive of manageable wage cuts only if the unemployment target is not set too low. Such advice is not very encouraging. Moreover, many researchers believe that the levels of economic growth required to make a major difference to the unemployment problem are unlikely to be sustained by most economies.

The United States and other countries could take other approaches to help reduce their unemployment rates (Ottosen and Thompson 1996). First, the methods of accumulation and dissemination of information on available jobs and workers could be improved. Ottosen and Thompson have suggested following the Swedish model, in which job centers have a nationwide, integrated database of jobs, employers, and available employees. This type of database could reduce the time spent by an average worker on the unemployment roll and thus reduce the unemployment rate. Second, unemployment agencies could tighten their job search and job acceptance requirements. Third, there could be improvements to the education and training provided to young people, with a greater focus on vocational skills. Finally, countries need to ensure that their welfare systems do not provide disincentives to work. Australia, for example, has strengthened the "Mutual Obligation" requirements (e.g., taking part in Work for the Dole projects) that eligible job seekers must meet in order to avoid loss of part of their income support.

There may also be a role for unemployment programs that target various groups of jobless persons. Carol West (1994) surveyed the unemployment programs aimed at reducing cyclical, frictional, seasonal, and structural unemployment in the United States. Some of these programs aim to change people to match existing jobs while others create jobs to match existing worker skills. The change in focus over time and the short duration of many programs make evaluation difficult. Many programs appear to do little more than reorder the line of unemployed people, though obviously they have the potential to fulfill an equity function in the labor market. John Piggot and Bruce Chapman (1995) suggest that labor market programs can be a cost-effective means of managing the pool of unemployment.

A number of other solutions to the unemployment problem have been advanced in the literature. For example, work sharing, early retirement, and reduced migration have been discussed. These policies affect the labor market by reducing the supply of labor. However, they have not won a great deal of support among economists.

See also: FAMILY POLICY; FAMILY ROLES; HOMELESS FAMILIES; MIGRATION; POVERTY; SCHOOL; STRESS; WORK AND FAMILY

Bibliography

Barling, J. (1990). *Employment, Stress, and Family Functioning*. New York: John Wiley and Sons.

Berry, A.; Mendex, M. T.; and Tenjo, J. (1997). "Growth, Macroeconomic Stability and the Generation of Productive Employment in Latin America." In *Employment Expansion and Macroeconomic Stability under Increasing Globalization,* ed. A. R. Khan and M. Muqtada. London: Macmillan.

Bregger, J. E., and Haugen, S. E. (1995). "BLS Introduces New Range of Alternative Unemployment Measures." *Monthly Labor Review* 118(October):19–26.

Britt, C. L. (1994). "Crime and Unemployment among Youths in the United States, 1958-1990." *American Journal of Economics and Sociology* 53(January):99–109.

Cantor, D., and Land, K. C. (1985). "Unemployment and Crime Rates in the Post-World War II United States: A Theoretical and Empirical Analysis." *American Sociological Review* 50(June):317–332.

Debelle, G., and Vickery, J. (1998). "The Macroeconomics of Australian Unemployment." In *Unemployment and the Australian Labour Market,* ed. G. Debelle and J. Borland. Sydney: Reserve Bank of Australia.

Finegan, A. T. (1978). "Improving Our Information on Discouraged Workers." *Monthly Labor Review* 101(September):15–25.

Gitter, R. J., and Scheuer, M. (1997). "U.S. and German Youths: Unemployment and the Transition from School to Work." *Monthly Labor Review* 120(March):16–20.

Haugen, S. E., and Parks, W., II. (1990). "Job Growth Moderated in 1989 while Unemployment Held Steady." *Monthly Labor Review* 113(February):3–16

International Labour Office. (1998). *Yearbook of Labour Statistics*. Geneva: Author.

Jackman, R. (1997a). "Unemployment and Wage Inequality in Advanced Industrial (OECD) Countries." In *Employment Expansion and Macroeconomic Stability under Increasing Globalization,* ed. A. R. Khan and M. Muqtada. London: Macmillan.

Jackman, R. (1997b). "Macroeconomic Policies, Employment and Labour Markets in Transition in Central and Eastern Europe." In *Employment Expansion and Macroeconomic Stability under Increasing Globalization,* ed. A. R. Khan and M. Muqtada. London: Macmillan.

Kenyon, P. (1998). "Discussion of 'Dimensions, Structure and History of Australian Unemployment' by Jeff Borland and Steven Kennedy." In *Unemployment and the Australian Labour Market,* ed. G. Debelle and J. Borland. Sydney: Reserve Bank of Australia.

Le, A. T., and Miller, P. W. (2000). "Australia's Unemployment Problem." *Economic Record* 76(March):74–104.

Liker, J. K., and Elder, G. H., Jr. (1983). "Economic Hardship and Marital Relations in the 1930s." *American Sociological Review* 48(June):343–359.

Ottosen, G. K., and Thompson, D. N. (1996). *Reducing Unemployment: A Case for Government Deregulation.* Westport, CT: Praeger.

Piggott, J., and Chapman, B. (1995). "Costing the Job Compact." *Economic Record* 71(December):313–328.

West, C. T. (1994). "The Problem of Unemployment in the United States: A Survey of 60 Years of National and State Policy Initiatives." *International Regional Science Review* 1 and 2(16):17–47.

Wooden, M. (1996). "Hidden Unemployment and Underemployment: Their Nature and Possible Impact on Future Labour Force Participation and Unemployment,"

National Institute of Labour Studies, The Flinders University of South Australia, Working Paper No. 140.

Yang, B., and Lester, D. (1994). "Crime and Unemployment." *Journal of Socio-Economics* (Spring-Summer) 23:215–22.

Other Resources

Bureau of Labor Statistics. *Monthly Data from Employment and Earnings*. Available from http://stats.bls.gov/cpsee.htm

Bureau of Labor Statistics. *Labor Force Statistics from the Current Population Survey*. Available from http://stats.bls.gov/cpsatabs.htm

California State University, Fresno. *Econ Data and Links*. Available from http://www.csufresno.edu/Economics/econ_EDL.htm.

International Labour Office. *Labour force statistics from ILO database LABORSTA*. Available from http://laborsta.ilo.org/

International Labor Organization. Web site. Available from http://www.us.ilo.org/.

Organisation for Economic Co-Operation And Development. *Labour Force Statistics*. Available from http://www1.oecd.org/std/lfs.htm.

World Bank Group. *Data by Topic*. Available from http://www.worldbank.org/data/databytopic/databytopic.html

ANH T. LE
PAUL W. MILLER

UNITED STATES

The first family system in America was that of the native peoples. This was actually a kinship system rather than a family system, for despite the wide variety of marital, sexual, and genealogical customs found in several hundred different cultures, most early Native-American groups subsumed the nuclear family and even the lineage in a much larger network of kin and marital alliances. Kinship rules regulated an individual's place in the overall production and distribution of goods, services, knowledge, and justice. Exogamy, the requirement that a person marry out of his or her natal group into a different clan or section, made each individual a member of intersecting kin groups, with special obligations and rights toward each category of relatives.

The kinship system of the Native Americans was disrupted by European colonization, and the nuclear family became more independent and more isolated. LIBRARY OF CONGRESS

This system was severely disrupted by European colonization of North America. Massive epidemics decimated kin networks, disrupting social continuity. Heightened warfare elevated the role of young male leaders at the expense of elders and women. The influence of traders, colonial political officials, and Christian missionaries fostered a growing independence of the nuclear family vis-à-vis the extended household, kinship, and community group in which it had traditionally been embedded. Economic inequities, legislation, and racial discrimination ensured that such independence led more often to downward than upward mobility for these newly isolated families.

The European families that colonized America had conceptions of wealth, private profit, state authority over families, sexuality, and power relations within families that differed sharply from Native-American patterns. Although there were considerable variations among the colonies by region, and the Spanish colonies had a particularly distinctive mix of caste, family, and gender hierarchies

(Gutierrez 1991), certain generalizations can be made. Colonial families had far more extensive property and inheritance rights than Native-American families, but they were also subject to more extensive controls by state and church institutions. The redistribution duties of wealthy families, however, were more narrow than those of Native Americans, so there were substantial differences in wealth and resources among colonial families right from the beginning.

Colonial families operated within a corporate system of agrarian household production sustained by a patriarchal, hierarchical political and ideological structure. The propertied conjugal family was the basis of this household order, but poor people without property tended to concentrate in wealthier households as apprentices, slaves, servants, or temporary lodgers, and the nuclear family did not occupy a privileged emotional or physical site in such households.

The propertied household, revolving around a single conjugal family, was the central unit of production, distribution, and authority. Thus, production and reproduction were tightly linked. The household head exercised paternal rights of discipline, including corporal punishment, over all household members; he was responsible for the education, religious instruction, and general behavior of his children, servants, and apprentices. Journals reveal the relative fluidity of household composition; as one or another member lived elsewhere for a while, servants came and went, and distant, relatives spent short stays. Yet the need for preservation of the family property demanded a strict hierarchy that left little room for independent reproductive and marital decisions.

Slaves, of course, did not experience this unity of family, work, production, sexuality, and reproduction. Slave families existed only at the discretion of the master, and traditional African kin ties were sundered by the processes of enslavement and sale. African slaves and their descendants, however, strove with considerable success to preserve or recreate kinship networks and obligations through fictive kin ties, ritual coparenting or godparenting, complex naming patterns designed to authenticate extended kin connections, and adoption of orphans.

By the last third of the eighteenth century, many economic, political, and religious forces had begun to undermine the colonial patriarchal, corporate order. Households gained more independence from neighbors and old social hierarchies; the tight bond between reproduction and production was loosened as land shortages disrupted old succession patterns; and the authority of fathers diminished, as witnessed by an erosion of parental control over marriage, an increase in out-of-wedlock births, and a new concept of childhood that stressed the importance of molding the child's character rather than breaking the child's will.

After the Civil War, the pace of industrialization, immigration, and urbanization quickened. As families adapted to the demands of an industrializing and diverse society, different groups behaved in ways that created some average trends, often lumped together as general characteristics of "modernization." Average family size became smaller; families revolved more tightly around the nuclear core, putting greater distance between themselves and servants or boarders; parents became more emotionally involved in child rearing and for a longer period; couples oriented more toward companionate marriage; and the separation between home and market activities, both physically and conceptually, was sharpened.

The gradual separation of home and work, market production, and household reproduction in the early nineteenth century, along with the emergence of newly specialized occupations, paved the way for a changing relationship between family activities and economic production, a growing distinction between private and public life, and a new conception of male and female roles that stressed their complementary but sharply divided responsibilities and capacities. This has become known as the doctrine of separate spheres.

By the late nineteenth century, both external and internal challenges to the domestic family and the concept of separate spheres had appeared. Victorian sexual mores clashed with the growing use of birth control and abortion, as well as with the opportunities for nonmarital sex associated with increased urbanization and changing work patterns for youths. Prostitution, once a safety valve for Victorian marriage, became a highly visible big business. A women's rights movement combined campaigns for seemingly conventional goals such as social purity and temperance with attacks on the double standard and demands for expanded legal rights for women. Debates and conflicts over sexuality became increasingly public.

These changes in sexual behavior and gender roles—interacting with the transition to mass production, a new corporate economy in which the role of family firms and personal reputation counted for less, and the rise of more centralized government institutions—had produced a new constellation of family types by the turn of the century. Many of the direct, class-specific family strategies aimed at preparing children for work, maximizing family security, and coping with illness, unemployment, or old age were obviated by new hiring and promotion patterns, the advent of unions, compulsory education, new patterns of housing segregation, the rise of specialized health and welfare institutions, and suburbanization. As families relied less on local, particularistic institutions such as craft, associations, ethnic organizations, religious institutions, and urban political machines, they related instead to more formal, centralized institutions of education, job recruitment and training, social services, and distribution. Personal ties and intensities that had been dispersed among several complementary institutions, and personal networks that mediated between the individual and the larger society, were increasingly concentrated in the family. New notions of family privacy developed, along with heightened expectations of romance and individual fulfillment in marriage. A youth culture began to reorganize older family-centered courtship patterns into dating rituals that eroded the intense same-sex friendships and mother-child bonds of earlier years.

The new family shifted its axis from the mother-child relationship to the couple relationship and put forward the nuclear family unit as a place for qualitatively different relationships than those to be found with kin or friends. It also assumed a different relation to the state, simultaneously claiming an expanded sphere of private life and becoming more dependent on state subsidies or government institutions. At the same time, the emergence of a public policy aimed at establishing a family wage led to new ideas about family self-sufficiency and to condemnation of "promiscuous" families that pooled resources or shared housing beyond the nuclear unit.

Tensions and contradictions were associated with the new consumer family from the beginning. Peer groups were necessary for romantic love and heterosexual dating, but they conflicted with parental supervision and older sexual mores; elevation of the couple relationship to the primary center of all emotional and sensual satisfactions made an unhappy union seem intolerable, leading to a sharp rise in divorce rates. The emphasis on personal fulfillment opened up potential conflicts between the sacrifices necessary in families and the consumer satisfactions that romantic fantasies promised.

These conflicts began to surface in the 1920s, which experienced a generation gap, sexual revolution, and sense of family crisis that was every bit as disturbing to contemporaries as later rearrangements of family life and sexual behavior have been. Following the stock market crash of 1929, however, such anxieties took a backseat to the exigencies of the Great Depression, followed by World War II. After the family conflicts, separations, and hardships of depression and war, people set aside their earlier reservations and wholeheartedly embraced the innovations of the 1920s' family ideal, attaching it to the leap in single-family home ownership and personal consumption made possible by an unprecedented rise in real wages and government subsidization.

The ideal family of the 1950s, portrayed in countless television sitcoms, is now frequently mistaken as "traditional." In fact, the family of the 1950s was a historical blip. For the first time in 100 years, the age for marriage and motherhood fell, fertility increased, divorce rates declined from a 1945 high when one in every three marriages ended in divorce (Cherlin 1981), and women's increasing educational parity with men reversed itself. In a period of less than ten years, the proportion of never-married persons declined by as much as it had during the entire previous half-century.

The young nuclear families that dominated the U.S. cultural landscape in the 1950s were not as idyllic as nostalgia makes them (Coontz 1992). The percentage of U.S. children who were poor was higher during the 1950s than during the early 1990s, and much higher than during the period from 1965 to 1978. A high percentage of African-American two-parent families lived below the poverty line. Social workers and prosecutors failed to act decisively against incest, child abuse, or wife battering, and pervasive discrimination against women led many housewives to report that they felt trapped. Alcohol abuse was widespread.

The composition of U.S. families changed dramatically throughout the second half of the twentieth century in ways that have important implications for the well-being of all persons, from the very young to the oldest old. Young adults are increasingly choosing to delay or forgo marriage, and those who do marry face a high likelihood of divorce. As a result, men and women are spending fewer of their adult years with a spouse, and children are spending a greater proportion of their childhood living with a single parent or in stepfamilies than ever before.

A number of important changes have occurred in the marriage patterns of women and men in the United States since World War II that have led to a general decline in marriage rates. While it is true that a large majority of men and women continue to marry at some point in their lives, the timing and duration of marriage have changed substantially (Bianchi and Spain 1986). More and more young men and women are opting to delay marriage, and for those who do marry, the risk of divorce has increased dramatically. In addition, those who have experienced divorce or widowhood are remarrying at lower rates. The net result has been a reduction in both the average duration of marriage and the total proportion of an individual's life that is shared with a spouse. One study suggested that U.S. men and women who reach adulthood around the end of the twentieth century can expect to spend more than half of their lives unmarried (Schoen et al. 1985).

While marriage is still highly valued (Bumpass 1990; Thornton and Freedman 1983), young men and women are increasingly opting to delay the start of their married lives. As illustration of this trend, the median age at first marriage (i.e., the age by which exactly half of all persons marrying for the first time in the specified year were married), has increased steadily since 1960 for both men and women. For women, the median age at first marriage increased from 20.3 in 1960 to 24.1 in 1991. The median age at first marriage for men, which is typically higher than that for women by about two years, also increased during this period (U.S. Bureau of the Census 1991b; U.S. Bureau of the Census 1992).

Despite sharp declines in marriage rates since World War II, the United States still has one of the highest rates relative to other countries at similar levels of social and economic development (United Nations, 1992).

As is true for patterns of first marriage, rates of remarriage (expressed as the ratio of the number of marriages involving persons who were previously married to the number of previously married persons in any given year) have declined for both men and women. For example, between 1973 and 1987, the remarriage rate declined from 133.3 to 90.8 for men and from 40.6 to 35.8 for women (National Center for Health Statistics 1991). Throughout this period, rates of remarriage for men remained considerably higher than those for women, although the differential narrowed somewhat due to the much sharper decline in rates for men compared to women.

Part of the decline in rates of remarriage is attributable to the fact that persons who have experienced marital dissolution through divorce or widowhood are less likely to remarry than they once were (Bumpass 1990). In addition, just as women and men have delayed the timing of first marriage, they have also extended the length of time between marriages.

Perhaps no other demographic trend has raised more concern than the increasing prevalence of divorce among U.S. couples. Divorce is not a new phenomenon in this country, however; in fact, divorce rates have been increasing in the United States since as far back as 1860 (Cherlin 1981). What is unique about the latter decades of the twentieth century is the pace at which divorce rates have increased.

Following a century characterized by a slow but steady rise, divorce rates increased dramatically during the 1960s and 1970s, to reach an all-time high in 1979. The divorce rate (expressed as the number of divorces per 1,000 married women fifteen years of age or older) more than doubled between 1960 and 1979, from 9.2 to 22.8. During the 1980s and early 1990s, the trend leveled off, and divorce rates actually declined slightly to 21.2 in 1992 (National Center for Health Statistics 1993a). Unless divorce rates decline substantially, however, researchers estimate that as many as 60 percent of first marriages occurring since the late 1980s will end in divorce (Bumpass 1990).

Throughout the history of the United States, widowhood, not divorce, was the more common outcome for married persons. However, beginning in the mid-1970s this balance shifted, such that the number of marriages ending in divorce each year actually exceeded the number ending through the death of a spouse (Cherlin 1981).

The practice of men and women living together as an unmarried couple (i.e., cohabitation) became increasingly common during the latter half of the twentieth century. Defined as households containing only two adults with or without children under fifteen years of age present, the number of unmarried-couple households increased from 523,000 in 1970 to 2.9 million in 1990 (U.S. Bureau of the Census 1991b).

In the United States, single-parent families are more likely to be headed by the mother. A growing number of children are spending at least part of their childhood with only one parent. ANNIE GRIFFITHS BELT/CORBIS

Childbearing

Children have always been and continue to be a central part of the U.S. family. Despite the profound changes that have occurred since World War II with respect to patterns of marriage and divorce, the vast majority of young women (more than 90 percent) still expect to give birth to at least one child at some point in their lives (U.S. Bureau of the Census 1991a). This does not imply that patterns of childbearing (or fertility) have remained unchanged, however. In fact, with the exception of a brief but dramatic increase in fertility rates during the postwar "baby boom," family size has declined fairly steadily throughout the nineteenth and twentieth centuries (Cherlin 1981).

The most notable aspects of childbearing patterns in recent decades are the pace at which fertility declined during the 1960s and 1970s, and the fact that fertility rates reached an all-time low during this period. A number of factors contributed to this decline, including an increasing tendency by young couples to delay the start of childbearing, to have fewer children in total, or to remain childless altogether. In addition to the general decline in fertility rates, the context in which childbearing takes place also changed during this period, as the proportion of births occurring outside of marriage increased dramatically.

In addition to delaying the onset of childbearing, an increasing proportion of couples are choosing to have only one child or no children at all. It is still too early to tell what consequences the sustained low fertility levels of the 1970s and 1980s will have for completed fertility levels, because women who entered their childbearing years during that period are only now starting to complete their childbearing. However, the experiences of women who had their children toward the end of the baby boom and who have now completed their families lend some insight into what might happen in the future. For example, the proportion of women age fifty to fifty-four who had only one child increased slightly between 1985 and 1991, from 9.6 percent to 11.1 percent. The percentage of women in this age group who were childless also increased slightly during the late 1980s, from 8.4 percent in 1987 to 9.3 percent in 1991 (National Center for Health Statistics 1993b). This latter figure is expected to increase rapidly, however, and researchers have projected that the proportion of women who remain childless may reach as high as

25 percent among women who will be completing their childbearing early in the twenty-first century (Bloom and Trussell 1984).

Childbearing in the United States has become increasingly separated from marriage. Sexual activity outside marriage, particularly premarital sexual activity, has risen dramatically among women since the 1960s, and women are becoming sexually active at younger ages on average than ever before (National Center for Health Statistics 1987). These trends, coupled with the fact that women are delaying marriage and spending a smaller portion of their reproductive years in marriage, have led to an increase in the number and proportion of births that occur to unmarried women.

Changes in patterns of family formation and dissolution and childbearing have translated into profound shifts in family and household composition for children and adults. The family model prevalent in the 1950s of breadwinner-husband and homemaker-wife raising their own children together in their own home is increasingly being replaced by a mosaic of alternative family types, including single-parent families, remarried-parent or stepfamilies, married couples with no children, and unmarried couples with children (Ahlburg and De Vita 1992). In addition, households comprised of persons living alone or with nonrelatives are becoming increasingly common.

Perhaps more striking are changes that have occurred in the composition of the family groups themselves. The percentage of families with dependent children that are maintained by two parents declined since 1970. The proportion maintained by a single parent (either mother or father) more than doubled during this period, from approximately 13 percent in 1970 to just under 30 percent in 1990. Single-parent families are much more likely to be maintained by a mother than a father. Although this pattern is starting to change somewhat, even in 1990 the vast majority of single-parent families (87 percent) were maintained by women (U.S. Bureau of the Census 1991b).

What the rise in single parenthood means from a child's perspective is that an increasing number and proportion of children are spending at least part of their childhood with only one parent. In 1992, more than one-quarter of all children under eighteen years of age (representing a total of 17.6 million children) were living in a single-parent family, up from 9 percent (or 5.8 million) in 1960 (U.S. Bureau of the Census 1991b, 1993). These figures relate to living arrangements at a given point in time; however, the proportion of children who have experienced or will ever experience living in a single-parent home is somewhat higher. Based on trends in marital dissolution and nonmarital fertility described earlier, researchers have estimated that the proportion of children expected to live in a single-parent household at some time before reaching adulthood will range between one-half and three-quarters (Bumpass 1984; Hofferth 1985). For some children this arrangement is only short-term, followed quickly by the parent's remarriage and the arrival of a stepparent; however, many children may spend a large part of their childhood years living with a single parent, because the parent either never remarries or experiences multiple marital disruptions (Sweet and Bumpass 1987).

Stepfamilies are also becoming much more prevalent in American family life, and it is important to keep in mind that children who are reported as living with two parents do not necessarily live with their biological parents

There is a great deal of uncertainty about what the future will bring for the family in the United States, as well as what the consequences of changes experienced thus far will be for individuals, family groups, and society at large. Demographic trends since the mid-1980s suggest a somewhat slower pace of change for the beginning of the twenty-first century. Furthermore, despite profound changes in its composition and function, the family continues to be highly valued in U.S. society, and the vast majority of young Americans expect to marry and have children at some point in their lives. Because the changes that have occurred have been so far-reaching, however, it seems unlikely that there will ever be a return to what Dennis A. Ahlburg and Carol J. De Vita referred to as the "seemingly well-ordered family world of the 1950s" (1992, p. 38). Hence it will be important to continue to focus efforts on developing a better understanding of the "new realities" of family life in the United States.

See also: AFRICAN-AMERICAN FAMILIES; AMERICAN INDIAN FAMILIES; ASIAN-AMERICAN FAMILIES; CANADA; HISPANIC-AMERICAN FAMILIES; MEXICO

Bibliography

Ahlburg, D. A., and De Vita, C. J. (1992). "New Realities of the American Family." *Population Bulletin* 47(2):1–43.

Bianchi, S. M., and Spain, D. (1986). *American Women in Transition.* New York: Russell Sage Foundation.

Bloom, D. E., and Trussell, J. (1984). "What Are the Determinants of Delayed Childbearing and Permanent Childlessness in the United States?" *Demography* 21:591–611.

Bumpass, L. L. (1984). "Children and Marital Disruption: A Replication and Update." *Demography* 21:71–82.

Bumpass, L. L. (1990). "What's Happening to the Family? Interactions Between Demographic and Institutional Change." *Demography* 27:483–498.

Cherlin, A. J. (1981). *Marriage, Divorce, Remarriage.* Cambridge, MA: Harvard University Press.

Coontz, S. (1992). *The Way We Never Were: American Families and the Nostalgia Trap.* New York: Basic Books.

Gutierrez, R. (1991). *When Jesus Came, the Corn Mothers Went Away: Marriage, Sexuality, and Power in New Mexico, 1500–1846.* Stanford, CA: Stanford University Press.

Hofferth, S. L. (1985). "Updating Children's Life Course." *Journal of Marriage and the Family* 47:93–115.

National Center for Health Statistics; Bachrach, C. A.; and Horn, M. C. (1987). "Married and Unmarried Couples: United States, 1982." *Vital and Health Statistics.* Series 23, no. 15, PHS 87-1991. Washington, DC: U.S. Government Printing Office.

National Center for Health Statistics. (1991). *Vital Statistics of the United States, 1987:* Vol. III, *Marriage and Divorce.* Washington, DC: U.S. Government Printing Office.

National Center for Health Statistics. (1993a). "Annual Summary of Births, Marriages, Divorces, and Deaths: United States, 1992." *NCHS Monthly Vital Statistics Report.* Vol. 41, no. 13. Hyattsville, MD: Public Health Service.

National Center for Health Statistics. (1993b). *Health, United States, 1992.* Hyattsville, MD: Public Health Service.

Schoen, R.; Urton, W.; Woodrow, K.; and Baj, J. (1985). "Marriage and Divorce in Twentieth-Century American Cohorts." *Demography* 22:101–114.

Sweet, J. A., and Bumpass, L. L. (1987). *American Families and Households.* New York: Russell Sage Foundation.

Thornton, A., and Freedman, D. (1983). "The Changing American Family." *Population Bulletin* 38(4):1–43.

United Nations. (1992). *1990 Demographic Yearbook.* New York: Author.

U.S. Bureau of the Census. (1991a). "Fertility of American Women: June 1990." *Current Population Reports.* Series P-20, no. 454. Washington, DC: U.S. Government Printing Office.

U.S. Bureau of the Census. (1991b). "Marital Status and Living Arrangements: March 1990." *Current Population Reports.* Series P-20, no. 450. Washington, DC: U.S. Government Printing Office.

U.S. Bureau of the Census. (1992). "Marital Status and Living Arrangements: March 1991." *Current Population Reports.* Series P-20, no. 461. Washington, DC: U.S. Government Printing Office.

U.S. Bureau of the Census. (1993). *Statistical Abstract of the United States,* 113th edition. Washington, DC: U.S. Government Printing Office.

STEPHANIE COONTZ (1995)
MARY BETH OFSTEDAL (1995)
REVISED BY JAMES J. PONZETTI, JR.

URBANIZATION

Urbanization, in conventional terms, refers to the process through which society is transformed from one that is predominantly rural, in economy, culture and life style, to one that is predominantly urban. It is also a process of territorial reorganization in that it shifts the locations, as well as the characteristics, of population and production activities. Typically, urbanization is defined by the simple proportion of a nation's population residing in areas that are classified, by national census authorities, as urban places. Since definitions of what is or is not urban differ from one country to another, however, so do interpretations of what the designation urban implies (United Nations 1996).

Urbanization, however defined, is much more than a simple matter of population or production accounting (Knox 1994). It reflects, for a start, a complex set of processes involving a series of linked transformations, not only in where people live and what they produce, but in how they live; in terms of economic well-being, political organization and the distribution of power, demographic structure (e.g. fertility), and social (and family) relations.

The Urbanization Process

It can be argued that urbanization represents the single most fundamental transformation of the

An immigrant family looks at the New York skyline, 1925. Urbanization is a social process as well as an economic and territorial one. It transforms the role of the family, relationships within families, and concepts of individual and social responsibility. BETTMANN ARCHIVE/UPI/CORBIS

twentieth century. Almost all other societal changes, for example, in levels of economic development, industrialization, the character of the family and fertility rates—indeed civilization itself—are contingent on the urban factor (Hall 1998). Although urban settlements—defined here as dense clusters of nonagricultural populations—have existed for perhaps 7,000 years, they seldom exceeded a few thousand people and only accommodated a very small proportion of the population of the territories they controlled.

In fact, it was not until after 1900 that any nation could be said to have a majority of its citizens living in urban areas. The industrial revolution in Britain, driven by the demands for a skilled and geographically concentrated labor force, and attracted by the economic benefits of agglomerating production facilities in dense settlements, produced the first truly urban nation in 1910 when more than 50 percent of its population was resident in urban areas. Other European nations followed soon after. The United States became predominantly urban, by this same measure, in 1920, whereas most Asian countries did not reach this stage until after 1945.

Prior to World War II less than 25 percent of the world's population was living in urban areas. Since then the process of concentration has accelerated, especially in the developing countries. By the end of the twentieth century roughly 48 percent of the world's six billion people lived in urban areas (United Nations 1996). Thus, the opening of the twenty-first century signals the beginning of another crucial global watershed: over 50 percent of the world's population will become urban dwellers.

Generally, the proportion of a country's population that is urban (i.e. the level of urbanization) is closely associated with the level of economic development—particularly the degree of industrialization—and the standard of living. In the advanced industrial economies today the urban proportion varies between 75 and 90 percent, in middle-income countries from 50 to 75 percent, and in the developing world from 10 to 50 percent. Recently, however, the long-standing association between levels of economic development and income per capita on the one hand and increases in the level of urbanization on the other has been broken. In many developing countries, unlike the industrialized world in the nineteenth century, the rate of urbanization has tended to out-pace the rate of economic growth. This has lead to a situation of over-urbanization, and the appearance of large mega-cities, often with insufficient employment opportunities, inadequate services, and intense poverty (Gilbert and Gugler 1994; Lo and Yeung 1998).

The Social Impacts of Urbanization

It is now widely accepted that urbanization is as much a social process as it is an economic and territorial process. It transforms societal organizations, the role of the family, demographic structures, the nature of work, and the way we choose to live and with whom. It also modifies domestic roles and relations within the family, and redefines concepts of individual and social responsibility.

Fertility rates. Initially, the societal shift from rural to urban alters rates of natural population increase. There are no recorded examples of where this has not been true. Contrary to public perception, however, it first reduces the death rate, despite the often appalling living conditions in many cities, as in, for example, nineteenth-century Europe and North America and in present-day cities in the developing world (Smith 1996). Only later does urbanization reduce the birth rate (i.e. the fertility rate). The time lag between declining death and birth rates initially means rapid urban population growth; subsequently, fertility rates drop sharply and the rate of growth of urban populations declines.

As a result, families become smaller relatively quickly, not only because parents have fewer children on average, but also because the extended family typical of rural settings is much less common in urban areas. Children are clearly less useful in urban settlements, as units of labor and producers, than in rural settings, and are more expensive to house and feed. In fact, fertility levels in developed countries have dropped so low that cities are seldom capable of reproducing their own populations. They grow, if at all, largely through in-migration from other cities or from rural areas—the latter is now a largely depleted source of population in Western countries—and increasingly through immigration.

Ironically, overpopulation in the Third World and historically low fertility levels in developed countries have combined to produce a massive immigration into those cities in the latter countries that serve as contemporary immigrant gateways or world cities (Sassen 2001; Castles and Miller 1998). Those cities, in turn, have been transformed, in social and ethno-cultural terms, as a result of this immigration (Polese and Stren 2000).

Families and living arrangements. The evolution to an urban society is also frequently equated with a decline in the status of the family, and with a proliferation of nontraditional family forms and new types of households. By nontraditional we mean those families without two parents and/or without children. This trend is in part a reflection of an increasing diversity in "choices of living arrangements." This concept is used in the scholarly literature to refer to the myriad of ways in which individuals in an urban society combine to form *collective units* (i.e., households). Those combinations may follow from marriage, the traditional arrangement, or from any other association of individuals within the housing system whether those individuals are related by marriage or blood, or are unrelated.

Historically, of course, living arrangements in the past or in rural areas were never as homogeneous or traditional as the literature would have us believe. Nevertheless, the last half-century, notably in the Western countries, has witnessed an explosion in rates of household formation and a sharp increase in the diversity of household and family types. For most of the period since World War II, rates of household formation—that is, the propensity to establish a separate household—has been much higher (indeed 50% higher) than the rate of population growth, and the rate of nonfamily household formation (whose members are not related by blood or marriage) has been higher still. This proliferation has many causes, including rising incomes, higher divorce rates, lower marriage rates, and alternative life styles.

The highest propensities to form separate households, however, have been within two principal groups: the young and the elderly. The former includes single parents, the most rapidly growing household type in Western cities; the growth of the latter has been facilitated by increased longevity and improved health and social benefits. In previous generations, and in most rural societies, many of these individuals would have shared accommodation, often as part of extended family groupings. The result, again with respect to Western countries, is that average family size is now fewer than four persons, while average household size is fewer than three. In many older central cities, in fact, average household size is below two persons. This is in part a sign of success, reflecting improvements in housing and in our ability to afford to live alone, but it also reflects dramatic changes in how we choose to live and in our attitudes to marriage, family life, and social responsibility.

Links to labor markets. This diversity in living arrangements and family composition in urban societies is also closely linked to shifts in the world of work—in the urban economy and in occupations. Not only does urbanization involve obvious changes in employment and working life, it alters the relationships between households (the collective units of consumption) and labor markets (the production sector). Individuals work and earn wages, but it is households (and families) that spend those earnings. Thus, the composition of families and households influences the changing well-being of the individuals in those households as much as the occupational status of its members.

Two countervailing processes are at work here in reshaping the linkages between living arrangement and work. One is that over the last half century the proportion of the population in the labor force—that is, the participation rate—has increased, especially among married women. Historically, of course, women always had full-time jobs in pre-urban societies, but through the process of urbanization much of that work became marginalized as "domestic" (and unpaid) work. Second, the decline in average household size has tended to fragment the incomes of consuming units, usually meaning fewer wage earners per household. One rather obvious result of this intersection of changes in family composition and the labor market has been a deeper polarization in economic well-being among urban populations, which is especially marked between households with two or more workers and those with none.

Domestic relations. Such labor market changes are also interrelated, as cause and effect, with shifts in domestic relations inside the household and family. The impact of these changes have been most obvious for married women. Not only has their involvement in the formal (paid) labor market increased, but so too has their economic position within the family. This gives women more autonomy in decision making, but it has not been without drawbacks. For many women the challenge of balancing work, domestic responsibilities, and the imperatives of everyday urban life, have increased, not decreased. Smaller families, and the dispersion of extended families in contemporary urbanized societies, have in combination also reduced the level of kinship support systems available to these women.

The Urban Future

The level of urbanization, as measured by the proportion of the population living in urban areas, has largely stabilized in the highly developed countries. This does not mean, however, that the urbanization process writ large has ceased. Almost everyone now lives in or near a metropolitan region, and thus shares many of the same values, living arrangements, and life styles. Population growth rates are also declining; in many western countries there is little or no natural growth. At the same time, within the urban size hierarchy, urban populations have continued to concentrate in the larger metropolitan areas; indeed, more than half of all Americans now live in areas with populations over one million. The concept *urban* now means *metropolitan,* and it implies a way of life, as well as a place.

Moreover, the social transformations that flow from that process are continuing. Families will likely become even smaller as fertility rates decline still further and the pressures of urban living become more intense. The proportion of smaller, nontraditional households will also grow. Cities, as a consequence, will depend for their future growth even more on attracting in-migrants.

Cities in developing countries face a far more daunting challenge a result of the continuing urbanization process in an era of rapid global economic restructuring. Although fertility rates are expected to decline, death rates are likely to decline even faster. Thus, urban populations will continue to grow rapidly. The magnitude of anticipated social changes in families, households, and living arrangements is immense. Indeed, the twenty-first century will be defined by the ability of countries to cope with massive urban growth and the parallel transformations in urban economies and social conditions. Most, but not all, countries will follow the urban path defined earlier by countries in the developed world.

Approximately 38 percent of the developing world population is currently classified as urban, at least according to their place of residence. If U.N. estimates (2000) are correct, this will rise to 60 percent within twenty years. Even with recent declines in fertility levels and thus reductions in family sizes in those countries, this projection means that a total of over two billion people will be added to the urban population of Third World countries. How well they will live, in economic terms, and in what types of social settings and family relationships, remains to be seen.

See also: IMMIGRATION; INDUSTRIALIZATION; MIGRATION; NEIGHBORHOOD; POVERTY; RURAL FAMILIES; WORK AND FAMILY

Bibliography

Castles, S., and Miller, M. (1998). *The Age of Migration: International Population Movements in the Modern World.* New York: Guilford Press.

Gilbert, A., and Gugler, J. (1994). *Cities, Poverty and Development: Urbanization and the Third World.* New York: Oxford University Press.

Hall, P. (1998). *Cities in Civilization.* London: Weidenfeld and Nicolson.

Lo, Fu-Chen, and Yeung, Yue-man, eds. (1998). *Global Urbanization and the World of Large Cities.* Tokyo: United Nations University Press.

Knox, P. (1994). *Urbanization.* Upper Saddle River, NJ: Prentice Hall.

Polese, M., and Stren, R., eds. (2000). *The Social Sustainability of Cities.* Toronto: University of Toronto Press.

Sassen, S. (2001). *The Global City: New York, London and Tokyo.* Princeton, NJ: Princeton University Press.

Smith, D.A. (1996). *Third World Cities in Global Perspective.* Boulder, CO: Westview Press.

United Nations. (1996). *An Urbanizing World: Global Report on Human Settlements.* New York: Oxford University Press.

United Nations. (2000). *World Development Report.* New York: Oxford University Press.

LARRY S. BOURNE

VENEREAL DISEASE

See SEXUALLY TRANSMITTED DISEASES

VENEZUELA

Venezuela is located on the northernmost tip of the South American continent. Its shoreline opens to the Caribbean Sea. The Venezuelan territory encompasses a portion of the Andes mountains chain, the Maracaibo Lake, and the Orinoco River basin and contains the regions of Guayana, Amazonia and the Plains. The capital city is Caracas. Venezuela has a wealth of raw materials—iron, asphalt, bauxite, water, coal, and above all, oil. The country is known worldwide as an oil-producing country.

Family, Society, and Culture

The axis organizing Venezuelan society does not lie in matrimonial alliances, mercantile practices, or religious ideology, but in the family. Based on the work of demographer James Mayone Stycos (1958), the definition of the family in the Venezuelan culture may explain Kingsley Davis's concern (1942) about Latin America as the *black* continent, speaking sociologically, with a social organization that is more unintelligible than Africa's. Characterized as matrifocal, Venezuelan family dynamics express one type of female-centered familism. Family conduct generally emphasizes the mother as the stable figure and decision-maker. Although families appear to be organized patrilineally, the cultural pattern is in reality matrilineal.

Conjugal forms of family and marriage are provided for in the civil and ecclesiastical codes that date from colonial times (Almecija 1992). However, these forms do not agree with the cultural reality. Various authors explain Venezuelan families in different ways (see e.g., Peattie 1968; Pollak-Eltz 1975). José L.Vethencourt (1974) considers Venezuelan family structure as atypical and as a failure to meet to bourgeois norms. His concept of *matricentrism* is conveyed in *machismo,* and both of these terms constitute conceptual poles in his structural analysis. Alejandro Moreno (1993) accepts Vethencourt's concepts but regards the family not as a failure to meet norms, but rather as an authentic Latin American family form. Rafael Lopez (1980) identifies this type of family with the Afro-Caribbean race, where the female is the focus of mythical and symbolic meanings in the kinship structuring process. The 1975 Congress on Family and Marriage in the Caribbean and Central America (Marks and Römer, 1975) discussed the matrifocal concept not mythologically but sociologically. The conclusion of this discussion was that concepts of matricentrism and matrifocality are insufficient to explain the reality of the Venezuelan family, that is, the powerful role of the grandmother figure.

Following a more sociological tendency, authors such as Gustavo Martin (1990), Manuel Briceño (1994) and Samuel Hurtado (1998) suggest that the Venezuelan family structure is ethnotypical—that is, it conveys the cultural pattern and explains the social structure. When the model cultural is so basic and strong, it affects societal rules. Society behaves as a family, characterized by an extremely pampering mother (Hurtado 1999). The neologism *matrisociality* defines the family-society relationship; however, the family structure interprets that relationship. Writers such as Alain Marie (1972), Audrey I. Richards (1982) and Karla Poewe (1981) have pointed to the tensions that exist in social organizations where the family structures tend toward a matrilineal system.

Excessive Motherhood

Economic and political strategies of the family determine patterns of social organization (Hurtado 1993, 1995). The matrifocal phenomenon can be seen in the figure of the grandmother. As decision-maker, her figure represents the principle of family reciprocity. The residence of the extended family is matrilocal, based on the grandmother's settlement. Low-income nuclear families live in or near the grandmother's household. Middle-class and wealthy families may reside elsewhere, but communicate with and visit the grandmother frequently, ensuring mutual help (Hurtado 1998). In one study in a Caracas shantytown, one-half of nuclear family groups of three related extended families dwelt in the grandmother's household (total 14), and another half (total 16) in the grandmother's neighborhood (Hurtado 1995)

Reciprocal systems depend upon the economic forms within family groups according to family composition and life cycle. There is mother, husband, wife, and filial economics, for example, and each has its specific function. There is a central function for mutual help among nuclear families related by grandmother. The contributions from the others make active a sort of semi-clan.

Matrifocality does not necessarily mean that the father is physically absent. However, the husband represents a marginal figure in the family group, even when married by civil norm and eccesiastical ritual. The husband is a lover of mother and a possible begetter of children, but there is no father figure evident in the cultural pattern. "A drinker husband is not a problem; the problem is a wicked son. The marriage is above all the children," is the attitude typical of a wife in this pattern (Hurtado 1998).

Venezualan society is matrifocal. Mothers and grandmothers are emphasized as the stable figures and decision-makers in the family. NEIL RABINOWITZ/CORBIS

The Venezuelan family consists of a group of women and children. It is a family without conjugality, where women only need men to procreate. The mother is worshipped at the expense of the father. Within this excessive motherhood, fatherhood and conjugal relations occur only in ritual forms and fantasy. The mother-child relationship with its overprotecting nucleus is the paradigm.

To be a mother defines the paradigmatic relationship. Scholarly studies (Vethencourt 1974, 1995; Rísquez 1982; Moreno 1993, 1994; López 1980, 1993; Hurtado 1998, 1999), looking at sociological facts as well as symbol, characterize the mother figure according to a fundamental threefold shape, or three archetypal models: a mother is a begetter, a virgin, and a martyr. Data for these studies are obtained not by statistical methods but rather by qualitative methods—for example, large interviews, life stories, biographies, and fieldwork. Each part of this threefold shape is explained as follows:

(1) The belief that *a woman is a mother because she gives birth* involves a cultural destiny that constitutes the begetter archetype. If the woman begets, she becomes respectable; otherwise the culture qualifies her as an *embittered* person. Motherhood is always emphasized. Pregnancy is welcomed with joy and celebrated by rubbing the future mother's belly. Ideally, a male child is expected for it reaffirms motherhood, even though a baby girl is desired. Part of this archetype of motherhood is a long period of breastfeeding. Samuel Hurtado (1998) has found that breastfeeding continues for one to two years (24 women), as long as the child wanted it (14 women), or until another baby is born (3 women). Any pediatric advice against this long period of breastfeeding is ignored under the intervention of the mother's mother (Torres 1996);

(2) The virgin mother defines the second archetype. The grandmother is the virgin mother raising children she has not borne. The grandmother wants and seeks more for her grandchildren than for her own children. The mother-son structural axis continues in the grandmother-grandchild relationship. The grandmother develops a feeling of ownership over her grandchildren that are stronger than her daughter's. A mother that never becomes a grandmother does not fully and happily realize her motherhood. This is similar to the phenomenon of the woman who shows more devotion to an adopted child than to her biological offspring. This symbolic transformation is inherent in every woman because Venezuelan culture makes her a mother from the time of her conception. In this manner, girls and young ladies feel their fathers and baby brothers are their children;

(3) From indulgence and abandonment emerges the third archetype: the martyr mother. Women radically despise men. The mother suffers because she has to let her son as a male leave her home. Husbands are almost an unnecessary burden. In the reciprocal husband-wife system, he is only a provider, whom society calls *family father*. If he abandons his wife but gives money to his children, he is not considered irresponsible. The passage to manhood is very hard, as it means that the young male will be removed from his mother's concern. A mother expects that her son will leave the home in search of amusement with other women, and yet never forgives him for being born male. The marital process has a similar logic. *Separation* means that a woman expels the man from the house. The woman, the symbol and reality of the home and in whose womb the families originate, remains with the house and everything inside, including children. The man departs in solitude without taking by any belongings.

Separation is not necessarily preceded by the interference of another woman. In spite of what they might say, Venezuelan women accept that the man has another woman. The explanation that is commonly offered is that another woman stood in their way—his mother, even though this may not be true.

Living Together

According to the cultural pattern, the world is divided into two halves: the feminine side, valued as good, and the masculine side, valued as evil. The woman is identified with the house, and the housewife is the *good woman*. The man is identified with the street, symbolically a no man's land. According to this pattern, if a man spends too much time at home he will become effeminate. His obligation is to play the *macho* with other women, who symbolically turn into *mean women* because they are exposed to the masculine libido. From this male-female pattern, three masculine types emerge (Hurtado 1998): the *man* who respects his home but has sex with other women on occasional basis; the *crook* who fails to respect his home because his sexual affairs with other women have been discovered; and the *marico* (effeminate) who is afraid of troubles with women and confines himself to his mother's house.

Living together in Venezuela does not coincide with concubinage or cohabitation without legitimacy. Civil marriage is the form with the highest degree of legitimacy and respectability, and reaches its apotheosis when blessed by the ecclesiastical rite. Here the woman is the traditional real bride in a wedding gown. This ideal form of the ecclesiastical marriage, or *main marriage,* is considered the "first" one by most people. Other forms of living together, however, are seen as legitimate, normal and respectable, even though they differ in degree. The second and successive women (those not married to the man, living in other households with their children), together with their respective families, are consubstantial with the multiple marital configurations, although from the legal point of view they may be linked to hidden concubinage, adultery, or other punishable cohabitation forms (Briceño 1994; Salazar 1985; Hurtado 1998).

The successive marriages show a general tendency to polygyny in men, and to polyandry in women, as characteristics of machismo (Vethencourt 1974). In spite of civil and eccesiastical codes and religious ritual, many people do not marry, but join in real significance. *Machismo* is not explained in its counterpart, *hembrismo,* but in maternalism and the mother-macho relationship. Both machismo and hembrismo originated in the mother-child dynamics. Machismo and patriarchy are not synonymous. According to the cultural system there is matriarchal machismo as well as patriarchal machismo.

Conclusion

There are the concepts of matricentrism, matrifocality, and matrisociality that purport to explain family relations in Venezuela, but social scientists are challenged in conceptualizing the Venezuelan family. Knowledge of the family is found in cultural behavior, which centers on social relations. Scholars point to the mother as the key figure. The mother figure as an archetype has implications for other family figures as father and children, and for conjugal relations. The apotheosis of this ideal motherhood is the grandmother figure, the family's primary decision maker. While the mother/grandmother is the center of the family, living together outside of marriage is common and is seen as legitimate and respectable.

See also: HISPANIC-AMERICAN FAMILIES; LATIN AMERICA

Bibliography

Almécija, J. (1992). *La familia en la provincia de Venezuela.* Madrid, MAPFRE.

Briceño, J. M. (1994). *El Laberinto de los tres minotauros.* Caracas: Monte Avila Editores Latinoamericana.

Davis, K. (1942). "Changing Modes of Marriage." In *Marriage and Family,* ed. Becker and Hill. Boston: Heath.

Hurtado, S. (1993). *Gerencias Campesinas en Venezuela.* Caracas: Consejo de Desarrollo Científico y Humanístico de la Universidad Central de Venezuela.

Hurtado, S. (1995). *Trabajo femenino, fecundidad y familia popular urbana.* Caracas: Consejo de Desarrollo Científico y Humanístico de la Universidad Central de Venezuela.

Hurtado, S. (1998). *Matrisocialidad: exploración en la estructura psicodinámica básica de la familia Venezolana.* Caracas: Coediciones de la Facultad de Ciencias Económicas y Sociales y de La Biblioteca Central de la Universidad Central de Venezuela.

Hurtado, S. (1999). *La sociedad tomada por la familia.* Ediciones de La Biblioteca Central de la Universidad Central de Venezuela.

Lévi-Strauss, C. (1975). "La Familia." In *Hombre, cultura y sociedad,* ed. H. L. Shapiro. México: Fondo de Cultura Económica. OT: *Man, Culture and Society.* London: Oxford University Press, 1956.

López, R. (1980). "The Matrifocal Family: A Critical Review of Scholarly Social Science." Master's thesis, University of Chicago.

López, R. (1993). *Parentesco, etnia y clase social en la sociedad Venezolana.* Caracas: Consejo de Desarrollo Científico y Humanístico de la Universidad Central de Venezuela.

Marie, A. (1972). "Parenté, Echange Matrimonial et Réciprocité" *L'HOMME,* XII, 3:5–46, 4:5–36.

Marks, A. F. and Römer, R. A., eds. (1975). *Family and Kinship in Middle America and the Caribbean.* Curaçao, Netherlands Antilles: Institute of Higher Studies; and Leiden, The Netherlands: Royal Institute of Linguistics and Anthropology.

Martín, G. (1990). *Homo-Lógicas,* ed. de la Facultad de Ciencias Económicas y Sociales de la Universidad Central de Venezuela, Caracas.

Moreno, A. (1993). *El aro y la trama. Episteme, modernidad y pueblo.* Caracas: Coediciones del Centro de Investigaciones Populares y la Universidad de Carabobo.

Moreno, A. (1994). *Padre y madre?* Caracas: Centro de Investigaciones Populares.

Peattie, L. R. (1968). *The View from the Barrio.* Ann Arbor: The University of Michigan Press.

Poewe, K. (1981). *Matrilineal Ideology*. Toronto: Academic Press.

Pollak-Eltz, A. (1975). "The Black Family in Venezuela." In *Family and Marriage in Middle America and the Caribbean,* ed A. F. Marks and and R. A. Römer. Curaçao, Netherlands Antilles: Institute of Higher Studies; and Leiden, The Netherlands: Royal Institute of Linguistics and Anthropology.

Richards, A. I. (1982). "Algunos tipos de estructura familiar entre los bantúes centrales." In *Sistemas africanos de parentesco y matrimonio,* ed. A. R. Radcliffe-Brown and C. D. Forde. Barcelona: Anagrama.

Rísquez, F. (1982). *Conceptos de psicodinamia*. Caracas: Monte Avila.

Salazar, M. (1985). *Geografía Erótica de Venezuela*. Caracas: Interarte.

Smith, R., ed. (1984). *Ideology and Kinship*. Berkeley: University of California Press.

Stycos, J. M. (1958). *Familia y Fecundidad en Puerto Rico*. México: Fondo de Cultura Económica.

Torres, M. (1996). "El complejo del destete y la aglactación." Ph.D. thesis, Universidad Central de Venezuela, Caracas.

Vethencourt, J. L. (1974). "La estructura familiar atípica y el fracaso histórico cultural en Venezuela." *Revista SIC* (February):67–69.

Vethencourt, J. L. (1995). "La Madre absorbente en Venezuela." *Heterotopía* 1(Sept.–Dec.):93–101.

SAMUEL HURTADO SALAZAR

VIETNAM

In both ancient and modern Vietnam, the family is considered the foundation of society. Grounded in Confucianism, the traditional patriarchal family was viewed as the basic social institution in which the welfare of the extended family outweighed the individual interests of any member. For Ho Chi Minh, the nation's revolutionary hero, the security of the state was rooted in the stability of the family. "It is correct to pay great attention to the family, because many families added together make up a society" (Himmelstrand 1981, p. 23). Ho's views were also clearly implanted in the constitution of the young Vietnamese republic in 1946. "The family is the cell of society. The State protects marriage and the family," reads Article 64 (Constitution of the Republic of Vietnam 1946, p. 26). Thirteen years later, the National Assembly adopted the first major piece of legislation related to marriage and families. It marked the beginning of four major reforms, discussed below.

Gender Equity and the Marriage and Family Law of 1959

The Marriage and Family Law of 1959 was, in many respects, recognition that women, as well as men, played a major role in defeating the French colonialists in 1954. In placing greater emphasis on gender equity, the 1959 Act contained four major provisions. First, for the first time in Vietnamese history, arranged marriages were abolished, and both men and women were granted the freedom to make their own decisions. Second, polygamy was declared illegal, and monogamy was adopted as the official form of Vietnamese marriage. Third, equality between men and women was to be practiced both in the home and in society in general. Fourth, the basic rights of women and children, such as freedom from abuse and oppression in the home, were to be protected.

Of the four provisions, however, the first two proved most successful. That is, by 1962 the proportion of arranged marriages fell in North Vietnam from more than 60 percent to less than 20 percent of all marriages. Today, the rate is near zero. A similar pattern emerged regarding polygamy. Except in a few rural areas where it may be difficult to apply the law, it is virtually nonexistent (Goodkind 1995).

The most difficult provisions to implement, however, were the latter two (Thanh-Dam Truong 1996). Both gender equity and the protection of children within families proved ongoing challenges for Vietnamese policy makers.

Although the Marriage and Family Law of 1959 focused primarily on the issue of gender equity, there was no mention of age requirements for marriage, nor was there any discussion of policies regarding cohabitation, rights and obligations of married partners, parental responsibilities, or divorce procedures. But new social forces were afoot over the next twenty-seven years that helped shape an entirely new set of marriage and family laws. By

A pair of Vietnamese women from different generations share a meal. Revisions to marriage and family law in 2000 addressed the importance of extended families by clarifying laws regarding relations with grandparents, nieces, nephews, and other family members. JOHN R. JONES/CORBIS

1986 the Vietnamese population was young, growing, and reproducing rapidly. Industrialization was pulling younger villagers toward cities and away from their extended families. Concerns over rising divorce rates in other developing Asian countries, and demands among teenagers for greater independence, drove Vietnamese policy makers toward major reforms of marriage laws in the mid-1980s.

The 1986 Law on Marriage, Parental Responsibility, and Divorce

The National Assembly passed the second major piece of legislation regarding marriage on December 29, 1986. The 1986 Law on Marriage and the Family, consisting of ten chapters and fifty-seven articles, is far more detailed than the 1959 law it replaced. Chapters I through III stipulate who may or may not marry, what are the specific obligations of married partners, and what rights and responsibilities they may have as a married couple. Men cannot marry until age twenty; women cannot marry until age eighteen. Cohabitation is illegal. Vietnamese from different ethnic or religious groups are permitted to intermarry, and those who are mentally ill, have a venereal disease, or are blood relatives, are prohibited from doing so.

With respect to obligations, married couples are required to abide by Vietnam's two-child family policy ("Husband and wife shall have the obligation to implement family planning") to raise their children in a wholesome manner ("a duty to make their children useful to society"), and to not ill treat spouses, children, or parents (The 1986 Law on Marriage and the Family, Chapter I, Articles 2 and 4).

A more interesting component of the 1986 code is found in Chapter IV, Article 27, which identifies intergenerational responsibilities within families. "Grandparents shall be bound to support and educate under-age grandchildren if they become orphans" (The 1986 Law on Marriage and the Family, Chapter IV, Article 27). Similarly, adult grandchildren have a duty to support their grandparents if the latter have no surviving children. Primarily because of decades of war, concern for orphans and isolated elderly runs deep in Vietnamese society.

Perhaps in anticipation of a problem in the future, the 1986 Law on Marriage and the Family includes a fairly lengthy chapter on divorce law. No-fault divorce is not possible; couples must document efforts to reconcile their differences and, to protect pregnant women, husbands cannot file for divorce until one year after the birth of the child. With respect to custody issues, Vietnamese law fluctuates between the "best interest of the child" on one hand and "the tender years' doctrine" on the other. Much depends on the age of the child. That is, nursing infants are consigned to the care of their mothers (the tender years' doctrine). The fate of older children is determined by the best interests of the child test.

The 1986 Law on Marriage and the Family was a direct response to, and coincided with, the major economic reforms that were converting the nation from state-sponsored socialism to free-market capitalism. To keep pace with major economic and social changes, specific laws were passed to clarify the obligations and responsibilities of married partners, identify specific responsibilities of parenthood, and reform existing divorce laws. What remained an unknown, however, was the extent to which these marriage reforms had an impact on Vietnamese families. This concern produced the 1994 Decree on Marriage and the Family.

Concern over Outside Influences: The 1994 Decree

The Vietnamese Ministry of Justice issued a special decree in 1994 that had two primary objectives: One, to clarify those sections of the existing codes that were confusing, and two, to focus on any potentially harmful influence foreigners may have on Vietnam's families. The latter point is not surprising in light of the recent growth in international trade and the corresponding increase in foreign visitors. The decree, issued on September 30, 1994, consists of seven chapters and forty-one articles.

Chapters I through III of the Decree pertain primarily to the regulation of marriage, with specific regulations concerning marriages between Vietnamese and foreigners. In short, any marriage on Vietnamese soil falls under Vietnam's marriage codes. Marriages performed outside the country must be approved by the Chairman of Vietnam's provincial People's Committee if one or both parties wish to reside in the country.

Perhaps even more indicative of Vietnam's concern about foreign influences is the government's effort to control foreigners' access to the nation's children. In 1992 the Council of Ministers issued temporary regulations on the adoption of Vietnamese children by foreigners, limiting such adoptions to Vietnamese children who are orphaned, abandoned, disabled, and are being institutionally cared for by government authorities (Council of Ministers 1992). Just two years later these temporary regulations were made permanent and expanded to include rules that restricted the teaching or tutorship of Vietnamese children by foreigners (The 1994 Decree on Marriage and the Family). In short, by actions set forth in the 1994 Decree, foreigners will be restricted by law in their attempt to either adopt or tutor Vietnamese children.

The 1994 Decree on Marriage and the Family clearly illustrates Vietnam's concern about the potential negative impact of outside influences on its families. On one hand, policy makers have pushed hard to modernize, and thus become more competitive in global markets. On the other hand, they are concerned that the traditional Vietnamese family, what Ho Chi Minh referred to as the "cell of society," will become endangered. According to this argument, a weak family structure will produce a weak nation. Thus, it is not surprising that Vietnam, in looking toward the future, is constantly evaluating its status with respect to family policy and putting in place new laws designed to protect families and stabilize society. It was within that context that additional revisions of national marriage and family laws were adopted in 2000.

The Revised Marriage and Family Law of 2000

On June 9, 2000, the Vietnamese National Assembly adopted the Marriage and Family Law of 2000. Consisting of thirteen chapters and 110 articles, the law revised the marriage and family code of 1986. Striving to preserve traditional values within progressive reforms, the new law recognized that a woman could have a child without a husband, forbade marriage between a foreigner and Vietnamese for mercenary reasons, and declared wife-beating and child abuse illegal. Prior to 2000, the law on these categories was either nonexistent or vague.

Article II addressed the emerging phenomenon of cohabitation. Under the 1986 statue, such living arrangements were illegal. However, the 2000 reforms stipulated that although cohabitation between unmarried couples was no longer considered a criminal act, neither would such arrangements be recognized as equal to marriage between a husband and wife. Other provisions of Article II clarify divorce procedures, encourage gender equity within marriage (including treatment of sons and daughters), and emphasize the equal treatment of children born within and out of wedlock.

Other additions to Vietnamese marriage and family law contained in the 2000 reforms recognize the existence and importance of extended families. Article V clarifies relations between grandparents, nieces and nephews, brothers and sisters, and other family members. Chapter VI addresses support obligations, and Chapter IX spells out the responsibilities of guardianship within intergenerational households.

Clearly, Vietnam has displayed a willingness to adapt its family policies to a rapidly changing social landscape. Today, with a population of more than 70 million people, half of whom were born after 1975 when the war with the United States ended, Vietnam serves as a fascinating case study of a developing nation struggling with modernization. After being subjected to centuries of colonial rule, thirty years of civil conflict, two major wars against modern Western powers, and a complicated reunification process that began in the mid-1970s, a major law was passed in 1986 that produced a deliberate shift from state-sponsored socialism to free-market capitalism. Clearly, the nation's families were affected by these developments, and specific marriage and family laws were adopted to reflect these historical influences. It is likely that more reforms will follow.

See also: ASIAN-AMERICAN FAMILIES; CONFUCIANISM; ETHNIC VARIATION/ETHNICITY

Bibliography

Council of Ministers (1992). "Decision of the Council of Ministers on Temporary Regulations on the Adoptions by Foreign People of Vietnamese Children Orphaned, Abandoned, and Disabled Living in Feeding Institutions Managed by the Labor, Invalids, and Social Affairs Authorities." Hanoi: Council of Ministers, Socialist Republic of Vietnam, No. 145-HBDT, April 29, 1999.

Goodkind, D. (1992). "Rising Gender Inequality in Vietnam Since Reunification." *Pacific Affairs* 68(3):342–359.

Himmelstrand, I. (1981). *Women in Vietnam.* Stockholm, Sweden: Swedish International Development Authority's Policy Development and Evaluation Division.

Kaufman, J., and Sen, G. (1993). "Population, Health, and Gender in Vietnam: Social Policies under the Economic Reforms." In *The Challenge of Reform in Indochina,* ed. B. Ljunggren. Harvard Institute for International Development. Cambridge, MA: Harvard University Press.

Thanh-Dam Truong. (1997). "Uncertain Horizons: The Women's Question in Vietnam Revisited." Working paper series no. 212. The Hague: Institute of Social Studies.

Tran Xuan Nhi. (1995). "Vietnam's Families." In *Worldwide State of the Family.* Tashknet, ed. A. Gafurov. Uzbekistan: Institute of Strategic and Interregional Studies.

Turley, W. (1993). "Political Renovation in Vietnam: Renewal and Adaptation." In *The Challenge of Reform in Indochina,* ed. B. Ljunggren. Harvard Institute for International Development. Cambridge, MA: Harvard University Press.

Vietnam Government (1986). *The 1986 Law on Marriage and the Family. Hanoi:* The Socialist Republic of Vietnam.

Vietnam Government (1994) "Decree of the Government Stipulating the Procedure of Marriage, Adoption of Illegitimate Children, Adoption of Children, and tutorship of Children between Vietnamese Citizens and Foreigners." Hanoi: The Socialist Republic of Vietnam, No. 184/CP, November 30, 1194.

Vietnam Government (2000). *The Revised Marriage and Family Law of 2000.* Hanoi: The National Assembly, June 9, 2000.

Wisensale, S. (1999). "Marriage and Family Law in a Changing Vietnam." *Journal of Family Issues* Fall (20):5–16.

Wisensale, S. (2000). "Family Policy in a Changing Vietnam." *Journal of Comparative Family Studies* 31(1):79–92.

Other Resources

Constitution of the Republic of Vietnam (1946). From an Outline of Institutions of the Democratic Republic of

Vietnam, Hanoi, 1974, 26. Available from http://www.cpv.org.vn/vietname_en/.

Vietnam Law Monthly (2002). "The Law on Marriage and Family." Available from http://www.vietnampanorama.com/.

Vietnam Population News. (2000). "Changes in Marriage and Family Concepts in Vietnam." N. 15, April-June 2000. Available from http://www.ncpfp.netnam.vn/tapchi/vietnam

STEVEN K. WISENSALE

VIOLENCE

See CHILD ABUSE: PHYSICAL ABUSE AND NEGLECT; CHILD ABUSE: PSYCHOLOGICAL MALTREATMENT; CHILD ABUSE: SEXUAL ABUSE; ELDER ABUSE; INFANTICIDE; INTERPARENTAL VIOLENCE—EFFECTS ON CHILDREN; RAPE; SPOUSE ABUSE: PREVALENCE; SPOUSE ABUSE: THEORETICAL EXPLANATIONS; WAR/POLITICAL VIOLENCE

WALES

See GREAT BRITAIN

WAR/POLITICAL VIOLENCE

Families are widely recognized as the "most basic institution within any society, because it is within [families] that citizens are born, sheltered, and begin their socialization" (Ambert 2001, p. 4). The importance and centrality of family is accepted across cultures. Families both influence and are influenced by the wider societies in which they exist. Violent societal-level conflicts affect societies at all levels, especially at the most basic: the family.

Definition of Family

Although there is widespread agreement on the importance of families, the definition of the term family remains under debate. Changes in marriage and parenting statistics prompt the need for definitions that are broad enough to recognize diverse family forms while still recognizing that families are unique compared to other social groups. Although various definitions emphasize different ideas, most include several basic components of families. First, families consist of at least two persons who are related and/or committed to each other and who live together in one household at some point in their lifetimes (Ambert 2001; Eshelman 1997; Olson and DeFrain 1997). Second, families perform specific important functions for society. In the 1930s, William Ogburn suggested that a family should perform the following seven functions (Ogburn 1938):

(1) Economic (meeting the basic physical needs of its members);

(2) Protection (physical as well as economic protection for children when young and for parent as elders);

(3) Prestige and status (providing a sense of place and belonging in the broader society);

(4) Education (formal and informal/socialization);

(5) Religion (providing traditions and religious identity);

(6) Recreation (play and fun); and

(7) Affection and reproduction.

More than sixty years later, Anne-Marie Ambert (2001) produced a very similar list of important family functions:

(1) Reproduction;

(2) Provision of basic needs for growth and development;

(3) A sense of personal belonging;

(4) Socialization; and

(5) Love and affection.

These lists, created several decades apart, indicate that expectations of families have remained fairly consistent. However, the extent to which a family fulfills these functions alone or with assistance from society varies across cultures and among individual families.

War/Political Violence

For this discussion about the impact of war and political violence on families, war is defined as violent, intergroup, societal-level conflict. It is "violence that is perpetrated by one set or group of people on another set or group of people who were often [but not always] strangers to each other before the conflict began" (Cairns 1996, p. 10). Other legal definitions of war are used by various government bodies, but those definitions often dismiss many areas of the world in which families are surrounded by political violence (e.g., Northern Ireland). War and political violence can occur between two or more states/nations or between groups (e.g., religious, ethnic) living in the same country or even in the same neighborhood or village.

Interpersonal violence (crimes against individuals, such as domestic violence, child abuse, or individual rapes) is not included in this definition of war. These behaviors often occur in areas of political violence, but the motivation behind such acts during war is a conflict between individuals as members of groups and involves societal-level issues usually related to one group wanting political power over the other.

War has changed over time. Throughout the late twentieth century and the beginning of the twenty-first century, "a new pattern of armed conflict has evolved, taking increasingly heavy tolls on communities and civilian populations" (Wessells 1998, p. 321). In fact, according to a study commissioned by the United Nations regarding the effects of war on children:

> Distinctions between combatants and civilians disappear in battles fought from village to village or from street to street. In recent decades, the proportion of war victims who are civilians has leaped dramatically from 5 percent to over 90 percent. The struggles that claim more civilians than soldiers have been marked by horrific levels of violence and brutality. Any and all tactics are employed, from systematic rape, to scorched-earth tactics that destroy crops and poison wells, to ethnic cleansing and genocide (United Nations 1996, art. 24).

At the beginning of the twenty-first century, many politically motivated violent conflicts were being waged around the globe—for example, the so-called war on terrorism led by the United States, the conflict in the West Bank between Israel and Palestine, the political violence in Indonesia and in the Congo, and the potential for a nuclear conflict between India and Pakistan, to name a few. Families in all of these conflicts are affected by the violence around them.

Impact of War/Political Violence on Families

The definition of family provided earlier will be used to examine the impact of war and political violence on families. How do violent, intergroup conflicts affect families' abilities to uphold family structure and perform the functions expected of them?

Related/committed persons who live together. Family members' shared lives are often disrupted by war, and members are often separated. Death is the most obvious and permanent form of separation. As established above, in the decade preceding 1996, civilians represented 90 percent of the casualties of war. The result was an overwhelming number of people in war zones who were separated by death from family members.

Families may be forced to live apart for other reasons. A family member or multiple family members may be involved as soldiers in combat. This could include voluntary or forced fighting and may affect families surrounded by the conflict (e.g., the Israeli-Palestinian conflict) or those far from the war (e.g., United States's military forces deployed in the Middle East).

Family members may be separated in refugee situations. The "unbridled attacks on civilians and rural communities have provoked mass exoduses and the displacement of entire populations who flee conflict in search of elusive sanctuaries within and outside their national borders. Among these uprooted millions, it is estimated that 80 percent are children and women" (United Nations, 1996, art. 26). In 1996, the United Nations identified more than 27.4 million refugees, and the number is estimated to have grown since then. At least half of these refugees and displaced people were children, and millions of them were separated from their families.

According to the United Nations (1996) report, parents living in areas of political violence can become so concerned for the safety of their children that they send them away from the family's home

Hmong refugees gather at the Ban Napho refugee camp in Thailand, 1996. Thousands of Hmong fled Laos for Thailand in 1975, fearing political persecution after the Vietnam War. A/P WIDE WORLD PHOTOS

to friends or relatives in another country or area. This may seem to be the best solution at the time, but unfortunately, some children are exploited by unscrupulous agencies that make money by illegally placing the children in adoptive homes. Other children experience long-term trauma from the separation itself. Thus, war separates families.

Economic function/provision of basic material needs. The goal of political violence is for one group to gain political power over another, which makes forcing economic hardship on one's opponents is common strategy of war. The idea behind this tactic is to require the opponent to use up all resources and suffer such economic hardship that it eventually will surrender. One common way to accomplish this goal is to use antipersonnel rockets and landmines. They wound many more than they kill, and this (theoretically) requires the opponent to use up resources in medical care and supplies. However, governments involved in political violence often delegate most of their available funds for military use during wars. Therefore, citizens are left on their own to obtain medical help (if it is even available). For individual families, the kinds of injuries inflicted by these weapons can drain them of all their available resources—especially because the weapons are most commonly used in poor countries, neighborhoods, and villages.

War has a more devastating effect on poor families than families with more resources. This may indicate that poor families are more vulnerable and are at risk for severe effects of war; it could also indicate that wealthier families have the resources to get out of harm's way to avoid many negative consequences. War can ruin a society's infrastructure (businesses, schools, utilities, transportation, etc), an effect that leaves many poorer families with an unemployed head of household. Therefore, "not only do the usual problems that [poor families] face not evaporate because of the onset of political violence, but it is likely that there is a cumulative effect with the negative consequences of political violence added to the effect of economic and social disadvantage" (Cairns 1996, p.71). During war situations, families can expend most of their efforts trying (and often failing) to meet the basic needs of their members. Displaced families (either in refugee camps or those staying with friends or relatives within the war zone) face a constant struggle to meet the basic needs of their members in a situation in which there are never enough resources to meet the needs of all.

Protection and safety. Protection and safety are of great concern for families involved in political violence. Trying to keep members safe from injury, exploitation, and death in a war zone can dominate a family's life. It is difficult and highly unlikely that families can provide for the safety of their members during wars. This is an especially salient issue for female-headed families, because women and girls often are targets of sexual exploitation as well as other forms of violence.

Sense of belonging/status/identity. Several researchers have identified a strong sense of belonging to a group with strong ideals (or ideology) as potentially protecting people from the negative effects of war. "As a worldview, ideology figures predominantly in successful coping under conditions of extreme danger" (Garbarino; Kostelny; and Dubrow 1991, p. 23). It provides what they view as a reason for the suffering and constant danger families endure. This has been highlighted in two areas of political violence with religious influences—Northern Ireland (McWhirter 1990) and the Gaza Strip (Punamaki 1988). However, James Garbarino and his colleagues also recognize that ideology can become so embedded that it may make it difficult to end the conflict.

Some family members, especially children who are separated from their families, are at risk of being stripped of their familial, cultural, religious, and national identity altogether (United Nations 1996). War victims also may face confusion and mixed feeling about their identities.

Education and socialization. Because schools are part of the infrastructure, they often are closed or destroyed in war zones. Therefore, families are expected to meet the educational needs of their members. However, other basic survival needs tend to dominate the time and energy of the adults. This leaves little time for extras such as education.

Socialization, or helping children learn appropriate behavior for the culture, may overemphasize issues related to the conflict during a war. Several authors have questioned whether children in war zones have a less developed moral sense compared to children who do not grow up surrounded by political violence (e.g., Garbarino; Kostelny; and Dubrow 1991; Punamaki 1987). "In such societies, children cannot be successfully socialized . . . in a period when the behaviour of their whole society is based on . . . the denial of basic human values" (Punamaki 1987, p. 33).

Recreation/play. Children need to play to reach their optimum development. Children learn through play. The danger and destruction that occur during war and political violence greatly deter or even prohibit children's play opportunities. Adults also need to participate in recreational activities to maintain good health. However, when basic needs and safety concerns dominate, recreational needs often are not met. The high levels of stress experienced by both children and adults in war zones also inhibit a family's ability to provide an atmosphere of playfulness and fun. These terms imply being carefree—a virtually impossible outcome of living in an area wrought with political violence.

Affection and procreation. All people need love and affection. This becomes particularly important in a war zone where they may feel especially insecure. Family members can be very important buffers to political violence by providing needed love and affection. However, once again, when adults and children are experiencing extreme levels of stress and are struggling to meet the basic needs of others, they may find it hard to express love and affection. In fact, Bryce and colleagues (1989) found that parents experiencing political violence became more restrictive and punitive with their children than when not experiencing war-related stress. The parents reported feeling overwhelmed with the responsibilities of taking care of their children in such extreme conditions. This led them to be less patient and to use physical punishment more than they had previously, during times of peace.

Conclusion

Families are the building blocks of societies. They perform important functions in providing and nurturing a culture's citizens. It is evident that families in war zones experience a great deal of stress. This inhibits their ability to meet the expectations of families as outlined by the definition of "family." War and political violence have a devastating effect on the family.

See also: AFGHANISTAN; DEATH AND DYING; GLOBAL CITIZENSHIP; IRELAND; ISRAEL; MIGRATION; POSTTRAUMATIC STRESS DISORDER (PTSD); POVERTY; RAPE; STRESS

Bibliography

Ambert, A. (2001). *Families in the New Millennium.* Boston: Allyn and Bacon.

Bryce, J.; Walker, N.; Ghorayeb, F.; and Kanj, M. (1989). "Life Experiences, Response Styles and Mental Health Among Mothers and Children in Beirut, Lebanon." *Social Science and Medicine* 28:685–695.

Cairns, E. (1996). *Children and Political Violence.* Cambridge, MA: Blackwell Publishers.

Eshleman, J. R. (1997). *The Family,* 8th edition. Boston: Allyn and Bacon.

Garbarino, J.; Kostelny, K.; and Dubrow, N. (1991). *No Place To Be a Child: Growing Up in a War Zone.* Lexington, MA: D. C. Heath.

Ogburn, W. (1938). "The Changing Family," in *The Family,* ed. J. R. Eshleman. Boston: Allyn and Bacon.

Olson, D. H., and DeFrain, J. (1997). *Marriage and The Family: Diversity and Strengths,* 2nd edition. Mountainview, CA: Mayfield.

Punamaki, R. (1987). *Childhood Under Conflict: The Attitudes and Emotional Life of Israeli and Palestinian Children.* Tampere: Tampere Research Institute, Research Reports.

United Nations. (1996). *Impact of Armed Conflict on Children.* New York: Author. [Document A/51.306 and Add.1].

Wessells, M. G. (1998). "The Changing Nature of Armed Conflict and Its Implications for Children: The Graca Machel/UN Study." *Peace and Conflict: Journal of Peace Psychology* 4:321–334.

KAREN S. MYERS-BOWMAN

WEDDING RING

Look, how my ring encompasseth thy finger,
Even so thy breast encloseth my poor heart;
Wear both of them, for both of them are thine.
Richard III *(William Shakespeare 1593)*

The ring could be the oldest and most universal symbol of marriage. There are many accounts of the meanings behind the use of wedding rings but the actual origins are unclear. The ring's circular shape represents perfection and never-ending love, and in the seventeenth century social pressure led to the preference of gold as the material because it does not tarnish (Ingoldsby and Smith 1995).

The ring gains even greater symbolism with the inclusion of a precious stone. The clarity and durability of the diamond make it the most popular stone, as does the idea that it represents innocence in the bride. It was a common saying that the diamond was forged in the flames of love. However, other stones have been assigned special meaning as well (Tobler 1984). The emerald guarantees domestic bliss and success in love. The ruby is a sign of love and a favorite for engagement rings. Its red color was widely believed to be a protection from evil spirits and nightmares. The amethyst was believed by the ancient Greeks and Romans to ensure a husband's love and was worn as a symbol of faithfulness. The sapphire represents truth and faithfulness and is said to bring good health and fortune. The garnet stands for true friendship. If you want someone to love you, then you should give them a garnet. Finally, the aquamarine was believed to make the ring wearer more intelligent and courageous, but more importantly it also gave the person the ability to read another's thoughts (something that might not be beneficial to a marriage)!

Some ancient people used to break a coin, with each partner taking one half. Modern jewelry still represents this idea of matching. We know that the ancient Egyptians, Greeks, and Romans all used wedding rings. Since most people are right handed the left hand was considered inferior. Therefore brides would wear their ring on the left hand as a symbol of her submissiveness to her husband. Men would wear their ring on the right hand to represent their dominance in the relationship. Today the ring is typically worn on the fourth finger of the left hand (the ring finger). No doubt this is because it is less likely to get in the way of other activities there. However, it was believed by some ancient peoples such as the Egyptians that there was an artery that went directly from that finger to the heart. This love vein, or *venis amoris,* made the fourth finger the proper place to wear the pledge of love (Chesser 1980).

Duncan Emrich (1970) has collected many of the folk beliefs concerning the wedding ring. One is that once the ring has been placed on your finger it should never be taken off until death, or at least until you have been married for one (or seven) year(s). The circle of the ring stands for the endless love of the couple, and the following couplet indicates how marriage is good for one's mental health: "As the wedding ring wears, So wear away life's cares."

The early Christian church gave religious meaning to the ring by making it part of the wedding ceremony. "With this ring I thee wed, and this gold and silver I thee give, and with my body I thee worship, and with all my worldly chatels I thee endow." The thumb and first two fingers of the hand were to represent the Father, Son, and Holy Spirit, and the fourth finger stood for the earthly love of man to woman.

In ancient times rings or other tokens were used as a pledge in any important agreement, and so it was with marriage as well. In Ireland a man would give his beloved a bracelet of woven human hair. Her acceptance indicated that she was linking herself to him for life. Marriage rings have been made with a great variety of materials, depending on what the people could afford, including leather, wood, and iron. But gold has generally been preferred because of its purity (Fielding 1942).

See also: MARRIAGE CEREMONIES

Bibliography

Chesser, B. (1980). "Analysis of Wedding Rituals: An Attempt to Make Weddings More Meaningful." *Family Relations* (April):204–209.

Emrich, D. (1970). *The Folklore of Weddings and Marriage.* New York: American Heritage Press.

Fielding, W. (1942). *Strange Customs of Courtship and Marriage.* New York: New Home Library.

Ingoldsby, B., and Smith, S. (1995). *Families in Multicultural Perspective.* New York: Guilford Publishing.

Tobler, B. (1984). *The Bride.* New York: Harry N. Abrams.

Other Resource

Effective Promotions Inc. "The Wedding Book." Available from http://www.wedding-book.com.

BRON B. INGOLDSBY

WIDOWHOOD

Losing one's mate is among the most stressful of all life events. It presents painful adaptational challenges to spouses and families. The loss dramatically marks the transition to *widowhood* and impacts an increasing proportion of the diverse aging population. Worldwide evidence shows a broad range of responses to widowhood. Cross-cultural variations among marital survivors reflect the changing cultural values of particular societies (Lopata 1996). For example, in the past Hindu widows were treated harshly in the highly patriarchal society of India. Loss of a husband meant a loss of status, economic dependency, and social isolation. Remarriage was not encouraged. Although still far from receiving equitable treatment in comparison to widowers, widows' situation has gradually improved over time. In Israel, which is also a strongly religious and patriarchal society, war widows are given greater recognition and preferential benefits in comparison with their civilian counterparts. Remarriage is not discouraged, as it was in India. In an earlier agriculturally based Korean society, becoming a widow resulted in lower status and a general prohibition against remarriage. Under the influences of growing modernization, including urbanization and industrialization, the cultural status of widows improved, especially for those who moved to the cities.

Widows in parts of the world undergoing modernization also find such conditions allow them a more flexible role compared to the past. It is difficult, however, to make international comparisons on this topic. Date gathered by the United Nations Statistics Division during the 1990s show considerable variation in the widowed population both within and between countries and regions of the world. For example, in Egypt three-fifths of those women sixty years of age and over are widows, compared to slightly more than two-fifths in Ethiopia. Moreover, the available rates are not systematically calculated in terms of age categories and time periods. Thus, for some countries, the percentage are based upon the widowed fifty-five years of age and over, whereas in other countries the base is fifty years of age or over.

Demography of the Widowed

There are more than 13.7 million widowed persons in the United States, over 11 million of these being women. (American Association of Retired Persons 2001) Female survivors have been outdistancing their male counterparts by a continually widening margin and now represent approximately 80 percent of the widowed population in the United States. In 1940 there were twice as many widows as widowers; by 1990 the ratio of widows to widowers had climbed to more than 4 to 1. This ratio is expected to widen in the future.

Several factors may explain the imbalanced gender ratio among the widowed. Women experience greater longevity than men. First, because their death rate is lower than men's, larger numbers of women survive into advanced years. Second, wives are generally younger than their husbands, a fact that increases their probability of surviving their spouses even without the differences in longevity. Third, among the widowed, remarriage rates are significantly lower for women than men. Therefore, many men leave widower status by wedding again, whereas many women do not, thereby adding to the surplus of female survivors.

Advances in medical technology, widespread sanitation and health programs, and improved living conditions have extended life expectancy. In the process, the probability of dying prior to midlife has greatly diminished. Consequently, widowhood has, for the most part, been postponed to the later stages of the life cycle. At the beginning of the twentieth century, about one in twenty-five persons was sixty-five years of age or older, as compared to one in nine at the end of the century. The gains in longevity have been more rapid for women than for men; hence, the growing proportion of elderly women in the population highlights the overall rates of widowhood. It has been estimated that about one-fourth of all married women in the United States will be widowed by age sixty-five, and that one-half of the remaining women will have lost their husbands by age seventy-five (Berardo 1992). Because there is little chance that the mortality differences between genders will be reversed anytime soon, the excess of women at the upper ages will continue to increase, and the older population will be comprised of a larger proportion of widows. Aware of these trends, researchers have focused their attention primarily on the conditions surrounding female survivors. Although comparative knowledge about the experiences and needs of males who have lost their spouses remains insufficient there are a few attempts to learn more about their experiences. (Blieszner 1993; Zick and Smith 1991; Lee et al. 2001)

Siham Thabet, a widow, sitting under portraits of her husband Thabet Thabet, a Palestinian dentist and political leader who was killed by Israeli forces. LAURENT REBOURS/AP WIDE WORLD PHOTOS

Bereavement and Adaptation

Most people are not prepared for the death of a spouse. Much of the stress of bereavement evolves from the loss of support of the deceased within the family system. The usually painful transition that occurs with the loss of a spouse begins as one assumes the new roles of a new status.

Roles and status positions must be shifted, values and goals reoriented, and personal and family time restructured in households with children who live with a widowed parent. The potential for role strains and interpersonal conflicts becomes evident as relationships are lost, added, or redefined (Pitcher and Larson 1989). Loneliness is a major problem. In the case of older bereaved spouse, in particular, loneliness and difficulties associated with the tasks of daily living are among the most common and trying adjustments encountered (Lund 1989). In many modern societies, this adaptive process typically proceeds with few or no guidelines (or even ambiguous signals) from the culture as to how to act. In this regard, the role of the widowed person tends to be in a "roleless" role, inasmuch as it lacks clearly specified norms or prescriptions for appropriate behavior (Hiltz 1979).

Although survivors face some common problems both within and outside the immediate family, it is difficult to specify a normative course of adjustment. This is partly because widows and widowers are a diverse group characterized by wide differences in social and psychological characteristics. It is also due to the fact that spousal loss evokes a broad spectrum of emotional and behavioral responses from the bereaved, depending on such factors as the nature of the marital relationship and the timing and circumstances under which death occurred. For example, a wife whose husband was killed on the battlefield, in an automobile accident, or in a robbery will respond differently than if he had committed suicide or suffered a long terminal illness. Many other types of such antecedent conditions, such as the quality of the marital relationship or the age of the deceased, affect bereavement reactions and coping strategies of survivors. In U.S. society, for instance, a young wife whose life is suddenly taken is mourned differently from a much older woman, married fifty years, who succumbs after a lengthy illness. As a result of such factors, responses to bereavement often show substantial variation.

Studies of whether anticipatory grief, or forewarning of the pending death of a spouse, contributes to bereavement adjustment have yielded conflicting results (Roach and Kitson 1989). Some suggest that such anticipation is important because it allows the survivor to begin the process of role redefinition prior to the death, whereas unanticipated death produces more severe grief reactions.

Those who experienced unexpected deaths of their marital partners report more somatic problems and longer adjustment periods than those who anticipated the loss. Anticipatory role rehearsal does not, however, consistently produce smoother or more positive adjustment among the bereaved. Again, the effects of such preparation vary with the age of the person, whether death occurs as an on-time versus off-time event, and other factors. In sum, the coping strategies of survivors vary with the timing and mode of death, which in turn influence the bereavement outcome.

In making the transition to widowed status, the bereaved are often confronted with a variety of personal and familial problems. They are not always successful in adapting to these circumstances. This is reflected in the findings that, when compared to married persons, the widowed rather consistently show higher rates of mortality, mental disorders, and suicide (Balkwell 1981). Although it is generally agreed that the bereavement process is stressful, studies of its effect on physical health have not yielded consistent results. The evidence does show that people who have lost their mates generally experience poorer health than those who are still married, but the reasons for this remain unclear.

Bereavement and Developmental Stages

The degree of adjustment encountered by widowed people in the transition to their new status varies by developmental stages. The death of a marital partner in young marriages is relatively uncommon; nevertheless, when it does occur it is apt to make bereavement and the survivor role much more difficult to accommodate than in later life "because of unfulfilled hopes and dreams, the lack of fit with other couples at the same life phase, and the lack of models of the same cohort" undergoing this experience (Walsh and McGoldrick 1991, p. 18). Typically there has been little or no emotional preparation for the shock and isolation of early widowhood. Being suddenly left alone to rear young children, for example, can be extremely trying, and at the same time impedes the progress of personal and familial recovery. The immediate and growing financial and caretaking obligations of single parenthood can interfere with the tasks of mourning (Levinson 1997). Adult friends and relatives can and often do provide assistance with everyday chores, such as cooking and housecleaning. Bereaved husbands, generally speaking, are more apt to receive these kinds of practical supports than bereaved wives. On the other hand, the wives are more likely to have a more extensive range of intimate family and friendship relationships that help to facilitate their emotional grief work.

Older people adapt more readily to widowhood because losing a spouse at advanced ages is more the norm and often anticipated, thus making acceptance of the loss somewhat easier. Research on surviving spouses over age sixty-five revealed that those who were more dependent upon their spouses show higher levels of anxiety than those who were not (Carr et al. 2000). Grief over the death of a husband or wife at older ages can be exacerbated if additional significant others also die requiring multiple or simultaneous grieving. This can cause *bereavement overload,* which makes it difficult for the survivor to complete the grief work and bring closure to the bereavement process. There is general consensus that the distress associated with conjugal bereavement diminishes over time. Grief becomes less intense as years pass, but this is not a simple, linear process. The emotional and psychological traumas of grief and mourning may sporadically reappear long after the spouse has died.

Gender Differences

The issue of gender differences in adaptation to widowhood has long been debated. The evidence does suggest a somewhat greater vulnerability for widowers (Stroebe and Stroebe 1983; Lee et al. 2001). Men are less likely to have same-sex widowed friends, more likely to be older and less healthy, have fewer family and social ties, and experience greater difficulty in becoming proficient in domestic roles (Lee et al. 2001). Higher mortality and suicide rates also suggest somewhat greater distress among widowers. It is important to note, however, that widows and widowers share many similar bereavement experiences and adjustments. There is considerable empirical support for the conclusion that although they do experience some aspects of grief differently, men and women have a good deal in common with respect to loss-related feelings, mental and physical health, and social life (Lund 1989).

Duration of widowhood has been associated with loss of income and increased risk of poverty. The death of husbands results in lower financial status for wives, many of whom become impoverished following bereavement (Hungerford 2001). Two-fifths of widows fall into poverty at some time during the five years following the death of their husbands. Widowers also suffer a decline in economic well-being, albeit to a lesser degree than their female counterparts (Zick and Smith 1991). People often fail to plan for the economic consequences of spousal loss. Elderly persons frequently have below-average incomes prior to the death of their marital partner. Once bereaved, their circumstances may worsen, especially if they have been stay-at-home wives who were highly dependent on their husband's income. They may be unwilling or unable to seek or find employment, and they are likely to face discrimination in the labor market (Morgan 1989; MacDonald 2000). Given their age, they may lack the education or skills required to compete for jobs. The younger widowed are more likely to have lost a spouse suddenly and may thus be unprepared to cope with lowered financial subsistence. Poor adjustment to being widowed, therefore, can often be attributed to socioeconomic deprivation. This is especially apt to be the case among members of disadvantaged racial/ethnic groups, whose recovery may be impeded by discrimination and inequitable social policies that affect their health and financial circumstances (Angel 2001; Berardo 2001; Blieszner 1993).

Regardless of the income level, the widowed person faces financial transitions upon the death of a spouse. These include dealing with: (1) immediate practical concerns that may take one to two weeks; (2) financial and legal concerns that might take one week to several months; and (3) settling tax concerns that may take one to two years. There are many published guidelines and web sites that hold useful tips, pitfalls, and checklists for this process.

Widowhood often leads to changes in living arrangements. Reduced income may force surviving spouses to seek more affordable housing. They may also choose to relocate for other reasons such as future financial and health concerns, a desire to divest of possessions, or to be near kin or friends. Most often, the people living alone are women—usually elderly widows. Isolation and lack of social support can lead to deterioration in physical and mental well-being. Compared to elderly married couples, widows and widowers are much more apt to live in poverty and are less likely to receive medical care when needed (Hungerford 2001).

As mentioned above, the probability for remarriage is significantly less for widows than widowers, especially at older ages. They may feel they are committing psychological bigamy and therefore reject remarriage as an option (DiGiulio 1989). There is also a tendency to idealize the former partner, a process known as *sanctification* (Lopata 1996). This makes it difficult to find a new partner who can compare favorably with the idealized image of the deceased. There are other barriers to remarriages for the widowed. Dependent children may limit the opportunities of their widowed parents to meet potential mates or to develop relationships with them. Older children may oppose remarriage out of concern for their inheritance. Widowed persons who cared for a dependent spouse through a lengthy, terminal illness may be unwilling to risk this burden again. Widowers remarry more frequently than widows (Berardo 1992). This is due to the lack of eligible men and cultural norms that degrade the sexuality of older women and discourage them from selecting younger mates. Many women manage to develop and value a new and independent identity beyond widowhood, leading them to be less interested in reentering the marriage market.

Social Support and Reintegration

Although social support is presumed to play an important role in bereavement outcomes and act as a buffer for stressful life events, the research is inconclusive. Nevertheless, there is evidence that the extent to which members of the social network provide various types of assistance to the bereaved is important to the pattern of recovery and adaptation (Ferraro 2001). Available confidants and access to self-help groups to assist with emotional management can help counter loneliness and promote the survivor's reintegration into society.

Much of the variability in bereavement response can be attributed to intrapersonal resources that make coping easier. For example, it has been found that a sense of optimism and belief that life has meaning is integral to how well the widowed adapted to their bereavement (Caserta and Lund 1993). Some other major factors that strongly influence the degree of difficulty experienced by widowed individuals include *self-confidence* (i.e., the belief that one will be able to manage the situation); a sense of optimism and self-efficacy, derived from having coped with previous life transitions; and strong self-esteem (Parkes 1988).

Widows and widowers show considerable variation in concluding their grief work, some essentially completing the process in months, others sometimes taking years to adapt to life without their mate. A small minority of people never get over the trauma of the loss. With help, however, the majority of the widowed are capable of eventually adapting to their new circumstances, managing their everyday affairs and maintaining a sense of purpose and a life of personal satisfaction.

See also: DEATH AND DYING; ELDERS; FAMILY ROLES; FILIAL RESPONSIBILITY; GRIEF, LOSS AND BEREAVEMENT; HEALTH AND FAMILIES; HOUSING; INHERITANCE; IN-LAW RELATIONSHIPS; LATER LIFE FAMILIES; LONELINESS; MARITAL QUALITY; POVERTY; REMARRIAGE; RETIREMENT; SELF-ESTEEM; SINGLE-PARENT FAMILIES; STRESS; SUICIDE

Bibliography

Angel, J. L. (2001). "Challenges of Caring for Hispanic Elders." *Public Policy and Aging Report* 11:11–15.

Balkwell, C. (1981). "Transition to Widowhood: A Review of the Literature." *Family Relations* 30:117–127.

Berardo, D. H. (2001). "Social and Psychological Issues of Aging and Health." In *Therapeutics in the Elderly,* 3rd edition, ed. J. C. Delafuente and R. B. Stewart. Cincinnati, OH: Harvey Whitney Books.

Berardo, F. M. (1992). "Widowhood." In *Encyclopedia of Sociology,* ed. E. F. Borgatta and M. L. Borgatta. New York: Macmillan.

Blieszner, R. (1993). "A Socialist-Feminist Perspective on Widowhood." *Journal of Aging Studies* 7:171–182.

Carr, D.; House, J. S.; Kessler, R. C.; Nesse, R. M.; Sonnega, J.; and Wortman, C. (2000). "Marital Quality and Psychological Adjustment to Widowhood among Older Adults: A Longitudinal Analysis." *Journal of Gerontology: Social Sciences* 44B:S197–S207.

Caserta, M., and Lund, D. A. (1993). "Intrapersonal Resources and the Effectiveness of Self-Help Groups for Bereaved Older Adults." *Gerontologist* 33:616–629.

DiGiulio, R. C. (1989). *Beyond Widowhood.* New York: Free Press.

Ferraro, K. F. (2001). "Aging and Role Transitions." In *Handbook of Aging and Social Sciences,* ed. R. H. Binstock and L. K. George. San Diego, CA: Academic Press.

Hiltz, S. R. (1979). "Widowhood: A Roleless Role." In *Marriage and Family,* ed. M. B. Sussman. New York: Haworth Press.

Hungerford, T. L. (2001). "The Economic Consequences of Widowhood on Elderly Women in the United States and Germany." *Gerontologist* 41:103–110.

Lee, G. R.; DeMaris, A.; Bavin, S.; and Sullivan, R. (2001). "Gender Differences in the Depressive Effect of Widowhood in Later Life." *Journal of Gerontology: Social Sciences* 56B:S56–S61.

Levinson, D. S. (1997). "Young Widowhood: A Life Change Journey." *Journal of Personal and Interpersonal Loss* 2:277–291.

Lopata, H. Z. (1996). *Current Widowhood: Myths and Realities.* Thousand Oaks, CA: Sage Publications.

Lund, D. A. (1989). "Conclusions about Bereavement in Later Life and Implications for Interventions and Future Research." In *Older Bereaved Spouses,* ed. D. A. Lund. New York: Hemisphere.

Morgan, L. (1989). "Economic Well-Being following Martial Termination." *Journal of Family Issues* 10:86–101.

Parkes, C. M. (1988). "Bereavement as a Psychological Transition." *Journal of Social Issues* 44:53–65.

Pitcher, B. L., and Larson, D. C. (1989). "Elderly Widowhood." In *Aging and the Family,* ed. S. J. Bahr and E. T. Peterson. Lexington, MA: D.C. Heath.

Roach, M. J., and Kitson, G. T. (1989). "Impact of Forewarning and Adjustment to Widowhood and Divorce." In *Older Bereaved Spouses,* ed. D. A. Lund. New York: Hemisphere.

Stroebe, M. S., and Stroebe, W. (1983). "Who Suffers More: Sex Differences in Health Risks of the Widowed." *Psychological Bulletin* 93:279–299.

Walsh, F., and McGoldrick, M. (1991). "Loss and the Family: A Systemic Perspective." In *Living Beyond Loss: Death in the Family,* ed. F. Walsh and M. McGoldrick. New York: Norton.

Zick, C. D., and Smith, K. R. (1991). "Patterns of Economic Change Surrounding the Death of a Spouse." *Journal of Gerontology: Social Sciences* 46:5310–5320.

Other Resources

American Association of Retired Persons. (2001). "Coping with Grief and Loss: Statistics about Widowhood." Available from www.aarp.org/griefandloss/stats.html.

MacDonald, J. (2000). "Careful Choices Can Help Brighten the Future after the Sudden Loss of a Spouse." Available from http://www.bankrate.com/brm/news/sav/2000530.asp.

FELIX M. BERARDO
DONNA H. BERARDO

WIFE

A *wife* is a female partner in a marriage. Most cultures recognize this common social status with a specific affinal kinship term. In most times and places, women have been expected to become wives at some point following the commencement of their childbearing years. The stage at which this happens varies greatly, however, as does the social role a wife plays within a family and her legal rights and obligations. Much depends on the typical form of marriage itself, gender role conventions, economic conditions, and religious and political edicts concerning marital roles. Despite such diversity, people often hold very strong opinions on the proper role of wives in marriages. This is notably so at the present time when marital roles have become the subject of often acrimonious debate between cultural and religious conservatives, feminists, social liberals, and sexual minorities pushing for legal recognition of alternative marriage styles (Coontz 1992).

Most women personally experience becoming a wife as a stage in their life cycle. They become familiar with the role and are groomed for it during their childhood by interacting with and observing their own mothers and other female caregivers. Most women living in contemporary Western countries enjoy considerable freedom in choosing when to get married or whether to marry at all. In societies where marriages are arranged between families, women have far less choice. In cultures practicing infant betrothals, a girl may become identified as a *wife* at a very young age and begin a long period of preparation for the full adult role. The common requirement of exchanges of wealth to confirm marital alliances, in the form of bride-wealth or dowry, likewise restricts choices and often dictates when marriage takes place (Fox 1967).

The social role a wife plays is largely determined by the nature of the larger family system. In most cultures, wives assume the greatest responsibility for childcare and food preparation. In precapitalist societies, where extended families tend to predominate, wives generally perform separate but complementary work to their husbands and contribute to the economic pursuits of the household as a whole. In polygynous families, two or more co-wives share these tasks. The advent of the Industrial Revolution in Europe brought with it a great expansion of individualized wage labor and a gendered distinction between paid labor, associated with men, and the now-privatized domestic sphere of the household, associated with women. These same economic changes encouraged a reduction in the typical family size. The ideal of the Victorian family, with the husband as the breadwinner and the wife in charge of the home, was never a possibility for poorer families. It was eroded further during the twentieth century as ever increasing numbers of women entered the work force and feminist activists successfully broke into male-dominated professions and reduced the wage disparities between males and females. Such developments have encouraged yet another view of the family as an equal partnership between wife and husband (Ruether 2000).

When they become wives, women move into a new status defined and constrained by ruling social conventions, religious teachings, and formal legal systems. Marriage provides a key means for conferring legitimacy upon children and thus allowing the orderly inheritance of property and the reproduction of the social order. Wives have tended to hold a higher status in societies where they have ownership over valuable property such as land. Among the matrilineal Dobu of Papua New Guinea, for instance, wives along with their brothers are the owners of clan lands while husbands are somewhat marginal "strangers" in the family system (Fortune 1932). In more patriarchal societies, such as have existed in much of Western as well as Islamic history, wives were seen at best as the junior partners but often as the property of their husbands, expected to obey commands and be punished if they did not. For many scholars, the legal status of wives has provided a key index for gauging the degree of equality women enjoy in a particular time and place (Yalom 2001).

See also: BRIDE-PRICE; DIVISION OF LABOR; DOWRY; FAMILY ROLES; GENDER; HUSBAND; KINSHIP; MATE SELECTION; MOTHERHOOD

Bibliography

Coontz, S. (1992). *The Way We Never Were: American Families and the Nostalgia Trap.* New York: Basic Books.

Fortune, R. F. (1932). *Sorcerers of Dobu*. London: Routledge and Kegan Paul.

Ruether, R. R. (2000). *Christianity and the Making of the Modern Family*. Boston: Beacon Press.

Yalom, M. (2001). *A History of the Wife*. New York: HarperCollins.

JOHN BARKER

WOMEN'S MOVEMENTS

Women's movements are among the most global of modern social movements. From nineteenth-century Canadian women's suffrage campaigns to recent direct actions for sustainable development in India, wherever women's movements have been established, national organizations and local grassroots groups have worked together for the interests of women and girls. Varied, even conflicting, understandings of women's interests arise from differences in gender, race, class, cultural, religion, and sexuality, as well as from global divisions of wealth and power. Nevertheless, the pervasiveness of oppression against women has led to the establishment of international women's movements with common agendas, connected to struggles for autonomy, democracy, and secure livelihoods around the world.

Women's rights demonstrators in Cuzco, Paucartambo, Peru. JEREMY HORNER/CORBIS

The goals and structures of women's movements reflect the commonalities as well as the differences among women. For example, *feminist movements* tend to be associated with the aspirations, and the opportunities, of middle-class women. Feminist movements include *women's rights movements* focusing on the goals of equal rights under the law and equal access to education, careers, and political power; *women's liberation movements* that challenge cultural patterns of male domination in the family and personal life through strategies that raise the consciousness of women of their own oppression, often within the context of women-only groups; *Black feminist movements* that address racism along with sexism; and *socialist feminist movements* that see women's empowerment as tied to the role of government, labor, and civil society in securing the entitlements of all citizens to equity and social security. The activists in *feminine movements* tend to be working-class women organizing to address problems of poverty and sexism and their devastating effects on the health and welfare of their families. *Womanist,* a term coined by the writer Alice Walker, refers to the confidence, strength, and wisdom of African-American women based in their cultures and long struggle to support their children and communities and to end racism and all forms of injustice.

Feminist and Feminine Movements in Brazil

Between 1964 and 1985, Brazil experienced repressive regimes and massive impoverishment along with the largest, most diverse, radical, and successful women's movement in Latin America (Alvarez 1990). Its success lay, in part, in addressing both strategic and practical gender interests. *Strategic gender interests,* such as overturning the gender division of labor, gaining control over one's own reproduction, and attaining legal and political equality, have emerged from various analyses of the roots of women's oppression. Health care, nutrition and shelter, potable water, and secure livelihoods, vital to the more immediate survival of women and their families, typify the *practical gender interests* that women would hesitate to sacrifice for more long-term strategic gender interests (Molyneux 1985). In Brazil, and Latin America generally, strategic gender interests inspire *feminist movements,* whereas *feminine movements* focus on practical gender interests (Alvarez 1990).

Mothers' Clubs, feminine movement organizations, called for childcare, health care, and affordable food and housing, and also for city services for their poor, mostly urban, neighborhoods. Middle-class, university-educated young women, including members of the militant opposition to the military government, and older professional women organized feminist movements around issues of economic discrimination against women workers, focusing their analyses on poor and working-class women.

As feminine and feminist movement organizations became increasingly militant, they created umbrella organizations for allied campaigns (e.g., the daycare movement). Feminine groups took up such issues as reproductive rights, domestic violence, sexuality, and family relations, first raised publicly by feminist groups. Both protested the crime-of-passion defense of men who had murdered their allegedly unfaithful wives.

The end of the authoritarian period in 1985 marked the beginning of antifeminist campaigns, such as opposition to women's reproductive rights and family planning. Nevertheless, women's movements continued to develop new forms, including organizations serving women's health, education, and legal needs; art and media groups; women's studies programs; women's labor union associations; and *popular feminism,* organized by poor and working-class women, to combine work on class and gender. Most recently, black women's organizations are challenging the interlocking oppressions of race, class, and gender oppressions. Many of these organizations participated in the first Black Women's Conference, held in Brazil in 1988 (Alvarez 1990).

Civil Rights and Women's Movements in the United States

The definition of women's interests in terms of individual rights is one that informs *liberal feminism* around the world and represents the mainstream of the U.S. *women's rights movements.* Set forth by white, propertied men to promote their interests, the rights discourse was adopted by the women's rights movement, as well as by the civil rights movement, the gay and lesbian rights movement, and most recently, the disability rights movement. The common language and philosophy of rights have facilitated cooperation and mutual progress among the various rights movements. Other groups, however, have criticized the women's rights movements because they were willing to reform the existing system rather than pushing to uproot the structures of inequality in the family and society.

The official beginning of women's rights movements is marked by the 1848 Seneca Falls women's convention and its resolutions calling for women's rights to legal adult status, access to all professions, and women's suffrage (the right to vote). Of the delegates, renowned black abolitionist Frederick Douglass and Elizabeth Cady Stanton, middle-class, white, feminist foremother, argued most strongly that women needed the right to vote in order to attain their other rights. The ideals of the women's suffrage movement drew on the liberal notion of the rights of the individual. In the 1970s, this same ideal was the foundation of a renewed, but unsuccessful, campaign for an Equal Rights Amendment (ERA) to the U. S. Constitution.

Through the *first wave* of the women's rights movement, which ended when women gained the right to vote in 1920, through the *second wave* of the *new women's movement,* which began in the 1960s, and the contemporary *third wave,* women's movements in the United States have been linked to the struggles for civil rights for African Americans. The 1964 Civil Rights Act, which prohibited sex discrimination (Giddings 1984), was particularly important. On the other hand, white women's rights activists have sometimes used overtly racist arguments to support their cause and failed to recognize how their conceptions of women's interests have been shaped by white, middle-class, and heterosexual privilege. For example, at the last meeting of the American Equal Rights Association in 1869, Elizabeth Cady Stanton and Susan B. Anthony proposed a resolution opposing the fifteenth amendment to the U.S. Constitution, which granted voting rights to Black men. This resolution and Stanton's subsequent appeals to racialist rhetoric have been interpreted as "constructing a hierarchy of rights, with those of white women on top" (Caraway 1991, p. 145).

Although the young, middle-class women of the *women's liberation movement* in the 1960s and 1970s, most of whom were white, did attend to racism as an issue, their small *consciousness-raising groups* were primarily directed towards their own personal and political concerns. Like the more mainstream National Organization for Women (NOW), founded in 1966, women's movement organizations in the late 1960s and 1970s tended to be independent of political parties and other women's organizations. Their mistrust of the state as an economic support for women and desire to set their own independent agenda may have contributed to tension between the women's liberation movement and other contemporary social movements. For example, women of color, lesbians, and working-class women organized their own women's movements (Johnson-Odim 1991).

Among these were the *welfare rights movement,* created by poor women for better public support for low-income families, and the Coalition of Labor Union Women, representing women in labor unions. As womanists, black feminists, and Third World feminists, women of color in the United States have developed independent movement organizations as well as multicultural coalitions. The National Black Women's Political Leadership Caucus was established in 1971 and the Organization of Pan Asian American Women in 1976 (Nelson and Carver 1994). The Indigenous Women's Network, the Center for Third World Organizing, and the National Black Women's Health Project represented U.S. women at the U.N. World Conference on Women in 1995 (Dutt 2000).

Nationalism and Women's Movements in Canada

Like most modern states, Canada shapes its national identity in the light of multinationalism. Organizing a pan-Canadian women's movement required bridging linguistic and cultural differences between French-speaking Canada, English-speaking Canada, and First Nations (indigenous nations). Although both the English and French Canadian women's movements have stressed government's role in their strategies, and both have created national umbrella organizations, their constituencies have been shaped by divergent national interests.

In English-speaking Canada, the women's movement began in the late nineteenth century, focusing on suffrage, pregnancy rights, education, and economic independence and divided by philosophies and class constituency. Nellie McClung and other, mostly middle-class, *maternal feminists* organized moral crusades for social reform based upon their roles as mothers of the nation, while *equal rights feminists,* under the leadership of Dr. Emily Howard Stowe and Flora MacDonald Denison, promoted women's equality with men. Working-class women's organizations like the Woman's Labor League of Winnipeg also supported women's suffrage as a means to improve working conditions (Adamson; Briskin; and McPhail 1988).

In Quebec, the women's movement began some thirty years later. Although Canadian women were given the right to vote in federal elections in 1918 and in the English-speaking provincial elections in the 1920s, it was not until 1940 that Quebec enfranchised women (Dumont 1992). Thus, Quebec suffrage leader Thérèse Casgrain was still active when a new women's movement arose. In 1966, she founded the Fédération des femmes du Québec (FFQ), an umbrella organization of Quebec women's groups.

At the same time, pan-Canadian women's rights organizations worked for the creation of the Royal Commission on the Status of Women, which was established in 1967. In 1972, they organized the National Action Committee on the Status of Women (NAC) as an umbrella organization of established women's organizations throughout Canada.

The *women's liberation movement* arose in Canada in the late 1960s with younger activists from other movements for peace, health and safety, native rights, and the new left. Largely independent of political parties, many were organized into small consciousness-raising groups; single-issue regional organizations working for access to abortion, birth control, and daycare; as well as student and socialist-feminist groups. They created alternative grassroots feminist organizations—rape crisis centers, shelters, women's centers, bookstores, counseling services, and feminist cultural and artistic alternatives—and deliberately distinguished themselves from the women's rights movement (Adamson; Briskin; and McPhail 1988).

In 1980, NAC began welcoming such grassroots groups and making its leadership more representative of Canada as a whole. It made equality in the federal constitution a high priority at a time when Quebec's constitutional relationship to the rest of Canada was being contested. Thus, most English Canadian feminists accepted NAC's federal strategy, while many Quebec feminists preferred a provincial approach (Black 1992). First Nations called for Canadian women's organizations to recognize indigenous rights in land and culture as inseparable from native women's conceptions of their own interests (Monture-Okanee 1993).

Autonomous and Affiliated Women's Movements in Nigeria

African women's organizations face the strategic question of whether to affiliate with governments and political parties or organize autonomously. In the postcolonial process of state formation in Africa, women's participation has often taken the form of women's auxiliaries of national political parties or umbrella organizations, supported by the state and composed of many local and regional groups. However, pointing to such autonomous women's movement organizations as Women in Nigeria (WIN), the Women's National Coalition (WNC) in South Africa, and Action for Development (ACFODE) in Uganda, Aili Mari Tripp (2000) argues that their autonomy has made it easier for members to work together across communal identities, which, in turn, has increased their effectiveness and led more women to see value in such forms of organization.

Before the British colonized the region in 1884, Yoruba and Igbo women in southern Nigeria had powerful political roles within dual-sex systems of female and male authority. Women were part of associations that were based on trade, age, and kinship. The Women's War of 1929, in which Igbo market women protested British taxation, is a notable example of women using their traditional power against colonial rulers. Grounded in their roles as mothers and provisioners of the family, women collectively defended their complementary sphere of authority within the extended family and wider community. Women's movement organizations in Nigeria continue to value the complementarity of women's and men's interests, an idea reflected in the strategy of Nigerian women's groups to demand reserved places for women in political offices (Okonjo 1997).

Before colonization, women's associations were formed within communal groups. In 1947, during the struggles against colonialism, the first *national* women's organization, the National Women's Union, was established, headed by Funimilayo Ransome-Kuti (Abdullah 1995). Since Nigeria's independence in 1960, most women's associations have continued to be tied to kin, ethnic, religious, or regional groups. Many are also members of women's coalitions, most importantly, the National Council of Women's Societies (NCWS).

WIN, established in 1982, is an exception in that it is an autonomous, national, and secular women's movement organization that eschews identification with any particular ethnic, regional, or religious group. It also accepts male members, thereby distinguishing itself from the traditional dual-sex approach to politics in which women operate within their own women-only organizations. WIN's independence has allowed it to openly criticize cuts in governmental social spending, mandated by international lending agencies' structural adjustment programs (SAPs). WIN has also taken up individual cases of sexual harassment, rape, domestic violence, and sex discrimination (Imam 1997).

NCWS, founded in 1958, includes more than 300 women's groups under its umbrella and provides some government support for their activities. Its priorities are to create more economic and political opportunities for women by promoting their education and training, legal equality in the public sphere, and proportional representation. Constrained by the necessity of developing consensual goals, NCWS has not addressed the issues of child custody, property rights, marriage, divorce, and sexuality. These are seen as too threatening to men's customary authority in the family and to Islamic law (sharia), governing family law and practice in northern Nigeria (Okonjo 1994). In Nigeria, where religious divisions have fanned the flames of civil war, NCWS's strategy is understandable. However, it means that leadership for change in familial customary and religious law has come from autonomous women's organization, Nigerian representatives of transnational nongovernmental organizations, and women's human rights' organizations.

Religious Communities and Women's Movements in India

Religiously diverse, multilingual, and caste-divided India also has one of the most vibrant and many-stranded women's movements in the world. One of their priorities is challenging patriarchal religious practices, while at the same time respecting religious differences. Another is alleviating the poverty and insecurity of women and their families.

The *women's upliftment* phase began in the late nineteenth century, first among elite Hindu men and women and, later, Muslims. Besides emphasizing education, they called for reform of the practices of widow remarriage, polygamy, purdah (the veiling and seclusion of women), property rights, and sati (the ritual suicide of widows). Women formed their own autonomous organizations, the most important of which was the All India Women's Conference (AIWC) in 1927.

In 1934, when AIWC introduced a bill for equality in marriage, divorce, and property rights, they drew upon the nationalist rights discourse; and after independence in 1947, women were granted constitutional equality. However, the Hindu, Islamic, and other religious communities retained jurisdiction over family law (Desai 2001).

The second wave began as grass-roots organizations focused not only upon gender but also upon caste, class, and culture as roots of women's oppression. The groups in this movement were affiliated with grass-roots labor, peasant, and tribal movements as well as leftist opposition parties. Among their activities were protests by tribal women in the Toilers' Union in Maharastra against alcohol-related domestic violence and by the Chipko movement of poor women in the Himalayas to protect their forest resources and highlight women's unrecognized economic contributions. The Self Employed Women's Association (SEWA), a union of women working as street vendors and rag-pickers and in home-based industries, established the first women's bank for poor women (Desai 2001).

Sustainable, grassroots development as a priority of Indian women's movement organizations is exemplified by the organization Stree Mukti Sangharsh (Women's Liberation Struggle). They envision development that promotes equality between men and women and overcomes the economic and environmental ravages of the rural areas precipitated by large multinational corporations whose focus on short-term gains have created unsustainable forms of development (Desai 2001).

In the late 1970s, autonomous, avowedly feminist women's movements arose. Outraged by the dismissals of cases of girls raped by police and by religiously sanctioned violations of women's human rights, their campaigns refocused on violence against women, dowry deaths (the murder of brides for their dowries), sex-selective abortions, and sati (Kumar 1995).

The success of women's movement organizations has met with an antifeminist backlash, which calls upon familial, communal, and religious identities to try to push back women's gains (Kumar 1995). Since poverty and insecurity fan the flame of reactionary fears, the feminist strategy of promoting grassroots-based sustainable development is a double-edged one—it addresses both the economic independence of women and the long-term security and well-being of the whole community.

Class and Women's Movements in Denmark

Danish women's movements have placed high priority on alleviating poverty, providing social support for women and children, and promoting gender equity in the family and society. Their success is tied to working-class women's demands that the public and private sectors accommodate women's employment and family responsibilities along with middle-class women's critiques of gender discrimination and male privilege.

Education, equal access to careers and business, and property rights were all goals of the nineteenth century middle-class women's rights movement. Established in 1871, *Dansk Kvindesamfund* (the Danish Women's Society) is still the most prominent national women's rights movement organization. It is explicitly nonpartisan and autonomous and has followed a strategy of promoting change through legislation.

At the same time, working-class women organized to improve women's lives through the formation of labor unions and the Social Democratic Party, the architects of the welfare state. Founded in 1885, *Kvindeligt Arbejderforbund* (Women Workers Union) organized unskilled women workers to fight for better working conditions and wages. Through union and party affiliations, working-class women's organizations have pursued state-supported programs, such as daycare, parental leave, health care, unemployment compensation, and old-age pensions.

Beginning in the late 1960s, a new women's movement arose, the most important branch of which was *RødstrømpebevÊgelsen* (the Redstocking Movement). Most of the members were young, middle-class, university-educated women; many belonged to new left parties. However, they maintained the Redstockings as an autonomous socialist-feminist movement organization and criticized the state as a form of public patriarchy.

The Redstocking Movement generated a national debate about the dominance of men over women in the family, the workplace, and political arena. In so doing, they contributed to a cultural shift that led to support for quotas on political party lists, women's centers and domestic violence shelters, women's studies programs, and expanded welfare services. Another result is that the state itself is less dominated by men. Danish women now make up 37.4 percent of the parliament, second highest in the world.

Although the Redstockings opposed it, Denmark joined the European Union (EU) in 1973. The EU is a new international power center whose bureaucracy is far more distant and opaque than the Danish state. New strategies of international feminist organizing are required to address it effectively (Walter 2001).

Globalizing Women's Movements

With the growth of the globalization of the economy and the development of international trade associations and governmental organizations, women have found it increasingly useful to organize across national boundaries. The United Nations has played a major role in making women's movements international and in defining women's rights as human rights. Women have used the opportunities provided by the four U.N. World Conferences on Women (in 1975, 1980, 1985, and 1995), the official ones and the alternative NGO forums, as arenas in which they could set goals, plan, network, and inspire one another to continue their work (West 1999). They have seized upon the various U.N. accords, especially CEDAW (Convention on the Elimination of All Forms of Discrimination against Women), as bases for demanding national changes.

Women have established regional networks, such as Women in Law and Development in Africa (WiLDAF) to implement U.N. policies and other regional human rights charters, including the African Charter for Human and People's Rights. In these efforts the Center for Women's Global Leadership, directed by Charlotte Bunch, acted as a coordination center for international women's human rights campaigns. These have focused on sex trafficking, issues of health and reproductive rights, female genital cutting (also known as female circumcision and female genital mutilation), and violence against women.

Regional meetings, such as the biannual Encuentros held in various Latin American cities to definc the issues of Latin American women's movements, have been a source of inspiration and strength for many feminist leaders (Sternbach et al. 1992). A 1984 meeting in India of women from different regions of the South led to the formation of Development Alternatives for Women for a New Era (DAWN) to focus on sustainable development to address the worsening of women's living standards as they relate to international lending policies (Stienstra 2000).

The first WAAD Conference, held in Nigeria in 1992, brought together Women in Africa, and the African Diaspora. Conference coordinator Obioma Nnaemeka (1998) affirmed, "Our faith in possibilities will clear our vision, deepen mutual respect, and give us hope as we *follow each other walking side-by-side.*" That kind of hope, determination, and egalitarianism, so critical to the success of grass-roots women's movements, is harder to sustain in more distant and bureaucratic international women's movement organizations; but it is just as vital.

See also: BIRTH CONTROL: SOCIOCULTURAL AND HISTORICAL ASPECTS; FAMILY ROLES; GENDER;

GENDER IDENTITY; LESBIAN PARENTS; MOTHERHOOD; POVERTY; WORK AND FAMILY

Bibliography

Abdullah, H. (1995). "Wifeism and Activism: The Nigerian Women's Movement." In *The Challenge of Local Feminisms, Women's Movements in Global Perspective,* ed. A. Basu, Boulder, CO: Westview Press.

Adamson, N.; Briskin, L.; and McPhail, M. (1988). *Feminist Organizing for Change, The Contemporary Women's Movement in Canada.* Toronto: Oxford University Press.

Alvarez, S. E. (1990). *Engendering Democracy in Brazil, Women's Movements in Transition.* Princeton, NJ: Princeton University Press.

Black, N. (1992). "Ripples in the Second Wave: Comparing the Contemporary Women's Movement in Canada and the United States." In *Challenging Times, The Women's Movement in Canada and the United States,* ed. C. Backhouse and D. H. Flaherty. Montreal: McGill-Queen's University Press.

Caraway, Nancy. (1991). *Segregated Sisterhood: Racism and the Politics of American Feminism.* Knoxville: University of Tennessee Press.

Desai, M. (2001). "India, Women's Movements from Nationalism to Sustainable Development." In *Women's Rights: A Global View,* ed. L. Walter. Westport, CT: Greenwood Press.

Dumont, M. (1992). "The Origins of the Women's Movement in Quebec." In *Challenging Times, The Women's Movement in Canada and the United States,* eds. C. Backhouse and D. H. Flaherty. Montreal: McGill-Queen's University Press.

Dutt, M. (2000). "Some Reflections on United States Women of Color and the United Nations Fourth World Conference on Women and NGO Forum in Beijing, China." In *Global Feminisms since 1945,* ed. B. G. Smith. London: Routledge.

Giddings, P. (1984). *When and Where I Enter, The Impact of Black Women on Race and Sex in America.* New York: William Morrow.

Imam, A. M. (1997). "The Dynamics of WINning: An Analysis of Women in Nigeria (WIN)." In *Feminist Genealogies, Colonial Legacies, Democratic Futures,* ed. M. J. Alexander and C. T. Mohanty. New York: Routledge.

Johnson-Odim, C. (1991). "Common Themes, Different Contexts: Third World Women and Feminism." In *Third World Women and the Politics of Feminism,* ed. C. T. Mohanty, A. Russo, and L. Torres. Bloomington: Indiana University Press.

Kumar, R. (1995). "From Chipko to Sati: The Contemporary Indian Women's Movement." In *The Challenge of Local Feminisms, Women's Movements in Global Perspective,* ed. A. Basu. Boulder, CO: Westview Press.

Molyneux, M. (1985). "Mobilization without Emancipation? Women's Interests, the State, and Revolution in Nicaragua." *Feminist Studies* 11(2):227–54.

Monture-Okanee, P. A. (1993). "The Violence We Women Do: A First Nations View." In *Challenging Times, The Women's Movement in Canada and the United States,* ed. C. Backhouse and D. H. Flaherty. Montreal: McGill-Queen's University Press.

Nelson, B. J. and Carver, K. A. (1994). "Many Voices but Few Vehicles: The Consequences for Women of Weak Political Infrastructure in the United States." In *Women and Politics Worldwide,* ed. B. J. Nelson and N. Chowdhury. New Haven, CT: Yale University Press.

Nnaemeka, O. (1998). "This Women's Studies Business: Beyond Politics and History (Thoughts on the First WAAD Conference)." In *Sisterhood, Feminisms and Power: From Africa to the Diaspora,* ed. O. Nnaemeka. Trenton, NJ: Africa World Press.

Okonjo, K. (1994). "Reversing the Marginalization of the Invisible and Silent Majority: Women in Politics in Nigeria." In *Women and Politics Worldwide,* ed. B. J. Nelson and N. Chowdhury, New Haven, CT: Yale University Press.

Sternbach, N. S.; Navarro-Aranguren, M.; Chuchryk, P.; and Alvarez, S. E. (1992). "Feminisms in Latin America: From Bogotá to San Bernardo." *Signs* 17(2):393–434.

Stienstra, D. (2000). "Making Global Connections among Women, 1970–99." In *Global Social Movements,* ed. R. Cohen and S. M. Rai. London: The Athlone Press.

Tripp, A. M. (2000). "Rethinking Difference: Comparative Perspectives from Africa." *Signs* 25(3):649–76.

Walter, L. (2001). "Denmark: Women's Rights and Women's Welfare." In *Women's Rights: A Global View,* ed. L. Walter. Westport, CT: Greenwood Press.

West, L. (1999). "The United Nations Women's Conference and Feminist Politics." In *Gender Politics in Global Governance,* ed. M. K. Meyer and E. Prügl. London: Rowman & Littlefield.

LYNN WALTER

WORK AND FAMILY

Because the two most important roles in life for many people are work and family, understanding the relationship between the two is crucial. Although work and family research in the 1960s and 1970s primarily focused on dual-career families and *working mothers,* research in the 1980s evolved into a multidisciplinary and multitheoretical area of study. Today researchers are still interested in the interaction between work and family, with a particular focus on the consequences of work for the quality of family life and the development of family members (Perry-Jenkins, Repetti, and Crouter 2000).

Theoretical Paradigms of Work and Family

Paid work has been conceptualized in various ways. Paid work typically consists of activities for which one receives remuneration or that an individual performs while occupying a position in an organization. This does not take into account the work that is unpaid and outside the formal economy.

Research on paid work and family life typically fits into one of two categories, depending on whether one focuses on the workplace or the family (Crouter 1994). Six different conceptual models representing multiple disciplines are presented: the *separate spheres model,* the *multiple roles model,* the *job demands model,* the *spillover/crossover model, compensation theory,* and an *interactive model.*

Separate spheres model. The separate spheres model sees family and work as distinctive systems, with the family as a domestic haven for women and work as a public arena for men (Zedeck 1992). Further, family and work should remain separate in order to function properly and the division of labor by sex should be maintained in order to avoid conflict. Although the separate spheres model is rarely used by social scientists in the United States and other industrialized nations today, it still informs the personal decisions as well as policy positions of individuals or countries that embrace more traditional family norms.

Multiple roles model (also known as the conflict perspective [Bowen 1991]). The precursor of the multiple roles approach was early research of the effects of wives' and mothers' employment on marital adjustment, power, and division of labor, as well as on child outcomes (Pleck 1995). The multiple roles perspective shifts from a special focus on wives' employment to viewing wives' employment as only one special case of a broader phenomenon, the possible occupancy of multiple roles by persons of either sex. Although the multiple roles perspective is broader than the older "wives' employment" approach, the multiple roles perspective does not incorporate contextual effects concerning, for example, the actual nature of the job held.

Job demands model. In the job demands model, negative outcomes on marital adjustment and other family variables are interpreted as a function of the structural demands (number, scheduling, and flexibility of work hours) and the psychological demands (pace of work, workplace conflicts, negative moods generated at work) of the jobs individuals hold. Underlying the job demands model is an implicit belief that the job demands most impinging on family life derive from a social organization of work that is structured rather arbitrarily. For example, if a study finds that long hours are associated with family stress, the interpretation made is that reducing hours would benefit families. Nevertheless, if the same study finds that having preschool children in the household is correlated with stress, no one draws the implication that families could or should reduce their stress by not having children.

Spillover/crossover model. Unlike the separate sphere model, which denies the connection between family and work, this model recognizes that either system may have spillover effects on the other (Staines 1980). Simultaneous membership in the two systems often entails strain and overload for individuals, families, and work units. In general, the spillover effects model shifts attention from the effects of social institutions on each other to the effects of family members on each other, ignoring the social and political consequences of the context in which family and work are located.

Compensation theory. This theory is the one most often contrasted with spillover (Zedeck 1992). It hypothesizes that there is an inverse relationship between work and family such that work and nonwork experiences tend to be antithetical. It further proposes that individuals make differential investments of themselves in the two settings (Champoux 1978), so that what is provided by one makes up for what is missing in the other (Evans and Bartolome 1984). Deprivations experienced in work are made up or compensated for in nonwork activities.

Interactive model. The interactive model "recognizes the mutual interdependence between family and work systems, taking into account the reciprocal influences of work and family and acknowledging their independent as well as their joint effects, directly and indirectly, on the psychological state and social conditions of individuals" (Chow and Berheide 1988, p. 25). Analyses utilizing the interactive model to describe system interdependence between family and work can be divided into two main types—Marxist and non-Marxist.

Marxists treat family and work as economic units and study their linkages to the larger economy. Non-Marxists tend to see family and work as social systems or structural units and examine the specific circumstances under which occupational and familial roles intersect.

These six models represent the various multidisciplinary and multitheoretical lenses through which issues related to work and family have been and are currently examined. They also illustrate the multiple and complex links between work and family spheres.

Historical Context and New Patterns

Most information written historically on work and family discusses issues related to the Western world or industrialized countries. In the preindustrial period of England and the United States, for example, the family was the unit of production. Men, women, and children worked in the home and in the fields. Life was characterized by an interweaving of the husband and wife's involvement with domestic life and with a productive work life. There existed an integration of work and family with the husband, wife, and children all working in the home (Coontz 1997; Hutter 1998).

With the Industrial Revolution, work was now separated from the economy. For men, it meant involvement in the outside world and in the expanding marketplace; for women, it increasingly meant confinement within the home. Legislation was introduced restricting employment hours for women and children, thus restricting women's employment opportunities and resulted in married women's staying at home to care for their children.

This ideology of women's confinement to the home originated in the middle and upper classes and is clearly a concept originating in Western family ideology that eventually extended to the working classes also, despite the fact that it ran counter to the economic needs of the family. The idea that work outside the home for married women was a "misfortune and a disgrace" (Oakley 1974, p. 50) became acceptable across all social classes. Nevertheless, although this ideology existed, families were still heavily dependent on the contributions of wives and children to the family budget and in many countries, such as Belgium and Spain, wives were gainfully employed (Janssens 1998).

Historical events, such as pressures of wartime economies, have led to the mass hiring of women in the labor force, causing a temporary relaxation of the gender divide. For example, the popular U.S. icon during World War II, *Rosie the Riveter,* signifies that women's efforts were seen as vital to the nation's survival. However, as soon as the men came home after World War II, the gender divide was restored. West Germany paralleled the United States in this phenomenon. In contrast, the East German government expected the war widows to replace the male breadwinner by seeking full-time employment (von Oertzen and Rietzschel 1998).

Changes that occurred in the United States from the 1960s to the 1990s include an increase in married women with children in the labor force, a slight decrease in men in the labor force, a greater incidence of early retirement, a continued decline in real earnings, the elimination of many formerly well-paying jobs, wage concessions in several unionized industries, and the establishment of a two-tier wage system that offers lower wages and slower pay increases to new entrants into the labor market. Cyclical unemployment and permanent job loss due to takeovers, plant closings, and layoffs also have increased. Traditionally male jobs (e.g., in manufacturing) are disappearing and the types of jobs women traditionally have held (e.g.,

Historical events such as war have led to the mass hiring of women in the labor force. During World War II, women's efforts were seen as vital to the war effort. CORBIS/ MINNESOTA HISTORICAL SOCIETY

in services) are increasing (Haas 1999). Many of the trends listed here have also occurred in European countries such as England and Greece (Brannen 1998).

Family and work are undergoing immense transformation as the twenty-first century begins. Today, alterations in the world economy are now affecting "every aspect of the employment scene—the work, the workers, the employers, and the typical career sequence" (Berger 1998, p. 528) in both developing and industrialized nations. In our postindustrial society, "the global economy is characterized by an advancing communications technology that dictates 'connectedness,' not only among nations, but also among individuals and within our overall social institutions" (Secret, Sprang, and Bradford 1998, p. 813).

In the poorest regions of the world, the shift is from agriculture to industry, as multinational corporations move in to take advantage of cheap labor (Berger 1998). Developing nations meanwhile are shifting from industry-based economies to information and service industries. As a result of all this change, certain job categories are appearing or disappearing, seemingly overnight; educational requirements for work are shifting every few years; and corporate strategies such as downsizing and outsourcing are becoming standard practices. Consequently the work path for individuals is much less predictable and secure than it once was, with a widening employment and income gap between those with knowledge and those without it (Berger 1998).

Technological change has also affected work and family. The growing use of computers, pagers, and cellular telephones, for example, meant that some employees could perform their work almost anywhere. Thus, home businesses and teleworking opportunities have expanded worldwide.

Although more U.S. workers were employed in the 1990s than ever before, many experienced an increase in work hours and job instability, and, for low-wage earners, a decline in real earned income (Mishel, Bernstein, and Schmitt 1999). The number of *contingent workers,* those holding jobs without long-term contracts, grew in both the United States as well as European nations (Drew and Emerek 1998; Rogers 2000).

The beginning of the twenty-first century found almost half the civilian labor force in developed nations to be female: 40 percent in Japan, 45 percent in Canada and England, 46 percent in the United States, and 49 percent in Sweden (U.S. Bureau of Labor Statistics 1996). In 1998, almost 64 million women in the United States were employed in the civilian labor force and more than 60 percent of adult women were employed. In comparison, 75 percent of adult men were employed (U.S. Bureau of the Census 1998, Table 645). Hispanic women were slightly less likely to be employed (57%) in the United States. Historically, African-American women have had higher labor force participation rates than white or Hispanic women. Between 1994 and 1996, however, African-American and white women had virtually identical rates—approximately 59 percent. Hispanic women participated at a rate of about 53 percent. Since that time, African-American women have edged ahead to a participation rate of 63.5 percent in 1999. White, Asian and Pacific Islander women, and Hispanic women participated at 59.6, 59, and 55.9 percent, respectively (U.S. Bureau of Labor Statistics 2000). The labor force participation rate for Cuban women was 53.3 percent; for Mexican women, 52.8 percent; and for Puerto Rican women, 47.4 percent (U.S. Bureau of Labor Statistics 1997).

In examining labor force participation of women ages fifteen to sixty-four in developing countries in 2000, notable differences were found around the world. In Northern Africa, 37 percent of women ages fifteen to sixty-four participated in the labor force in 2000; in Central America and Western, 42 percent of women ages fifteen to sixty-four participated in the labor force in 2000; in South America, 46 percent of women ages fifteen to sixty-four participated in the labor force in 2000; in South Central Asia, 47 percent of women ages fifteen to sixty-four participated in the labor force in 2000; in the Caribbean, 54 percent of women ages fifteen to sixty-four participated in the labor force in 2000; and in Western Africa, 58 percent of women ages fifteen to sixty-four participated in the labor force in 2000. The highest rates were found in Middle Africa (63%), in Southeast Asia (64%), and in Eastern Africa, where 73 percent of women percent of women ages fifteen to sixty-four participated in the labor force in 2000 (*Population Today* 2002).

Between 1960 and 1997, the percentage of married women in the United States labor force almost doubled—from 32 percent to 62 percent. During that same period, the number of employed married women between twenty-five and thirty-four years of age (the ages during which women are most likely to bear children) rose from 29 to 72 percent. Over 70 percent of married women with children were in the labor force in 1997, including 78 percent of those with children six to seventeen years of age, and 64 percent of those with children age six or younger (U.S. Bureau of the Census 1998, Table 654). In countries such as Belgium, France, Portugal, and Ireland, female economic activity peaks for women in their mid-twenties, and then falls as women leave the labor force to begin raising a family, whereas in Sweden and Finland rates continually increase for women until their fifties (Hantrais 2000). France has one of the highest female participation in the labor force rates for mothers, as well as one of the highest birth rates in the European Union (Fagnani 1998).

By 1990, nearly three-quarters of all divorced mothers also were involved in the U.S. labor force. The experience of women in the U.S. labor force follows that of their counterparts in Russia, Sweden, and Israel (Hutter 1998, 335). Many single-parent families are in poverty, however; for example, England, Australia, the United States, Canada, and Italy all have high rates of young children in single-parent families who are in poverty (Brannen 1998).

At the end of the twentieth and beginning of the twenty-first centuries, increasing ethnic diversity became evident in the workforce. In every developed nation—except France—the total immigrant segment of the labor force is increasing, with rates of 25 percent in Australia, 19 percent in Canada, 9 percent in the United States, Austria, and Germany, 3 percent in England, and 1 percent in two nations that formerly had virtually no immigrant workers, Italy and Japan (U.S. Bureau of Labor Statistics 1996).

Child labor is on the increase in the United States, especially those children in their teenage years (Zinn and Eitzen 1999). Almost all U.S. adolescents now work at some time during high school (Mortimer and Finch 1996). Unlike children from Western industrialized countries, many children in poorer countries, such as India, Pakistan, and Morocco, perform a wide variety of jobs and they and their families are dependent on this income. One of the most visible forms of child labor in large cities in countries such as Brazil, Kenya, and India is that performed by street children. In countries that have been agricultural communities in the past but are under pressure to industrialize—such as many of the countries of Latin America, Africa and Asia—child workers engage in both traditional work and modern industrial production. Tourism is also a major employer of children in many countries (Hobbs, McKechnie, and Lavalette 1999).

During the last several decades, the U.S. family has undergone dramatic changes that have had an effect on work and family. Similar to trends reported in the majority of developed nations, the U.S. family has become increasingly heterogeneous (Fredriksen-Goldsen and Scharlach 2001).

Dual-career families now outnumber traditional families (those in which the husband but not the wife is the earner) 2 to 1 in the United States (Zinn and Eitzen 1999). Alternative, noninstitutionalized family forms are becoming more common, particularly in Sweden, Denmark, and France, whereas patterns of family formation remain much more conventional in southern Europe, particularly Portugal and Greece (Hantrais 2000).

Other notable changes affecting the U.S. family include a decrease in overall fertility, an increase in family dissolutions, and a shift in economic roles within the family (Fredriksen-Goldsen and Scharlach 2001). In a reversal of traditional roles, some husbands relinquish the role of breadwinner to their wives. *Househusbands* are those rare men who stay home to care for the family and do the housework while their wives are the wage earners.

However, these changes are not limited to the United States. The role of women in many cultures has been changing. Traditionally, married Brazilian and Filipino women stayed in the home and performed housework and childcare while husbands worked outside of the home and were responsible for the family's economic support (Sroufe and Cooper 1988; Szanton 1982), but an increased rate of women in the work force has been observed in Brazil (Schmink 1986) and the Philippines (Eviota 1982).

In underdeveloped countries working mothers become more an issue of survival than of social significance. Among developing countries the housewife's income is likely to be an important addition to the material support of the family. As noted above, in many countries the income of children is also significant for the family.

Links between Work and Family

Impact of employment on families. The structure of work and work roles has direct effects on family roles and family life. Among the most significant aspects of work that influence family life and family roles are (Gelles 1995; Zinn and Eitzen 1999):

(1) the amount of time worked and the location of work;

(2) the nature of the work schedule;

(3) the geographic mobility associated with work;

(4) work-related travel; and

(5) type of work.

Generally, in the United States in the early twenty-first century, both women and men work longer hours than they did twenty years earlier (Zinn and Eitzen 1999). Hours have risen for men as well as women, and for those in the working class well as for professionals (Zinn and Eitzen 1999). Married men work longer hours than unmarried men, but the reverse is true for women, with unmarried women working longer hours than married women (Voydanoff 1987). Fathers of younger children work longer hours than those of older children (Moen and Moorehouse 1983). More than a third of employed men with younger children in England work fifty hours a week or more (European Commission Network on Childcare 1993), a figure surpassed only by Ireland, and significantly above the European average (Eurostat 1992).

Throughout the industrialized world, the end of the twentieth century saw a change in work times. The United States, Canada, and Japan tend to give firms more independence and authority in determining working hours so there is greater disparity between enterprises. In Japan, there is no general working time standard, whereas in the United States the normal work schedule is a seven- to eight-hour workday during the daylight hours Monday through Friday. The two most common deviations from this norm are *shift work* and *flex-time* (Gelles 1995). The prevalence of shift work (afternoon or evening shifts that begin around 3 P.M. and end around 11 P.M. or the "graveyard shift" that begins around 11 P.M. and end around 7 or 8 A.M.) is growing for both women and men (Zinn and Eitzen 1999). As of 1985, one out of every six working mothers with children under fourteen and one out of every five working fathers held an evening or night job or worked a rotating shift (Zinn and Eitzen 1999). Thus, "one out of every six two-income couples with children under the age of six had work hours that did not overlap at all" (McEnroe 1991, 50). Shift work often precludes the sharing of routine family activities. Levels of temporary, shift, weekend, and homeworking tend to be similar for women and men within European countries, unlike rates of part-time employment, in which there is a consistent divergence in men's and women's rates (Drew and Emerek 1998). This divergence also exists in the United States. Estimates suggest that one-fifth of the U.S. labor force is involved in part-time work; the majority of these are women.

Alternative arrangements, such as flextime (a flexible schedule around the traditional or normal core working hours of 9 A.M. to 5 P.M.; flextime workers may choose to arrive early and leave early, or may report to work later and work later), allow workers to spend more time with their children and spouses than do regular-hour workers. However, the amount of total contact U.S. parents have with their children has dropped 40 percent since 1965 (Mattox 1990). Surprisingly, flextime workers spend less time alone with spouses (Winett and Neale 1980). Men are slightly more likely than women to work flextime hours, and married men and men with children have higher rates of flextime work than married women and women with children (Nollen 1982). Weekend working is more common and important among male workers and men are much more likely than women to work evening and night shifts in Europe (Drew and Emerek 1998).

Geographical mobility may affect families. The two most common forms in U.S. society are job-related moves and transfers and work-related travel (Zinn and Eitzen 1999). In general, the worker who moves has an easier time adjusting than his or her spouse and children. However, the level of stress experienced by the family is uncertain other than high levels of geographical relocation engender family stress (McCollum 1990). Geographical relocation in countries such as Italy, Spain, Portugal, Greece, Ireland, and France includes older people being left behind while younger people go searching for work (Eurolink Age 1995).

Work-related travel can also have a significant impact on family life. For example, the majority of U.S. workers work and live in different places. Commuting can make fulfilling family-related roles, such as companionship with spouse and children, household responsibilities, and attending family and school functions difficult as commuting extends the workday. Frequent or extended absences of family members can make it difficult for them to perform their family roles and obligations and may lead to estrangement from their families, such as is in Singapore because of the economic strategy of internationalization (Chia 2000).

In addition, the type of work one does has implications for family well-being. Jobs vary in wage levels and other benefits, such as health insurance, Social Security, private pensions, disability, and unemployment insurance (Zinn and Eitzen 1999). Generally, occupational prestige and income increase marital stability and marital satisfaction. Inadequate resources, monotonous and unchallenging work, unsafe working conditions, dead-end jobs, the unrelenting threat of unemployment, and low self-esteem also affect family life. Specific occupations have been singled out for their high rates of negative carryover. For example, problems associated with family disorganization and personal stress—divorce, family violence, and alcoholism—are particularly common in the families of urban police officers (Hoffman 1987).

Effects of family on work. Family roles and family structure also influence work and work roles. Although variations do exist, the following general trends exist in the Western industrialized world. Two of the most significant aspects of family life and family roles that influence work are (1) parenthood and other dependent care responsibilities and (2) marital dynamics (Gelles 1995; Haas 1999).

Having children does affect labor market behavior. For example, women who earn a high proportion of family income before childbirth or who have high-status jobs have been found to be more likely to return to work sooner after childbirth than other women (Yoon and Waite 1994). However, involvement in family roles seems to reduce women's tendency to be involved in careers (Haas 1999). Mothers are also more likely than fathers to miss days of work and research suggests that up to 40 percent of parents miss work because of childcare responsibilities (Ferber and O'Farrell 1991). In the Caribbean (as in other countries), many women quit their jobs because of an inability to find appropriate childcare (Massiah 1999). Others work evening or weekend shifts (when husbands can care for children) or leave the workplace for home-based employment. In fact, women account for an increasing share of the self-employed in many postindustrial nations (McManus 2001). In single parent households, extended family members may assist with childcare, such as the case in Botswana where the grandmother may be the main caregiver for her daughter's children while the daughter works (Ingstad 1994).

There is a continuing reliance on the family, particularly middle-aged and older women, as well as increasing numbers of older men, to provide elder care in industrial countries with increasing numbers of elderly persons. Although men participate in elder care, throughout the world the majority of caregivers are women and responsibilities for elderly parents affect labor force behavior (Haas 1999). Generally, women experience more interruptions in their work due to elder care responsibilities than do men (Neal et al. 1990), which include a decrease in work hours, rearranging work schedules, taking unpaid leave, being late or leaving work early, and working less efficiently because of stress. Daughters of elders who require substantial assistance with daily living are often forced to quit work entirely (Barnes, Given, and Given 1995).

Marital dynamics also influence work behavior and performance, particularly for women. For example, having a lower-earning husband and being in an unstable marital relationship increases women's chances of being in the labor force (McLanahan and Booth 1991). The requirements of the husbands' job or their desire for occupational achievement can also affect women's involvement in the paid labor force (Fowlkes 1987). Marital distress likewise affects work productivity, particularly for men (Haas 1999).

Employer/workplace responses. Policies affecting workers' abilities to manage their work and family lives fall into four areas: family-related leave, childcare, adult dependent care, and alternate working arrangements. Nations vary in their family policies. Some provide every resident free childcare, universal health benefits, and paid maternity leave, sometimes for a year; others mandate that employers provide such benefits; others, such as the United States, furnish only minimal support, such as the first *family leave* law, not passed until 1993, which legalized maternity leave—but only for twelve weeks, without pay, and only if the employer has at least fifty full-time workers.

Work-family policies also have different levels of effectiveness because of cross-cultural differences in family structure, standards of living, infrastructure, and cultural beliefs and practices. For example, in England, the lack of paid leave for sick child care, minimal provision of publicly funded child care and the prevailing philosophy of care in the community, which relies heavily on informal care of the elderly and vulnerable, all derive from the assumptions that there is someone (i.e., a woman) at home to provide this sort of care or that a woman's income is not essential for the family. Elsewhere in Europe, social policy is based on the assumption of a modified single-breadwinner family, with women as secondary earners (e.g., Germany and the Netherlands) or on the dual-career family as the norm (e.g., France, the Scandinavian countries and Eastern and Central Europe in the former communist countries) (Lewis 1997).

Future Directions

Themes that emerged from the work and family literature of the 1990s were maternal employment, work socialization, work stress, and multiple roles (Perry-Jenkins, Repetti, and Crouter 2000). New terminology that was introduced into our language since the 1960s includes *Mommy track, glass ceiling, second shift,* and *third shift.* We have also seen a rise in part-time and contingent work as well as individuals choosing home-based employment.

Possible directions for work and family research in the future are (1) issues of definition and meaning regarding the terms of "work" and "family"; (2) a need for more cross-cultural and comparative studies; (3) an examination of our theoretical research models: are they universal or are they only applicable in certain contexts?; (4) a need to build better measures of family processes, family relationships, and employed adults' interpretations and constructions of their work and family roles into studies of occupational conditions; (5) research that investigates the role of children; and (6) use of experimental research designs (Perry-Jenkins, Repetti, and Crouter 2000). Other emerging issues include the psychological consequences of job insecurity, the acceptance or rejection of long work hours and the polarization of *work rich* and *work poor,* blurred work-family boundaries, and the impact of the changing nature of work on gender equality (Lewis and Cooper 1999).

Work and family connections are complex and change in both expected and unexpected ways over the life course, adapting to cultural and societal developments. It is imperative that future research continue to reflect the complexities of the nature of this relationship for men, women and children.

See also: CHILDCARE; COHABITATION; COMMUTER MARRIAGES; COMPUTERS AND FAMILIES; CONFLICT: MARITAL RELATIONSHIPS; DIVISION OF LABOR; DUAL-EARNER FAMILIES; EQUITY; FAMILY BUSINESS; FAMILY ROLES; FATHERHOOD; HOUSEWORK; HOUSING; INDUSTRIALIZATION; MIGRATION; MOTHERHOOD; POVERTY; POWER: MARITAL RELATIONSHIPS; MARITAL QUALITY; RESOURCE MANAGEMENT; RETIREMENT; RICH/WEALTHY FAMILIES; SINGLE-PARENT FAMILIES; STRESS; SUBSTITUTE CAREGIVERS; TIME USE; UNEMPLOYMENT; URBANIZATION; WOMEN'S MOVEMENTS

Bibliography

Barnes, C.; Given, B.; and Given, C. (1995). "Parent Caregivers: A Comparison of Employed and Not Employed Daughters." *Social Work* 40:375–381.

Berger, K. (1998). *The Developing Person through the Life Span,* 4th edition. New York: Worth.

Bowen, G. (1991). *Navigating the Marital Journey—MAP: A Corporate Support Program for Couples.* New York: Praeger.

Brannen, J. (1998). "Employment and Family Lives: Equalities and Inequities." In *Women, Work and the Family in Europe,* ed. E. Drew, R. Emerek, and E. Mahon, London: Routledge.

Champoux, J. (1978). "Perceptions of Work and Nonwork: A Reexamination of the Compensatory and Spillover Models." *Sociology of Work and Occupations* 5:402–422.

Chia, A. (2000). "Singapore's Economic Internationalization and Its Effects on Work and Family." *SOJOURN: Journal of Social Issues in Southeast Asia* 15:123–138.

Chow, E., and Berheide, C. (1988). "The Interdependence of Family and Work: A Framework for Family Life Education, Policy, and Practice." *Family Relations* 37: 23–28.

Coontz, S. (1997). *The Way We Really Are: Coming to Terms with America's Changing Families.* New York: Basic Books.

Crouter, A. (1994). "Processes Linking Families and Work: Implications for Behavior and Development in Both Settings." In *Exploring Family Relationships with Other Social Contexts,* ed. R. D. Parke and S. Kellan. Hillsdale, NJ: Lawrence Erlbaum Associates.

Drew, E., and Emerek, R. (1998). "Employment, Flexibility and Gender." In *Women, Work and the Family in Europe,* ed. by E. Drew, R. Emerek, and E. Mahon, London: Routledge.

Eurolink Age. (1995). Caring for Older People: A European Issue. Report for a Eurolink Age seminar, Bonn, Germany.

European Commission Network on Childcare. (1993). *Mothers, Fathers and Employment 1985–1991.* London: Author.

Eurostat. (1992). *Labour Force Survey 1990.* Luxembourg: Office for Official Publications of the European Communities.

Evans, P., and Bartolome, F. (1984). "The Changing Pictures of the Relationship between Career and Family." *Journal of Occupational Behavior* 5:9–21.

Eviota, E. (1982). "Philippines." In *Women in Asia,* ed. R. Jahan. London: Expedite Graphic.

Fagnani, J. (1998). "Recent Changes in Family Policy in France: Political Trade-Offs and Economic Constraints." In *Women, Work and the Family in Europe,* ed. E. Drew, R. Emerek, and E. Mahon. New York: Routledge.

Ferber, M., and O'Farrell, B. (1991). *Work and Family—Policies for a Changing Work Force.* Washington, DC: National Academy Press.

Fowlkes, M. (1987). "The Myth of Merit and Male Professional Careers: The Roles of Wives." In *Families and Work,* ed. N. Gerstel and H. Gross. Philadelphia: Temple University Press.

Fredriksen-Goldsen, K., and Scharlach, A. (2001). *Families and Work: New Directions in the Twenty-First Century.* New York: Oxford University Press.

Gelles, R. (1995). *Contemporary Families: A Sociological View.* Thousand Oaks, CA: Sage.

Haas, L. (1999). "Families and Work." In *Handbook of Marriage and the Family,* 2nd edition, ed. M. Sussman, S. Steinmetz, and G. Peterson. New York: Plenum Press.

Hantrais, L. (2000). "From Equal Pay to Reconciliation of Employment and Family Life." In *Gendered Policies in Europe: Reconciling Employment and Family Life,* ed. L. Hantrais. London: Macmillan.

Hobbs, S.; McKechnie, J.; and Lavalette, M. (1999). *Child Labor: A World History Companion.* Santa Barbara, CA: ABC-CLIO.

Hoffman, L. (1987). "The Effects of Children on Maternal and Paternal Employment." In *Families and Work,* ed. N. Gerstel and H. Gross. Philadelphia: Temple University Press.

Hutter, M. (1998). *The Changing Family,* 3rd edition. Boston: Allyn and Bacon.

Ingstad, B. (1994). "The Grandmother and Household Viability in Botswana." In *Gender, Work and Population in Sub-Saharan Africa.* London: International Labour Office.

Janssens, A. (1998). "The Rise and Decline of the Male Breadwinner Family? An Overview of the Debate." In *The Rise and Decline of the Male Breadwinner Family?,* ed. A. Janssens. Cambridge: Cambridge University Press.

Lewis, S. (1997). "An International Perspective on Work-Family Issues." In *Integrating Work and Family: Challenges and Choices for a Changing World,* ed. S. Parasuraman and J. Greenhaus. Westport, CT: Quorum Books.

Lewis, S., and Cooper, C. (1999). "The Work-Family Research Agenda in Changing Contexts." *Journal of Occupational Health Psychology* 4:382–393.

Massiah, J. (1999). "Researching Women's Work: 1985 and Beyond." In *Gender in Caribbean Development,* ed. by P. Mohammed and C. Shepherd. Barbados: Canoe Press.

Mattox, W. (1990). "The Family Time Famine." *Family Policy* 3:2.

McCollum, A. (1990). *The Trauma of Moving.* Newbury Park, CA: Sage.

McEnroe, J. (1991). "Split-Shift Parenting." *American Demographics* 13:50–52.

McLanahan, S., and Booth, K. (1991). "Mother-Only Families." In *Contemporary Families,* ed. A. Booth. Minneapolis, MN: National Council on Family Relations.

McManus, P. (2001). "Women's Participation in Self-Employment in Western Industrialized Nations." *International Journal of Sociology* 31:70–97.

Mishel, L.; Bernstein, J.; and Schmitt, J. (1999). *The State of Working America.* Ithaca, NY: Cornell University Press.

Moen, P., and Moorehouse, M. (1983). "Overtime over the Life Cycle: A Test of the Life Cycle Squeeze Hypothesis." In *Research in the Interweave of Social Roles: Family and Jobs,* ed. H. Lopata and J. Pleck. Greenwich, CT: JAI Press.

Mortimer, J., and Finch, M. (1996). "Work, Family, and Adolescent Development." In *Adolescents, Work and Family,* ed. J. Mortimer and M. Finch. Newbury Park, CA: Sage.

Neal, M.; Chapman, N.; Ingersoll-Dayton, B.; Emlen, A.; and Boise, L. (1990). "Absenteeism and Stress among Employed Caregivers for the Elderly, Disable Adults, and Children." In *Aging and Caregiving,* ed. D. Biegel, and A. Blum. Newbury Park, CA: Sage.

Nollen, D. (1982). *New Work Schedules in Practice.* New York: Van Nostrand Reinhold.

Oakley, A. (1974). *Women's Work: The Housewife, Past and Present.* New York: Pantheon Books.

Perry-Jenkins, M.; Repetti, R.; and Crouter, A. (2000). "Work and Family in the 1990s." *Journal of Marriage and the Family* 62:981–998.

Pleck, J. (1995). "Work Roles, Family Roles, and Well-being: Current Conceptual Perspectives." In *The Work and Family Interface: Toward a Contextual Effects Perspective,* ed. G. Bowen and J. Pittman. Minneapolis, MN: National Council on Family Relations.

Rogers, J. (2000). *Temps.* Ithaca, NY: Cornell University Press.

Schmink, M. (1986). "Women and Urban Industrial Development in Brazil." In *Women and Change in Latin America,* ed. J. Nash and H. Safa. South Hadley, MA: Bergin and Garvey.

Secret, M.; Sprang, G.; and Bradford, J. (1998). "Parenting in the Workplace." *Journal of Family Issues* 19: 795–815.

Sroufe, L., and Cooper, R. (1988). *Child Development.* New York: Alfred A. Knopf.

Staines, G. (1980). "Spillover versus Compensation: A Review of the Literature on the Relationship between Work and Nonwork." *Human Relations* 33:111–129.

Szanton, M. (1982). "Women and Men in Iloilo, Philippines: 1903–1970." In *Women of Southeast Asia,* ed. P. Esterik. DeKalb, IL: Northern Illinois University Center for Southeast Asian Studies.

U.S. Bureau of Labor Statistics. (1996). *Comparative Labor Force Statistics for Ten Countries, 1959–1995.* Washington, DC: Author.

U.S. Bureau of Labor Statistics. (1997). *Employment and Earnings.* Washington, DC: Author.

U.S. Bureau of Labor Statistics. (2000). *Employment and Earnings.* Washington, DC: Author.

U.S. Bureau of the Census. (1998). *Statistical Abstract of the United States, 1998.* Washington, DC: Government Printing Office.

von Oertzen, C., and Rietzschel, A. (1998). "Comparing the Post-War Germanies: Breadwinner Ideology and Women's Employment in the Divided Nation,

1948–1970." In *The Rise and Decline of the Male Breadwinner Family?,* ed. A. Janssens. Cambridge: Cambridge University Press.

Voydanoff, P. (1987). *Work and Family Life.* Newbury Park, CA: Sage.

Winett, R., and Neale, M. (1980). "Modifying Settings as a Strategy for Permanent Preventive Behavior Change." In *Improving the Long-Term Effects of Psychotherapy,* ed. P. Karoly and J. Steffan. New York: Gardner.

Yoon, Y.-H., and Waite, K, (1994). "Converging Employment Patterns of Black, White, and Hispanic Women: Return to Work after Childbearing." *Journal of Marriage and the Family* 56:209–217.

Zedeck, S. (1992). *Work, Families, and Organizations.* San Francisco: Jossey-Bass.

Zinn, M., and Eitzen, D. (1999). *Diversity in Families,* 5th edition. New York: Longman.

DEBRA L. BERKE

Y

YORUBA FAMILIES

The 22 million Yoruba who live in southwestern Nigeria are one of the four major sociolinguistic groups of contemporary Nigeria. The others are the Igbo to the east, and the Hausa and Fulani to the north. Subgroups of the Yoruba in Nigeria include the Awori, the Ijesha, the Oyo, the Ife, the Egba, the Egbado, the Ketu, the Ijebu, the Ondo, the Ekiti, the Yagba, and the Igbomina. These subgroups have been described as belonging to a distinct cultural category because of such binding factors as a generally intelligible language, myth of common origin, and basically similar political structures. Besides the Yoruba in Nigeria, subgroups of Yoruba descent exist in other areas of the world as a result of the Atlantic slave trade and the artificially drawn international boundaries. In French Dahomey, now known as The Republic of Benin, the Yoruba are known as the Nago. In Cuba, they are known as the Lukumi. In Sierra Leone, they are known as the Aku, and in Surinam as Yoruba (Warner-Lewis 1996). In Brazil, the Yoruba culture influenced a religion known as Candomble (Murphy 1994; Voeks. 1997). In North America, particularly in Miami, Florida, Yoruba-influenced syncretistic religion is known as Santeria (Gonzalez-Wippler 1998).

Yoruba Culture and the Meaning of Marriage

Yoruba culture is not static. At the same time, every generation tries to preserve aspects of the indigenous tradition. This effort is counterbalanced by the pragmatic desire of the Yoruba to appropriate change in the garb of tradition. The dialectical relationship between the unchanging aspects of Yoruba culture and the dynamics of change are fueled by two sources of human interaction. The first source of change pertains to the new conflicts in human interaction that cannot be explained by Yoruba tradition. The second is the permanent effect of contact with Islam and the West, expressed in such institutions as law, marriage, religion, education, and public health services. Tola Olu Pearce has drawn attention to the importance of situating the present resistance to women's efforts to participate in the democratic process in Africa in the context of precolonial, colonial, and postcolonial times if it is to be fully understood. As she noted, "What is of theoretical import is the fact that elements of all three historical periods interact in the present" (2000). For example, Yoruba marriage forms have been influenced by Christian and Muslim marriage practices in all the three phases even as the steps to Yoruba marriage project a decidedly traditional outer form. In marriages in contemporary Yoruba society, the modernized Yoruba cling tenaciously to this outer form as a proof of loyalty to the original culture. Traditional Yoruba courtship and marriage must be understood in the context of the impact of the precolonial, colonial, and postcolonial periods.

The family is the most sacred and significant institution to the Yoruba, who are child-centered, ruled by the elderly, and controlled by adults. The family is an effective unit of political control, religious affiliation, resource allocation, and assurance of safety. It is also the most effective agent of socialization. The family teaches the first lessons in

Yoruba chilren in Ibadan, Nigeria. Many Yoruba proverbs stress that the dead give birth to the living, and the living are responsible for nurturing the children who represent the future. OWEN FRANKEN/CORBIS

discipline, personal gratitude, and affection. The family is where young people are exposed to their first preferences and prejudices. In the family, the lessons in honor and shame are learned, just as are the first lessons in dissembling to avoid the truth that may injure the well-being of the community. More poignantly, it is in and through the copious lessons in religious symbolism learned in the family that one comes to understand the cyclical and connected way of life in the here and now, the future, and the hereafter. Many Yoruba proverbs reiterate the view that the dead gave birth to the living, and the living ought to give birth to and nurture the children who represent the future.

The Yoruba further cloak these sentiments in the garb of religious obligation by insisting on a notion of afterlife whose reward is the opportunity for those elders who died well or properly to come and visit their progeny on earth. They attach their soul to the two other souls of the child to be born (Bascom 1956). *Eleda,* the first soul, is every individual's share in divine essence. The *ori* is that which is unique, or that which distinguishes one from any other person. In and through the child that is born, the dead are reincarnated to temporarily be with and bless the living. The sociological significance of this notion of birth and rebirth lies in its usefulness as a social welfare policy (Zeitlin; Megawangi; Kramer; Colleta; Babatunde; and Garman 1995). It ensures that children are wanted, nurtured, and brought up to be fine examples of what the Yoruba call *Omoluwabi*—the well-bred child. If a parent believes a son or daughter is a reincarnation of the parent's mother or father, the parent will not abandon the child. Seen in this context, marriage for the Yoruba man or woman is a necessity. As Nathaniel Fadipe noted:

> For a man or a woman who has reached the age of marriage to remain single is against the mores of the Yoruba. Men get married even when they are sexually impotent in order to save either their faces or the faces of their immediate relatives, as well as to get one to look after their domestic establishment. There are a few cases of confirmed bachelors; men, who have reached middle age without getting married even though they are in position

to do so. But they are a product of modern times with its individualism, and are most invariably Christians. (1970, p. 65)

Ideally, marriage should establish the foundation of the family. When it does, marriage is a union not only of the two spouses, but the two extended families to which they belong. Marriage itself is the proof that both spouses are good products and ambassadors of their families. By successfully going through the demanding steps to the Yoruba marriage, the spouses are a good reflection on the quality of character of their families. They have shown restraint as people who are well brought up, focused, enduring, reliable, disciplined, and people who are able to defer gratification until they are ready for the responsibilities of adulthood. As the Yoruba say, "It is easy to get married; what is difficult is to provide daily food for the family" (*Ati gbeyawo, kekere; owo obe lo soro*). In other words, the ability to satisfy the hierarchy of human needs was critical to the Yoruba evaluation of the spouses' readiness to be united in marriage. They ought to be able to provide food and shelter and safety. They ought to have the level of commitment and patience needed to inculcate a sense of belonging and self-esteem in their children. The test of the level to which one has internalized a sense of belonging and self-esteem is manifest in the desire to excel and find self-fulfillment in the service of the family. To ensure that the spouses have the requisite level of the skills that will enable their family to find its own balance, an elaborate system of calibrated steps and activities tests the endurance of the spouses. These steps reiterate the fact that the selection of the spouse is a communal affair that involves several symbolic steps (Babatunde 1992).

Steps That Lead to Marriage

Six important steps lead to the traditional Yoruba marriage:

- The time for seeking a potential spouse (*Igba ifojusode*);
- The approval of the oracle-divinity (*Ifa f'ore*);
- The release of the voice of the young woman (*Isihun*);
- The request for the young woman's hand in marriage (*Itoro);*
- The creation of the affinal bond (*Idana*); and
- The transfer of the wife to the husband's lineage (*Igbeyawo*).

When the young adult male is between twenty three and twenty-eight years of age and the female is between eighteen and twenty-five, they are both expected to be identifying potential spouses. At this time, the male is expected to have acquired skills that will allow him to provide for his family. The Yoruba socialization ensures that the daughter learns, from the age of seven, to serve as a little mother and child-caregiver to her younger siblings. By the time she is preparing for marriage, the Yoruba female would have learned some of the preliminary skills she will need to be a wife and mother from watching her mother and other women in her family.

Because Yoruba society in male-oriented, it is structured in favor of men taking initiative in the steps that lead to marriage. Thus, it is the man who formalizes his desire to proceed to the next level of courtship by visiting the house of the spouse-to-be. It is the man who pays his prospective to *Isihun*—payment to release the voice of the female so that the couple can talk with one another (eesee *Ishihun*). It is the suitor's male relations who take the initiative to institutionalize the marriage by first going to ask for the hand of the spouse. The suitor's male relations plan for the ceremony that creates affinal bond between the two families. Finally, the spouse is transferred from one group of patrilineal kin to another.

Oja Ale

In traditional Yoruba society, the forum for meeting the potential spouse is the evening marketplace, *Oja ale*. During this period of seeking a spouse, it is a cultural obligation for mothers of young female adults to find a reason for them to go to the market. Often, among the highly entrepreneurial Yoruba, some commodity is found for the female to sell in the evening marketplace. The female continues to go to the evening market until a serious prospect is identified. The seriousness of the prospective spouse is determined, when after many meetings in the evening market, the young man offers to go and visit the young female in her parent's home. Among the Yoruba, avoidance is part of the etiquette regulating one's interaction with one's affinal relatives. The determination to visit the house of one's potential spouse is a final proof of readiness to engage in a serious relationship. However, before the suitor takes this important step, he should inform his father about his intentions. The father of the suitor then informs the eldest male member of the extended family, *Idile,* who is known as the elderly father (*Baba agba*).

The suitor's father communicates the message to the eldest member of the lineage in symbolic language, "Elderly father, your son has seen a beautiful flower that he thinks he wants to pluck" (*Omo yin ti ri ododo elewa ti o feja*). The elderly relative then replies, "Can our family members pluck a flower from that family tree?" (*Nje awon ebi wa leja ododo lati iru igi bee*). The father of the suitor answers that from inquiries already made, members of their extended family can pluck flowers from the said tree. Then the elderly father gives his blessing by appointing a wife of the family to serve as the go-between (*Alarena*).

The choice of a very respected wife as the *go-between* has complex sociological implications. As an affinal member of the lineage, she has the immunity of an outsider with a proven record of excellent service as a wife and a role model for new wives of members of the lineage. The Yoruba, who are very secretive and status-conscious, would find it offensive for a family member of the husband to take on this sensitive job of finding background information about the family history of the prospective wife. Because the go-between is an outsider acting on behalf of the male descendants of family, the culture accords her the immunity to carry out her assigned duty as a neutral party. Yet the main condition for her selection is her intense loyalty to the extended family into which she married. The office of the go-between is also a mechanism for the smooth integration of the wife-to-be into her family of marriage. If things work out, the new wife is not completely alone in her new family. She has an ally in the go-between.

The go-between tries to discover information that will assist the elders of the suitor's family in deciding whether the spouse would be a good companion for their son and a good resource in the extended family. If the go-between finds out that members of the spouse's family are lazy, that their womenfolk are stubborn and incorrigible in their marital homes, or if men in the extended family of the spouse are notorious debtors or have been known to have debilitating diseases, this information will be passed on to the elders, who will subsequently bring pressure to bear on their son to discontinue the relationship. If inquiries reveal that the spouse's family members have a reputation for hard work, respect for elders, a great sense of nurture and motivation to induce their children to excel, every effort will be made to move the courtship to the next step in the process. The male elders direct the father of the suitor to find out from the oracle the future prospects of the union. The Yoruba are pragmatic. They want to know ahead of time whether the endeavor is worth the effort. The oracle is an instrumental use of symbolic inquiry to fathom the profitability of a future enterprise.

Select male elders of the suitor's lineage would consult the oracle divinity (*Orunmila*) who serves as the refraction of the supreme being, *Olodumare.* The intention is to find out whether the marriage will benefit the extended family. Symbolic presents are made to the priest of *Orunmila.* The priest of *Orunmila* is known as the Keeper of Secrets or fortune-teller (*Babalawo*). The gifts include a goat, two fowl, two pigeons, a tortoise, and a snail. This ritual consultation serves as an occasion for the redistribution of meat, a scarce commodity in Yoruba society. Parts of the goat, such as the head and the hind legs, are sent as present to the elderly members of the consulting family. The rest of the goat is cooked for the members of the extended family of the fortune-teller. The other items serve as the consultation fees for the service rendered. Again, it is very rare for the results of the oracle divination to contradict the general mood of the extended family modeled on the findings of the go-between. It is not without reason that the pragmatic Yoruba proverb emphatically asserts that one ought to use one's hands to repair one's fortune (*Owo eni laafi ti tun ara eni se*).

If the oracle is positive, the process of courtship, until then private and secretive, now becomes a public event with all the formality for which the ancient, dignified Yoruba culture is known. If the portent is negative, elders dig up some forgotten past occurrence that has prohibited marriage between members of both families. The sociological significance of this step in the marital process has to do with the desire to cloak the wishes of the extended family in the present in the garb of tradition so as to make the results more final and readily acceptable to the parties. It would be unthinkable in the traditional close-knit Yoruba society for the spouses to take the only choice left to them by refusing the pronouncement of the oracle and opting to elope. In the Yoruba traditional society, one's fortunes and safety are guaranteed only as a member of one's group of ascription. To separate oneself from the group by elopement would amount to social suicide.

Once the approval has been given, the suitor is then allowed to visit the home of the prospective spouse. The visit takes place at dusk and is accompanied by an extreme show of cordiality. The suitor is always accompanied by a male peer. The visitors greet every senior member of the household, male and female. Upon the conclusion of the elaborate greeting, seats for them are placed in a conspicuous place. The two sit patiently and endure being ignored for about an hour. They then begin the elaborate ritual of departure, which includes completely prostrating themselves flat on the belly for one senior member of the house after another. Upon the conclusion of this ritual, the suitor goes out and waits patiently for the spouse to emerge. When the spouse arrives, the male companion moves to a safe distance.

A unique aspect of the first six visits is that only the male speaks. By the seventh meeting, the male pays the female the equivalent of two dollars and ten cents to release, literally, the voice of the spouse to converse (*si ohun*). This ritual establishes a hierarchy of superordination and subordination. The wife-to-be is already conceding to the prospective husband the right to be the head of the family. These visits continue for six months, after which the time is set for the crucial ceremony of *Itoro*.

Itoro—begging for the prospective spouse's hand in marriage—is conducted between the male elders of the suitor and the spouse. The man's family members pay a visit to the compound of the extended family of the prospective spouse. It is important that the visit be unannounced, even though everyone involved seems to be in the right place at the right time. It is important too that upon arrival at the woman's house, her father uses symbolic language to tell the visitors that it is not his right, but that of his elders, to give his daughter in marriage. He proceeds to take the group to the eldest member of the family. At the house of the eldest member, all the senior members of the prospective spouse's lineage are waiting. This deference of the father to the eldest member of the family is a demonstration that the marriage of a member of the family is the business of all the members of the extended family because the suitor and the spouse are ambassadors of their extended families. The two families become united in a very special way by the union of the two people in marriage. Before the parties depart, a date is set for the most important ceremony, the *Idana* or creating the affinal tie.

The *Idana* ceremony centers on the payment of bride-wealth. This payment officially transfers the two crucial rights in the woman to the extended family of the suitor. Although the Yoruba term for bride-wealth literally translates *Owo ori* as "money for the head," in actual fact, this practice has, among the Yoruba, little to do with the transfer of economic resources as price for the wife-to-be. Yoruba families would cringe at the idea of putting monetary value on the head of a daughter. The presents involved in this ceremony have very little economic worth. Their significance has to do with the symbolic value they reiterate for enhancing the goals and objectives of the Yoruba family.

The anthropology of bride-wealth has identified prime and contingent obligations as the two categories of bride-wealth (Fortes 1962; Babatunde 1998). Primary obligations are essential to marriage because they transfer the core rights in the woman as a mother to the house of her husband. This core right is the procreative rights of the woman. Contingent obligations, however, transfer the rights to the woman as a homemaker.

The items involved in the Yoruba primary obligations are not negotiable. They have been fixed by tradition, and their use is not restricted to marriage because the culture tends, generally, to repeat rituals continuously to reinforce the aim, intention, purpose, and acceptable practices deemed crucial to the survival of the group. These items that are used in other rituals of the Yoruba life-cycle retain the same symbolic function. They include honey (*oyin*), salt (*iyo*), palm oil (*epo pupa*), kola nut (*obi*; *kola acuminata*), and bitter kola (*Orogbo*). Each item serves as a motif for prayers that reinforce what is desirable and necessary to make a marriage, and, indeed, life itself successful. Examples of prayers include:

(a) This is honey; the quality of honey is sweetness. May your married life be sweet, that is, happy by being blessed with many children and money to take care of them.

(b) This is salt. It preserves and sweetens, may you be preserved in your lives so that you live long and see your children's children.

(c) This is palm oil. It reduces the harsh taste of pepper in the soup. May the harsh impact of difficult times be ameliorated;

(d) This is kola nut. It produces prolifically. May you wife be as fertile as the kola nut tree and be blessed with many children who survive and do great things in life;

(e) This is bitter kola. It means that you will live long and see your children achieve great things in your lifetime;

(f) This is a pen. We use it to write. Education is the means to greatness. May you learn to read and write and become famous through achievement in education;

(g) This is the Bible/Koran. It is the holy book of power. May your faith provide direction to you in life;

(h) This is candle. It lights the way. May the word of God provide the light that will guide you through life;

(i) This is money. Money is needed for fulfillment and enjoyment of life. May you be blessed with plenty of it in your lifetime.

The property or quality of each item in the ritual repertoire is used to attempt to achieve a similar effect in the couple about to get married. This is based on the twin magical principles of the effect of like producing like and on effect by contact. The special quality of the ritual item is used as a motif in the prayer to reinforce the purpose and expectation of marriage. Taste is transformed to a condition of living in terms of what the Yoruba regard as happiness. Thus, a life that is sweet is equal to one that is happy. Yoruba understanding of happiness includes wealth, demonstrated in long life, begetting many healthy children who outlive their parents, having many wives, large cash crop farms, and status in the community.

The secondary obligations consist of duties that are periodically performed by the son-in-law to parent-in-law. The husband performs these duties as a continuous demonstration of his indebtedness to the family that has provided him with a wife. These duties include the provision of free labor to weed the farms, thatch leaking roofs, and harvest farm products, and political and economic support in times of competition for the various achieved status in the Yoruba community.

Co-Wife and Sibling Rivalry

Rivalry between co-wives and between siblings is useful for the maintenance of patrilineal ideology. To prevent the conjugal tie from threatening loyalty to the lineage, a wedge is put between husband and wife (Babatunde 1983). From the start, the wife understands that the Yoruba monogamy is the commencement of a possible polygyny (Sudarkasa 1996). The thought of sharing one's beloved with other wives reduces the intensity of the conjugal tie. A second source of rivalry is the practice that a man can marry two or more wives. The division of children within the family according to mothers creates competing groups within the family. Children of the same mother (*Omo Iya*) are often set against those of other mothers. The term that describes all the children who belong to the same father is *Obakan*. The relationship between the *Omo-Iya* and *Obakan,* respectively, must be understood in the dialectical terms referred to by Edward Evans-Pritchard as "fusion and fission" (1940). Children of the same father, *Obakan,* unite to protect their father's property and their common interests. When competing for resources within the family, they subdivide into groups of children of the same mother to protect their interests at this level. Yoruba fireside tales, told while the evening meal is cooking, often reiterate the lesson of the jealous co-wife who, in the attempt to hurt the children of her co-wife, ends up killing her own children. The Yoruba practice of having co-wives and all children eat from the same big bowl of food is both a way to prevent internal divisions within the family and to lessen those that already exist.

Monogamous marriages also have sibling rivalry, especially in contemporary times. Because seniority exerts some political control in the group, the assumption is that elders know more. As long as the society remained agrarian, the arrogation of roles and statuses sought to respect the function of seniority in the articulation of control. Morally contradictory practices like efforts to deliberately tell lies to protect the integrity of the senior were condoned. The ability to dissemble was seen as a proof of cultural suavity. With modernization, individual achievement and merit replaced the privileges of ascription and seniority. Ability, not age, became the most important factor in seniority. Conflict arose because many junior siblings seemed to succeed more in the new order. This change made the position of the senior son or daughter precarious. The significant amount of mistrust and conflict between senior and junior siblings in contemporary Yoruba families is the price that is being paid to resolve the transition from the predictable agrarian culture to the complex modern culture.

Birth Control and Childrearing

Among the Yoruba, the weaning practice maintains a three-year gap between births. Subtle cultural methods of reinforcements are brought to bear on the female to observe this method of spacing and birth control. Since the Yoruba social structure is male-oriented, some of those methods of enforcement of traditional forms of birth control are asymmetrical. They impose the duty of control on the female while excusing the male from the same rigorous disciplinary expectations. To satisfy his sexual cravings at this time, the Yoruba man is allowed to take another wife, with the supposed assistance of the first wife. If a wife gets pregnant within one-and one-half years of giving birth, she is made the subject of jokes and made to look like one who belongs to *the wild,* one whose hot passions were not tamed as she grew up. Not only is she the focus of jokes, but by extension, her extended family is blamed, too. The husband is not exempt from blame, but is excused to begin a relationship that can become formalized into a marriage.

A more positive method of birth control is the cultural obligation of continence for the mother once her daughter begins to give birth to children. This expectation is related to the expectation that the mother spends between three to six months to assist the daughter in nursing and postpartum care. When they see the need, the Yoruba use innuendo, derisive songs, and open avoidance to show disapproval for mothers who compete with their daughters to have children.

Morality, Childrearing, and Food Distribution Among the Yoruba

Anthropological literature on African infant care practices (Babatunde 1992) reiterates that children are being prepared to seek group survival through acquiring a sense of belonging and loyalty to the group. Living in a harsh environment with rudimentary technology, other people constitute ones' technology (Turnbull 1974). So Yoruba parents teach their children obligatory sharing. They also teach them practical lessons by withholding portions of meat, eggs, and other animal foods from children because they believe that when children acquire tastes in these expensive and scarce commodities, the desire to satisfy them will make children steal (Ransome-Kuti 1972). From a more pragmatic economic perspective, it was also considered most uneconomical to eat an egg that could produce a chicken, which would in turn produce more chickens. Thus, in the attempt to teach discipline, self-denial and deferred gratification, this pattern of food distribution within the family leads to unintended nutritional crises. Although claims about these crises were made in qualitative research studies, only in the 1990s were the claims empirically confirmed by quantitative research findings (Setiloane 1995).

In a study conducted as part of UNICEF's Child Development Project in Nigeria from 1986 to 1989 entitled *Child Development for the Computer Age,* quantitative research using anthropometrics measures was conducted in rural and semirural settlements along Ifo-Otta, in Ogun State, forty-five minutes from Lagos. To be eligible for this family study, the mother had to be Yoruba; the child had to be between twenty-two and twenty-six months old; the child could not be a twin. The researchers also required that the child have a birth certificate to verify its age and that both mother and child lived in the household. A systematic sampling frame specified that every second house was to be selected, with daily starting points. Sample size for the cross-sectional field research totaled 211, including a census sample of 181 mothers and their children and an additional subsample of thirty households screened for the presence of malnourished children.

Survey instruments included a fifty-two item questionnaire that asked how frequently foods were consumed, as well as structured observations of feeding and play; the Bayley Scales of Infant Development (Bayley 1969); a socioeconomic and attitudinal questionnaire containing the Caldwell H.O.M.E Inventory (Cadwell and Bradley 1984); an ethnographic study of ten households, and, finally, anthropometrics measurements of weights and heights of children. The impact of beliefs on withholding meat and nutrient-dense foods for children was surveyed in a section with the question: Is there any reason why you don't think a child of this age should have more meat? The participants answered yes or no to the following choices: (a) more might cause child to have worms; (b) more might cause a child to steal; and (c) more could spoil child so he expects too much when things are scarce. This section also included the question: Do you believe that a child of this age (two years) should have more meat if you can afford it?

Responses to questions on stealing, spoiling, and moral character were combined together using factor analysis to create an index. The score of any respondent could range from a minimum of 0 (0 on all 3 items) to a maximum of 3 (1 on all 3 items). The index was subsequently condensed to a dichotomous variable representing mothers who had abandoned all beliefs about meat and moral training (0) and those who retained one or more (1). Each of these variables was used alternatively as a measure of mother's beliefs.

The data collected show that the distribution pattern gave available meat to fathers and mothers at the expense of their children. Among adults, men were favored over women. The median values of mothers' allocation rules deprive the children relative to their protein requirement needs when they need it most—between age one day to two years—and gives adult males more than their nutritional requirements. Although this outcome was predictable given the Yoruba male-oriented ideology, what was surprising was the result of the data on the impact of modernization on food allocation. A more in-depth examination of the meat allocation rule through cluster analysis showed that the total amount of meat mothers allocate changes with modernization. However, the ratio of meat relative to the total available remains the same, and adult males still get much more than their nutritional needs. But because modernization makes more amount of meat available, the children get more meat to meet their requirements. The data prove the saying that the more things change, the more they remain the same.

See also: NIGERIA

Bibliography

Babatunde, E. D. (1983). "Kinship Behavior and Patrilineal Ideology: A case study of the Ketu, Yoruba." *The Journal of Business and Social Studies* (n.s). 6:51–65.

Babatunde, E. D. (1992). *Culture, Religion and the Self: A Critical Study of Bini and Yoruba Value Systems in Change.* Lewiston, NY: Edwin Mellen Press.

Babatunde, E. D. (1998). *Women's Rights Versus Women's Rites: A Study of Circumcision among The Ketu Yoruba of Southwestern Nigeria.* Trenton, NJ: Africa World Press.

Babatunde, E. D. and Zeitlin, M. F. (1995). "The Yoruba Family: Kinship, Socialization and Child Development." In *Strengthening the Family: Implications for Development,* ed. M. F. Zeitlin, R. Megawangi, E. M. Kramer, N. D. Colletta, E. D. Babatunde, and D. Garman. Tokyo: United Nations University Press.

Bayley, N. (1969). *Manual for the Bayley Scales of Infant Development.* New York: The Psychologic Corporation.

Caldwell, B. M., and Bradley, R.H. (1984). *Home Observation for Measurement of the Environment.* Little Rock, AR: University of Arkansas.

Evans-Pritchard, E. E. (1940). *The Nuer.* Oxford: The Clarendon Press.

Fadipe, N. A. (1970). *The Sociology of the Yoruba.* Ibadan, Nigeria: Ibadan University Press.

Fortes, M. (1962) *Marriage in Tribal Societies.* Cambridge: Cambridge University Press.

Gonzalez-Wippler, M. (1992). *The Santeria Experience: A Journey into the Miraculous,* 2nd edition. St. Paul, MN: Llewellyn Publications.

Kemmer, I. A. (1989) Research results from phase I: *Child Development for the Computer Age Project.* Nigerian component of the Tufts-UNICEF-JNSP Three Country Positive Deviance in Nutrition Research Project. New York: UNICEF.

Murphy, J. (1994). *Working the Spirit: Ceremonies of the African Diaspora.* Boston: Beacon Press.

Ransome-Kuti, O. (1972). "Some Socio-Economic Conditions Predisposing to Malnutrition in Lagos." *Nigerian Medical Journal* 2:111–118.

Setiloane, K. (1995). "Beliefs and Practices Regarding Meat Distribution and the Nutritional Status of Children in Lagos State, Nigeria." Ph.D. dissertation. Boston: Tufts University.

Sudarkasa, N. (1996). *The Strength of Mothers, African and African American Women and Families: Essays and Speeches.* Trenton, NJ: Africa World Press.

Turnbull, C. M. (1974). "Introduction: The African Condition." In *The Child in His Family, Children at Psychiatric Risk,* ed. E. J. Anthony and C. Koupernik. New York: John Wiley and Sons.

Voeks, R. (1997). *Sacred Leaves of Candomble.* Austin: University of Texas Press.

Warner-Lewis, M. (1996). *Trinidad Yoruba: From Mother Tongue to Memory.* Tuscaloosa: The University of Alabama Press.

Other Resources

Pearce, T. O. (2000). "Gender and Governance in Africa: A Conceptual Framework for Research and Policy Analysis and Monitoring." A draft paper presented at The African Knowledge Networks Forum Preparatory Workshop, 17-18 August 2000, Addis Ababa, Ethiopia. Available from http://www.uneca.org/aknf/pub/gengovern.htm.

EMMANUEL D. BABATUNDE
KELEBOGILE V. SETILOANE

Z

ZAMBIA

Zambia is a landlocked African country. Its population in 1995 was about 7.4 million. The average number of children in a Zambian family is about 6.5. The country occupies about 0.752 million square miles and has a density of fifty-four persons per square mile.

The Structure of the Zambian Family

A Zambian family, like families elsewhere, can be thought of as a group. The most important duties of this group are to reproduce, nurture, and educate the young to become productive members of the family and the society at large. This training process is also referred to as socialization. The head of the Zambian family can either be the father or a maternal uncle. If it is a maternal uncle, the mother, more than the father, plays a crucial role in decision making within the family. These matrilineal families are very common in Zambia. In matrilineal families, the authority and power to make decisions rests with the mother and her relatives. In some family types, the father is the decision maker. These patterns of authority and power are passed from one generation to the next in Zambia.

In the patrilineal system, the transfer of wealth is from father to his children. In matrilineal families, children belong to the maternal uncle. In some instances, the father may have more than one wife, although this polygamous type of family is rare in Zambia.

A larger proportion of Zambian families are matrilineal than are patrilineal in organization. Within the country's nine provinces, most households in the four provinces of Central, Northwestern, Luapula, and Copperbelt are matrilineal. The Namwanga and the Ngoni in the Eastern province, the Lozi in the Western, and the ILA in the Southern province are patrilineal. These groups are also patrilocal. That is, after marriage, the couple lives in the husband's family house or close to his father's household. Daily activities such as eating and educating the young are seldom conducted in the privacy of one's house. Zambian villages have a central place governing the village. This place is called *Insaka* or *Nsaka*. In the matrilineal villages, the Insakas are located at the village center.

Fostering is common in Zambia. When couples fail to have children, they often become foster parents. It is also very common among siblings to foster care; that is, children are fostered by aunts and uncles. A survey of households in Kitwe, the second largest city in Zambia, found that about 14 percent of all children aged fourteen and younger, and nearly 18 percent of children aged to ten to fourteen years were not living with their parents (Ahmed 1996). The estimates of the extent of fostering in other African countries, such as Ghana, are much higher. Often fostered children are considered and treated as though they are biological offspring. When families are forced to adopt children following some misfortune, foster children may become victims of abuse and neglect.

Family Formation

Families are often formed through marriage. Almost all Zambians eventually marry. Very few remain unmarried throughout life. As soon as a boy is recognized as an adult and brings his marriage intention to the attention of his parents, the boy's parents become involved in marriage arrangements. In matrilineal societies, the maternal uncle plays a very important role in arranging marriage. In patrilineal societies, boys are required to present a certain amount of money, material goods, or both, called *labola,* demanded by the bride's family. Matrilineal families do not follow the practice of giving labola. In a few matrilineal groups in Zambia, marriage alliances from outside the group are discouraged. Indications of lack of virility and male impotence are grounds for terminating the marriage after the couple's first night. If the marriage is not terminated, the man is invited to the *Insaka* where he eats with the village elders. The new husband resides with the bride's family (matrilocal) and he works the fields and engages in village life. The matrilocal extended family is composed of a man and his wife, their married daughters, and their husbands and children (Richards 1969). Over time, however, a great deal conflict develops between the sexes. This is because men want or have more control over resources. (Poewe 1978).

Socialization

In Zambia, the communal way of life is widespread among matrilineal households. Community members participate in the socialization of the young, initiated by family members. In these *Insakas,* the young are rewarded with praise and acceptance if they show respect for people who hold power and authority, become proficient in age- and gender-related activities, and demonstrate the capacity to assume adult roles in the family and the community. For example, among the Luvale, a matrilineal community, a newly married young man is likely to be judged by assessing his capacity to share chicken meat equally among the members at the dining place in the *Insaka*.

Children are socialized not only by parents, but also by village elders. Socialization is often segregated by both age and gender as children mature into their early and late teenaged years. Children in matrilineal families learn that their father has little responsibility for them. Children are socialized to acquire desired familial values. Qualities such as honesty, bravery, and trustworthiness are valued in boys. They are also trained to show respect to the elders by allowing elders to eat first in the *Insaka* and by keeping the *Insaka* lights illuminated. Boys in matrilineal societies assist the elderly in firewood collection. As boys mature, they are expected to show bravery and gain skills necessary for making a living. Boys who do not posses desired social and personality traits often become alienated. These boys, among the Bembas in Zambia, are called *Nibalaya*. The term means *it is that one—the outcast.* Girls are socialized to acquire values and skills necessary for caregiving while learning to be independent as far as possible in terms of farm management and participating in market activities.

Beliefs

The collective life in the Zambian family is shaped by both living and dead family members. Those who are dead influence decision making indirectly. It is believed that the dead exist as spirits. There are good and bad spirits. Whether the dead entered the world of good or bad spirits depended upon how their funerals were handled. For this reason, most Zambians believe that it is important to bury their dead in accordance with the customs, norms, and rules. In matrilineal societies, all adults are expected to attend funerals and initiation ceremonies. The presence of either positive or negative spirits is associated with the desirability of outcomes from actions taken by people to either maintain or enhance family and community well-being. For example, at the christening ceremony, if the infant is named after the wrong ancestral spirit, it is believed that the infant will cry endlessly. There are three types of spirits: ancestral, evil, and possessive. The last kind is believed to cause illness through possession. Maintaining respect for ancestors is an important family function. Belief in and practice of witchcraft is another essential aspect of Zambian family life, particularly in matrilineal societies.

Urban Families

Families in urban areas such as Lusaka and Ndola in Zambia do not resemble their counterparts in the rural Zambia. A typical urban household may consist of children of the spouses from earlier marriages, elder rural-based visitors, friends of the spouses, and promising young relatives of the spouses who attend local schools (Schuster 1979). Because husbands may be employed only intermittently, during the period of unemployment,

Zambian families at a festival at Mongu. JASON LAURE/LAURE COMMUNICATIONS

they may move into households of either the husbands' or wives' relatives. A household under these conditions is like an open kin group. Individuals move in and out of the households, and the definition of the family is broad enough to accommodate even unrelated friends. The composition of the urban households in Zambia is continuously changing.

Bibliography

Afaque Ahmed. (1996). *Fostering of Children in Zambia.* M. A. thesis. Department of Sociology, University of North Texas, Denton, TX.

Poewe, K. (1978). "Matriliny in the Throes of Change, Kinship, Descent, and Marriage in Luapula Zambia." *Africa* 48:353–367.

Richards, A. I. (1969). *Bemba Marriage and Present Economic Conditions.* Manchester, UK: Manchester University Press.

Schuster, I. M. G. (1979). *New Women of Lusaka.* Palo Alto, CA: Mayfield Publishing.

VIJAYAN K. PILLAI

ZERO POPULATION GROWTH

See FAMILY PLANNING

ZIMBABWE

See ACQUIRED IMMUNODEFICIENCY SYNDROME (AIDS); RICH/WEALTHY FAMILIES; RURAL FAMILIES

INDEX

Page numbers in **bold** indicate the main article on a topic
Page numbers in *italics* indicate illustrations
Page numbers followed by *f* indicate figures
Page numbers followed by *t* indicate tables

A

B

D

F

G

I

J

K

M

O

P

Q

R

S

T

U

V

ISBN 0-02-865676-8
90000
9 780028 656762